From Small Lochs To Great Lakes

From Small Lochs To Great Lakes

The Remarkable Story of a First World War Soldier,
Sailor and South Uist Crofter

Donald MacDonald
Dòmhnall Ghilleasbuig Sorcha

For The Right Reasons

1

First Published in 2016 by
For The Right Reasons
60 Grant St
Inverness
IV3 8BS

ISBN: 978-1-910205-82-2

British Library Cataloguing-in-Publication Data
A catalogue record of this book is available from
the British Library

Typeset, Printed and Bound by For The Right Reasons

Contents

Index of Pictures with Referencing

Remaining documents and photographs were provided by the family.

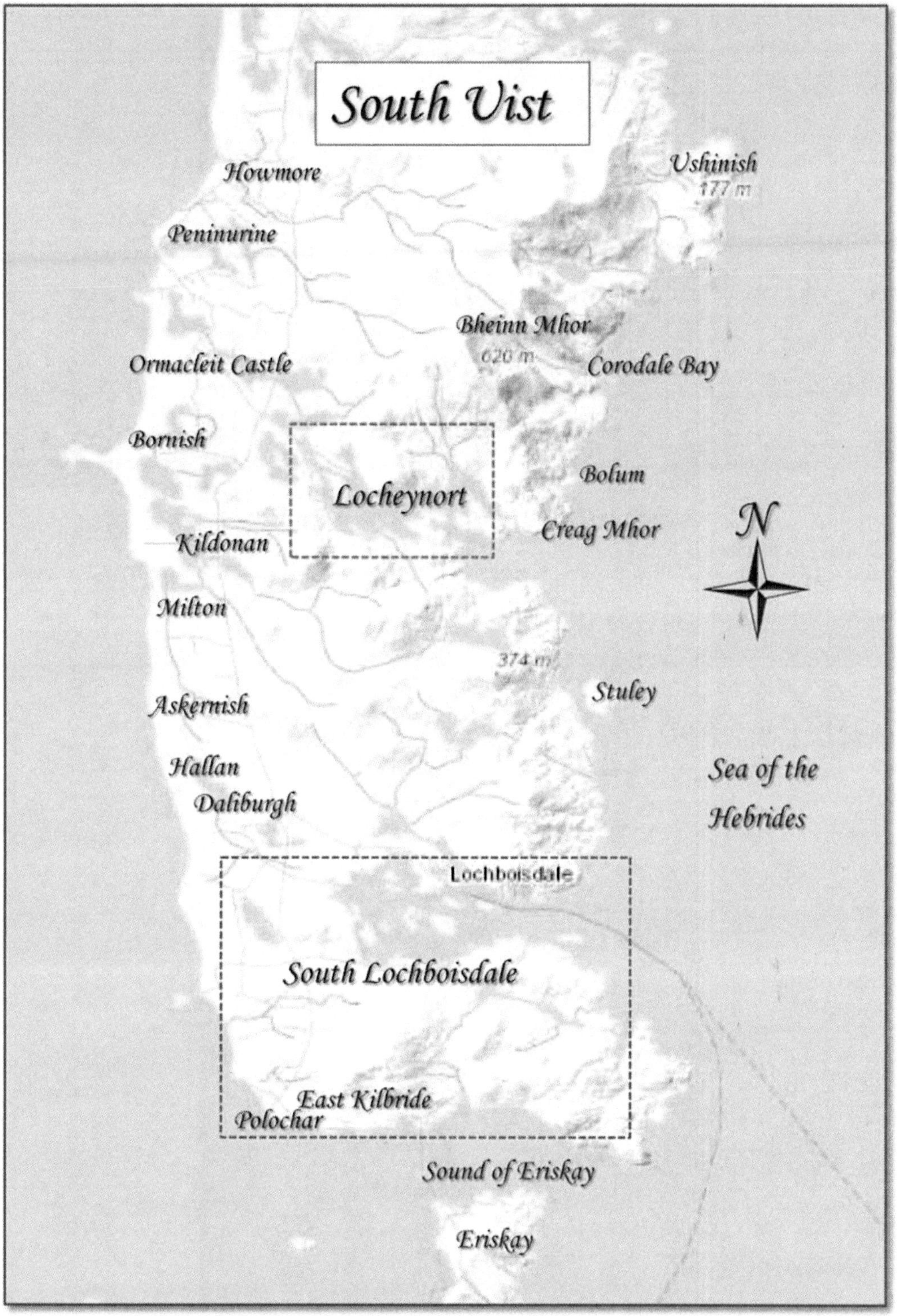

South Vist

Howmore

Ushinish
177 m

Peninurine

Bheinn Mhor
620 m

Ormacleit Castle

Corodale Bay

Bornish

Bolum

Locheynort

Creag Mhor

Kildonan

N

Milton

374 m

Askernish

Stuley

Hallan
Daliburgh

Sea of the
Hebrides

Lochboisdale

South Lochboisdale

East Kilbride
Polochar

Sound of Eriskay

Eriskay

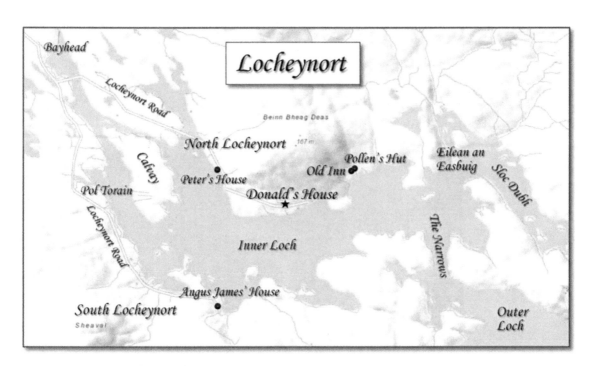

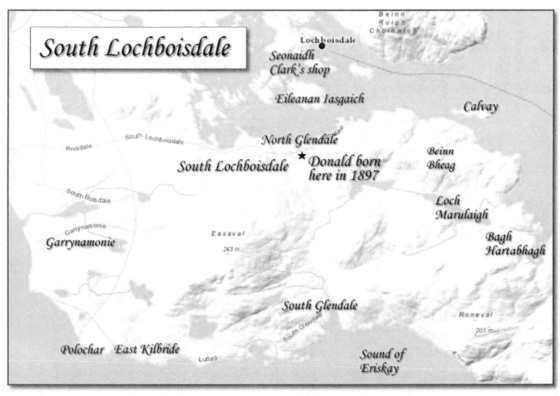

Introduction and Acknowledgements

Donald MacDonald wrote these memoirs when he was in his eighties. They are remarkable for his total recall of conversations and situations which occurred throughout his long life, and his account of the Battle of the Somme gives an insight into the horrendous conditions involved. Serving throughout the war, he tells of real men trying to cope with its brutality, and leaves behind an honest, personal and somewhat different account.

Not all his siblings survived childhood, and his mother died when the remaining children were still young, leaving his older sister to take over the running of the household and successfully keep the family together. It has been our wish that our father's story should be maintained as he wrote it, to remember how he, in his turn, when our mother died at an early age, held his own young family together, though there is little doubt that we would have been sent away to children's homes had we lived on the mainland.

Throughout his memoirs, all aspects of his life are illustrated through the medium of his stories and adventures from all over the world, through which he demonstrates the hopes and aspirations of an ordinary man looking back over a more than full life.

Prior to his death in 1985, having completed the handwritten manuscript, my father left it to me, his only daughter. The family are grateful to Sir Walter and Lady Pollen for their friendship and support and. in particular, their encouragement of our father to embark on the enterprise of writing his memoirs. Our thanks to their daughter-in-law, Patricia Pollen, who undertook the task of transposing the handwritten copy into a typed form, a laborious and time consuming task.

Eventually, with the advent of technology it became possible to have the manuscript digitised whereby it was electronically available to allow further progression towards publication. In this regard, I am grateful to Margaret Watt for computerising the manuscript. In addition, mention should also be made of the previous research undertaken by the author's granddaughter, Mairi Thomson and in particular certain illustrations used within this book.

Having pursued publishers over the years to take on this task to no avail, I was delighted that Richard Burkitt of For The Right Reasons was extremely enthusiastic and supportive in this regard. From the start he brought hope and confidence to this project and I am grateful to him and his team of talented young people for all their help. A special mention goes to Sonia Cameron Jacks who, from the beginning, was so enthusiastic and spoke so highly of my father's work. She worked tirelessly in proof reading and correcting the manuscript.

This indeed has been a labour of love and I would never have got to where we are without the help and patience of my husband, David. We are still together so it can't have been that bad. I'm sure my three children, Stephen, Colin and Mairi, will be delighted to have reached the end of a long journey as they have been pestered over the last year to provide all sorts of technical assistance in preparing the manuscript for publication, especially Colin for providing the customised maps and I thank them all for their patience.

Finally, after long family discussions regarding a title, my thanks to Scott, my son-in-law, for his flash of inspiration regarding lochs and lakes as they figured so prominently in my father's journey through life. How could it have been anything else?

My father, Donald MacDonald, was the most resilient man I have ever known and had we, as a family, known our mother, Mary Ann, our lives would have been so much more enriched.

Fois shiorraidh thoir dhaibh, a Thighearna

Donald MacDonald (Dòmhnall an Òir – Donald of the Gold as he was known after returning from the States) started to write his story while staying with me in Glasgow. I will be eternally grateful to him for leaving behind this legacy for all the family and for generations to come.

Peggy T. Imlach

1   Childhood Pranks and Fort George

My name is Donald MacDonald, and I was born on the Island of South Uist in the year 1897. Many of my friends have been trying to persuade me to write my memoirs and I have now agreed that I will attempt to do just that.

My first recollection of life was when I discovered a bottle of whisky in my father's chest. After having a few tries at it to make out what it was, I ran outside the house but kept going back and forwards to the bottle until I had drunk a fair amount of it. My father saw me from some distance away and wondered what I was doing and, as he came towards me, he realised I was not playing and that something was wrong. When he came towards me, he right away smelt the whisky and realised that I was drunk. My father and mother then carried me into the house and put me to bed without giving me a thrashing, which I considered was rather unusual. That was my first recollection of life, also my first introduction to whisky.

My father was a crofter and fisherman, that is, he owned part of a croft between himself and his brother Roderick. There were nine of us in our family although only six lived to full maturity. Life was very hard in those days. The houses were very poor and the way of life extremely hard in comparison to today. Our house was very old and was situated in a township called South Lochboisdale. Despite its age, it had one distinction in that it was the only house which had a glass window. This window was about a foot square and any other daylight gained access through holes in the house walls, which could be closed off with wooden shutters. It was at least 50 feet long and about 14 feet wide, with a very low thatched roof. Inside, apart from my father's chest, there was very little in the way of furniture. My mother also had a chest which stood end to end with my father's and contained her clothing, although all she possessed only half filled it. My father's chest was a bit fuller but only because he kept herring nets in it along with his clothing. The nets were new and unused, as they had come from the mill. The remaining furniture consisted of a bench, three beds, one chair and a few stools arranged around the fire, which was built in the centre of the floor.

We had an apparatus fitted to the roof which, if all the windows were closed, allowed the smoke out of the house. The apparatus consisted of four posts each about 18 inches high and in total was about 2 feet square. Leaning against these posts was a square of wood about 18 inches high which had attached to it a shaft hanging down into the room. The wooden square was positioned into the wind and accordingly drew the smoke up the chimney. If the wind changed direction, then the square of wood could be turned by the hanging shaft to meet the wind. This functioned perfectly well until the rain came and because of the 18inch square hole in the roof, a lot of rainwater could get in. This problem was overcome when a large basin was put on the floor, this caught all the water coming through the chimney. The fire was extinguished every night and in the morning it had to be rebuilt. A chain hung down from the rafters right above the fire and each morning when rebuilding the fire, it had to be laid right under the lowest point of the hanging chain.

The method of resetting the fire each morning was to lift a cinder with a pair of tongs, place it under the lowest link of the hanging chain and let it drop. The centre of the new fire was built where the cinder landed. Sometimes we would play pranks and move the chain so that the person building the new fire would build it 6 inches off centre having performed the cinder test and amid a lot of laughter the fire would have to be rebuilt.

Although the houses were poor in structure and lacked all the amenities of life as we know them now, they were warm in the winter and cool in the summer. Wear and tear did occur to the roof and periodically the house had to be re-thatched using turf in order that the gales and inclement weather did not penetrate. The best turf was the one that had been washed by the tide and was obtained by digging it from the ground and carrying it to the house. A roof would require about 100 18 inch square pieces put on just the way slates are with the top turfs overlapping those underneath. This created a water and wind-tight seal.

Thatching, Eriskay, 1936. **Russell, (A Different Country, Page 68)**

Thatching was different, using either bracken, rushes or heather, of which heather was by far the best and although it grew in abundance around us, only certain types were any good and that type was in short supply. For this reason usually it was bracken we used which was available in any amount and was easy to lay on but had to be replaced each year or so. When thatching a roof, the thatch had to be tied down securely and as wire and wire netting were unknown to us, it was rope that was used. Rope to buy was beyond our means so nothing else for it we had to manufacture our own from heather. The long winter nights were passed in making the rope.

When thatching time came around, two men usually tackled the job, as it was very difficult working on one's own. The existing material on the roof was used as a base with the new bracken being laid on top. The bracken was laid in rows along the roof and up its slope to the top until complete, when the whole roof was secured using the homemade heather rope. This was placed over the roof in a latticed pattern each low point having an anchor, usually a large stone, attached to it.

The people who lived and worked in these conditions were unfortunately lacking a good education, which was not then available to them; however they were a very intelligent race. I remember one time during the last war when I was employed in Glasgow at a time when shipping was being sunk by magnetic mines. We were installing degaussing gear on a ship lying in Princess Dock which previously was hung on the outside of ships although it functioned just as effectively when placed within the ship. This was a great advantage as it was regularly damaged when ships came alongside a dock or quay. At this time we were placing the gear into slots within the ship's hull, which was then welded into place. The installation had reached the after-quarter of the ship when it was finishing time and so everyone stopped work leaving part of the gear not yet inserted into its casing. There was a stout rope which was fed into the casing, and by this manner the degaussing gear was pulled into place. On returning to the job the following morning, it was discovered that the rope was missing and accordingly the gear could not be placed in its channel, which measured about 4 inches square.

The foreman said, "Well, there's nothing for it but to get welders to cut open the top of the plates to allow access" and was about to summon the welders when one fellow in the squad said that that was not necessary. "You think you're able to get the gear into place without cutting the plating" the foreman said. "Yes, I think so," said the man. "If you're thinking of pushing wire through the casing, that won't work." said the foreman. "There are several bends in the channel and wire won't go through." "No," said the man, "I wasn't thinking of that at all." The foreman said, "I'll bet you two bottles of whisky that you're wrong, no matter what you're thinking." "Well," said the fellow, who was an islander and had been brought up in the same conditions as I had, "I can do it and there are only two things I need, a ball of string and I'm going off to look for the other." After a while he returned with the ship's cat, which he found in the galley. He tied the string around the cat and pushed the animal into the small 4 inch opening, thereafter pushing some burning waste in after it. Of course the cat took off along the channel and was caught at the other end by another man. "There you are," said the fellow, "all you have to do is tie a stronger line to the string and pull it through." "Well" said the foreman "there certainly seems to be more in the islands than drunken seamen" and needless to say he paid up with the whisky. That was only one small incident, although I can think of many more which demonstrate that the highlanders and islanders of Scotland are possessed with agile minds which are as good as those found anywhere and, given the educational opportunities, could have been greatly improved.

The school I went to was situated in Garrynamonie. It was over three miles from our house and there were three ways of getting to it. One was over the crest of a fairly high hill, the second was to cross the hill at a lower brow and the third was to go around the hill by road. Of course the shortest way was the most used, except on very rare occasions. One such occasion was the first day I went to school. My mother dressed me up in my best clothes because memory tells me I was wearing a kilt that day. Anyway, off I went with my brother and sister who were already attending school, having been warned that they were in charge. Now there was a whole drove of children going to school from my township and one of the boys was the undisputed leader and all had to do what the leader said. On this occasion we were en route over the lower brow of the hill where we passed a croft belonging to an uncle of mine. He had a garden on his croft situated by the roadside in which he grew vegetables.

There was a patch of turnips growing in his garden, I was ordered by the 'leader' to go into the turnip patch and take as many turnips as I could carry in the apron of my kilt. Of course, I had to obey orders and so off I went. I gathered as many turnips as the apron of my kilt could hold and was walking away when I heard sounds behind me. I looked round and there was a big dog coming after me. It appeared that my uncle had sent his dog after whoever was pilfering his vegetables. I kept going as fast as I could run but that wasn't fast enough because the dog quickly caught up with me and seized hold of my kilt. There was I with the turnips in my kilt to the front of me and the dog pulling my kilt to the back of me. Suddenly my uncle appeared and when it seemed that the dog might hurt me, he called it to him. By that time though the dog had had the best part of my kilt and I had succeeded in hanging onto two turnips. When I caught up with the rest of the group, they were all sitting resting. I was praised by the 'leader'; he said that I was very fast and that by the following year I would be faster than the dog. I had my doubts about that. Anyway, he cut up the turnips and gave a slice to every member of the group and we carried on our way to school.

On arriving at the school, I was taken in front of the headmaster who asked my name. I told him that it was Donald. The headmaster, who was an Englishman by the name of F.G. Rea, did not at that time speak Gaelic. He said "Donald, Donald who? What's your other name?" I didn't know what other name he meant so I said, "No, my name is Donald." in as much English as I could manage. He called my sister out and he said to her "Is this your brother?" "Yes" she replied. "Well," remarked Mr. Rea, "his name must be Donald MacDonald. We have so many Donald MacDonalds in this school that in future he will be known as Donald MacDonald E." I presume that there already was an A, B, C and D. For evermore throughout my schooldays I was known as Donald Macdonald E.

My teacher was a Miss MacAskill, whose father was Robert MacAskill, owner of the Polochar Inn. My first task was to learn the A.B.C. Most children knew the alphabet before beginning their schooling, but as neither of my parents could read or write, I could not expect any help from that quarter. There was nothing for it but to plod on with the alphabet until I mastered it. The school itself was very small, consisting of only two rooms, a main room and a classroom for the infants. I made good progress and began enjoying school. The teacher was very kind and did not punish anyone unless he or she deserved it. She had a very bad temper however, and when it was aroused, anyone on the receiving end felt it. I found out just how bad her temper was. One day she was teaching us the musical scales, doh, ray, me, etc. and the class was all standing. She was out in front and pointing to the scale on the blackboard with a long brown, wooden pointer. Well, I happened to be standing behind a girl who was a very good singer and for some reason this annoyed me. I had a safety pin in my jacket, which held it closed due to the lack of buttons, which we had ripped off to play pitch and toss and it seemed a good idea to me to jab her with the pin. That was what I did and it resulted in a very loud howl from the girl. Of course, it wasn't long before I was found out.

I was taken to the front of the class and the first stroke I received was across the legs with the pointer. I was trying to be brave and didn't cry. The next stroke I received, the pointer broke but I still didn't cry. She carried on belabouring me with the broken point and at that some of the older boys began laughing while some of the younger children began to cry. The school was in bedlam by this time and Mr. Rea came in to investigate. By this time I had slipped onto my knees. He asked Miss MacAskill what was wrong and she explained. He looked from me to the broken pointer and said to her "I think he's had enough. Just keep him in at playtime." I was made to remain in the classroom until all the rest returned from their play, when I was made to apologise to the girl into whom I had stuck the pin. When it was over, Miss MacAskill and I became good friends. I always liked her, as did all the other pupils. She was very different from another teacher we had, a Miss McMullen, who had a bad habit of shaking pupils and pulling their ears for the slightest misdemeanour. None of the children liked her.

My attendance at school was bad at times, and I was told by Miss MacAskill that had it been better, my studies would have progressed much quicker. On many days, I did not attend school because I had to remain at home to herd cattle. On other days the weather would be so bad that I couldn't go. There were other days, of course, when I just didn't go and played truant in the hills. I have tried to roughly total my time at school, taking everything into account, and all in all, I don't think that I spent more than two years there.

Apart from the reasons I have already mentioned for not going to school, there was also the fact that because we lived more than three miles from the school, we were not compelled by law to attend. We probably did not go more than one day a week, two days being reckoned as good attendance. It follows, therefore, that when I left school at 14 years of age, my education was nothing to speak of. My education as far as learning has never really improved to this day, and most of what I have learned has been by experience in many different parts of the world. This is maybe not the most satisfactory way, but it certainly is more enjoyable.

In Rea we had an excellent teacher, a first class educationalist but a very strict disciplinarian particularly about fighting which was very common among the older boys. The punishment he meted out for this 'crime' was sometimes rather severe. His method was that he would take the offender outside to the porch of the school building and make him bend down and place his head between his (Rea's) legs. The offender's head was then firmly held by his legs. The boy's trousers were then lowered to his ankles and thereafter a leathering with a strap was administered on the bare buttocks. All the boys used to bind up their trousers with hemp rope to make it more difficult for Rea. This punishment was used to great effect for some time until one of the oldest boys who was undergoing the punishment suddenly jerked his head up causing Rea to over-balance, bang his head on the top of the porch and fall, landing with a clatter on the floor. The youth concerned made off immediately into the hills and did not appear back at school for some considerable time. This incident put an end to that particular form of punishment.

Although it ended then it was too late for me as I had already, although only once, suffered the humiliation of having my trousers pulled down and punishment administered. Despite being a very strict person, he was also very fair and each and every one of us deserved what we got. If children were punished nowadays as they were then, I doubt very much if their parents would stand for it although it did none of us any harm, in fact, it probably did us some good. The same schoolmaster wrote a book entitled 'A School in South Uist'. It tells of conditions prevailing at that time on the island, of life in the school, and of the life of the schoolmaster, and because I was part of those times, I can vouch for its complete authenticity.

In the summer evenings, coming home from school, it was always a delight to look westwards out into the Atlantic Ocean, and see the fishing fleet out at sea. These boats were all under sail as engines had not at that time been fitted to that type of craft. There would be sails stretching almost to the horizon, all tacking back and forward and this, together with the always pleasant smell of seaweed tangles burning on the shore, has left a picture etched firmly on my mind.

I was still attending school when I began to earn my living. I was hired out by my parents to herd cattle on the west side of the island. My wages were to be 30/- and a pair of boots and the employment was for the period May to September. This wage I never received as I only remained in this job for a few days. In the mornings the cattle were let out of an enclosure where they were penned at night. It was my job to take them down to a nearly loch and water them and,

13

thereafter, to the machair, the fertile land on the west coast of the island. To reach the machair I had to drive them along a corridor of land which had oats growing on one side and potatoes growing on the other. I was to prevent the cattle from eating any of those growing crops. The corridor of land through which I had to pass was about 150 yards long and 80 yards wide and with about 10 cows it was no easy task to curtail them. Some beasts were worse than others and they would go from side to side picking at the crops. Whilst I chased one, the others would go to the opposite side and begin grazing.

Eventually I would reach the shore with the cattle and have a rest, passing the time by drawing diagrams of boats and animals in the sand with the herding stick. After playing around for some time I thought I had better put the cattle back on the grazing and face the wrath of the owner who was soon due to relieve me for school. When he did, he was very angry seeing patches of the corn eaten. He said if I did not do better, he would not keep me so 'off you go to school.' As I had already had my breakfast, I was given a mug of sour milk and a piece of rye bread and another of rye to put in my pocket. I was an unhappy boy going to school that day, wondering if I should run away home that evening or stay and see if the next day improved. I did go back but the next day was not any better as the cattle kept wandering into the corn and so ended my first brief attempt to earn my own living. Herding cattle was a job that a schoolboy could hope to get at that time. I had three seasons of it. If there was a large area to graze the cattle on, it was pleasant work.

My next place as a herder was in my own township, not far from home. I was happy there; small stock with much grazing space and the fact that they had a small sailing boat which, without permission, I used to take out while the cattle made good use of the corn. If caught, I was in for a good scolding but no thrashing. Playing pranks on people was a hobby that I was well known for and often for good reason.

There was an old lobster fisherman, Donald Gillies, who always left his new boat moored near where I was herding. His young nephew David stayed near me, and both of us used to meet the boat when they came in, as nearly always they would have crabs. I noticed that the nephew was getting the best and the most, however there was nothing I could do. I decided to try and change this situation, so one day I took away the rowing pins, and the next day, as usual, we met the boat. We asked if they had crabs. They said, "Yes, plenty, but none for you, why did you take the pins out of my boat and what did you do with them?" We said we were never near the boat. "I don't believe you. This will be reported to the Police." We did not get any crabs that day. When, on my way home, the owner said to me "Donald, did you see anyone near my boat or at the shore?" "No" I said, "I only saw David at the shore. I did not see him in the boat, I don't think it was him that took the pins away." "Well Donald, if you find them, I will give you all the crabs every day and that rascal will get none". This was on a Saturday. That night I replaced the pins.

On Monday we both met the boat. I got all the crabs they had. David was told to go home and never to come near the boat again. Unknown to Donald, while the ban lasted, I gave David his share as soon as the owner was out of sight. My wages in that second herding job were £2 from May till November. They did not hire me for the next season, I think on account of the sailing boat problem. Instead, I went to people on the west side of the island, where I stayed for two seasons. My wages were £3.10 shillings and a pair of boots. They were the first pair that I had ever owned. Although there were more cattle to herd, there was a larger area to graze on.

My first day there nearly ended in tragedy. There were two small children in that family, one a two year old, the other a baby at the crawling stage. The mother asked me if I would look after the baby while she was away on an errand. She brought a large tartan plaid and spread it on the shingles in the sun at the back of the house, and placed the baby in the centre saying, "He will be alright there but keep your eye on him." There was much shamrock growing around there, and to pass the time I began to look for a four-leaf clover, said to be lucky. The baby was happy playing with his toys. I soon found a four-leaf clover. I also saw that the baby had left the rug and was now among the shingles with his face black and blue and choking. I tried to reach the pebble with my finger but could not and by then he was in spasms. I then had an inspiration and caught him by the ankles, raised him up and shook him hard, and was I glad when I saw the stone dropping out of the wee mouth that was gasping for breath. Perhaps the luck of the Irish had done it. When his mother arrived he was trying to tell her what I had done to him. She could not understand. He shunned me for a long time after that. They were fine people to work for and saw that I got to Mass every second Sunday.

Different to the story I heard of a man living in the same village who also had a boy herder who was not happy on account of the harshness of the master who had two sons, one was called Big John. It was an unfailing routine of the master to say the grace at every meal. The grace was always the same, "God bless this house, myself, my wife and my son, Big John and no one else." The boy herder, who was not happy there, was asked one day by the master to say the grace, "Just say it in your own Catholic way" and when the boy hesitated, the master said "Go on, you are wasting time." "Alright" said the boy, "may the Devil take you and your wife and your son Big John and nobody else."

When all the crops were in I, like most of the boys, started gathering whelks. We had to walk five miles across the hills to where we could get them. It did not matter in what kind of weather so long as it was spring tide. I went partners with my cousin Donald who was older than me. The most we gathered in a tide was a bag full of about 140 lbs. We were getting a shilling a peck which was very poor, considering the hardship of carrying them on our back for five miles. When we all took whooping cough, it did not stop us. When the spasms came on, we just laughed at each other. One day on our way to the gathering we came upon a coble hidden in the heather on the bank of a long loch. We did not know whom it belonged to. It would not have made any difference if we did, as the place was miles from habitation and off the beaten track. We considered our find a piece of luck. It had a flat bottom and to get it on the water we had to roll it. We got it afloat without any damage and later we learned that it belonged to the hotel and was there for the use of anglers fishing the loch.

We found pieces of wood on the shore, which we used for paddles. It was an ideal thing to ferry the whelks on the loch that stretched homewards. We used it for that purpose many times, and for the pleasure of sailing it when we got a mast and sail made. As it had a flat bottom, it did not sail well, and many a dooking we got. When it often capsized, we had to swim ashore. Winter and summer we kept a box of matches in a dry place on the shore, and we would make a large fire of heather then strip off and dry out our clothing. We had so many escapes from drowning that we at last decided to sink her. We took her to a deep place and filled her with stones and when sinking we pushed her off. Years later she was found on the loch side badly damaged. The owner of the hotel was giving a £5 reward for information as to who took her. He had a shepherd in his employment whose territory was in the area where the boat was and knew well who took her away, and although he often saw us in her, he would not come near us. Privately he used to say he was glad when she sank, as she would likely drown the lot of us.

This shepherd was Roderick O'Henly and he himself did not escape pranks played on him. He had the strange idea that a shepherd always followed the same path in the hills, and that assumed path crossed a ditch that required a jump to cross it. We would dig a large hole in the centre, fill it with slush and cover it with an enticing piece of thin turf. Donald and I made many of these but we never found out if Roderick ever took the bait.

It was different with Angus Beag (Wee Angus), a cousin of ours, who had at that time got himself a new navy blue suit, and all in the village knew about it. We decided to play the same trick on him. Late on Saturday we dug the hole, knowing that Angus would be going to Mass next day. After filling it with muddy water, we made it again as enticing as we knew how. With other flat stones leading to it, the ditch was in his direct path and to miss it he would have to detour some twenty yards. We did not think he would do that. We were wrong. When he came to it he tested the first stones, he found them firm, but not so sure of the one he could not reach, he made the detour and tested the other side and continued on his way to Mass. We were a disappointed pair but only on his return would we be sure of our failure. We left our hiding place only to return there, to watch for him coming, when we were sure after walking the seven miles he would be tired and glad in not needing to go round. He made for the stepping-stones and jumped to the centre, where down he went to his hips in liquid mud that splashed over his head. We made a fast getaway before he could see us but eventually I got the blame.

During the whelk gathering I was involved in an incident that nearly ended in tragedy. We had a good lot of whelks for transportation, and since we lost our means of part-transport when the coble capsized, we were obliged to carry them on our backs. However, on coming into view of the bay, we saw a small boat anchored on the far side. We did not know her or who she belonged to, and as there was no one around, we thought it would be a good idea to take her out for a sail. On boarding her we saw there was no mast or sail in her but four oars and also a spade, a lot of rabbits and a basket containing a lot of food. Off we went rowing towards Canna, which was clearly in view on the other side of the Minch. We were delighted and surprised when no one came down to call us back. The sea was flat calm but as Canna, which was thirty miles away, didn't seem to be getting much nearer, we decided to turn back. When we reached the shore, expecting to be met with an angry crowd ready to give us a sound thrashing, there was none of that as there was no one to meet us. We could not understand the reason for such silence. The reason was that the crew was in hiding. They had set out to poach rabbits, which were plentiful at that time, and of course they had dogs with them.

The shepherd, Roderick, did not like the sheep being worried. One loud blast on the whistle and barks from his dogs soon drove the poachers to hiding, where they stayed all day till dark, but when they reached where the boat was kept, it was gone. They had nothing to eat since they left home and all the food was in the boat. In the meantime, we thought it would be good sport to take the boat and the whelks home with us, which we did, leaving her moored safely below Angus Beag's house. We ate some of the food but left the rabbits. We carried the whelks the rest of the way.

As we were passing his house, Angus Beag saw us "Where did you find that boat and who does it belong to?" We said, "On the shore and we did not think it belonged to anyone." "Where did you find her?" We told him, "It belongs to Ronald Calum, North Lochboisdale."

16

"You will be in prison for this." "We hope you will not tell on us." "Well, if you will promise you will come and work for one day each, I will not say a word about seeing you near her" and off we went without the whelks. In the meantime, the crew was searching along the shore for the boat till it was dark, when they had to give up and make for the nearest house. They were tired and hungry, and to make matters worse, the owner of the boat was old and infirm with a heart condition. They had to carry him most of the time, and his chances of survival were slim.

The nearest house was Angus Beag's house and when they arrived exhausted, they were made welcome and asked if they came by boat. "Indeed no, our boat is lost, stolen from Bagh Hartabhagh and we are after walking all the way from there." "Well," Angus Beag said, "I was in at the shop and when I came back I saw a strange boat moored down in front of the house. I thought you had called for a cup of tea or something, and when you weren't in the house, I then went to make sure!" When they heard this, two of the ablest went down to make doubly sure, and they found it was there with no damage done and everything in its place. They were happy and as for reporting it to the police, they dared not on account of the rabbits. Angus Beag kept his word and I did a day's work carrying wet seaweed on my back for him. It was years before they found out who did it. I was then in the war and past being dealt with.

When the 1st of April came around, everyone would be trying to send people on a false errand. It was on such a day when the neighbours were busy at the spring work, and knowing full well that it was April Fools Day, I had made everyone (at least a dozen), leave their work and run up a steep hill. The cattle were grazing and I had already taken them to the hill out of sight. I left the workers and pretended I was going to see the cows. I went past the top of the hill and stayed there a while before appearing on the top again, this time shouting at the top of my voice that there was a cow in a bog and naming whose cow it was. At first they hesitated, but when I urged them on, they started up in ones and twos till I had the whole crowd running. If any faltered, I would shout his name. I had to laugh at seeing them discard their outer clothing. I moved that cow to a hollow where it took them some time before they found her eating away quite contentedly. That April Fools Day was remembered for a long time in South Lochboisdale.

The merchant, Donald Ferguson, had a fish curing station just below Angus Beag's house, where he salted and cured herring and white fish when they were in season. There was a fleet of boats landing their catches there. Fish was very plentiful and we used to meet the boats for fish. They had no use for small codlings, cod roe and skate so we got as much as we could carry for nothing. The leftovers were thrown back into the sea, which brought other small fish to the jetty to feed on. These fish were called cuddies; they also were nice and good to eat and we used a small mesh net to catch them. The net was round and about five foot deep while its mouth had a circular area of more than twenty feet. There was a circular piece made of light rods at the top with two other light rods to form a ladle. For bait we used any kind of shellfish we could get. That had to be beaten in a hollow on a rock till it was smooth, you then dipped the ladle in the sea to a depth of 12 feet and held your shoulder to it with your leg half round the pole to keep it steady, then you took a handful of bait and began spreading it on the sea with the aid of your thumb. To throw it out in chunks would scare the fish that would be inside the circle. When the fish started feeding and following the bait to the bottom, it was time to gently pull up the pole and once the ladle surfaced you had them safely inside, but sometimes it would take two men to haul them in. If there was a crabbit man at the net I would creep behind him and throw a handful of pebbles into the net and in a flash all the fish were gone, and so was I, but with an oath and a promise that I would get a good belting when he caught me, and when caught that promise was fulfilled.

The net itself was a valuable piece of gear. It had to be hand made, very fine mesh, and it took a whole winter's night to weave it, but with care it would last many years. Many people from the west side of the island who used to come out to the cuddies, were dependent on our net and took as much as they could carry home on their backs. On one occasion, a neighbour called John came out and got a large bag of cuddies. There was no net involved on this occasion. It was late in the evening before he started on his homeward journey. He called for tea at a house that was like ours, with the opening for the smoke in the centre of the roof. Ronald, the old man of the house wore what was called a blue shirt, commonly worn by old men in those days. It was made of navy blue flannel and tucked in the trousers with the braces over it, which made it rather bulky, but when sitting and the braces let down off the shoulders, it was quite comfortable.

Another John and myself followed him at a discreet distance to this house. As usual the cuddies were left on the rock outside. He climbed to the smoke opening where we could see what was going on around the fire. The household were sitting around there with John and Ronald sitting on the bench having a cup of tea. It was too early for us to put our plan into operation, which was to take the bag of fish to this opening, ready to capsize it as soon as John was leaving and standing under the hole. We waited until he had announced it was time to go. Ronald got up to see him off and did not bother to raise his braces but held his trousers up with both hands. When they both were under the hole, we capsized the bag of fish over their heads. There was a rain of cuddies over them. Ronald had to let go of his trousers with the result that much of the fish poured into them. We were well away from the house before they let their dog loose on us. I think that was the last trick I played on that John, who had a large family and in later years emigrated to Canada where he took to farming and prospered. Sadly he met his death by being gored by his own bull. He was, of course, not the only one we played tricks on; anyone was a subject if the opportunity was there.

One of them was my Uncle Seonaidh. On a certain day, he and his wife Peggy were busy stacking the corn when three of us were going by on our way to school. We offered to help them saying we did not have to attend school that day. The offer was gladly accepted and we started carrying the corn on our backs nearly half a mile till we had it all in and stacked. After a long ceilidh and storytelling with them we left, but on our way home we tumbled down all the stacks. Fortunately it was a windless night with no rain. Next morning on our way to school, we were not surprised to see Peggy and Seonaidh hard at it, restacking the stacks we had tumbled over the night before. "It is a fine morning," said Seonaidh "but it was blowing hard last night. It knocked down all the stacks we had worked on yesterday; I hope that's the last of the gales. Did your father have his blown down?" "No." "Ah well, the wind can strike anywhere, I am lucky it did not scatter it about." We stayed a while, helping, and were very late for school for which we got a good belting. Seonaidh was wise and I am sure he knew of our prank.

Come springtime, everyone would be busy cutting seaweed and carrying it in creels on their backs to lazy beds. Lazy beds are parallel strips of land, banked in the middle with deep furrows in between for drainage purposes and to separate each lazy bed. Seaweed was carried from the shore and uniformly spread over the lazy bed to improve the soil. That was left for some three weeks or until the grass came through. The ground was then turned over on both sides of the bed and it was ready for planting or filling in on the top of the weed, leaving it

18

higher in the centre. That done, you had a 3 foot wide lazy bed ready for planting which was done with a dibble by pressing it down with your foot. When withdrawn, you aimed a single seed in the hole it left, with six inches apart. It was a backbreaking job. I recall one day planting three full bags, I thought my back would never straighten again.

Another task was cutting the peats and its preparation, which was removing turf and cleaning to open a new peat bog. It had to be six foot wide by law so that any beast falling in would have space to turn round. After the turfing and cleaning, it is ready for cutting. In those days it took 6 strong men to give you a year's supply of peats. The method was two men to an iron or treisgeir, one cutting the peat, the other picking it out and placing it flat on the ground, the longer the bog, the better. The first layer is thrown out and scattered on the surrounding ground leaving a space for one row of peats at the edge of the bog. The next four or five layers are built on this space with a gap between each peat to form a wall, the spaces to allow air to circulate for drying purposes. It usually took about 9 hours of very hard work before all the cutting was finished. It then lay for three weeks or more before it was ready for lifting and then, when dry, it was stacked beside the house. The women always provided a hearty meal and a dram if available at the end of a hard day's work.

Donald's relatives cutting peat in North Glendale.
(Shaw, folk songs and folklore of South Uist).

My father had an old boat and when afloat none of us children, unless along with himself, were allowed to board her. Of course, if he was away from home we were in her often and used to take her out on sails regardless of the many knocks on different rocks she got. In this way we learned where the rocks and reefs were, good training, but severe on the boat. She had a mast and lug sail with which we also became accustomed. I think that rough training helped me in later years when handling a boat.

One day when father was out fishing for lobsters, I took her out on my own. The wind was not strong then, but increasing. I was going to take her to the pier at Lochboisdale, where I wanted to return a parcel to Seonaidh Clark's shop. The wind was getting stronger as I was leaving the shelter. I had full sail on and was short of ballast. Before reaching the pier I had to make a half turn. The wind was on the starboard and much stronger now. I was obliged to jibe the sail, and not yet being fully wise to the finer points in sailing, I omitted to take in the sheet before making the turn, thereby leaving all the wind in the sail. I made the turn and over she went, the gunnel went under and the sea came in, in waves. The sheet was pulled out of my hand, which I think saved her from capsizing. She slowly came back to even keel and I got the sail down and started baling her, I had plenty of ballast in her but of the wrong kind. I had her baled dry before she reached the pier. In the meantime my father's boat turned back as it got too rough for lobster fishing, and while passing near Angus Beag's house he was told that Donald or some other fool alone went across the loch with his old boat and very near capsized her. He should go after him before he starts back and drowns himself.

Seonaidh Clark from the shop saw me coming in and gave me a hand from preventing her being smashed against the concrete pier. Before we got her moored my father's boat arrived. I thought I was in for it, but I wouldn't rush to leave the boat and run. He looked at me and without a word jumped in the boat and pushed her out to anchor, while the rest of the crew moored their own boat, and when both boats were made safe, my uncle said, "It's a wild day Donald, I think we should all go for a dram," and up we went. Not a word was said to me as to why I took the boat out. We had one dram when uncle said it was time for leaving before the wind got stronger. Father and I rowed our boat to a sheltered area where we could put some ballast in her, and after hoisting the mast and trying the sail we were on tack as the wind was then blowing hard against us. The boat was not in sailing condition and at the first squall the sheet went. We were in lee of the shore and heading near the rocks. My father shouted, "Now you have put an end to everything." We were lucky, we managed to clear the rocks and make the tack. Coming back we only made where we left and I suggested that we should put the sail in the stern and let out a reef as well he knew, but was afraid I could not handle the sail. He would not trust me with the tiller, "Alright" he said, "if you can shift the sail." I said I could. We made good progress on that tack and once more we were clear of the shore, with fair wind home. My father was in good spirits in seeing how capable I was in handling the sail, "Where did you learn to sail a boat?" "From the loch at the back of the house with a toy boat." "I don't believe you, but wherever it was, you surprise me, I did not expect you could do it." If he had known of the many times I had been out with her and other boats he would have understood.

Although I had played many tricks on him, he never thrashed me; he left that chore to my mother who did not spare the rod. Many's a broom she wore out on my legs and backside and yet I loved my mother more than him. My father was a kind, honest, hardworking and God fearing man. I like to think he has passed on those sterling qualities to his children. My mother was a hard working cheerful person; she was always full of song and laughter. My memory of her is being very kind, industrious and good living. She died of cancer, after suffering much, at the age of 52. I was broken hearted. I loved her most sincerely and was always sad at not having anything worthwhile to give her.

When a schooner loaded with salt came alongside the jetty, there was some work to discharge the salt from the ship. Being a strong lad, I got a job carrying bags of salt on my back to a shed some 40 yards and up four stone steps. The pay was sixpence a day which was from 8.00 am to 6.00 pm. Men got a shilling a day. The work was hard and as the school was closed, I stuck it out to the last. With that and a few pence I had from the whelks, I owned the handsome sum of 7 shillings. I kept it in my pocket and liked to hear the jingle, but for many reasons it was not safe there.

To keep the money safe, I decided to use a large raw potato, by pressing the shillings and sixpences inside, it was safe as there was a hole in my pocket. When I found it was rather bulky there I looked for a hiding place. I thought if I bury it shallow in the ground a cow might step on it. I felt if I stuck it under the thatch on top of the house it would be safe there, and under the thatch it went with a small stone on the top to mark its location. Every day I watched the stone for disturbance which came after the house was shaken in a gale. That ruined the hiding place and I began to take the thatch apart, and had just found it when my father appeared in a rage. I was up to the top and down the other side before he could catch me. I didn't get off scot-free. My mother saw to that. The potato and its contents became too troublesome. I gave the lot to her and got a new jersey costing one and sixpence out of the potato contents.

Ceilidhs with singsongs and dancing were our only recreation. There was also plenty of story telling, mainly of ghosts and far away places, as many of the men were old sailors and some of the people had the gift of the second sight. Each one had to take his turn. Donald Currie, our neighbour, I think because of hearing too many ghost stories, was afraid to go out alone any distance in the dark. On account of that he always went with someone. On this night, when the township was getting a new highland bull from the mainland, Donald and Roderick were at a ceilidh near the bull's house. Those that went to the steamer to meet the animal found him tired after the long sea journey but he was able to walk the eight miles to his destination, where he was glad to lie down. It was a very dark night and Donald and Roderick were obliged to take a lighted peat with them. Torches were unheard of and lanterns were rare, but a lighted good peat with a piece of wire or a knife stuck in was not too bad so long as there was wind and no rain.

There was no road but they were making good progress till the wind dropped and the rain came on. The peat went out. They kept on falling till they drifted apart. After a while like that, Roderick let out a cry "What is it Roderick? What are you seeing?" "I don't know, I think it is the devil, I got him by the horns." "Oh for God's sake Roderick, hold him there till I get away." Roderick did actually walk in between the bull's large horns. The bull was too tired to move. Many were the stories told at those ceilidhs, and when scholars were present they listened more attentively than they would do in class, perhaps an education in itself.

I am not sure when or why I was nicknamed 'a Ròn' (the seal), I think because I was always wet and did not mind it. The little clothes we had on during summer or winter did not afford much protection. They consisted of a shirt or jersey and a pair of trousers, which were so patched it made the original hard to make out. It was nothing for Donald and I to break the ice before us when we went swimming in the lochs and bays in the sea. On one of these occasions when I swam far out in the sea and landed on a small rock to rest, a boat passing by saw me and took me for a seal. They had no gun with them, which was lucky for me, and the nickname held till that generation passed on. Many a time my hard upbringing stood me in good stead. In particular the time when I was in a section of trenches we were defending on the Somme front line. The trench was full of mud and water to our waists and everyone but me went down with swollen bodies. There was not a shot fired as the Germans were in the same position. I came out after four days with not even a slight cold but minus my kilt. More of that later.

I was now doing my last month of herding. My mother was very ill and not getting better. I used to run the three miles home every night to see her. I came home at the beginning of November with my wages, which I gave her, but she was not able to use them, she died shortly afterwards. I was broken hearted like us all. There were six of us in the family, three girls and three boys, the others having died young. Mary, Peter, Sarah, John, Annie and myself. Mary was the oldest and John and Annie were still at school. On Mary fell the burden of caring for us and although she did well, she could never take the place of mother. I think I then became hard to manage. I had given up my prank playing. One day I decided to leave home and go and live in the surrounding hills, but first I had to take John into my plans which were to build an earth hut in an out of the way glen and live there for ever. John was quite agreeable, as he did not like school. We waited until one day when father, Peter and Mary were away cutting seaweed. Sarah was left at home to do the cooking and the caring of the house. Our plan was that as soon as she was finished with the baking, we were to take her to the room, close the door, tie it with a string as there was no key, then gather up all the bread in the house, tea and sugar, a pot and some potatoes. Then, with a spade, a fire in a bucket and the dog for catching rabbits, we felt independent and off to the hills we went. We were not yet out of sight when we heard Sarah calling the dog. He left us in a hurry under protest, but we carried on to the glen and built a small earth hut with the spade. We then went to Glendale where we got plenty of shellfish. We cooked them with the potatoes and had a great feed.

When darkness fell we could hear shouts, "Where are you Donald? Where are you John? Come back and all will be forgiven." They had called the neighbours out to search for us. We were afraid they would see the glow of the fire from the doorless hut and thought it best to evacuate. We made our way through the line of searchers unseen and when we got to the house, Sarah was there. She ran towards the others shouting, "They have come back." Mary wanted to give me a sound thrashing but my father wisely took me to his brother's wife Kate. "What shall I do with him Kate? Shall I give him a good thrashing?" "No" said Kate, "he is so foolish, a thrashing will not do him any good. Make him promise he will not do the same thing again." That I promised, and I was let off. But John was not so lucky. He got it from Mary who could handle him.

Our neighbour Donald Currie had a son Roderick who was a sailor. On one wild night up aloft he was hit on the head, which afterwards affected his health till he went mental. After a spell in hospital he was let home, but bad spells used to come on him. In one of these he attacked his father, grabbing him by the throat while sitting at the table. The daughters sent for my father who was nearby to help save them. They managed to release his hold and tie him down, he started laughing at them, saying they were poor sailors if they could not make a better job of tying him. In between these spells he was quite normal and a very likeable man who would not normally harm man or beast. When in his good spells working, carrying seaweed in a creel on his back, us children around him, he always carried us in turns when the creel was empty. At that time we had a harsh dog that my mother wanted to be put down. One day she asked Roderick if he would drown him.

Drowning was the method we used for putting down old and unwanted dogs, as there was no vet. The method was to take the dog to a deep place on the shore, tie a rope with a slipknot round his neck and a heavy stone tied on the other end. Both stone and dog had to be thrown in the sea together. It was a quick death and preferred to shooting. Roderick said he would do it and asked me to go along with him. Roderick with the rope and I with bread in my hand set off with the dog following us. Roderick put the loop around his neck and held him. He said, "Can you tie the stone on?" I said I could and did, in a fashion. "Now" he said "I'll throw the dog and you throw the stone when I say heave." We did and the dog went to the bottom. After a moment's struggle, the dog appeared on the surface swimming towards Roderick, who thought it was going to jump on him and in his hurry to get away, he slipped and fell in the water. When up, climbing on the rocks, I took a look at him, and fearing that I would be the next for the heave, I beat a hasty retreat. The dog was home before me. His near miss did him no harm and soon afterwards he became quite tame and died a natural death.

Roderick was in one of his bad spells when one day I came upon him praying out loud at the back of a large rock near the shore. He asked me what I was doing there. I said I was going out to see the masterpiece. This was a two masted schooner owned by a local man, Dougal Campbell. It was moored in a bay between four hawsers. He said, "Have you ever been on board her?" "No" I said. "Well, come with me and I'll take you on board her." I didn't have the sense to be afraid of him and off we went. There was no one on board her, so with an oarless small boat, which we pushed off the shore, we went alongside her. She was high out of the water and I could not get on board. He then took hold of me and flung me skywards. I landed on my backside on the deck. He did shout, "Are you alright?" When I said yes, he said "Get a piece of rope and put the middle of it round a cleat and let me have both ends. I don't trust your knots."

This done, he hauled himself up on the rope. He then took me up the mast to the cross tree and showed me all the ropes and explained what they were for. My father, wondering where I was, went in search of me. He had thought I might be out there and he came in sight of the ship with Roderick and myself sitting on the crosstree yard. He was greatly alarmed and dared not shout or show himself but hoped for the best and that the mad man and I would somehow come down and ashore safely. And safely we did, perhaps through his ardent prayers. Shortly afterwards poor Roderick had to be sent back to Craig Dunain where he died years afterwards. I used to visit him there when I joined the army and bring him tobacco which he would not accept and he did not appear to recognise me, perhaps on account of my having grown up and the fact that I was in uniform, kilt, red tunic and white spats. I would give the tobacco to the other inmates who would take it aside and start laughing at me. I would feel embarrassed and be glad to leave them.

There was a small loch at the back of our house. It was partly covered with reeds. Flocks of birds of different kinds used to come and feed in the reeds. In the autumn, it made good sport for the gentry who would be staying at the hotel and I used to follow them, gathering up the empty cartridges. One day there were five guns and two dogs out. Among the party was Professor Hodson of the Edinburgh Royal Infirmary. He was the man who looked after my mother when she was there twice for surgery; he was very kind to her but could not cure her. They saw many birds landing in the reeds, but on account of their thickness, the dogs were unable to swim through and put the birds in flight. They called me over and asked would I wade out through the reeds and chase the birds. Although my English was poor, I understood what was wanted and into the reeds I went and soon had some on the wing. The firing was heavy and scattered. I was much alarmed when many shots were fired at a low flying bird, when the pellets would be singing in the reeds near me, I thought I had better clear out. On my way I picked up two ducks that fell in the reeds, which I handed over. They gave me a row for staying out there so long. Not knowing where I was, they had missed good shots. They also gave me a shilling, which I gave to my mother.

This incident was to be remembered and talked about years later when I was a wounded patient in Craigleith Hospital in 1914. Professor Hodson was the head of the Royal Infirmary, Edinburgh. He and another crowd were visiting and inspecting our hospital. I was a bed patient and when they arrived at the foot of my bed, the matron said to the Professor that I was the youngest wounded soldier in the ward and had just arrived from France in the last convoy. He at once walked to the head of the bed where my chart hung "You are a Cameron Highlander. What battle were you wounded at?" I told him. "Where are you from?" "South Uist." "What part?" "Lochboisdale. "North or South?" "South" "Do you know a lady, Catherine Campbell, there?" I said she was my mother "She is dead now." " Do you remember seeing me there?" "Yes" I said,

First World War army recruiting poster.

"I remember well the day you nearly killed me." "Where was that and how?" I told him of the day. "I well remember that day. It was a very enjoyable day. You were in no danger, I'm sure you had more escapes from bullets in France." He turned to the Sister and said, "Look after him Sister." In his party was a gentleman who gave me a half golden sovereign, which was a fortune to me in those days.

I was not yet sixteen when a sergeant from the Cameron Highlanders came to recruit. He was staying at a house near Lochboisdale pier and when I heard this I decided to enlist. Other boys had already done so but how could I get away. I knew my father would not let me go as they were leaving for Inverness that night. I had to plan fast. I was lucky, I had a fairly good suit and when I asked my sister Mary if I had a clean shirt, she looked and said, "Where are you going?" I said "Nowhere." I got the shirt and then I needed a haircut badly. It was not safe to ask Mary, who used to cut it. I went to Kate next door and asked her. She said she would but said, "What's wrong with Mary, doesn't she always cut your hair?" I said we had broken the scissors. "Come on then, I'll do it." She got a sack and put it round my shoulders and started on one side. She had just finished that side when Mary came in and shouted "Don't cut his hair, he is going to run away to join the army." "Well if that's the case, I'll cut no more and he can't go away like that" and off my shoulders came the sack. I ran home, had a quick face wash, changed into the fairly good suit and took my father's cap off a nail and started running the mile to Angus Beag's house, hoping to catch him before leaving for the pier, and when I saw them, he and his wife were at the boat ready for leaving. I shouted and waved and they waited for me, and when they asked what was wrong, I said "Nothing, only my father before he left for the creels this morning said that I was to go to the shop for nails but there was none there, I thought I would try the shops on the pier." "Alright, jump onboard we are not going to be long. What is your father doing with the nails?" "I don't know for sure, but I think he is making more creels." "No, it can't be that at this time of year."

We had a light following wind and soon landed at the pier, where they told me again that they were not staying long and that I must be at the boat waiting when I got the nails. I said I

would and waited till they were gone when I made enquiries about where the recruiting sergeant stayed. On being told, I made my way there and knocked on the door. A stout lady answered. I asked if the sergeant was in. She said no, that he was down on the pier but would be back soon, would I wait inside. I would, and she gave me tea and scones. She asked me who I was and the reason why I wanted to see the sergeant. I told her and she gave me more scones saying she knew my mother well. She was and had the reputation of being a very kind person. Her name was Lexy

After a while the sergeant came and had a look at me and when I said I wanted to join the army, he said "You look small, but I'll put you on the measuring scale. Take off your boots." That did not help. "No," he said, "you are half an inch short." I could have cried with grief. But when he said, "I'll take you on as a boy." I was very happy. He asked who cut my hair, I said my brother but the scissors broke. He said "I'll cut it for you, I can't let you stay like that." He did, and when finished the cap came down over my ears so I threw it away.

"I will now have to take you to the doctor for medical inspection, and to the priest to take the oath. Were you thinking of going away with the crowd that is leaving tonight?" I said that was my intention. "Do you have to go home again?" "No." "Well, we better go to the doctor now, we shall have dinner when we come back." He was Sergeant Bowie from Benbecula, a nice man but he was killed in action early in the war.

When we arrived, after walking the three miles to the doctor's house, he was not in. His wife said he would be late as he had a call to Eriskay. We carried on to the Priest. On the way he asked me if I had ever been ill. I said that apart from measles and whooping cough, I very seldom took a slight cold. He said, "You look healthy enough, we won't bother with the doctor." The pastor at St. Peter's Daliburgh was Canon Alexander MacDougal, and after looking at me he asked "Are you joining the army? You are very young, have you got permission from your father?" and when I said "Yes Father" he said he did not believe me and that I did not need to raise my hand while taking the Oath, just repeat the words after the sergeant.

There was another young boy there for the same purpose, he was along with his father and had permission to join. I had good reasons to remember his father as he was the truant officer. He winked at the sergeant and said "The army is the best place for him." Like himself, his son John could play the pipes. After the war he joined the City of Glasgow Police Force and became Pipe Major of the band, which he taught to become many times champions of the world.

Of all the young, hopeful crowd going away that night, only John and I are living, some killed in action, some died of wounds.

When the sergeant and I got back, Lexy had a good dinner waiting for us. The steamer had not yet arrived. When he asked if I had money to go away with, I told him I had none. He gave me six shillings, which saw me to Inverness with the travelling warrant. The steamer was coming to the pier and then we left to meet the rest. I was on the pier watching for any boat coming from the south side waiting to detain me. After a while I did see such a boat, within it also the most feared man in the township and others. Ignoring the rest I made for the steamer, now alongside. I went on board and descended to the bottom where I hid in a coalbunker and stayed until the engine started. It was safe to go on deck where I was told that a search had been made for me. The boat was drawing away from the pier. I could see my father in the crowd and waved to him. If he saw me he did not wave back. I was told afterwards that the feared man, Angus, had to be restrained from giving the sergeant a beating for enlisting me without permission. The sergeant was willing to tear up my papers if they could find me. At last we were on our way.

The boat called first at Lochmaddy, then Dunvegan in Skye, then Harris and round the north end of Skye to Portree where she was to meet the paddle steamer *Glencoe* which went to Kyle of Lochalsh. We landed at Dunvegan at 11.00 pm. It was a calm moonlight night, freezing hard with ice on the road. We didn't like the idea of staying on the boat until she got to Portree at seven in the morning. Instead we decided to walk the twenty miles or more to Portree and would be in plenty of time to catch the boat before 7.00 a.m. We all agreed and started walking. None of us had a watch, and after what seemed hours of walking and sliding on the ice, we came to a place where another road branched off. We didn't know which one to follow; however there was a light shining from a house near by. The man who answered our knock gave us the right direction. A voice from within said, "Who is that, Iain?" "Oh" he said "a crowd of young boys going to Inverness to join the army." "Oh Iain, see that the boys are not hungry." We said we were not, thanked them and left, sure that we were on the right road.

Hours after that, with many miles behind us, most of our boots were beginning to fall apart. One boy had the sole of one boot completely off. Fearing the same would happen, we all took them off and tied them around our necks, as for walking bare footed we were quite used to it. We kept on till we came to where again another road joined, but there was no house or light to be seen. We took the branched off road for surely this would be the right one. The moon had nearly gone and it was getting dark. We had been walking a long time when we met a man with a horse and light cart. We stopped him. "Are we on the right road to Portree?" we enquired. "No" he said, "you are over five miles on the wrong road." He asked where we came from. We said Dunvegan. He said that's where he was going. We asked would he take us in his cart. He said he would but that some of us would have to walk and ride turn about. This was agreeable, as the horse did not look strong. When we asked how much he was charging, he said three pence each. "No" we said, "that is far too much," that we would pay him one penny each. "No, no, I don't want to kill the horse for five pence" he said. The horse did not seem to have long to go; it was doubtful if it could reach Dunvegan.

Judging by the pails and tins he had in the cart, we took him to be a tinker. We carried on backwards till we reached the fork of the road. We were tired and sleepy so we lay down in the long, dry heather and soon were asleep. Sometime afterwards, I woke up cold. I had matches in my pocket and thought it a good ploy to set the heather on fire. This I did, luckily on account of the frost the heather was not very dry but it made plenty of smoke. When I saw the rest standing up coughing, spluttering and swearing, it was time for me to run with a boy of my own age after me. He caught the tail of my not so good jacket, which tore with the tear ending at the collar. In retaliation, I got after him with the result one of the sleeves came off his jacket. We did not fight, I imagine because we had more important things on our minds. Beside us was a burn where water was still running. We splashed our faces in the icy water and were ready for the road again.

The date was the 21st January 1913, daylight was coming on fast and soon we could make out the town of Portree in the distance. When we approached its outskirts, there were many trees growing there. Apart from one of the boys, Murdoch, who had been to the mainland, the rest of us had never seen a tree before. We were awed and amazed at the thickness and height of them. The urge to climb them was too strong to leave. I chose a tall one and began to climb. When I got to the top I carved my name there. Murdoch pleaded with us to come down or we would miss the boat. As I was coming down, I made another long tear in my trousers.

We got our boots on and tied the sole of John's boot on with a piece of string and started to where we hoped to find the boat. When we enquired about her from a policeman, he told us she had left hours ago. We were rather disappointed but not downhearted. He asked where we came from and what we were doing there. We told him how we had left the steamer at Dunvegan, walked from there, lost our way, slept in the heather and missed the boat to Kyle. "Have you got warrants to take you to Inverness?" We said yes and showed them. "Do you know people here?" "No, nobody." "When did you eat last?" We told him before we left home. "Then you must be very hungry. I'll take you to a place where I think you will get something to eat. What happened to your clothes and boots?" We said playing on the way and sliding on the ice. He laughed and said, "I understand."

He took us to a house in the square. When a middle-aged lady came to the door, she looked at us, and at the policeman and said, "Are you taking them to prison, Angus?" "No," said the policeman, "they are going to join the army and have missed the ferry." Could she give the boys a meal and maybe give them a place to sleep for tonight? She said she would but did not have much room. We thanked the Officer and he left, laughing. The lady invited us in and showed us the sink to wash. She then had our breakfast ready, two large kippers, three large plates of scones, butter and tea, with a second helping for any who wanted it. We asked her if she would let us have a needle and black thread. She said "Yes, why?" to which we said. "Our clothing needs mending." "Off you go to your beds, leave your clothes outside and I'll mend them for you."

We went to bed three in one, two in the other. There was another small bed in the room. The lodger, a stonemason who was out working, used it. No sooner in bed, we were sleeping like logs, not a murmur except snores. She woke us up in the late afternoon with our clothes on her arm, mended. She told us that dinner was ready. We got up, had a quick wash. It was salted ling, potatoes milk and plenty of it, all of which we enjoyed. After that we went for a walk in the town and were greatly surprised at the many shops we saw and at their nearness to each other. There was one that had black sugar candy made into ladders, pipes and watches showing in the window, beside other trinkets. We went inside and bought many ladders and pipes and other useless things. Euan Walker bought three watches and ate them all before we got back late, filled with sweets, lemonade and black candy. The landlady asked if we wanted supper, we said "No." "Well you better go to your beds, you have to be up at six in the morning for the boat." We went upstairs. The lodger was in his bed, he looked a big man and if awake did not say anything.

We went to our beds but had no need of sleep as we kept talking, giggling and pulling blankets. We kept at it till the lodger said in anger that we had better quieten down or he would call up the landlady. We did become quiet and in vain tried to sleep. When the laughter and giggling broke out again the lodger got up, and when we saw the size of him, we thought we were in for a thrashing. Instead, he put his hand under his bed and brought out a large chamber pot and started to use it. There was louder laughter then, which brought the landlady up. She was very angry and told us if we did not behave she would send for the policeman and throw us out. We did as wanted and slept till she woke us at 6.00 am as promised. We had kippers again for breakfast and plenty of scones. When we asked how much she was charging, she said 10 pence each. We paid her and gratefully left for the ferry. I have not been to Portree again, but had I been I would have gladly called on her.

The ferry was waiting. Before we boarded her, we had to pay a penny and pass through a turnstile. Ewen was the last to pass and he did not have a penny to drop, the man attending the stile said he would not let him through without paying and we told Ewen he would have to turn back home. Ewen started to cry. I at last paid the penny. We went on board and amused ourselves on the short passage to Kyle. When we arrived there Murdoch took charge. He led us to a place with two seats and a rack above them. We took it to be a waiting room. Murdoch said he was going to a shop to get us something to eat on the way. "Stay where you are and don't open the door till I come back." It was not long before he was back with two large loaves of bread and a large jar of jam. He cut one in thick slices with his pocketknife and spread jam on them. We were eating when we felt that something had hit the room with a very hard bang. Fearing it would fall on the top of us, we made for the closed door. Murdoch got hold of us saying, "Sit down you fools, this is the train you are on." We had a good laugh while we indeed felt foolish. It was our first time on a train and we wondered at the speed it was going at. The train journey was very tiring and we were glad when we arrived at Inverness. Murdoch knew the way to the Barracks. On the outside of the town we came upon a small confectionary shop, and Murdoch bought us some ice cream. We had never seen or tasted the likes before, and when we took the first bite, we thought we were burned and that Murdoch was playing a huge joke on us. We were going to throw it away when Murdoch said, laughing, "Eat it you fools, it is not hot, lick it". We had rounds of it before we left. I think it cost a penny a slab.

We arrived at the guard room where they took our names and addresses and after that to the Quartermaster's store where we were given a pair of blankets, a knife, fork and spoon, and then to the receiving hall where each were allotted an iron bed which could be drawn out and made into a sitting place when not in use. We were told we could go to bed till teatime if we wanted. Instead we strolled around the grounds, fascinated at what we saw. Tea was announced by a piper playing, 'Come to the Cook House Door Boys'. With our knife and fork we crowded to the dining hall. It was kippers again but this time only one each. We could do with more and as we discovered a coffee bar, we regretted having squandered so much money in Portree.

We slept well in our new single beds till the piper woke us at reveille playing the tune of 'Hey Johnnie Cope' followed by a sergeant shouting, "Show a leg there". One of the boys got up, sat on the bed and pulled the clothes well up off his legs and stayed there. The sergeant roared "I don't want to see your legs, you damn fool, you are in the army now. Show a leg means get up and get dressed, you are going to the Quartermaster's store to be fitted out in uniforms." We were put in a line and walked there. I can't say marched, as we didn't know how. When we got there the Quartermaster's sergeant took over and started to fit us out.

The kit comprised of a pair of shoes, two pairs of spats, one pair of hose, two pairs of socks, one pair of trousers, one kilt and plaid, one khaki tunic, one red tunic, one white tunic and belt, one housewife holdall, two towels, two shirts and a kit bag. The rest of the equipment was to be issued later on. It took some time to fit one out. I thought, behind the sergeant's back I would be smart and began to fit myself out. I had the kilt on when the sergeant caught me "You stupid fool" he shouted "leave all those things strictly alone, you've got the kilt on back to front." After giving me a scolding he said, "Now it's your turn." His name was Walsh and I think on account of that incident he was to remember me and I him at a later time when no one in the depot knew me. But for him, the course of my life may well have been very different.

At last we were fitted out and taken this time to a room in the barracks where we changed into uniform. That day, sporting tartan trews and khaki tunics, we were taken on to the parade ground where we were put in charge of an instructor, Sergeant Cranston, who had no Gaelic and many of us in the squad had very little English, in fact, the oldest soldier in our crowd could only understand his own name and Regimental number in English. The sergeant, when he got us into a straight line, began his talk saying "You're in the army now and you've got to do exactly as you're told. When you're on parade, when I say 'attention', you snap your heels together." Some did, many didn't. After many trials he said he would number us off, "By that I mean you begin from the right, the first man says one, the man on his left says two and so on to the end of the line."

There were eight in the line and when numbering came to 8 he kept on saying 9, 10, 11, 12. The sergeant shouted, "You idiot, stop numbering at the end of the line, let's start again, Squad numbers." We did better this time. "Now I want you to try marching. You start off when I say 'quick march' and always by the left foot. Squad quick march." Some did, others looked dumb at the sergeant who said, "You bunch of fools, that command is for you as well." We understood better and off we went after the rest. Before we caught up, he gave the command 'About turn.' We kept going till a man was sent after us to turn us back before we reached the barracks wall. When we got back, and after a long lashing from the sergeant at our stupidity, he said where did we think we were going? There was no answer to that but there was plenty of laughter from the rest. The sergeant soon put a stop to that; he decided instead of letting us loose on the parade ground, to keep us marking time, left right, left right in the same spot for the rest of that afternoon.

In the evening we heard that a party of new recruits from Lewis were coming. Another boy and I went down to the guardroom to see what they were like. They were lined up, about a dozen of them, in front of the guardhouse. Their clothes were nearly the same as ours before we got into uniform, except for one boy about my own age. He was dressed in a navy blue flannel shirt, which reached down well past his knees and with only part of his fingers showing out of the sleeve. He had a cap on that came down over his ears, otherwise with red rosy cheeks he looked the picture of health. It was not at him as a person that I began to laugh, it was rather the comical dress he was in. He caught me looking and laughing at him and without hesitation stepped out of the rank and socked me on the nose. There was much blood, of course, I retaliated and before we were parted, I had already got the worse of it, as I well deserved.

Fort George Barracks

There wasn't much damage done. After a few days in which I kept out of his way, I was ready for a proper fight and this time I would not be taken unawares. I saw him in the distance and ran up to him. I asked him "Are you as good as you were at the guardroom the other day?" "Yes" he said, "do you want more?" We stood toe to toe and the slogging match began in earnest for some time till he said, "That's enough for today." We were both much bloodied and I too was glad to call it a day as I had felt the victor, but not for long, only till we were healed, and then on the slightest provocation and little warning, the fight was continued. There were very few days that we did not fight. It wasn't a crime so long as we were privates. To hit an N.C.O. was a different matter. During all of our six months training, the fighting continued and when our time was up at Fort George, he was let away earlier to avoid trouble on the train. His name was John Montgomery. I regret I was never able to find out what part of Lewis he came from. I was not to see him again till I met him in a nearby trench at the first battle of Ypres. I think it is better to leave this part of my story, which I will relate when I come to it.

Meantime, it's back to the Square and Sergeant Cranston who by then must have been feeling sorry for himself and vowed he would make soldiers of us or break our hearts. After he had got us to turn about together at that command, he said he would teach us to form fours. "First you number off, that is to say the front rank, then those in the rear rank take the number of the man in front of them. Now when I say 'form fours', the odd numbers remain at attention, the even numbers take one pace backwards and one pace to the right, you are then in fours. To return to your original position, I will give the command 'form two deep', and you take one step to your left and one step forward." It took us some time before we mastered that.

There would be many squads on the square. I think ours was the worst as the sergeant kept us in a corner drilling before he would risk letting us fifty yards away from him. We were often told we were stupid, and worse than that, we were the laughing stock of the square and that we would be the cause of him being sent to the mad house. Sometimes we would laugh at our own folly. There were the times when old Cranston would start to pull his own hair. He was an old soldier with many battle ribbons on his breast to show for it, yet he was a kindly man. One day he took us outside the Barracks for an exercise in judging distance and when we gained a good idea of the length of a hundred yards on account of our good eyesight, the rest became easy to us. He was very surprised and no one was called stupid that day. "Boys" he said "that's what I want to see, when you get your rifles on the rifle range, that you move according to the object you are aiming at and if the distance is wrong, you will not hit the target. The target is the man you are shooting at. Take it from me boys, there will be a war between us and Germany within two years." How right he was, and it is then you want to make every bullet count. After that day he never called us the stupid squad but we were still the awkward squad. The drill was slowly progressing mainly because we were getting used to his English.

Barrack routine was reveille at 7.00 a.m. when we washed in ice cold water, dressed for P.T. training, a mug of cocoa and then on to the Square to run a mile. After that it was breakfast and we could always eat more. The fact that most of us could only understand and talk very little English meant we were made the butt of any horseplay and jokes. This was carried out relentlessly by the older boys until an eighteen-year-old Arisaig boy joined us. His name was James Campbell. He was over 6 ft. in height and built in proportion. The army had no shoes or clothing in the store that would fit him, everything had to be hand made for him, and once in uniform he certainly looked a giant. He was fluent in English and Gaelic, he took us under his strong wing and after that no one dared to touch us. One night around the fire, a big boy from his own township was getting rough with us. James told him to stop and leave us alone and when he would not, James caught him by the breast in one hand, picked him off the floor and flung him away, sliding him under three beds. After that incident he and the others took the hint and we were left strictly alone.

Every Friday the barrack room floor had to be scrubbed with soft soap and pails of hot water and then dried and sprinkled with dry sand, which we got by digging outside the barrack's iron railings. It was one of these days when three others and myself were detailed off for sand. Robert MacInnes being the oldest soldier was in charge of us, and he still only understood little or no English. We climbed over the railing and filled two large buckets of sand. On the slope below us stood the Millburn Distillery, which had a flat roof. As we had never seen a flat roof on a house before we were fascinated at the sight and went to inspect it. As it was low, we were well able to reach up. It was covered with ice and the temptation to slide stones on its icy top was too great. This was an enjoyable play until some of the stones overshot the wall near a door. A man in white overalls came out shouting.

We beat a hasty retreat over the railing thinking that bed would be the best hiding place. We went there only to be discovered shortly afterwards by a sergeant who took our names and told us to report to the Orderly Room the next day. This we did and were lined up to be dealt

31

with; our crime was a serious one, 'throwing stones at civilian property to the danger of their lives.' Two officers and a sergeant major came out of the Orderly Room. The officer began by saying "Private 5540 MacInnes, you are the oldest soldier, it was up to you to see that those under you always behaved themselves." Poor Robert did not understand a word of this and as I was standing beside him, he bent his head and whispered towards me "What is he saying Donald?" I said, "Do you see that tree in front of the cook house?" "Yes," "Well, as you are the oldest soldier, he wants you to run as fast as you can and go round that tree and salute it, then turn back here and stand to attention. That's to be our punishment." Off went Robert as fast as he could. The sergeant major roared, "What's the matter with that man, come back here you fool.". Robert never looked back but continued to do as I told him. When he went round the tree three times, saluting it every time round, the officers could not contain their laughter and had to go inside. Robert came back running and almost out of breath, took his place in the rank and stood to attention.

A Major Gunn, who could speak good Gaelic, came out of the Orderly Room from where much was going on, and asked in Gaelic why he had run and circled that tree. "Well" said Robert "that's what the officer said, he said too that was to be our punishment for throwing the stones." "Who said that?" "Donald here, he has plenty of English." The major went inside from where much laughter could be heard. Soon the major came out and he spoke to us in Gaelic telling us of the danger of throwing stones when we did not know where they might land. "You were very lucky no one was hurt. Do you see that high stone wall at the end of the parade ground? That's the miniature range, you can throw as many as you like on that wall. Keep away from the Distillery or you will be severely punished. You are admonished, off you go and behave yourselves." I did not get off so easy with Robert who was much taller and older than I. We were making slow progress at the drill. Old Cranston had still some hair left on his head. One day he took us to the miniature range and we surprised him that day too.

Inverness is a cold place in the winter. The barracks were no exception. Our room was large and draughty, and a fire was not allowed till after 3.00 pm. There was no hot water and lights had to be out at ten, and no talking after that. After we learned the different commands of the drill, we were issued our equipment, rifles, bayonets and dummy cartridges. We began training in rifle drill and kept at it for long hours. In the morning it was always physical training and gymnastics.

We had an Irish boy training to be a boxer. He used to be the first in the washroom and would fill four large basins of icy water, which he would raise, one after another and tip them over his head. He would be blue and could only stutter for a while afterwards. One morning I thought I would have a go. I filled three basins, which were too heavy for me to lift over my head, so I had to pour some out. When the Irishman saw what I was doing, he said, "Begorrah man, you will kill yourself." He was nearly right. It took me some time to get my breath back to normal and I only managed one that day. I did not give in but three was the most I could manage and that was daily. It was worse than the times when cousin Donald and I used to break the ice in front of us when swimming. All day after the ice shower I would feel very warm, even when the big boys would be rolling and covering me in snow, I would laugh at them. This would be after throwing snowballs if the opportunity was there, snow down the back of their necks or in their beds. All this time the fighting between Montgomery and myself never let up and neither side gave in, until our camp broke up in June.

The camp was held at Fort George under canvas where we joined up with the old hands doing their annual training and us doing our musketry, at which the old silly and awkward squad proved themselves to be the best on the firing range. I myself at 150 yards put a 2-inch group on the target and at 300 yards, four bull's eyes and 1 inner, all out of five shots. We were all marksmen, that is, all who came from the Western Isles. Old Cranston was dancing with joy. He took us to the coffee bar and gave to all lemonade, ice cream, cakes and buns, all we could hold. But he would not let us go near the canteen, claiming that beer was bad for young boys, a thing we very seldom indulged in.

Money was always short. My pay was nine pence a day till I got a rise of three pence for being a good shot. We used to have much fun on pay night going round the tents, when many of the older hands would be well oiled on strong beer which then cost one penny a pint. Two of us, with a mallet each, would look for tents with a bulge on them, preferably the nearest two. We would then together give the bulge a good tap with the mallet and run. Whoever got the tap in both tents would make a dive for the entrance, trying to catch the culprits. Nobody in sight, one blamed the other and often a fight would start while we watched in our own tent, laughing. We had strict orders to slacken the guy ropes on the tents at night. After lights out, we would go round and tighten many of them with the result some of the poles would come through the canvas and down the tent would come. The occupants would be up for punishment next day. All this depended on it raining that night.

Our six month's training was coming to an end. We were in the best physical shape, well trained and well able to take our place alongside the best on parade, and as we were having lots of fun, we regretted leaving. Looking back on it, I can honestly say it was one of the best six months that I have ever spent in my life. I would have no hesitation in recommending army training for any young boy. At last the day of departure came. We handed in our kit, uniform, equipment and rifle and got into our civilian clothes. Mine were much too short and tight but it had to do. Montgomery was let off with the early train as already said. There were no more fights or meetings until we met in the front line in France. We got the train, which was not strange to us now, to Kyle of Lochalsh and steamer to places in Harris and on to Lochmaddy and Lochboisdale, our last port. Some of my people were waiting and I got a warm reception.

2   Early Sea Days and War Training

I was soon able to buy a new suit. I was now approaching manhood but there was no work to be had. My father and uncle Seonaidh and his nephew were fishing lobsters and were doing fairly well. Uncle was always troubled with the toothache and as there was no dentist on the island he had to go to Glasgow for treatment. I took his place, not as skipper, but as a very green hand. Lobsters were very plentiful in those days. We used to have sixty pots out with one eye in each pot. That was the method from time immemorial. We used to catch five to six dozen a day, using gutted salt mackerel as bait. The size of a creel was 2 ft x 14 inches and it was accepted that it could not be improved. Time has proved that the same type of creel would be quite useless today, when they are using creels of 5 ft. x 2 ft. wide with five eyes, 2 on each side and one inside called the parlour. It is not baited and I am told that that is where most of the lobsters gather, no one seems to know exactly why, only that once they are in that trap it is almost impossible to escape.

Lobster fishing is a very lucrative form of making a living, that is providing you are lucky and you save your boat and gear which you can lose all or part of in any storm. Replacing loss is very expensive. Now, you can have your catch weighed, sold and paid for that day or when you wish. In my day, we had to construct boxes to carry three and four dozens lobsters packed in straw, bracken or dry heather, then to be taken by boat to Lochboisdale to be shipped to Billingsgate, to take what the salesman felt like giving in return. With the slow and warm transportation, many would be dead and unfit for human consumption. One such time, I sent twenty-four dozen lobsters, a week's fishing, away to Billingsgate and in return only got seven shillings and sixpence, with a warning not to send food that was unfit for human consumption. That was the usual excuse for what the salesman pocketed. We had no protection.

It was late autumn before my uncle took over and I was out of a job. I had another uncle, called Iain, he was a stonemason and I got a job along with him. I thought seeing that he was my uncle I would have an easy job. I was wrong. He was not as bad as Cranston but not far off it. When 6.00 pm came, he used to say, "Now Donald, it's six o'clock, our time is our own and we can do as we like with it. We've done a good day's work, now we will go for a dram." I was allowed one dram while he took a couple. He was a kindly man, a splendid stonemason and a very good bard. Some of his songs are still in demand. It was mostly repair work and the job did not last long.

I was getting restless. In late 1913 I had a notion of going to sea. I did not need to ask for permission this time and when another lad called Roderick from the township decided to go to sea and was going to Glasgow, I went along with him. When we reached Glasgow, we were to stay at a boarding house and were met by a Barra man at the station. We got the tramcar and placed our kit bags under the stairs thinking they were quite safe there. We had only gone a few car stops when a youth boarded the tram and away he went with one of our kit bags. Someone shouted "Stop the car, a thief is away with a kit bag." We saw him in the crowd running with the bag on his shoulder. The tram stopped and the Barra man got out and ran after the thief. He was soon caught and given a good slapping, as there was no policeman in sight.

When we got to the boarding house, we got a semi cool reception due to the fact that times were bad and jobs both on sea and land were very hard to get. However, when we said we had enough money to keep us for a while, the atmosphere got warmer. The Barra sailor was just

34

back from a long voyage, he used to take us round the docks to every ship. There were no jobs to be had, many ships tying up for lack of trade. Before the end of the week Roderick signed on as a seaman on a ship going to Spain. I gave up doing the docks and shipping office and turned my quest landwards. I kept at it, shipyards, factories, anywhere I thought there might be an opening, till at last one morning while passing a lumber yard I went to the office and enquired. "Yes" they said, they had one vacancy. "Can you start now?" I said, "Yes, what's the wages?" "Eighteen shillings a week, three days' lying time kept off. The hours are from 7.00 a.m. till 6.30 pm with half an hour for breakfast, one hour for dinner; at the end of the month your wages will be a pound a week." I said I would take the job. The landlady was charging twelve shillings; I had to be very careful with the other six shillings.

The yard was on Shields Road and was called *'Potters Saw Mill'*. The work was not too heavy, stacking up cut timber and moving logs to the sawing platform. A small steam crane was used for this purpose. The yard was in a hollow with a wooden stairway going down. The steam crane was fired by wood, which gave off many sparks. One windy morning as I was descending the stairway, I got a spark in my eye. I did not think much of it at the time, but afterwards it gave me much trouble and again, could well have changed the course of my life.

At the end of the first month there, I reminded the foreman of his promise of a rise. He said, "times are bad, many are walking the streets idle. I can get as many as I want of better men for less wages than you are getting". I said, "alright, get your slaves, I want my money now" "Alright, I'll tell the timekeeper to make up your time." I got that and the three days' lying time.

Not wanting to face the landlady and lie to her that I had left my job, I decided to take another run around the docks. At last I came on a ship loading coal. I enquired if they needed an ordinary seaman. The man said, "ja, ja," and I wondered if I heard right. However, he pointed to a door and I knocked. The man asked what did I want. I said "a job as an ordinary seaman." "Have you been to sea before?" I lied and said "yes." "Let me see your discharge book." I said I was sailing on MacBrayne ships and they don't give discharges. "Alright, we are sailing with the tide at noon, are you ready to sign on?" I said "yes, sir." it was the first time I had said 'sir' since I left the army. "Alright, come along with me to be signed on." He took me to an office, which I knew was not the shipping office I used to go to. However, I was signed on.

He asked if I wanted an advance in wages. I said I did and understood then that he was the captain. He asked if I had oilskins. I said that I had no gear. He then took me to a shop where I bought an oilskin, a straw pallet, a blanket, towel, knife and fork and spoon, an enamel mug and plate and some soap. These were put into a bundle and I took them on board the ship where I found an empty bunk. I noticed painted on her bow the name was *Ivanhoe*. I went to the lodging house to gather my kitbag. The landlady said that I was too early for dinner, when I told her that I had left my job and signed on a ship, she said I was very lucky and asked the ship's name. When I said the *'Ivanhoe'*, she said, "I know her, she belongs to MacLay and McIntyre and she goes to Hull and Lisbon, coal out and iron ore back, you'll be away for over a month." She knew most of the ships' names and their ports of call, as all her lodgers were sailors. But she was wrong this time, like myself, in assuming that the ship was British, when in fact she was Norwegian and did not call in these ports.

We were well down the River Clyde before I found that out. I asked several where we going, but I could not make out their answer, till at last I enquired from a man whom I understood very well. He was surprised I didn't know. He said the ship was Norwegian, and we were going to Algiers. He said there was a Glasgow chap and himself from London, all the rest of the crew were foreigners. He also told me to be aware of the Glasgow lad that he had been along with him on the last voyage.

It wasn't my watch and so I went to my bunk. The shifts were four on and four off. I made myself as comfortable as I could and slept part of the time. On deck it was my first watch ever. While the rest of the watch was busy squaring down hatches and gear, I was more in their way. The fact that I couldn't understand a word of what was being said to me made me appear to be a lot more stupid than I was. I was being pushed and dragged most of the time. I noticed that the Glasgow lad, who was in my watch, was having fun at my expense. Not a word of advice came from him. All I could do was to keep my eyes open, it seemed that the ears could not help. I was glad when eight bells came and the watch was over.

I think it was the longest watch on deck I ever did and when I again went on duty we were in open sea. It was blowing hard and I began to be seasick, and although it was fish, I couldn't eat the food that was brought to the fo'c'sle. Someone asked if I could steer, I said that I could steer a sailing boat. I was ordered to take the wheel. I went up on the bridge and was given the course. I kept her there for a few minutes. The Captain who was on the bridge said, "You will have to do better than that." He blew a whistle for another man to take my place. I was sent off in disgrace. The other man was the Glasgow chap who did not forget to torment me. When the watch was over and I said I would learn, he said, "No, you are a Highland man and they are all stupid." I asked him how long he had been to sea? He said "Nearly two years." I said "You are still an Ordinary Seaman, that doesn't seem very bright to me." He retorted "One more word out of you and I slap you" and he did. I thought of retaliating, but he was too big for me and I had to suffer it.

The gale blew itself out before we were through the Irish Sea, and we had good weather till we came to the Bay of Biscay. It was real rough there and we had three days of it. She was heavily loaded, the rail under the water most of the time and I was seasick all the time, but that was no excuse I had to work whenever possible. Down the coast of Spain and on to Gibraltar, the weather was much warmer and we were mostly engaged in repairing the damage done in the Bay, such as damaged iron ladders and ventilators. I had no idea of the power of the sea when at its worst. Even in calm weather I was still very ill and only cold potatoes would stay down. I was in no shape to defend myself against the Glasgow hooligan but come what may I vowed some day I would be his match. I tried it once but all I got was two black eyes. He had spent some time on a training ship and he was taller, longer in the arms and had some boxing experience. I had to wait till the eyes cleared up before I was provoked and could no longer suffer him. This time I got to grips with him and did better by getting him down, and giving him a bloody nose, but still it was not good enough. When he got up, he gave me another pasting but only one black eye this time. I felt I was doing much better and was delighted to see him going about with a swollen nose. The rest of the crew did not interfere, the London boy I am sure would, but he was afraid of the big bully.

After we passed the Straits of Gibraltar, the days were very hot and my eye was giving me much trouble, I think mainly due to the heat and the fact that my aggressor poured a full bottle of ink over my face while I lay asleep in my bunk. This time I went after him in good style with the aid of a hatch batten, and with my army training in fencing and bayonet work I gave him a good slapping he would have reason to remember. It was on our trip from Iceland that we had the next fight. I was walking along the deck with a pot of red lead paint that I was working with, when from behind he tripped me. The paint spilled on the deck and I fell. When I got up, I made a dive for him, the deck was wet with paint, he slipped and I fell on the top of him. I was in much better shape then and knew what to expect and before he gave in, the deck was wet with more than red paint. After that he left me alone for a long time until on the next ship when I had the misfortune to be along with him, which I will relate later.

When we arrived at the port of Algiers, we were too deeply loaded to get alongside the pier and had to anchor off shore in the bay. It was very hot and I was ordered to be the watchman, my duties were to ferry the Captain and any member of the crew back and forward to the pier and also to keep a fire going in the galley and keep a good look out.

They started to unload us the next day and a swarm of Arabs came on board to do this, and except for the working of the winches which the crew did, we discharged to a barge on each side of the ship taking over a week to unload. Every day other boats used to come alongside us. One day a young boy came aboard with two large baskets, one of fruit the other containing brooches, rings, bracelets and many other trinkets of Egyptian ivory. He had to be clear of the ship and ashore before sunset but had stayed in the fo'c'sle selling his wares too long and there was no way he could get ashore except through me the boatman. He began to bargain about taking him ashore and would give me anything I wanted out of the baskets. I chose three articles, a brooch, bracelet and ring and a promise to bring me a bottle of wine the next day. I rowed him ashore.

I watched him coming on board the next day and sure enough he had the bottle under his coat. He climbed with his two baskets on to the bulwark and jumped on deck. The bottle slipped and broke to pieces when it hit the deck. There was a general cry from the workmen who blamed the kid for bringing and selling such stuff on board. I stepped in and said the bottle belonged to me and that it slipped out of my pocket and had nothing to do with the kid, and that I would report them for interfering with a member of the ship's crew. That seemed to do the trick. The kid was allowed to go about his business. After a while he took me aside and told me I could have anything I wanted out of the baskets, that I had saved him from six months in jail and losing his licence. He could talk good English. I got more trinkets and oranges. I intended sending the lot to my three sisters when I would arrive in the U.K. again. I thought they would like the decorations, however I never got to do it, instead they nearly got me into trouble on two occasions before I parted with them, more of this later.

I was beginning to be friendly with a Russian called Finn who could talk a little English. Although we had already got a sub from the Captain we again approached him but there was nothing doing, he wouldn't give us a cent, and so we went ashore broke. All we could do was window shop and watch others going into pubs. As we walked up a street, we saw a well-dressed lady ahead of us. She was leading a small poodle dog on a long leather leash and when passing the first lamppost we were beside the dog when he sniffed the post and lifted his leg. The lady turned her back and stood. Finn the Russian, in a flash, took out his sheath knife, cut the leash, took a turn and a half hitch around the post, picked up the poodle and placed it under his jacket without a yelp. We turned back and walked fast towards the ship. The small boat was at the shore and we rowed fast to the ship. The Russian said, "He will make good company for the big dog." This was a Great Dane that the Captain had. We felt he would buy the poodle, but first we had to swear that we had won it at a raffle. I am sure we only got less than what it was worth, but enough for another headache and hangover. He was a real playmate for the Great Dane. Sadly we lost him overboard in a storm going to Iceland.

We left Algiers for the Balearic Isles to load salt for Iceland. Cleaning the holds from coal to salt was our main task on the short trip there. When we arrived, they began loading up. It was all, or nearly all, women's work, carrying baskets full of salt on their heads, coming on board on one plank and when above the hatch, a tilt of their head the basket would fall off but was caught by a hook at the end of a short stick, then stepping off that plank on to another which took them ashore to their loading rack. There was the distance of a pace between each person and they carried on like an endless chain. We had one winch working with a barrel. I was surprised to see that the women were putting more salt on board than the barrel. It was a very small port and it took four days to load her. I went ashore to see where the salt was coming from. It was an open cast mine with a light railway leading from it to a crusher at the dock. The salt came down in very large blocks. There seemed to be a large amount of salt on the ground and also fruit trees, especially fig trees.

We left there in March and called into Portugal for fresh water. A lighter came alongside. We got the hose ready but when the tank in the lighter was opened, it smelled really bad with sulphur. The Captain would not take it. We left at once and all taps and pumps were padlocked. We were allowed a pint and a half for drinking and nothing for washing.

We had very good weather in the Bay this time and made good passage to Troon where we bunkered with coal and fresh water. I went ashore, broke as usual. I took all the trinkets with me intending to sell them on the street. I approached a tall, well-dressed man and told him I had a lot of jewellery I would sell him cheap. He asked to see them and when he examined them said, "Where did you steal these from?" "I never stole them, I bought them in Africa." "I don't believe you, I am a policeman, you better come along with me." I said "If you come down to my ship I can prove it to you." "Are you off that ship?" I said, "Yes." "Well in that case I am inclined to believe you, but stop selling them or you might get into trouble." I took his advice and went back on board, disappointed. The next time I gave them away, which I will explain later on.

We left in good weather but getting colder the further north we went. Going round Barra Head, I was at the wheel, by then I was a good steersman. We passed a fleet of local boats fishing with great lines. We could see the fish being hauled in. The Captain asked me if I lived on one of these islands. I said "Yes, South Uist." "Do you know Uisinish?" When I said I lived not far from there, he said they were very bad people there. I at once knew that he was referring to the ill-fated ship 'La France' that was wrecked on that shore. It was alleged that some of the crew got ashore, but were very badly looked after. Their common grave is still easy to see. She was from Latvia.

I still remember our course from Barra Head to Reykjavik in Iceland. The weather held good for a day and night, when we ran into a gale and then a storm. The height of the waves was terrifying. I recall being at the wheel and every time she rolled she used to dip the corner of the flying bridge and take in tons of seawater. When she came to even keel, I would be up to my knees in water. No work except steering could be done.

In Troon we got a replacement Second Mate. The old Second Mate whom I got on with very well had taught me many things and I was sorry that he had left us. The new Second Mate was a different kind. He was just out of navigation school and had less experience than was necessary for the working of a ship. He went by the book but I went by the 'Ivanhoe' and on many things we did not agree with the result my life was made miserable by his rank. I got every dirty job that was going.

I recall once after that storm and after repairs had been done, he ordered me to get a pot of paint and an arm full of dry rags and to dry the fo'c'sle deck and paint it. I had it half done when a wave came over the bow. I jumped onto the windlass and held on fast while the paint and all went splashing down the deck. At once a whistle came from the Bridge. I answered it and was asked by the Captain if I was trying to commit suicide. I said I was ordered by the Second Mate to do that, he said, "Get something useful to do, we haven't got that much paint to waste." I reported what he said to the officer who said, "You are the Captain's boy." I said, "No, but I am nobody's fool." He was not any better after that and I vowed I would get my own back.

Before we entered the port of Reykjavik, there were patches of ice on the sea. It was bitterly cold and I was ill clad for it. The Captain gave me a pair of leather gloves and an old jacket for which I was grateful. Reykjavik then was only a small fishing port where all ships had to lay at anchor in the bay. We anchored about half a mile out and they started unloading us the next day. There were many women in the work force. They were in the hold shovelling the salt into sacks, eight bags to a sling, which was hosted by the ship's derrick basket over the side and lowered to a barge alongside. The girls, perhaps over twenty, were pretty even when they took snuff, which could be seen in brown rivulets from their noses. They wore only a net on their heads and drank a lot of cold coffee.

About a mile inland we could see a cloud of vapour rising from the ground. I was told it was evaporation from the hot water springs, which Iceland is famous for. I decided at first opportunity I would visit them. I again was picked for watchman, perhaps because I could row well. I had a longer and harder row this time, and had to keep a stricter look out in case she began to drag her anchors, and if so, I had to call the Second Mate at once. After work I rowed them ashore and took them back before midnight, all nearly drunk including the Second Mate. He told me to call him if the wind got stronger.

I had my vow in mind, and had not intended to let him have any sleep that night, so after a quarter of an hour in bed, I shook him awake and told him the wind was rising fast. He only turned over with a grunt. I called again soon afterwards but there was just another grunt. After that I said the ship was dragging the anchor. He said "To hell with her." I kept at him like that throughout the night but as far as I know, he never got out of his bunk. He was an angry man in the morning and said he was reporting me to the Captain for disturbing his sleep. I said I would report him for being drunk and refusing to take a look when I thought the ship was in danger. "You can report me if you want to." I knew he would be afraid to do so as neither the Captain, nor the First Mate thought much of him and until he was sacked, I gave back as much as I got. I heard no more of the incident.

The next day I went ashore on one of the barges. The town was small and mostly built of corrugated iron. When we got ashore we saw the largest mound of fish I had ever seen. I would say it was 100 ft. long, 50 ft. wide and at least 12 ft. high, all split, salted and frozen. I stayed a while gazing in amazement at its size. Most of it was cod and ling. On my way towards the hot springs I saw a railway engine standing on the rails. There was no steam and no one was about as far as I could see. The rails were partly covered with snow. I thought it only ran in the summer time to another town and left it at that.

Many years afterwards I was taking a party out for a day's fishing. They knew I had been a sailor. The conversation drifted to many parts of the world including Iceland, and I said they had a railway there. The schoolmaster in the party said "No Donald, there is no railway in Iceland." I said, "Yes, I saw it." His brother who was an engineer in the party began to laugh and said, "You are right Donald, at least partly. I was at the building of that steam engine. It was built at Greenock and sold to the Icelandic people along with rails by someone who was trying to promote a railway there. I did not know it actually arrived there.

I was now less than half a mile from the hot springs and though the sky looked dark and greenish overhead, I carried on. There was a track branching off the road with a small riverbed beside it heading towards the hot spring pool which appeared to be 50 yards x 20 yards with an 8 foot high corrugated wall all around, there was no roof. The path led to a door and on opening it I saw two large swimming pools, parted by a low wall. There were also cubicles arranged at its end. In fact, there was a man swimming in one pool. I felt the water, which was like a hot bath. I decided to take one and started to undress. I was ready to dive in when the bather came up to me, grabbed me by the arm and led me back to where my clothes were and very angrily pointed to them. I took the hint, as he was a big man. When dressed he took me to the door and pushed me out.

On my way back a blizzard came up. I could see the ship out in the bay and took a bearing on it before visibility was nil and stayed there in a shelter for a long time, keeping the circulation going. At last it eased so that I could see the masts, I knew I couldn't go wrong. I met the search party from the ship as I was nearing the shore. They had some rum with them and gave me a good rubbing. I didn't catch a cold after my adventure although my eye was giving me a lot of trouble, I daresay on account of the cold weather. I asked the Finn who could understand some of their language, why I was not allowed to bathe in the pool. He said since I was a foreigner, I could have some disease and that is where they got the household water from. That was quite understandable

The next day it was blowing strong and I was ordered to relieve on one of the winches. This was easy when loading the barge on the lee side, but when on the weather side, they had to push the sling of eight bags over the bulwark against the wind, four men pushing. There was a man with a raised hand giving the signal when to heave away. It had to be done in a second or the sling would not clear the bulwark. The signal was given to me too late whereby they were unable to push the bags out far enough with the result they came down on top of them. As it was salt, no one was hurt badly but although it wasn't my fault I was still chased from the winch.

The next day we left in a following gale. The old man used to be in sailing ships. He ordered four sails to be rigged on her and, as long as they lasted, she was going like a train and we made fast time round the Pentland Firth to Blyth. The crew had gone ashore and all got drunk and demanded to be paid off. The Finn went mad and started to break things up. The Police were called and took him to the lock-up. I had some time to go before serving my six months contract and the Captain was refusing to pay me off on that account. When I told him I was in the Army and was due for my annual training, he said he would let me go. My wages were 30 Kroner a month with a few deducted. I got a lot less than that. A few of the foreigners stayed on and the ship sailed off in a fashion. The Finn was fired but managed to get a British ship in South

Shields where shipping was better, I never saw him again. Three of us got a place to stay in the Sailors Home, the Londoner, myself and the Glasgow bully. There were another two sailors staying in the Home. One was Harry Shields, he was about thirty and I rather liked him, I forget the name of the other. The home was clean and tidy and the grub was not bad either, and although my eye was getting worse, there was nothing wrong with my appetite. There was a maid serving at the long table and she always gave me large second helpings, I liked her for that. I went to the drug store and bought an eyeshade and that helped to keep the glare of the sun out, but still it was a bad advertisement for one seeking employment. I used to take it off when going to the shipping office.

I still had the brooches and trinkets from Africa and thought it was time to part with them. I felt indebted to the maid for her kindness, so one day after she cleared the table I showed them to her and asked if she would care to have them. At the sight of them she was taken aback and said they were very pretty but said, "I can't take them, I have nothing to give in return." I said, "You have been very kind to me and I want you to have them. You don't need to be afraid, I got them in Africa, quite honestly." "But what will Harry say when he sees them? You know we are going to be married when he comes back from his next voyage." I said, "He will be glad for you to have them." She took them and I think would have kissed me only I was too bashful. Harry was not so happy as I soon found out when at a pub's door where I used to take him in for schooners of beer. Harry was broke from the time I had known him. I asked him in for a schooner. He angrily said, "No, I will not drink with you" and when I asked why, he said, "You ought to know, I thought you were a friend of mine." I said, "I thought so too, what's wrong?" "Do you deny giving my intended wife some jewellery that you got in Africa?" "No" I said "I don't, what's wrong with that?" "Do you know we are going to be married when I am back from this voyage?" I said, "Yes, she told me so and I wish you both every luck." "Then why have you given her that present, have you been out with her?" "No, I have never been out with her or any other girl in my life. I think she is a very nice girl and kind to me, you must have seen how she loads my plate at the table. I had to do something in return. I was glad she accepted them and that's all there is to it." "In that case" he said, "we are still friends." I said, "I hope so, let's go in."

Over the beer he told me that *the Dart* was signing on sailors and he was getting a job on her, and also that he would have an advance in wages which was then raised from £2.10 to £5.10 shillings a month. "I'll have plenty of money then to return your drinks" and he kept his word. There was a celebration, all the sailors in the home were signed on except me, and I thought the eye was the reason. The day before *the Dart* was due to sail, Harry took me aside and told me a friend of his had signed on as a seaman but had changed his mind. "If you are down on the dock there is sure to be a job for you, be there with your bag. I will put in a word for you."

I was down at the dock very early. I was now broke and owing the landlady a week's board and if she saw me leaving with my bag she did not try to stop me. Her name was Edwards, a very fine old lady. I could see the men working and making the vessel ship shape. I wished to be among them and didn't have long to wait, when I was called on board and into the Captain's cabin where he and the Shipping Master were standing. They asked if I was looking for a seaman's job and if I had my kit bag handy I said "Yes Sir, on the dock." When they saw my discharge papers from the Ivanhoe, they were satisfied and I was signed on as a seaman, wages £5.10 a month. I asked for an advance of a pound. The Captain said, "There is no time for you to go ashore." I said I owed Mrs. Edwards 10/- for board. "I am giving it to the Shipping Master to pay her and something for himself, if he'll do that". He said he would and would not take anything for himself. I was richer by 10/-.

The Dart was very old and she belonged to the Mercantile Shipping Co. London. She had a flush deck, no fo'c'sle head; her anchors were of the sailing ship type with two winches to haul them on board. The living quarters were forward and down a ladder. There was very little protection when she was heading into heavy seas, with the result that much seawater would be pouring down the ladder entrance into our living quarters. Sometimes everything there would be afloat before bailing it out in buckets carried up the ladder, we had much of that before we reached Gibraltar, at best she could only do about eight knots. It took us twenty-eight days to reach Constantinople, as it was called then. We signed on for a three-year voyage. Of course, if she entered any British port within that time we could claim to be paid off. We had part coal for the first port, the rest for Poti on the Black Sea then taking grain from there to China, and back to the U.S.A. It was to be a long voyage and I was already counting all the money I would have at the end of it, if I stayed that long. I had no intentions of doing that as already the Londoner and myself were making plans to desert the ship whenever she hit the U.S.A. and join the Texas Rangers. This came about by reading some of Zane Gray's cowboy stories, but again, the schemes of mice and men gang aft agley.

I got on very well on that ship and I was by now a good enough steersman with no complaints on deck although my eye was getting worse in the hot sun. One day after passing Malta, I was at the wheel. The sea was like glass, the Captain was on the Bridge and the ship was steering well. Towards the end of my two hours at the wheel the bad eye went blind and the other with tears streaming down was almost useless. I could not see the compass and the ship went far off her course. The Captain came over and said, "Watch your steering." I said, "I can't see the compass Sir." He looked at me and saw my condition and at once blew the whistle. I was released and told to rest. Next day I was put on day work where I stayed until we reached Constantinople.

The Glasgow hooligan stayed clear of me, till one day as we were entering port he hid and pushed me. I fell heavily but was not badly hurt. Harry, whom I had already made aware of his misdeeds towards me, did not like the Glaswegian. He saw this and set about giving the hooligan a sound thrashing that he would not forget. I felt he had got what he deserved.

That night I was told to see the Captain who said I would have to see a doctor in the morning about my eye. He asked if I got hurt on board the ship. I said "No" and told him how I got it. He said that I should have had it seen to long ago "Anyway, the shore watchmen will take you to the British Seamen's Hospital and they will look after you." The way to hospital was long and it was all walking through the city's narrow streets where I had a chance to observe what was going on. I was surprised at the number of beggars who seemed to out-number the shops. They were in fact travelling shops. I saw a woman carrying a large crate on her back with many shelves fitted on it, it was loaded with every kind of ware and eatables. She carried it with a bridle around her shoulders. A man whom I presumed to be her husband, walked behind her with a small bell, and when a customer came, he rang the bell for her to stop. Her face was covered with a black veil. I took pity on her and I don't know if they took turn about.

We arrived at the Hospital, which was in fact an old converted fortress. I handed over the letter from the Captain and waited. Soon a doctor with my letter in his hand came and told me in plain English and with a Glasgow accent to follow him to a room where he began to examine me; there was hardly any vision. The examination took some time and he told me I would have to stay in the hospital for treatment. I said I couldn't stay, that the ship was leaving the next day. "Well" he said "I can't let you go back to the ship with your eye in that condition. As it is, you may need an operation to save your eye, or, on the other hand treatment may do, in any case, going to work is out of the question." That settled it and also shattered my dreams.

The ward was large with at least a dozen beds on each side and some at the end. They were all in use by many nationalities, who were employed on British ships. I was given a kit of hospital blue and a pair of heelless slippers, three sizes too big, which I was unable to keep on while walking. When I asked the Greek orderly for an exchange, he said "None in store" he could talk a little English. I was put to bed for three days, and on the second day Harry came to see me. He told me that the hooligan said he had been up yesterday and that I had died and he wanted to share out my kit. Harry was glad it was not so and he would send my kit up to me by the watchman, which he did. All was there except a jersey, which perhaps the Glaswegian swiped. I also had a visit from the Captain. He wanted to sign me off and said that I had no claim on the ship for any damage. I refused to sign off, hoping somehow that I might be able to get back on her when she returned from the Black Sea. He said the doctor told him that I needed an operation on my eye or long treatment and that he had already taken a man on in my place. My hopes were gone as he said he was obliged to sign me off himself.

The hospital fare was not too bad. It was either stew or salad and when I asked for porridge in the morning, the Greek said, "Don't know how to make it for one man." Lying next to me was a Turkish soldier with a bayonet wound in his side, and when he was being dressed I could see his innards. Little did I then know how familiar I was to become with such cases. He was in the Balkan war about 1912. There was a big American sailor there with whom I used to play cards and be friendly with. One day as I was sitting by my bed I saw a stretcher case coming up the ward with four men carrying it. It was a great big black man whose legs were hanging over the end, his hospital kit in a bundle on the top of him and on top was a pair of slippers, they looked my size. The black man appeared to have a broken arm besides the rest. I had my good eye on the slippers, thinking he would never use them. In any case they were, judging by the rest of him, far too small for him, and if he was alive in the morning I would swap. When I woke up next day he was still in bed so I went over to him and said, "How are you John?" There was no answer, I knew that he was alive but I thought he did not have long to go.

The slippers were lying in the open doorless locker. I did not want to waken him or disturb him, so I exchanged the slippers in full view of all in the ward. I thought it was not stealing as I left my own in his locker. The slippers were a good fit. They treated my eye with Atropine, three drops a day. It showed no improvement so they advised me to have it operated on, I would not let them and carried on with the treatment although they said I was in danger of losing my eye. There was a small library at the end of the ward with a collection of old books, among them I came across a small Gaelic songbook and although not a Gaelic scholar, I could follow the songs I knew. The find made me very happy and I read much of it over and over again. The walls of that building were very thick and the room was near sound proof. The doctors were keen that I should undergo this operation but I still refused. They said that they could do no more for me and would have to send me home on the first available ship. I said that was what I wanted and I would have the operation in the Eye Infirmary in Glasgow. "Is that where you left from?" I said, "Yes," "Well let's hope a ship will turn up to take your there soon." I was to wait for another week for a ship, which was a Turkish passenger ship going to Alexandria. Meantime I was kept on the same treatment and also kept going to the library.

One day there, reading my songbook with one leg crossed, the door opened and in walked the big black man. I had forgotten about the slippers. His arm was in a sling and he kept walking towards me. As he closed the door behind him, I knew I was in trouble. He took the slipper off my raised foot and hit me hard over my head with it. I thought when he raised it again that I was finished, but at least I would go down fighting. I grabbed his broken arm and started pulling and pushing him round. He picked up the heavy armchair I was sitting on. Although I was stunned, his pain must have been awful and I felt sorry for him. I dared not ease up on him and kept dancing him around so that he was not able to hit me with the chair. I kept crying for help but the wall and closed door were too thick for me to be heard.

I was near giving up when the door opened and in walked the big American. He took in the scene and said, "What's the big black bastard doing to you Scottie?" "I think he is trying to kill me." At that the Yank took a swing, which landed on the black man's jaw. He went down like a sack of potatoes and lay there. The door was now open; they heard the commotion in the ward. It took four strong men and a stretcher to carry the black man, to his bed. After that near escape, I was afraid that he might have another try. He never did. Before I left the hospital, I got a letter from Mrs. Edwards thanking me for the 10/- and saying money or not, she would put me up. I never went there again and never heard any more of the *Dart* or any of her crew.

There were three of us being sent home, a Welshman who was a hard case, so the doctor gave a supply of Atropine and a dropper to the West Indian, who was an educated man. He took over the eye treatment and was making a tidy job of it. We three joined the Turkish passenger ship and left. Before leaving, the doctor gave me a letter for the Eye Infirmary in Glasgow saying I would be well looked after there. The ship was crowded and called at many islands in the Aegean Sea. The Welshman got drunk on wine for the passengers, he also sang and danced for them. It took us two days to get to Alexandria. I was not sorry leaving her, she was full of bed bugs and sanitation was almost nil.

On arriving we went to the Sailors Home, except the Welshman who joined a crowd of Arabs at the dock. He had a good suit of cloth on and a hard hat. When we saw him again at the British Consul office next morning, he had nothing on but a short pair of ragged trousers, no shirt, boots or socks, his body all covered with mosquito bites and half drunk. It appeared that he was robbed and stripped of his clothing and left naked for the mosquitoes to eat. His condition was a sorry sight, he was sent to a hospital and I never saw him again. We stayed in the home about a week. I had only a few coins of Turkish money so our time was spent mostly in walking round the sea front. The West Indian left so I chummed up with a boy from Manchester who also was being sent home the same way. He took over the atropine.

My eye was getting better and the sight slowly returning. One day at the mouth of the Nile I went swimming. It was full of large fish. I swam for a while when I saw a small rowing boat heading towards me. They came alongside me and said in good English to come on board. They were in uniform so I knew I had to obey. They asked where my clothes were, I told them and they rowed me over and said to get dressed. I did that and weighed my chances of making a run for it. I thought better of it when I saw one of them pulling out a revolver and ordered me to come on board. I did and asked where they were taking me. They said to jail for bathing in a prohibited area. "This place is full of sharks and other man-eating fish, you were lucky, did you see any sharks?" I said I did not and did not believe them, but afterwards I heard they were right. We were nearing the shore when one of them asked if I had a match. I had a full box and when it was handed back I told them to keep it, as I would not need it in jail. He thanked me and said "We will let you go this time but remember, no more bathing here." Needless to say I took their advice.

Near the dock was a steep incline of cobblestone road and a small urchin boy. I watched him trying to make a poor looking horse draw a four wheel wagon of scrap iron up the incline, the horse, shoeless, was slipping but making a big effort, but no go. A big Arab that I took to be the father, came on the scene and instead of taking the rein he got hold of the boy and commenced to thrash him on the legs and almost bare bottom with the horse whip, the kid howling in pain. Then the horse raised his foot and down it came on the big Arab's foot and stayed there. It was his turn to do the howling and crying. The horse would not raise its foot, the Arab was held there. The kid was now in screams of laughter and I joined him saying "It serves you right you big bully." The horse decided to raise his foot and the Arab was free to sit down and nurse his foot. The kid had vanished. I made my way back to the Sailors home, where word was waiting for me to join a ship the next day. She was the SS Favonian bound for London. The Manchester boy and myself joined her, and we left the next morning.

After an uneventful passage we arrived in the Thames in late June. We were passengers but we volunteered to work to pass the time, we got paid for that. My eye, thanks to atropine was now almost back to normal. We went to the shipping office and got our clearance money and rail fare. I said goodbye and good luck to the Manchester lad and headed for Euston Station, where I deposited my kit bag and went for a meal. The place had a bar and after the meal, a maid got very talkative. I told her I was a stranger in London and that I had just left a ship and was on my way to Glasgow, she seemed interested in my talk. I asked for a glass of whisky. It took some time before I got it and it did not taste good but I drank it and left at once for the station. I did not get far, I began to feel dizzy and felt I was going blind but I kept going, I saw a policeman on a corner and made for him. When he turned into two I collapsed at his feet. When I came to, he said, "Where did you get it?" I said, "I am not drunk officer." he said, "You are drugged, I watched you along the street, where did you come from?" I told him. "Would you know the place again?" I said that I thought so. "We'll take you there and I'll deal with her." I was afraid I would miss the train and decided not to tell him. He got my bag and saw me on the train but would not take anything.

Next day I went to the Eye Infirmary and handed over my letter. The doctor examined me and told me my eye was healed now and that I could start work any time. "By the way, how is Doctor Andrews, he is a brother of mine?" I said that he was well; that he looked after me well and that he told me I would be well cared for here. "Well" he said, "Your eye had a growth and the Atropine cleared that up."

About the beginning of August 1914 I got a job as an A.B. on one of the Robinson coastal ships. The wages were 32/- a week. We had to feed ourselves out of that and do our own cooking. We went light to load stone from North Wales to Brighton. We had on board an Irish lad, an Ordinary Seaman, on his first trip and never in my life did I see a man who could eat as much. He was on my watch and we shared the grub between us. This day I went ashore in North Wales, for our weekly food. When I got on board, I told Paddy to cook the dinner, take his own and then relieve me. After a long while he took over and I went for my dinner. He had left very little for me, I thought, the rest of the food would be in the locker, but it was not. I ate what he left me and went back on deck. I asked him where was the rest of the food. "Begorrah Scottie, the food was that good I ate and ate but I left some." "You big glutton, what you left won't take us to Brighton, I am dividing what you left and after this you will look after your own grub." The Captain on hearing that I had deposited a pound in my Post Office Savings Account would not advance me any money. It was mostly potatoes for me till we got to Brighton. Paddy I think was worse off.

Shortly before we arrived at that port we were stopped by a destroyer and boarded. It was Sunday the 4th August 1914. They told us that the British had declared war on Germany and asked if we had any Naval Reservists on board. There was none, they did not want the Army Reserve. The ships in port and the whole of the town were decorated with flags. We hoisted our flag. It was a fine sunny day with no wind. The flags got twisted around the mast and I was ordered to free them. I went shinning up the mast, past the rigging. Coming down I got a shower of hot water from the winch. The exhaust extended some 8 feet in the rigging and I got my backside soaked in hot water. I thought it was done on purpose and told the Second Mate whom I did not like, what I thought of him. As he was an old man I let it go at that. We finished unloading the crushed rock and went to Rochester for a cargo of cement for Port Glasgow and then up to Glasgow for bunkers.

Before leaving Rochester we heard that the cruiser 'Amphion' had been sunk. She was to be the first ship sunk in the war. The war had been on for a few days and it was only going to last three months at the longest, some said a month, although late at night when we arrived at Glasgow I went to the old digs to see if my friends were away to the war. They were gone. In the morning I told the Captain that I was leaving for the war and wanted to be paid off. He did not want to let me go but when I told him I was an Army Reservist he had to let me go. I got paid off and besides sending money to my father, I also sent him a large box of carpenter's tools, which he greatly valued, and today I have a small plane left of that collection, still in use after 64 years.

I reported to Maryhill Barracks where I was given a pound and rail fare to Inverness. I arrived there late at night. I well knew my way to the Barracks where I got a knife, fork and spoon and a pair of blankets. In the morning I went to the Orderly Room to report. They did not have my name on any of their books and I did not see anyone in the depot that I knew. They told me I did not belong to the Cameron Highlanders. I said that I did but they did not believe me and told me to clear out, that they did not want me and if I kept pestering them, they would get the police after me.

I was near giving up when one day I saw Sergeant Walsh, I knew him at once. He asked why I was not in uniform, when I told him he said, "Come along with me to the Orderly Room." The same crowd was there and when he vouched for me, they were told to fit me out in uniform. We left the Quartermaster's Store and he said "I remember the first day you were fitted out, I think you will be able to put the kilt on right this time." I have already said that were it not for my chance meeting with Sergeant Walsh, the course of my life may well have been changed, as I would have gone back to sea again. Instead, I was the next day sent to the feeding Battalion for the First Cameron Highlanders at Invergordon. The First Battalion was somewhere in France.

In Delny in tents, we mostly dug trenches and put up barbed wire in turnip and potato fields, anywhere a stupid officer saw fit, regardless of the damage done to crops and land. There were rumours of a spy around. The next night I was picked for guard duty. We had a tinker on the guard who was very nervous. In the guard area stood a church in a small enclosure. On that enclosure a Shetland pony grazed. I was relieved of sentry duty by the tinker at 1.00 a.m. and everything was quiet and I could sometimes make out the pony. I lay down beside a hedge and was dozing to sleep when three shots rang out. The guard was called out. The sentry reported seeing a spy in the churchyard and as he did not stop when challenged, he had to fire on him but he got away. There was more firing now till the Corporal of the guard ordered "Cease fire, we will get the body in the morning." In the morning there was no body, the pony was still there. But there was much damage to the church, hardly a window escaped the brave soldiers, the pony was unharmed, the tinker was admonished.

We stayed outside the village of Delny till mostly all the ground was trenched or barbed wired, and the tinker incident was the first shots I heard fired in the war. We moved to Invergordon where there was a large field of tents, they were also putting up huts for the winter. It looked as if the war was going to last more than the three months prophecy. There was a draft going to France every week and later, every other day. The method of choosing was that a bugle would sound the 'fall in' and almost everyone in the camp would do so. An officer would pick out the most likely looking in age and height, about fifty at a time. I used to fall in with the rest. The officer would not even look at me. All were keen to go to France.

They were building large oil storage tanks for the Navy on one side of the village and these had to be guarded day and night. There indeed were spies in that district, looking for a chance to blow them up. Three sentry posts guarding them with rifles, bayonets, live ammunition and strict orders to fire if not halted when challenged. There would be three men to every post, two hours on and four hours off. On our particular guard most of us were from the Islands. We also had a native sergeant in charge and a lance corporal, all Gaelic speaking. We asked the sergeant if we could splice up a bottle of whisky, he said only one. The village was out of bounds for troops so we got a worker to get it for us. All went well and we drank the whisky, which did not impair our ability. It was still broad daylight when the Orderly Officer called on his visiting rounds. The sentry at the first post saw him coming and knew him well. He foolishly thought there was no point in challenging him when he knew him and it was broad daylight.

The Officer, who was young and extra strict, approached the sentry and asked his orders, which said, "Challenge anyone approaching. Guard all government property. Open fire if the person doesn't stop." The Officer left for the two other posts and I think he was again challenged. On his way back he told the Sergeant that he found the guard very slack. We thought nothing would come of it, however the next day after being relieved the same Officer inspected us. We were looking for some sleep and to be dismissed. Instead he told us that he was giving us an extra guard on account of our slackness the night before so no sleep for us. Quick march, and off we went, and when out of sight and hearing, we called him all the names we could think of. We relieved the others who just laughed at us.

I was on the far away post, a post with a road running through it with tanks on each side full of oil. The road was barricaded at each end with barbed wire and no one was allowed on this road after daylight and if anyone was seen there, the sentry had strict orders to fire without challenge. Shortly after midnight that night, I was on sentry duty on the far away post when I heard the first sentry challenging. I heard the response "Orderly Officer." I was getting ready for him. The middle sentry challenged and then I heard him creeping slowly towards my back.

The night was very dark and I judged him to be twenty yards behind me. I let him come on and I don't know if on purpose or not, but he made a noise when he was about twelve yards from me. In a flash I turned round and called out as loud as I could "Halt, halt, halt" at the same time working the bolt of the rifle at my shoulder before he could answer me. He was only a few paces in front when I shouted "Put your hands up and advance to be recognised or I will blow you to hell." It was then he found his voice and said "For God's sake sentry, don't shoot me, I am the Orderly Officer. Is everything alright?" I said "Yes Sir." He had to call at the guardhouse on his way out where he asked the Sergeant if the sentry on No. 3 post was very nervous. The Sergeant said he did not know. He said the Orderly Officer was very pale and shaking. "What did he find wrong this time?" I said, "He did not even ask me my opinion, he left in a hurry and tripped and I nearly laughed." There was no more extra guard for us.

Routine was much the same as before, route marches, digging trenches, putting up barbed wire, sometimes taking us out at night on long route marches in the woods, dismissing us and telling us to find our own way back to camp and report. Those of us brought up in the Islands could always find our way in the dark and also the sense of taking observation as we went along, with the result that we were always the first back in camp. There was the usual 'fall in' for overseas draft, which was then attended by many more than required, and although I attended every one, no one even spoke to me or asked my age, I felt I should have gone back to sea when I had the chance.

A great many were in the camp without uniform, they were known as 'Kitcheners'. There were not enough uniforms to supply them and there was a great demand for tailors. In my tent were two tailors whom I was friendly with. They were old soldiers with many battle ribbons on their breasts. They always had plenty of money while I most of the time was broke on 1/3d a day. They used to stand me drinks of beer. On one such a day we were at the canteen drinking till it closed and the pipes for dinner had gone. On our way towards our tent we passed the guardroom. In front of it stood a tree, white washed in lime for show. The tailors were half drunk, I was just happy. The tailors stood below the tree and started to urinate against it. I stood aside waiting when I saw the Duty Sergeant watching us. I called to the other two and got off my mark, walking fast. The Sergeant saw me and shouted "Fall in you for escort duty." I thought it hard lines after all the beer the tailors gave me. I now had to escort them to the guardroom.

I just kept going and the Sergeant kept after me. He started to run and I started to run till I slowed down at the tent. "Where do you think you are going?" "I am going for my dinner, I am running because I am late." "Why did you not stop when I ordered you to fall in for escort duty?" "I did not hear you right. I thought you were saying hurry up for your dinner." "You know damn well what I was saying, I don't care if you never get dinner, fall in for escort duty for your friends." I had to go. In the meantime the Corporal of the guard got another two for that duty and we followed them inside the guardhouse, where the two tailors were put in the detention room with their boots taken off. The two who were doing the escort duty asked if they could go for their dinner and the Sergeant said "Yes." I asked if I could go, but he said "No, you are going with the prisoners on a very serious charge, refusing to do escort duty." I was put in with the tailors and my boots taken off. I knew I was in for it and started to make up a story on how to plead.

The next day I was taken before my Company Commander and when my crime was read out, the Officer shook his head and said, "What is his crime record?" When he was told that I had a clean sheet, he said, "Even so, his crime is far too serious for me to try." I was remanded to the Commanding Officer. I was sunk, only the very worst crimes were sent to him. I had to think fast, I knew that he could speak Gaelic well and when I was brought before him and the charge read out, he asked me what I had to say for myself. I started by saying in a mixture of English and Gaelic that I no understand her, she speak too fast for me, no have much English nearly all Gaelic, she no speak the Gaelic. I no understand her, me, indeed very sad for her Sergeant Major. The Officer said, "What is this man's crime record like?" They got the sheet. "He has a clean record Sir," replied the Sergeant Major. "In that case, it is plain to me he did not understand what was being asked of him. Case dismissed."

As I was ordered about turn, I felt sure that I saw him winking at me. When I got outside there was a rank of prisoners there with the Sergeant taking their names and punishments. I walked past and smiled. "Hey" shouted the Provo, "where do you think you are going? Line up along with the rest there, what punishment did you get? I'll soon find out, stay where you are." He went into the Orderly Room and came out with a bright red face and said, "You Heiland buggers are clannish but I'll get you yet." He never did. The tailors got off lightly, weak bladders was their story.

It was now towards the end of September. The war was nearly two months old and no signs of me going to France, regardless of how often I tried by lying about my age, saying I was now past eighteen when in reality I was seventeen. All I got was a shake of the head. I was due leave if I could pay my own fare. I only had 7/6 saved. I had been caught laughing on church parade, not, I may say, in disrespect to the Minister but in another incident in which he was involved. Mixed church parades were held in the open air. On Saturday those that were putting up the make-do pulpit of two large 50 gallon empty hog sets of beer, saw to it that the bottom of one, the far away one, would not bear the weight of the Minister. There were steps climbing to the first one. The next day, Sunday, the parade was formed at a short distance round the Minister who climbed to the solid hog set and started off with a prayer and took his text for his sermon from the words "in a little while you will see me and again in a little while you will not see me." He coughed and stepped onto the loose barrel and down he went. The parade, in gales of laughter, was dismissed in disgrace. I was caught running away and for that crime I got four days pay stopped which amounted to 5/- which I could well be doing with, but this did not deter me.

I had enough and a few pennies over my rail fare to Kyle of Lochalsh. Let the boat fare look after itself. There was another lad from Howmore along with me. He had enough to pay rail and boat fare and 9 pence over. We boarded the ship and I went into hiding till she was well clear of the land. Between Skye and Harris, I ran into the Purser, who asked to see my ticket. I told him I had none and no money to buy one. He asked where I was going. I told him Lochboisdale. "Then you will have to walk there from Harris for having the cheek to board us without any money. Do you think MacBrayne is going to give you a free ride?" I said "No, but I will pay you on my return." He took out a notebook and pencil and asked my name, regiment, where I was stationed and name of my Commanding Officer and the date of when I was returning. "If I am not paid then you will hear more about it." I was free to show myself.

On account of mines and submarines in the Minch, there was only daylight sailing and when she came to Lochmaddy, she tied up for the night and we were not allowed to stay on board. There was a small waiting room at the pier; it had a long bench and a fire, which was nearly out. Having not eaten since we left Invergordon, we were really hungry. We went to a

49

nearby shop and bought a loaf of bread and a jar of jam, we ate half and left the other for the morning. To pass the time while we still had a few pence between us, we went to the pub near the pier and ordered two glasses of beer. The bar was empty; we took our order to a corner table and nursed it for some time. We were just doing that when a tall, well-dressed middle-aged man came in.

He had on a starched shirt collar and tie with a pin in it and golf cuff links and a walking stick with gold bands on it. He wore a bowler hat and looked a regular toff. After buying a drink for himself and chatting with the barmaid, he glanced our way and said, "You are not drinking boys, drink up and have one on me." We thanked him and said we were not able to return the treat. He said, "Never mind that." He brought over a whisky and beer each and then took his own over. He asked what part of Uist did we belong to, I said South Lochboisdale and the other boy Howmore. He asked me if I knew John Campbell the mason. I told him he was my uncle. "Well boy, if John Campbell is your uncle, drink up at once, any kin of John is a friend of mine, more drinks, tell me have you ever seen or remember me?" I said "No." "Well my name is Seonaidh Morrison, your uncle composed a song about the two of us when we were building an addition to Garrynamonie school." I said, "Yes, I know you now and I know part of the song." He made me sing it more than once. It was a witty song telling about the kind of boots they were wearing and them earning big money.

He asked where we were staying that night. We said in the waiting room. "No, you are not, you are coming along with me to a wedding. I am best man and I am inviting you, you have no excuse about not being invited." "But" I said, "we need a wash." "You will get that at the hotel here." We had nothing to lose and after a wash and tidy up, to the wedding we went. We were given a place of honour next to the bride and bridegroom. Seonaidh made a speech in which he included us. After what we drank in the pub and at the first table, my memory of the rest is blank, even going on board the next morning or how we got there. Seonaidh indeed looked after us, even the half loaf and the jam jar was in the haversack. She was nearing Lochboisdale when I woke up and after a slice of bread and jam, the leftovers went through the porthole. Seonaidh was a good and very well known stonemason. He went to the U.S.A. and made a lot of money at the San Francisco earthquake, and that was him, newly back home. I got a very warm welcome at home and greatly enjoyed my short stay. I got money to pay the purser, who did not forget what I owed him. I felt sorry at seeing my sisters crying when it came time to say goodbye. It was back to Invergordon again and to trench digging, drill and the everlasting barbed wire.

3   Off To War at Last

It was then into November and one day in the draft picking, the officer said, "How old are you today?" I said "Nineteen, Sir." "Alright, you have been pestering me long enough, do you want to go to France?" I said "Yes Sir." "Alright, I'll give you a line for the Medical Officer and if he passes you, I'll let you go." I went to the M.O. and he passed me. I was seventeen. I was put in the draft and did heavy field training of long route marches with full kit and loaded with ammunition. It was a relief to get away.

The day of our departure was a Sunday. Throughout the week a band would play the draft to the station. This being Sunday, no band or even a piper was allowed to play. As a concession, the Colonel ordered a piper to lead us but he was not allowed to play. Such was the strict Presbyterian influence in the district. It was like a dead march and for many indeed it was to be true. We boarded and the journey to Southampton was long and weary. When we stopped at any station for food, crowds waving small flags and handkerchiefs cheered us. One young girl shouted "Kill all the bastards, they have killed my brother." Someone replied "That's what we intend to do." Some would throw us fruit and cigarettes. When we got to the dock, a large troop ship was alongside. As we were the first there, we were taken down to the very bottom where we were allotted a small space each, and by the time all the troops embarked, there was not a square yard of space left from top to bottom, and when we felt the vibration of the engine we knew we were on our way to France.

We had gone about an hour when a shout came down the companion way "Everyone on deck, a submarine is chasing us." There was a mad rush for the stairway, which soon became completely blocked. There were many other stairways to the top, I expect the same as ours but one could only wait for the torpedo and death, no way to avoid it. Three of us from the Islands decided to lie down and wait, as there was plenty of space then, and sleep if we could. We lay down and were soon dozing away as we were very tired. There was a loud roar and rumble, which woke us, but the stairway was as choked as ever. There was no water coming in although we were well below the waterline. We could only wait and pray. Some did, loudly, and after what seemed an eternity, a shout came down the stairway that the ship was back at anchor. The roar we heard was the ship letting go the anchors and the noise of the chains as they flew down the spurling pipes above us. Many were brave then and even swearing as we missed the torpedoes fired at us.

We left again at dawn and made Le Havre without further interference. There was a crowd at the dock entrance, and lining the streets some girls with scissors would snip a piece out of our kilts. I am told when those long before arrived in kilts, the girls often looked under to see if it was a he or a she. We marched up the brae to tents deep in snow, where we stayed for a few days. The French had a canteen run by civilians and they had a horse-drawn wagon to take bottled beer up in crates for which they charged a high price, and we had little or no money. In the tent we planned on how to get beer.

The wagon always came up at sunset and later all we had to do was to stop it at a bend before passing the graveyard. I was to hold the horse's head while two grabbed the Frenchman and put a hand over his mouth, the one on the wagon handing down the crates to the one below. I did not agree to take part, but I had to. The plan was put into operation the next night. Instead of wearing our usual head cover in the form of a Glengarry, we used cap comforter gear down over

51

our faces and the great coat over the kilt. We waited for the Frenchman and stopped him. I took hold of a quiet horse and the man offered no resistance. I turned the horse and wagon round. We took five cases. The Frenchman, unharmed, was told to return home. We each carried back a crate and buried it in the deep snowdrift. Next day an identification parade was held. The Frenchman was there trying to pick out the culprits. He had made out kilts and our draft got the blame. We were not identified. The French to make good their loss put up the price.

Next day a long queue formed at the canteen, which was a large tent; however, those at the front of the queue would not pay the extra charge. The large marquee tent had a long bar inside but no one could get in unless he paid the extra price in advance. Someone shouted, "Let's rush it." In an instance, the walls were pushed aside and beer was carried out in crates and bottles. The Red Caps were not yet formed and any civilian around was soon pushed aside. I only got what I drank and one bottle of beer. Our tent was too far to carry a crate in the open although we also had what was hidden in the snow. We again got the unproven blame for the canteen rush.

In the evening we were ordered to 'Fall In', we thought for another identification parade but no, we were to leave camp at once for being troublemakers. We had time to gather our kit but very little of the stored beer could we take with us on account of the usual inspection. We were marched to the station, passing the scene of the hold-up. I recall thinking it was not worth it, and never since have I taken part in any hold-ups. We entrained to cattle trucks and after a long, slow journey, landed at Borre, twenty miles behind the front line. We could occasionally hear the gunfire.

There we were billeted for about a week. One day we were to be inspected by King George V. It had been raining heavily all day and from daylight we were busy clearing the road of mud and were made to stand for a long time at attention while the rain came down in buckets. When he came he wore a coat and high knee boots, I don't think he even looked at us. There were the usual route marches and drill from Bore. There were no signs yet of going up the line, until one Sunday, when we were some five miles away on a route march, an orderly with a note came to the officer in charge. He ordered us to about turn and told us that the Germans had broken through and that we were wanted up the line as fast as we could get there. We were not allowed to go into our billets to collect any of our valuables. We were given a tin of bully beef between two, and some hard tack biscuits and were not allowed to sit down to eat, but as soon as we had finished, we were off to the war at last.

It was a long march along the twenty miles to the front with only ten minutes rest every two hours. It was almost unbelievable that we passed a group of the Bengal Lancers going the same way on the same errand, horse weary. I did not know how far they had come, most likely much further than us. When we got to within rifle fire hearing, we were told to rest. Many of us went on the sick parade and I did too, all with swollen feet. The treatment was that you were not allowed to take your shoes off because, once off, you could not get them on again. You had to place one foot in a large bucket of surgical spirits, keep it there a moment, take it out to drain and do the same with the other. We wore shoes and spats in those days. I must say the rough cure helped a lot. Too soon we were on our way and came under fire before crossing the bridge on the La Bassee Canal. The first war casualty I saw was a cow, which got a shell to herself and somehow foolishly I thought that shells were meant only for animals!

52

The first human being I saw killed was piper Willie MacKenzie, playing us across the bullet-swept bridge. After that there were thousands, some got across, many did not, those that did took shelter in an open shed where farm implements were kept. A boy in front of us was hit by a sniper, I managed to get him into a shed and thought nothing of it. The sniper hidden in a high chimney was inflicting many casualties on us. I and another were detailed to try and get him, one covering the other by firing while the other ran forward. We got inside the tractor and looked up the chimney. He was up there and two shots brought him down and we took his cap to prove it. An officer at once took hold of my arm and took out his indelible pencil, spat a few times on my shoulder and said, "We are very short of N.C.O.s, what do you want to be, corporal or lance corporal, you are too young to be a sergeant." I said, "I've got very little English, all the chaps will only laugh at me, I would rather not take it." The other fellow was older and took the promotion. There is one thing about being promoted in action, it takes the King's command to reduce you to the ranks and any crime against you meant only pay stopped. Although many times I was recommended for promotion, I never took any. I started off as a private in 1914 and ended with the same rank in 1919. I felt if I was an N.C.O., most likely sometimes I would have to order others to dangerous places and maybe to their death. I thought number one was enough to look after.

Our platoon was ordered to advance and find out how strong the Germans were in the village ahead of us. It was called Givenchy, a village the Germans had taken from an English regiment. We advanced in sections, one covering the other. My section was the first to reach the edge of the town, which we did without losing a man and waited for the others to join us. While waiting a man appeared at our side from nowhere who had neither rifle nor sword. He asked us where we were going. We told him and he said, "Don't go there, the town is full of Germans." He vanished in a flash. It was still not quite dark and I always thought it was a warning. When the others joined us, the young officer with them asked our sergeant what he was waiting for. When the sergeant told him what the stranger said, he said, "You are afraid" and the sergeant replied "No." "Then follow me, men."

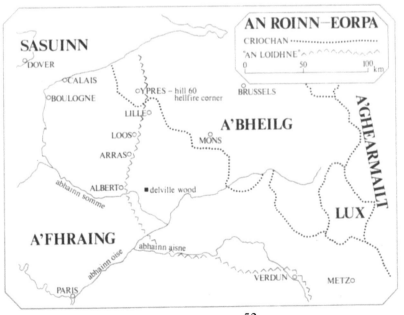

Gaelic Map of France

Into Battle. (Pròisect Muinntir nan Eilean, An Cogadh Mòr: 1914 – 1918)

We were already well in the village when the enemy surrounded us. I saw the officer falling. His last order was "Give at them men and keep the bastards down." We were in single line and I was the third from the front. There were sixteen of us when we were surrounded and when the sergeant saw there were only three left standing, he shouted "Retire men, three men can't stand up to three thousand." The two ahead of me fell, we did not have our bayonets fixed, my rifle was empty and I could touch the Germans. It was dark and how I got out of that I will never know. Only three of us came out, the sergeant, myself and another lad who was sent back to report that the enemy in large numbers were in the village. The sergeant and I lay behind a wagon drawn across the road. We were then between the two fires with splinters coming off the wagon, but neither was hit. We fired at them until the rifles were too hot to hold, and must have done much damage as the enemy advanced no further; then our main body came up and we attacked them in force.

The battle was long and bloody with much of the fighting done inside the houses. The Germans who were alive were cleared out of the village and beyond, but not for long. They counter-attacked and drove us out. Our losses were great, however we formed up again and with fixed bayonets we attacked. The slaughter was awful but we took the village the second time and held it. The battle started in the afternoon and this was the next day of continual fighting.

54

There was a lull after we had taken our objective. Myself, and my pal from Lewis, Angus MacDonald, were ordered to go out into no-mans land to watch and listen for any signs of the enemy attacking. We were only to be out there for an hour when we would be relieved. We went out and found a deep shell hole where we kept watch. We saw a German patrol but as it was not coming our way, and not wanting to give our position away, we did not fire. We thought it was much longer than an hour so I crawled back to enquire. When I got to where the rest were and asked about our relief, a Corporal asked me, "Who sent you out there?" I said "Sergeant Turnbull." He said, "He was killed a while ago, did you get your rations?" I said "No, and we have not had anything to eat since yesterday." "Did you get any rum?" "No." "Well, if you crawl back till you come to many dead and I don't mean dead drunk, you will find a rum jar. Be careful and don't take much of it or you will be in the pile with the rest. I will have you relieved soon."

I found the jar as he said and took a good swig. I nearly filled my canteen and crawled back. I found Angus and told him about the relief and the rum. It was the strongest and best rum I had ever tasted and it soon began to take effect. We took our packs off and sat on them. After a while Angus said, "Do you know this song Donald?" and began to sing at the top of his voice 'Leaving Stornoway Pier'. I joined in but the noise we were making was giving our position away to the enemy. I distinctly heard the order at the back of us for two men to go out there and have us shot for being drunk and giving the position away to the enemy. I sobered up as if a bucket of ice water were thrown over me. I can't explain it, but I was as sober as could be at that moment. I said, "Come on Angus, let's get out of here." We left in a hurry and crawled in a wide circle and joined the rest from the back. The execution party did not find anything and we dared not enquire.

At dawn we were to attack the German trench. The order was that 'A' Company was to attack the trench. We in 'B' Company were to support them if needed. Angus and I went along with the rest. We were about twenty-five yards behind 'A' Company who took the small trench without resistance. The Germans had left and as there was no room for us, we were ordered back to where we left. We were settling down there when there was a huge explosion in the trench and all of 'A' Company were blown sky high. The Germans had left the trench mined. The awful sight is still in my mind, and when everything came down, the bushes and hedges were covered with pieces of khaki and tartan kilts. There was no mercy shown after that. When the shelling started, Angus was hit badly in the arm. I was doing my best to bandage his arm when a stretcher-bearer saw us and came over. He asked "Is he bad?" I said, "Not too bad, his arm is still on." He looked at me and said, "You are wounded too?" I said "No." "Look at the blood on you." "That" I said "is from Angus." "No" he said, "Look at your leg." I looked and there was the calf of my right leg blown off. I remember it was funny seeing the diamond hose top with a chunk of flesh sticking to it lying on my shoe. It was then I felt the pain. It's hard to believe it, but that's the way it was. Angus was well able to walk away while I needed help.

Now there were many from my native island in that crowd, among them also was John Montgomery, my old foe. The stretcher- bearer asked would anyone help me but no one would. I did not blame them as it was daylight and bullet swept. It was then that John Montgomery jumped out of his protection and said, "I will help you Donald." There were shouts from some of the others "Let the bugger go, don't risk your life, he wouldn't do it for you." But John never

55

heeded them, he helped me under heavy rifle fire to a house where the wounded were gathered. John felt it was too draughty, so he took me further in. He left me there saying "We will not fight again Donald." "No" I said "You were always the best man, now I'm sure of it." He was not long gone when a shell came and landed at the open end among the wounded. I never saw John again regardless of the many enquiries I made trying to trace him. I felt, and still do, that I owe him a great debt, and since I could not find him, I vowed that if ever I came across any Lewis man or woman needing help, I would be glad to do that in fond memory of John.

Years passed during which I met many Lewis people, both men and women. However, at this point I am obliged to take you many years ahead in my life story. I never let up on my quest to find John and once I felt sure I had him. In Detroit a piper friend of mine told me of a John Montgomery who lived in that city. When I visited him and asked if he was in the Cameron Highlanders during the war, he said he was but that he had joined up in Canada in the Canadian Camerons. Another blank.

One day on a ship in Ashtabula, Ohio, where I was on deck watch, I saw a small man coming up the ladder. I took him to be the replacement for my opposite number, who had been sacked. He went to his cabin and I called him at 12 noon for his watch on deck. When I entered his cabin there was much coughing and hard breathing and when I shook him and remarked that he had a bad cold, he said "No, its asthma and I've been troubled with it for a long time." He then asked, "What kind of ship is this? I noticed she has wooden hatches, if I had known that I wouldn't have joined her." He told me he was from Lewis and I told him I came from South Uist and that I was the only other Scotsman on board. His name was Kenneth MacKenzie; he was a very quiet man and relieved me after he had his dinner and when I got mine, the others on his watch were busy putting on the hatches which were heavy wooden oak, each taking two men to handle.

When I finished dinner and checked, I could see Kenneth was far behind, sitting down and coughing and breathing hard. I went to him and told him to take a good rest, that I would do it for him and also any other hard work when needed. "I think," he said, "When we get to the head of the lakes I'll get off. This is too much for me and I can't let you do the hard work for me." I said, "It's time enough for you to say that when I complain and I am not complaining."

Kenneth made that trip and another besides until he got a few dollars together and I lent him some with which he got some gear, but I could not persuade him to make another trip. He wanted to pay back more than I gave him but I would not accept any. When he asked why, I said, "Forget about it, it's too long a story." He left and I did not see him again until we called in port, when I was able to help him with a meal or two and some cash to keep him going for a while. I said goodbye as the ship was leaving soon and I never saw him again. I felt though that I had at least been able to help another Lewis man in memory of John Montgomery.

I was still in the torn building with sounds of crying and moaning of the wounded and dying, waiting for a stretcher bearer to take me to the first field dressing station if we could reach it, which was just a hope perhaps as the area was swept with machine gun and shell fire, but we made it without being hit. Previous to that, and while the Germans were after us, a lad from Daliburgh, South Uist, Ewen MacKenzie, was running with me. Ewen fell laughing, saying it was his knee and also his foot. I looked but there was no blood. Then I looked at the sole of his shoe, and there was a bullet lodged in the instep of the shoe. It was at an angle and did not penetrate the leather, his knee was knocked out of place but he was all right and got safely back. While getting his knee fixed I could see the Scots Guards retiring. They had to mark time to wait for the rest under machine gun and rifle fire, the height of stupidity and worse, all for the sake of discipline. I finally got to the first field dressing station, but there were many needing more urgent attention than me. Our Commanding Officer, Craig Brown, was there with a bullet in his stomach. At last my turn came, when I was taken this time to the advanced field hospital where I was dressed properly and then taken by ambulance to Rouen Hospital to await, if lucky, to be sent to the U.K. I was lucky and was sent to Craigleith Hospital near Edinburgh.

In that battle which started in the early afternoon till late the following day, when roll was called of the 1st Cameron Highlanders, out of nearly a thousand men that went into action, only 123 answered the roll call. It was a terrible slaughter and every other regiment suffered as much. The Bengal Lancers that we passed on the way up were almost wiped out and no wonder, as they were on horseback. In Craigleith Hospital, I was the youngest wounded soldier and much petting was made of me. I was there about a month and my leg was healing up fine. The night before I was marked out for convalescence, we had a singsong party with all the nurses and orderlies. It went on late at night; there was lemonade but no beer or whisky. The next evening I arrived at the home in Langholm, near Dumfries, which was a church with beds along each side like the ward I had left, only this one had a pulpit and the bed I had was almost under it. This was Saturday and a service was to be held in that Presbyterian Church the next day.

I was never in a Protestant church before save at that church parade that I spoke of. I was nervous that I would not do the right thing since I was a Catholic and there was no Catholic church in Langholm. The Minister went into the pulpit and said the opening prayers, he then said. "We will now sing a hymn." The tune of the hymn sounded to me like some of the songs we were singing the night before. When the hymn ended I, with my befuddled head, started to clap and clap and I wondered why the others were not clapping. It suddenly dawned on me that I was in church. I got up amongst the nurses' laughter and made for the door, wishing that the floor would swallow me. The matron followed me and caught me at the door in a state of collapse. After that the minister came down and was kind and understanding. He said good laughter in these times was as good as a sermon. Langholm was a free town to us wounded. They wouldn't take a single penny for any service or any goods we bought, even drinks in pubs were free. I stayed there some three weeks as my wound still required dressing, and shortly after that I went home on sick leave for fourteen days.

They were glad to see me, more so because I was the first wounded soldier to be home in the district and I was held in awe by some. Many of the Lovat Scouts were home on sick leave after contracting measles. None had been abroad, they had been given an extension of a month when their leave expired by the local doctor who, when I applied through a misunderstanding, turned on me rather nastily and was actually pushing me through the door. When I asked him why would he not give me an extension as he was giving the rest, the least he could do was to give me a clean bandage. "What do you want a bandage for," he asked. I told him I was wounded in France. "Come inside laddie, why didn't you tell me that at first, I thought you were a Lovat Scout." "I am a Cameron Highlander." "I'm sorry" he said, "I haven't any bandages but I will give you a line to take to the hospital and I have no hesitation in giving you a month's extension. Come and see me again if you need more." I did not go back for more, as I was restless to be along with the rest, but not to volunteer again for France. I think only a mad man would do that. It was about this time that the townships of Ormiclate and Locheynort were divided into crofts. My father got a croft in Locheynort and we were making the removal by our boat, with many trips as the boat could not carry much at a time, and all depended on the weather. It is worth noting that the place where my great great grandfather lived is where my house stands now. They were cleared out at the time of the Highland Clearances, and we were the next to occupy it. I used to help them with the spring work, which my father was in a big hurry to get done and get on with the building of our home, as we were living in a crude shack while the house in Lochboisdale was being dismantled. One day, I got hold of an old shotgun and went along the shore where I saw a young seal basking. I shot and slightly wounded him. I got hold of him before he entered the water and started to pull him up on the grass. I could not do that on account of the bad leg. Peter, my brother, heard the shot and came running along. We were both playing with the seal when father came and was angry at the delay and us laughing. He said, "Lift it by the rear flippers, help to put it on my back and I'll carry it myself, this is wasting time." We got it on his back and the seal started to wriggle about. He had then started to walk away with it but the wriggling brought him to a halt. It was then that I raised the gun and said, "Father, hold it a second till I put another shot in him." Father looked back and saw the raised gun. He dropped the seal and ran for his life, the gun of course was empty. Later he said to Peter, "You cannot trust anyone who's been to France." Peter and I took the seal to the house and made good use of it.

It was goodbye to my people and to Uist, and I headed back again to Invergordon where they found me medically fit and I joined the everlasting drill of route marches, trench digging and erecting barbed wire. That and bayonet practice on dummy straw bags arranged and spaced apart. It was a hard course. After a week of that training, my name came out in orders for a draft overseas. Gone were the days when they only had to blow the bugle and the whole camp fell in for a draft. The wounded, as they came back, told their own story and very few of them would volunteer, hence the reason for me being picked out so soon. We were to do a week's field training and that was the toughest of the lot.

I wrote home to inform them that I was going to France again. There would be no time for a reply. In charge of our draft was a captain, Lord James Stewart Murray, a very hard and strict officer who just couldn't get enough of training. At the corner of the road where we turned into camp there was a clump of thick bushes. He sometimes would order us to keep going on past the camp while he himself would hide in the bushes, and us dead tired. We used to call him all the names we could think of, luckily he was not in my company and I heard later that he was wounded and taken prisoner.

The appointed day for the drafts departure came. We lined up on the parade ground. The Colonel had given his farewell speech that we were a fine body of men and he was sure that we would uphold the honour that the Cameron Highlanders had held in every battle and country. He looked upon us as second to none, just the same as he did with all the other drafts. We were numbered off and it was then that a runner from the Orderly Room arrived with a telegraph to the Colonel. Having read it he called out my name and number to step out of the rank. I did so and he came over and said, "How old are you?" I told him, "Past seventeen." "Were you in France before?" I said, "Yes Sir." "What happened?" I said, "I was wounded Sir." "How did they send you out so young?" I said, "I volunteered." "Are you volunteering this time?" I said, "No Sir." "Well we can't send you out again till you are past eighteen." A law was passed to that effect and my father found out about it and had a wire sent to the Commanding Officer who then called for another man to take my place.

Shortly after that luck, I was sent to Inverness for garrison duty, guarding trains and loading and unloading shells for the Navy in Scapa Flow. There was very little drilling going on, it was guard duty all the time. There were three sentry posts and they were far apart. On one wet dreary night I was on guard duty on the railway post from 2am till 4am. The sergeant, Colin McAulay, was in charge of the guard and he was noted for his strictness. I had no watch and could only imagine that I had been on sentry duty for about an hour. All was quiet except for trains being shunted. The rails along the path on which I was walking up and down were empty, and soon a passenger train was shunted onto them. I opened a carriage door and climbed up. It was warm and cosy inside. I decided it would not be too risky to spend the rest of my time on sentry in the warmth and comfort of the carriage.

First I had to be sure there was no engine attached to these carriages that might take them away. On being satisfied, I again boarded her, taking my rifle and equipment with me. I closed the door and sat in the warm corner next to the window, keeping a good lookout for anything moving, or noise, also thinking that if found that I had left such an important post unguarded, the consequences would be very grave. On active service it would be the firing party. With thoughts of that in my mind, and reluctant to leave my cosy corner I dozed off very pleasantly until I was awakened by a hard jolt. When I opened my eyes and sensed where I was, the train was already moving out and gathering speed and before I got the door open, I felt it was too risky to jump out in the darkness. I held on hoping it would slow down, but instead it was increasing its speed and to jump could only mean death. I was not ready for that.

I knew there was a junction much further down the line and that she would have to slow down when passing over it. I would jump then and take my chances. The question was if I did escape being hurt, would I be in time at my post before my relief came? I had no watch and no way of knowing how long I had been asleep. There were poles along the line that I could make out in the darkness from which I tried to judge the speed and when I felt it was easing down I threw my rifle out and did the same with the rest of my equipment. Soon after that and in pitch darkness, I opened the door and took a jump forward and away from the train. I landed on all fours on the cinder track and somersaulted down the embankment. When I came to a halt, I found that apart from a few scratches, very little was wrong with me. I started back, praying that I would find my gear and be in time for my relief. In that and in many other situations of danger, I felt that my prayers were answered. I found my gear and rifle intact and as I marched towards the sentry box, the same train was being backed to her original place with perhaps some carriages taken off. When I was approaching the sentry box, I heard footsteps coming my way. I challenged them, "Halt, who goes there?" "Sergeant relieving guard." "Advance to be recognised." They did and asked my orders. I was in time and my worries about that incident were over.

The post at the dockside where the ammunition for the Navy was loaded into small coasting ships was very closely guarded. No one could board or leave these ships without a pass showing their picture and their authority to be there. In order to board the vessel one had to pass through a narrow gate that allowed only one person through at a time after his credentials were checked. If the sentry stood at ease, his rifle and fixed bayonet barred the way to anyone trying to enter.

Nearly all at the depot were old soldiers, too old and unfit for active service. I was the youngest, and when I reached the age of 18, I was sent to Invergordon again, where I was picked out for an overseas draft and at once put on field training. It was the usual long route marches, digging trenches, bayonet fighting and running with full pack till one was glad to be away to face the real thing. There were two from my native Island on that draft, Sandy Campbell and Roderick MacLeod, and the three of us stayed together till Roddy was killed and I was wounded.

It was night-time when we arrived at the embarkation port of Southampton. The troopship was alongside waiting for orders to start embarking. The delay was caused on account of many submarines sighted in the Channel. We were kept in large sheds on the pier where a concert party was brought in to entertain us in the hope that we would not break out. All doors were closed and locked. The pubs were still open and the entertainment was getting stale. We had to get out somehow. There was a long heavy pole nearby and many willing hands grabbed and lifted it. With a rush, we rammed the door, and we poured out and made for the pubs, staying there until a company from an English regiment came to arrest us. It was more gathering than arrest, all pubs were closed and we were shepherded back to the ship, some drunk, some just merry. There were no arrests in our draft and we started boarding at once and landed in France without any further incidents.

In tents in Calais we stayed several days. There was plenty of beer if one had money. We had little or none. There was a large contingent of Australian troops in camp and none of them yet had been under fire. There was very little discipline among them. They had plenty of money and were free with drinks. I was asked by one of them if I would sell him my cap badge and if it was in action. I said, "It was in many battles and I will sell it for five francs but I must keep it till the canteen closes or the Sergeant might spot me without it." "That's alright, I want to send it to my girlfriend in Australia." I sold the same badge five times that night at the same price and terms and no one came to claim it. The last one that wanted it I gave it to him for nothing. It kept us in beer and buying drinks for others that night, with some left for the next day.

A fight broke out to free some Australians that they had detained in a large tent. We joined in and soon the tent was pulled down and the prisoners freed. For that, and another incident in town where a certain house was burned down in which some of our draft was involved, we were sent to the front and out of mischief. No individual was caught.

When we reached our destination we were not needed for reinforcement. Instead we were sent to a pioneer battalion whose mission was to dig trenches and put up fences about a mile behind the front line. The camp where we were sent was in a wood, some four miles behind the front line. There was no drill or much movement in the camp during daylight hours and no lights were allowed at night. This was a precaution against being seen from the air. There were many posters stuck on the trees warning anyone caught cutting down branches or trees would be severely dealt with. The trees at that time were sprouting leaves and affording some protection. The tent allotted to us three was very crowded with much bad language, so we decided to find some other place. No other tents were available.

One very wet night, an officer's tent fell down as, through ignorance, stupidity or neglect to slacken the guy ropes, the tent pole came through the canvas. It was left lying there. We thought if we could steal it we could make a good bivouac out of it. Roderick volunteered for the job while we two kept watch. Roddy dragged the tent across and we hid it till we could get a long light pole for the top. Such a pole was hard to get unless we would risk going into the wood where there were plenty. I volunteered for that job. I selected a limb and hacked it down with my jack knife, along with slender rods. I had the lot trimmed when I heard footsteps coming. There was no place or time to hide my work and when the Commanding Officer came into view, I knew I was in trouble.

When he saw the damage, he said, "Did you cut that down?" I had to admit it and said that since it was a small branch with no leaves on, it would not be of any harm. "What were you intending to do with it?" I told him. "You will hear about this." As I was walking away he said, "Take it with you, it is no use lying there." I took the lot with me and we made a comfortable place with three bunks, seats, flooring and a large mirror all taken from a large empty house not far away. From the garden of that house we plucked many beautiful flowers, which we stuck in the mud around our shack. On camping inspection day, when everyone stood beside his own tent, we stood beside our lot and when the high command came, the Commanding Officer looked in and smiled. The doctor said it was a better place than he had and complimented us for its tidiness. There was no charge for cutting the branches.

It was all night work at that camp. During the day we took cover under the trees and when darkness came, we went up the line near the front to dig and repair trenches with sandbags. Sometimes we would come under shellfire. When these times occurred, a very frightened officer would tell us to clear out and everyone for himself. If this happened early in the night, us three made for the Estaminet, which was a small French café selling food and drink, if we had any money. From these trips we would always bring something new to our dwelling.

One dark night when shelling was unusually heavy, Sandy and I were working together, one holding the sandbag open, the other shovelling the sand in. The one holding the bag had to carry it when full, some fifty yards away. We took turns about. It was my turn to carry and the Sergeant was eager to get the job done and clear out. He was rushing everyone. After carrying half a dozen bags, I decided to play a trick on Sandy who was shovelling. I cut the bottom of the empty bag I brought to be filled and held it open. As soon as he had a few shovels put in, I gave the bag a jerk. Sandy kept shovelling but the bag was not getting filled. The Sergeant came over and gave us a bad row for being lazy, and when he turned on me in anger I said, "The bag is not full yet." He felt it and gave it a tug. The bag came away empty. "You damn fool, do you know this bag has no bottom?" I said, "No, Sergeant, I can't see in the dark." Sandy was angry but when he calmed down we decided to compose a song about our dugout, which we did.

As there were no route marches or drill to keep us fit, some bright or not so bright officer came up with the idea that a swimming pool should be built or rather dug. It was to be 50 ft x 20 ft and 5 ft deep. All had to be dug and moved away by shovelling. It was a slow process. The clay was very sticky. Every day a party of 15 would be at the digging. It was our turn one day and in charge was an English Sergeant.

We worked hard for a spell until someone threw a handful of wet clay while the Sergeant's back was to us. That was repeated and, when he became aware of it, he thought it was good fun and joined in by throwing an occasional ball. We did not want to hit him, but when he said we were very poor shots I challenged him to take off his jacket. This he agreed to and detailed one man to keep watch in case the Orderly Officer might come. The match was to be between him and Roddy, whom I picked as the best shot among us. They stood one on each side of the pool, with the helper making ready the wet clay. The match started by Roddy scoring a hit on the Sergeant's face, who soon matched it, and I would say they were about even, both covered in mud and neither side would give in. All of us, including the man on watch, were enjoying the clay fight when we heard a roar near us, "What the hell is going on here? Where is the Sergeant – is this another Bannockburn?" He told us to clean up and get on with the work for if the Commanding Officer caught us like that, we would all be in for it.

The pool was only a few feet dug when we were drafted into the Argyll's who needed reinforcements after a hard battle. They were in the front line at Hulluch, a village one mile north of Loos in northern France where we joined them. It was trench warfare with neither side gaining ground. We did sixteen days and nights in the trenches and eight days out, when we would sometimes be deloused, get a bath and a new shirt, which was as lousy as the one we took off, although new from the bale.

I recall after a long time in that sector of the line, we came out for an eight-day rest. We were to be inspected by the General. We were lined up on parade and ordered to attention by the sergeant. When the Colonel was approaching on horseback, the horse was shaking itself. The rider was trying to get it to stand still when he saw a man shaking himself in the ranks. He called out in anger, "What's the matter with that man in the ranks Sergeant?" The Sergeant came over and asked him. The man said he was lousy. The Sergeant went to his stance in front but did not report. The Colonel again shouted, "I want to know what is wrong with him." The Sergeant replied, "He is lousy sir." "Lousy" said the Colonel "I am lousy, my horse is lousy, the General is the same, the whole of France is lousy, take that man's name." It seemed that no one was quite clean there.

Much of the time in the trenches we would be engaged in repairing and consolidating when and where it was bombarded. There were always two to a bay on sentry. That part of the line was on high chalk ground, and so a dry place to lie on when there was an opportunity. As neither side could advance, both sides began tunnelling to each other to be blown up. As many as three a day went up in our sector. Seeing the effect one of these had on the ground some distance from the actual explosion, I tried to compare it with anything I had seen before. The comparison I arrived at was like a place I knew at home where the spring tides ran strong, and if a gale of wind was against it, the waves were very high. Such were the waves of earth that the exploded mine had set in motion. I thought that if I came out of the war alive that would be the image and description I would have to tell. Before that I had the impression that everything, after reaching its highest point, came down straight. Not so with human beings or what was left of them, they came down spiralling. It took some time before the ground calmed to its original position. I was very lucky as none went up near me.

On one occasion in the front line, where our position had to be held at all costs, we were doing the usual sixteen days in the trench. Early on the fifteenth day, we felt and heard the underground knocking. We reported it to the headquarters, hoping that we would be withdrawn from that area. Our hopes were ignored. All we could do was wait for the blast. With an ear flat to the bottom of the trench, we listened, trying to judge the distance of the sound and its direction. As it became louder, we dared not make any noise, the talk was in whispers with no moving about, but inwardly praying and hoping they would not reach below us before our relief came the next day. It was a nerve wracking time, a dragging age, with still the knocking not quite under us when we were relieved by the Tyneside Scottish to whom we made aware what to expect.

We were almost out of the communication trench, a matter of about twenty minutes' walk, when the blast came and the position we were holding went up. We were ordered back in a hurry, trying to catch the Germans before they occupied the crater. Some had, but none got back. The task of consolidating by hacking through the bodies of those who, a short time before, had relieved us, is something I don't want to remember. All this was done under heavy machine gun fire. The next day we were relieved. For our eight days' rest while I was in that area, no large-scale battles took place, but there were raids in plenty. Some of us would be picked out for wire cutting, some for grenade throwing, some as bayonet men but all of us went on every raid. The drill was, the wire cutter ahead in no man's land cut the barbed wire, the bomb thrower, if within reach of the trench, threw his grenade in and the bayonet man after allowing some four seconds, jumped in and dealt with anyone alive there with the help of the wire cutter who had a stout wooden club with many spikes through it. The same club was strapped to the right wrist by a piece of leather to allow it to drop when not in use.

The operation continued that way till our ammunition was gone or we were out of action. If lucky, we made our way back under rifle and machine gun fire from the then alerted trench. Some would not return and these were reported missing or killed in action. Not all such raids were successful. At last the hard ground in that sector was so pulverised with mines and shellfire that no tunnelling was possible. To us that was a relief.

In the trench every night when darkness came, if possible a party left to bring up the rations for the next twenty-four hours. These usually consisted of loaves of bread, tins of bully beef and hard tack biscuits. Sometimes there would be candles. The sergeant divided them if and when the party came back; very seldom did we have enough to eat. If we were in a quiet sector, the cooks would risk a charcoal fire. Then we got a hot meal or stew, sometimes tea and bacon at breakfast, four to a small loaf was the commonest thing. At other times, if part of the rations did not arrive, we would be down to ten and eleven to a loaf. Water for drinking was carried in two-gallon petrol tins. There was no water for washing. If it rained for a spell there would be water in the shell holes. We used that and when they dried up, I hate to say what was at the bottom.

We slept fully clothed with boots and equipment in recesses in the walls of the trench facing the enemy ready for instant action in case of a surprise attack. There were very few deep dugouts at that time; one part of the line we held in that sector was only 25 yards from the Germans and each side could hear the other talking. In daylight we used dummy heads as decoys to draw their fire when our own snipers were in hidden positions. To raise your head above the parapet in daylight was like asking for a bullet. We used mirrors fixed on top of the fixed bayonet to see across to the enemy. The only advantage of being in the front line there was being too close for accurate shell fire. Our mail came up with the rations and it is hard to say which was more welcomed. Once I got a letter from home while in 'No-Man's-Land' going to the attack. There was a ten shilling note enclosed which I thought at the time was bad luck but held on to it. I read to where it said they were all well, then pocketed the letter and turned my mind to the business ahead.

4   The Somme

Towards the end of July 1916 we were force marched to the Somme in very hot weather in full marching kit, loaded with ammunition and short rations. I don't remember how many days we were on that march. It was said that thirty of our Brigade died by the roadside from sheer exhaustion. None was allowed to remove his pack. I passed many on the way in that state; such was the discipline in the 8th Argyll's and 15th Division. We were glad when we came within hearing of the big gun, for at least this ordeal, which the enemy had nothing to do with, would soon be over. Without any rest, we went into the line and took over a position that was to be held at all costs. The Somme was a terrible place; perhaps the worst place in the whole war. Going up to the front line you passed through a long stretch of the communication trench made up entirely of bodies, friend and foe. It was sometimes impossible to pass without stepping on them, and if you were going that way in the dark and stepped on a decayed body, the stench can only be imagined. It stayed with you for a long time. You did not enjoy your food that day.

One night while in the front line, four of us were detailed to bring up two coils of barbed wire to repair a gap that was broken in front of us. We got down and found the wire, which was already made into coils about 2 feet in diameter; two of us to a coil, they were not heavy but awkward to carry in the dark. My friend and I decided on a plan how best to carry it. With fixed bayonets we put both rifles through the coil and put it on our shoulders. The other man was shorter and the coil kept slipping on the top of him, and when he complained, I said if he would carry both rifles I would carry it myself. He agreed and set off to catch the other two, who had a good start. I put the coil on my shoulder with my arm through it, keeping clear of the sides of the trench.

My progress was slow but steady till the barb caught in a sand bag. If it was rotten a jerk would free it, if it was strong, it would take some time to clear it. Most of them were rotten. I knew I would soon be coming to the patch of packed bodies and wondered how I was to get the coil past without getting stuck in them. Before I reached there, I got stuck in something I thought was another sand bag. It did not tear or come away with my second pull, which only made the barb go deeper in my shoulder straps and it hurt. I gave it a stronger tug and everything came down. I fell on my side with the barbed wire stuck in my kilt and also in the not too badly decayed body of a German that I recognised by his top boots. It took me some time before I got the wire off the shoulder and my arm clear of the coil to loosen my kilt and get out of it. It was impossible to clear it in the dark, so I left all three stuck together and made off for the front line. It was easy to get another kilt, there were plenty of them around unburied.

On being relieved tired, weary, hungry and dirty, we were met at the end of the communication trench by a piper who played ahead of us to our destination. The stirring tunes did much to cheer us, boost our morale and lighten our dragging feet that no other instrument could. That was well known to all in these circumstances. I was to witness some touching scenes while liberating towns and villages towards the end of the war. Meantime, and on the subject of the charms of the bagpipes, I will relate a story to that effect. Like all tall stories, I doubt if it is true.

During the First World War, a Scottish soldier lay, seriously wounded, in a hospital in France. He was the only Scottish man in his ward, all the rest were English. The soldier was putting up a strong fight for his life and the doctor and sister thought it was a losing battle that

64

would soon be lost. One night after the doctor inspected him, he called the sister aside and told her that he did not think the Scots lad would last till morning, "You can give him anything he wants. If he wants a glass of Scotch whisky, you can give it, it won't do any harm, it won't do any good, it may help on the way out." "Alright" said the sister "I'll do that doctor." After a while she went to his bed again and asked, "How are you tonight Scotty?" "I am not so good sister." "I am sorry to hear that. Is there anything you would like, anything at all, how about a glass of good Scotch whisky?" "No sister, I never touch it." "Is there anything else then?" "Well sister, I would like to hear a tune on the bagpipes." "Well Scotty, if I can manage, I will get a piper to play for you." She was alone in the ward and yet she dearly wished to grant the dying boy this last request. She told the sister in the next ward of her intentions and would she look after her ward while she was away getting a piper.

It so happened that a Canadian Scots regiment was nearby and there was no trouble or delay in getting a piper who was able and willing to fill her request and as soon as they got to the bedside, the piper began playing the tunes the soldier liked best who, after much play, fell asleep. Next morning when the doctor came on duty he met the sister and said, "Morning Sister, how are things?" She replied, "So, so Doctor" and told of the piper. "I suppose" he said, "Our friend is away?" "No indeed, he is sitting up in bed after eating a plate of porridge. But Doctor, fourteen of my English patients died last night." "Well, well" said the doctor "I never thought bagpipes were so powerful." As already said, I am not vouching for the truth of the story.

There were many rumours and speculations as to when the war would end. On the Albert front (a major control centre for the planning of the battle of the Somme) where we were for a long spell, the famous statue of the Madonna and child hung from a church spire that was hit. It was firmly believed that when it toppled down, the war had ended. After every bombardment we watched eagerly but nothing happened.

In a heavy bombardment, with death and desolation around you, your heart pounding like a piston, thinking the next shell would be yours, you thought the end of the world had come, and when the shelling stopped and a brave little skylark rose high above us with her sweet song of hope and courage, you felt there was a God. No other bird came and she will always be among the birds of the air to have the warmest place in my heart.

Later on in the same sector, when bombing from the air started, the warning was given by a blast from a police whistle. In daylight you took cover wherever you found it. In darkness, all lights had to be put out. At the back of the line, where we used to have our rest, there was a café that did good trade selling fried eggs and chips. Madam would have two large frying pans on a huge stove meeting the demands of some Canadians who always had money. My friend, Alex MacMillan, and myself were flat broke and hungry.

This night Alex said, "Donald, do you know who is on sentry?" I knew. "Do you think he will let you have the whistle for a short while?" I said that I was sure he would, "Why the whistle at this time of night?" "Here is the plan and it's easy. We take our canteens to the café, and I will order four fried eggs and chips with the others, and when she turns them over you give me your canteen, wait till I give you the signal by raising my balmoral and scratching my head; then you will slip out and, at a short distance from the door, you blow the whistle hard. I will be near the stove, Madam will have to put the lights out, and I will scoop up everything on the pans before the rest move. It's dead easy." Everything went according to plan. We had a good feed with some left over. After that everything had to be paid for in advance.

Again on the Somme we were engaged in fierce fighting. The position had to be held at all costs. Instead of the sixteen days in the line, as the casualties were heavy, we were relieved every four days and two out. On this occasion we were long past the four days, no relief could get through the barrage of shellfire at the back of us, and no ration party that tried got back. Our emergency rations were long eaten; we were working as hard as we could, trying to keep the trench open. When a shell landed, digging out survivors, removing the dead out of your way, there was no time and no use in burying them, as they would soon be thrown up again. It is no wonder those surviving were weak, hungry, thirsty and exhausted. Many a time, after much chewing on my leather belts, I wished I was near my native glen where I would be satisfied if I could only get a bellyful of heather. There was not a blade of grass or any roots growing there. Searching the dead for any food they might have, I only got the heel of a loaf that was badly soaked in blood. I scraped some off and offered half of it to my mate. He would not take it saying it would not stay down, but when he saw that I had eaten it with no ill effects, he asked if I had any left. I said, "Yes, you can have half" and when he had eaten that he said it was alright and wished he had more of it. That sustained us for a while.

There was no sign that rations might get through, those that were killed and wounded had nothing left. I made my way back over the top to where my friend Sandy Campbell was in the support group, knowing if he had anything to eat, I would get some. All the way I was badly shelled but it did not seem to matter. By a piece of luck I came upon Sandy, who saw me coming staggering and falling. He called out in Gaelic, "Where did you get the rum Donald?" I said, "I'm not drunk Sandy, only starving, have you got anything to spare?" He said there were no rations getting up to them either, but that he had some of his emergency left. It was hard biscuits broken to almost powder; he gave me a handful and I thought it was the best feast I ever had. I made my way back more carefully.

Shortly before this event, another chap and I were sent down the line for a box of small ammunition. Our way took us through the shattered village of Contalmaison, which was then about a mile from the front line. It was out of machine gun or rifle fire range but not shellfire. We got out of the trench to have a look. It was desolation. There was only one corner of a house left standing, consisting of seven bricks and five bricks high. There was the usual cross that you see in French graveyards. This one was about fifteen feet high; all around it the graves were shattered, strewn in every direction with their contents, and almost unbelievable, the wooden part of the cross was hardly touched, and on the figure of Christ I could not see a scratch, as if to say 'you can destroy all but you cannot destroy me'.

I felt a pang of sorrow for the remains of the nuns in what was left of their brown habits. The other lad who walked ahead while I gazed on the cross, shouted, "Hey Donald, have a look at this." I looked and saw a large mound with the usual rifle stuck in the ground and the bayonet forming a cross. This one was in the form of a cross with a card that had an epitaph in large letters, which read, "Here lie four square headed bastards." I wondered at the mentality of the man who wrote it. I gazed back to the figure on the almost untouched cross and remembered his almost last words, 'Father forgive them for they know not what they do'.

I got back safely to the trench. My mate had found two biscuits that I had overlooked in the pocket of our now still and shattered friend. Early that morning they stepped up the shelling of our trench on which it seemed they had an accurate range. With our heavy losses in killed, wounded and buried alive, our position became untenable. We were ordered to withdraw from

66

that part. I was lying down in the trench, waiting for the rest coming. I was reading part of the Mass in my simple prayer book when a heavy shell landed a few yards away. I was hit in the shoulder and leg with my right buttock nearly blown off, all on my right side. I was in shock and dazed. I don't know if any of the rest was hit but I was fortunate. We still had two stretcher-bearers with us and they, although short of bandages, did their best for me. They carried me about a quarter of a mile to the advanced field dressing.

The Somme

We were always under shellfire and they had to drop me whenever a shell burst near us. I don't recall how many times they had dropped me to take cover. I was in a very poor state from starvation, loss of blood and these drops. When we reached the dressing station, I was left on the stretcher at the outward edge of the crowd, some dead, some dying, and some crying in pain. I was not in great pain. When an orderly came near me and saw the blood pouring over the stretcher, I think he thought that I was finished and not worth looking at. There was only one doctor and the shelter could only take one stretcher at a time.

After the doctor had a look at the patient he had to decide whether his state was worth the involved risk of taking him to the next dressing station. The way there was also under constant shelling. The stream of wounded joining us had eased. I knew that some who had been brought down after me had already been taken to the doctor and I wondered why I was left. Were the others worse hit than I was? I had no way of knowing. Sometimes I would doze off to sleep as I was in no great pain. I thought I had been there a very long time when an orderly from the station came near me. He knelt down beside me and said, "Would you like a cigarette?" I said, "No, I am a pipe smoker." "Do you think you could smoke a pipe?" I said, "Yes, sure." "What kind of tobacco do you smoke?" I said, "Black Twist." "Have you got a pipe?" I am afraid in your condition it would be very wet now, I'll see what I can do." He went away and I heard him calling to the doctor that he had a man wounded badly who wanted a smoke of a pipe. "He smokes black tobacco but has no pipe." The doctor called up "If he can smoke black tobacco take him down and I'll have a look at him." They did so, and when he saw the damage he said I had a good chance and should have been taken down long ago. He swabbed the wound with iodine and gave me an injection.

They put me on a dry stretcher and we started down on the stretch to where the horse ambulance came up. I only remember being dropped three times; the last time was the worst. It was on rubble stone in front of a deep dugout and they, quite rightly, made a dive for it when the shell exploded a few yards from me. I was not hit, I think because I was so close that the pieces went above me. At the mouth of the dugout were two Australians who came to my aid; they took me to the shelter of the dugout to await the horse drawn ambulance. No cars could get up that far.

The journey to the advanced hospital was indeed painful with the horses racing through shell and potholes. I passed out and came to again on the theatre table, where they properly dressed me, and sometime later put me on a Red Cross train along with the cries of the wounded. There was a tall nurse standing with a large syringe, giving an injection to those in agony. I got my issue and don't remember any more of that painful long journey to a hospital in Rouen where they kept me for two weeks to gain strength for the crossing to England.

I was well cared for and made rapid progress. The day came when I was marked and labelled for embarkation. I was taken on the stretcher to await the ambulance that would take us to the hospital ship. Facing me on the ground was a lad of my own age, and when I asked was he hit bad, he said not too badly in the back. When he asked about me, I said in the leg, shoulder and hip but not very bad. He told me his regiment and division and they were in the same area. When I said that the Germans were bombarding us with unusually heavy shells, he heard that it was because they knew the tanks were hidden scattered in that area and were about to attack. It was a well-kept secret from us, yet the Germans knew all about the tanks, but not their places of concealment. The attack was made on the 21st August, the day after I was wounded, with some success.

Soon the ambulance took us to a different part of the hospital ship. We landed at Folkestone without any incident that concerned me. The Red Cross train that I was numbered for was going to Wales. In a mistake I was put on a train going to Scotland, and when that was discovered, they wanted to take me off saying that I could not stand the long journey. After much protesting and pleading, they let me stay. The journey to Perth was long and painful and I ended up in a poor house converted into a military hospital. When I woke up the next day, the lad that I talked to in Rouen was in the next bed facing me as before. His name was Harry Metcalf. He was a miner and came from the Durham area. We became good pals and whenever he got a parcel from home, he gave me a share.

Apart from x-rays and dressing, I was left alone. The leg and shoulder showed some shrapnel, but the buttock was clear of iron. I was too weak to be operated on to remove the shrapnel and to this day it is still there. The buttock wound was six inches long, 4 inches wide and 3 inches deep. The problem was to fill that hole. There was no plastic surgery, plasma or blood transfusion in those days. They decided to draw the wound together and put double stitches in it. That night, when the effects of the chloroform wore off, with the stitches top and bottom pulling through the flesh, I was howling in agony. The ward doctor was called. He ordered the stitches to be taken out otherwise I would not survive the night. It took many days before I got over that ordeal. The wound was left to heal and when that started, parts of it grew out like warts and these had to be burned by bluestone or caustic, which was not pleasant. Harry and I used to laugh and make fun of our condition and would sometimes keep those near us awake. They thought there was not much wrong with us.

We were there over a week when a new night sister came on duty. She was a tall heavy woman and when she walked past our beds, although the floor was of concrete, the beds vibrated and we would be in agony. We did not want to tell her, but kept our faces screwed up till she passed, and then we laughed. With many trips up and down the ward, she caught us at last laughing. She came over to the beds and said, "What are you two laughing at me for, what do you see so funny about me?" "Nothing Sister, we're not laughing at you." "Yes you were, I heard you every time I pass your beds and if I hear you again, I shall report you. What is wrong with you? Are you up patients?" We said, "Yes sister." Alright, I'll see that you are up early to wash tomorrow." The chap in the next bed said, "They are not up patients. They are badly wounded and plain daft." "Right, I'll see in the morning what's wrong with them." She stayed on till after the day shift started the dressings. When it came to our turn, she was awed at what she saw. She said she was sorry at being angry with us last night, "But tell me what were you laughing at?" "Well sister" I said, "You are a heavy person and when you pass our beds, they vibrate and we are in agony. There is nothing we can do except to laugh when you pass." "I had no idea, but now I can understand. After this I shall walk in the centre until called for." Like most nurses, she was real nice and often, when we could not sleep, she would bring us some of her own tea.

In the ward was a titled V.A.D, (Volunteer Aid Detachment), nurse, Lady Brooks. She wrote and stamped my letters. I didn't have the then penny postage. A month before then I had plenty more than I knew for a while. It happened we were a long time unpaid. One occasion, while out of the line for a long rest, we were paid in full. That night we were ordered back to the trenches, and very little of our money had been spent. It was always considered unlucky to have much money in your pocket going into action, yet there is something about money to make you hesitate to throw it to the wind no matter what the circumstances are. In the trench under heavy shellfire, someone had a pack of cards. We spread a waterproof sheet and started to play the game of banker. I was winning and losing till I won the bank and kept it for some time, turning up aces, my great coat pockets crammed full of francs, some of high denomination. I thought my luck was out and any time a shell would land among us and I wished to lose the bank, which at last I did. With no regret I started to back my card heavily which did not matter, high or low. I began to lose until at last I had only ten francs left. I put it on and lost. I was quite happy. During the playing time no one was hit. I was wounded a few days after that and broke.

One day the same nurse began talking about the war. She said her fiancé was a prisoner of war since 1914. He was in the 1st Cameron Highlanders and when I asked his name as I had been in the Camerons then, she said Captain James Stewart Murray. I was glad that I remembered that she had already said he was her boyfriend because this was the man that used us so harshly doing our field training when we first went to France. We did not like him. I said I knew him well, that it was he who took our draft out in 1914, that he was a gallant officer. I knew he was taken prisoner. After that talk she seemed nicer to me all the time I was there.

69

Although we were badly injured, and despite being in pain most of the time, Harry and I used to joke and laugh a lot to the annoyance of some of the staff and other patients. Shortly after that the ward was cleared out for distempering, and when they moved our beds they made sure that Harry and I were well separated. I was placed at the head of the ward while he was placed at the other end. That night when we were both restless our temperatures went up alarmingly. Long before his time the duty doctor was called. He asked why we were parted. They told him we were laughing too much, "Put them back again or you will not have them for long. Laughter is the best medicine I could order."

We got together again, but it was some time before we were back to normal and inclination to laugh came. My leg and shoulder had healed. The other required burning every second day and was slow to heal. They said Harry was doing better, but they let me up before him. One day after the doctor had passed, I saw his wound. Unless seeing it, it was hard to understand how he could have survived. I could see some of his internal organs in a long wide gash and so seeing, I felt proud of him at his patience in his suffering.

At last the day came when we were both marked for convalescence. We were sent to Strathallan Castle, part of which was taken over by the Red Cross and staffed by V.A.D. nurses. There were twenty-four wounded patients from the hospital we had left, only a few needed treatment and dressings like myself. I was still getting the burning treatment to which I was now well used. The castle stood in large grounds with an avenue of trees leading up to it. Part of it was said to be the oldest standing in Scotland. Sir James Roberts, who had made his fortune in the Lancashire mills, owned it then. After a week there I could walk 25 yards and thought it good progress. I was in no hurry to be again sent back to the carnage in France to where eventually I had that misfortune to go. They treated us well and the food was good and plentiful.

The nurses often invited us to tea parties in the many castles and big houses in surrounding areas. They had a donkey at the castle; he was a small beast, no higher than a ten-month-old calf. They had a harness for him and a carriage was got for my use to ride and drive in the castle grounds. I had to feed and look after him. I had no trouble in harnessing him and got on board. I took the reins and looked forward to a fast gallop, but it wouldn't move regardless of my efforts. After a long time trying, the housekeeper arrived. She said, "He won't move unless you give him a cigarette." I thought she was joking but I gave him one and he started to chew it and off he went at a walking pace and kept on for about 100 yards when I had to give him another. I tried him with two, hoping to get more speed, but he just took one at a time. Before the packet was empty we had a good distance behind us.

I thought at this rate we would be very late getting back, but he knew the way better than I and when I turned him he went off at a gallop. The way back was very enjoyable. It was the same drill every time I had him out. Some days if I was short of cigarettes he would try to capsize the buggy by shying suddenly to the other side of the road, but before doing so he always looked behind to see if I was watching. One day on the homeward stretch he caught me unawares. The buggy was capsized and I landed in the ditch. I was not hurt and thought I could catch him. Before I got out he was away with the upturned buggy, galloping in the centre of the road all the way back. Those at the castle saw him coming empty and the search party found me hobbling my way home. Except for my clothes there was little damage but the carriage was beyond repair and so ended my joy rides.

As a result of an epidemic which broke out in the Perth Hospital, where we all came from, there were no replacements for those who were sent home on leave. At last only two of us were left. I was marked out for home leave and was to go the next day. That evening we were invited to a tea party with the Matron and nurses. After the singsong and tea, someone suggested reading the cups at which the lady of the house had a good reputation. Cups were passed to her and when it came to my turn Matron said, "Pass your cup, Donald, to see what kind of a passage you'll have tomorrow crossing the Minch." I did and after what seemed a long time she said, "I don't see any sea here, but I see a large house more like a hospital. I see many beds and I don't think you are going tomorrow." "Yes he is" said the Matron "I have his leave papers and travelling warrant in my desk." To that the lady of the house could only say "Ah well." We thought no more about it. Before going to bed that night the Matron told me a telegram had come while we were away, to notify her that I was to be sent for further treatment to a hospital in Dundee the next day. While I don't give much credit to cup reading, we were amazed at the accuracy without fore knowledge.

I arrived at the hospital and was kept on the burning treatment, as the wound was not yet healed. After a week they put me on a different kind, and this stuff was hot and like treacle. One nurse always put it on too thick and when I said so she became angry, saying it was taking far too long to heal. I took some of it off in the bathroom and when she saw me coming out and that I had taken most of the stuff off, she reported me to the Doctor. When he asked what was wrong, I said that the nurse was putting too much of the burning stuff on me, more than I could stand. He looked at the wound and said it was filling up nicely, "Try that ointment on light every second day, it's hot stuff." He left and the nurse redressed me. She was not the same after that incident and many times made things unpleasant for me. I can truly say she was the only nurse I didn't like among the great many who cared for me during the thirty six times I had been a patient in hospital.

My wound now healed, I was looking forward to being discharged, but they said I was to be sent for further convalescence. I pleaded with the ward sister to use her influence with the doctor to send me home instead. They finally agreed and said they would send me home on fourteen days sick leave. At the end of that time they would send me a travelling warrant to where they wanted me to report back to, as I was likely to need more treatment. I was quite happy with that arrangement. I was sent home with a single travelling warrant. I was welcomed warmly at the steamer after having gone through so much since they last saw me. The house my father was building had not yet got a roof on and so I helped whenever I could. My father was not an easy man to get along with, perhaps thinking these young fellows don't know much, and I think was glad when I would take the shot gun and dog to the hills for rabbits or along the shore bird hunting.

I passed most of my fourteen days doing that, and when they ended, no word to report back came. I waited for over a month, but still no word and I did not want to question why. I felt it was their business and I was following their instructions and I knew I was in the right. At last I was reported to the policeman of the district as a deserter from the army. The policeman, without a warrant, came to arrest me and take me to the steamer that night. When I told him my orders on leaving the hospital were to stay at home till sent for, he would not believe me. He said, "Get ready, I am taking you to the steamer leaving tonight, under arrest." I said, "You or nobody else is taking me under arrest, I will go on my own when they send me a warrant and orders to report.

71

I have already been to France twice, I saw things and did things there and you would be well advised to remember that. I have nothing to lose." "Alright" he said, "I'll put in a report about you and you'll be sorry for this." I told him as far as I was concerned he could go to hell. He left in a hurry, having to walk miles to his bike and then home. I knew his report could not be in the mail in time for the steamer, I also knew someone was leaving the village for the mainland. I wrote a short letter to the hospital I had left, asking what they intended to do with me, and gave it to the man to post on the mainland. It would be ahead of the police report.

The next mail brought me a warrant and letter to report at Stirling Castle and if unfit to travel, to report to the nearest doctor; I was fit enough and left with the next boat. I arrived at Stirling Castle expecting to be put under arrest at once. I passed the sentry on guard who did not question me. I reported myself to a sergeant inside. He said, "We have been looking for you, you should be under arrest, but I am short of a man for guard duty, will you do that till we find out more about your case?" I was taken to the guardroom and asked to relieve the sentry on duty at the gate. This was the young man who had let me in. After about half an hour on sentry, the telephone in the guardroom rang and surprisingly there was no one there that knew how to answer it. Telephones were rare in those days. They asked me if I knew how and when I did another man took my place. The voice said, "Take the prisoner D. MacDonald you have there to the Orderly Room under escort." I said "I am D. MacDonald, I am on guard duty just now, what shall I do?" There was a pause. "Stay on duty till an escort is sent for you."

The escort duly arrived. I was marched to the orderly room and in front of the Commanding Officer. The charge of absent without leave was read out. "What have you got to say for yourself for this long absence?" I told him my story, and all the time he kept reading a report he had in front of him. He raised his head and looked at me, "Sergeant Major, what is this man's crime sheet like?" "There is none against him that we know of Sir." "Then it appears to me that the hospital neglected their duty towards this man, no blame can be charged to him. Therefore, the case against him is dismissed." I was lucky. I did not expect to get off so easily. They only kept me there for two days, then I was sent to a camp outside Colinton near Edinburgh.

After about a week there, I was put on field training for a draft for overseas and when this was finished and before we were to go on draft leave, volunteers for a three weeks' course of signalling were called for. At that time a soldier going overseas was entitled to 36 clear hours at home and the course was to begin as soon as we came back from this leave. I volunteered for the course and then thought I could not be back from leave in time to start with the others. In any case it was only three weeks since I had been home so I decided to forego the leave in order to be on time. I saw the sergeant major and explained my position. He saw my point and said he would put it to the C.O. I was then told that I was taken off the list of those going on leave, and when they had gone and the parade was formed up, my name was not on the roll as I was supposed to be on leave. I did not attend parades after that. Instead I used to hide myself in the Y.M.C.A.

I had to turn out on the many false alarms we used to have. On the last one of these, the alarm went before dawn. We were ordered in a hurry to start packing up everything we had and all blankets were to be rolled up in bundles of ten. Emergency rations were handed out, and as things had not gone this far before we wondered what it was all about. When the huts were empty, we were given some hard biscuits and a tin of bully beef between two. We thought this nonsense was over and that we would be ordered back to the huts and a few hours sleep. Instead we were ordered to fall in and were numbered off and told to march. It was then well into daylight. After marching for about half an hour, we met a detachment of Irish soldiers, some carrying rifles although most had none. Their appearance and marching was much below our standard and when we asked where they were going, none knew. As we approached Edinburgh, not having been told anything, we felt this was not an ordinary route march. As soon as we reached Waverly Station we entrained. There was no doubt then, we were going somewhere, but where? It was anyone's guess. Some said France, some Greece, some Egypt. The only thing they told us officially was that we were under sealed orders which did not mean anything to us.

After a long time on the train, we were given a meal, the usual hard tack and bully beef. We also had tea. That took us to the end of the train journey, which ended at Holyhead. We saw the sign and knew where we were. We were then marched to a field on the outskirts of the town. The town was put out of bounds to us. Cooks provided us with a hot meal from a field kitchen. Sentries were posted around the enclosed area, no passes were allowed. In the evening after the meal, Ainsley, an old soldier and an ex-sergeant who had been reduced to the ranks many times for being drunk, asked me if I knew any of the tailors. I said I knew one well, "Ask him to give you a pair of sergeant stripes, and a needle and thread, I am taking a party to town, but don't tell him, and you will be one of them if you want." While I was away searching for the tailor and getting the stripes, Ainsley was picking out his party.

All had to have a little money, all were to be in full view of the sentry at the gate when he would shout out loud for the sentry to hear, 'Fall in the fatigue party'. The stripes were sewn on the jacket, all was ready and in place, when the now Sergeant Ainsley walked smartly and stopped near the sentry and in a loud voice said 'Fall in the fatigue party' pulling a list from his pocket, most likely a blank. He began calling out names, to which all answered 'Here Sergeant'. He told the sentry that he had orders from the Sergeant Major to take this party to the station to unload baggage. We were to march smartly to attention as we may well be the first kilted troops to enter the town for a long time and should conduct ourselves to leave a good impression. He numbered us off, formed fours and quick march, and when passing the sentry he gave the order 'Eyes left'. The sentry returned the salute by coming to slope arms and slapping the butt of his rifle. Once out of sight, Ainsley told us to walk as we liked, but keep a look out for any officer who might be on the road. When we reached town he said, "You are on your own now, don't get drunk and don't mention me if you are caught." We broke away and I am afraid the good impression that we made fast disappeared in the pints in the alehouses while money lasted. As far as I can remember, none of us were caught getting back to camp.

We embarked on a ship next morning and were at sea at least an hour before they told us that we were bound for Ireland, landing at Dublin, and that our final destination was the old fort of Kinsale where the Irish we met on the way to the Edinburgh station were from. The reason for their lack of rifles was that they had sold them to the Sinn Fein. When we disembarked at North Wall in Dublin, we were greeted by a large crowd of men, women and children, with catcalls and three cheers for the Kaiser. There was no stone throwing or rotten fruit. Fearing that, they took us through a back street to the station with the insulting crowd following, and when the train was full, it was pulled to the outskirts of the city, where we stayed for some time before we got some rations of corn beef and biscuits.

When we arrived at the Fort we found that it was manned by a skeleton guard, but what they were guarding I don't rightly know. We took over, and it was guard duty for me, all the time I was there. At first and in daylight, fearing being attacked, we were only allowed out in small groups, each carrying a rifle, but after a few days like that without any incidents, we could go out in pairs but with side arms and a bayonet.

There was no church parade for Catholics but if one wanted to, he could go at his own risk. I went with side arms, although at first I felt scared with everyone looking at me, as I was the only one in uniform. After Mass I talked to many people outside and not an angry word was spoken to me. They asked where I had come from, and when I said South Uist, they said, "That is a Catholic island. Why are you fighting for England?" I said that I was in the war for Scotland. "Do you like this place?" "Yes, it reminds me of home with all these fishing boats in the loch, the place is very pretty." "And do you like fishing?" I said I did, "Then why don't you desert your regiment and stay with us, we will hide and protect you and you can fish with us." I must say for one on the verge of going to the carnage in France for the third time, the offer was tempting, but I would have nothing to do with it.

I was there for a little over a week when, coming from the canteen, I was met by the Sergeant Major. He said, "Where have you been, I have been looking for you since we left Scotland." I said, "I was here and didn't think I was wanted." "You are now. Come with me to the quarter master's store to draw your overseas kit, you are for the next draft, you escaped the last one." I said, "That was not my fault." "I know all about that. You are entitled to a draft leave if you want, starting the day after tomorrow." I said I wanted to go on draft leave as the signalling course was cancelled. I was fitted out and no crime was put against me for over-staying my hospital leave.

I had a lot of accumulated pay coming to me. I went to the paymaster to see if I could draw all before going on leave. He said "Yes, and as it is a tidy sum, you will be the last to be paid so that none of those going on leave will know you have that much on you." The tidy sum was only £20.00. I thought it should have been more, but that itself was a fortune going on leave. As I knew it was impossible to be back on time, and in order to make this clear to the company commander, I got a map of the west coast of Scotland and marked off the many islands in the Minch where the boat called, and of course adding some to them. It was all daylight sailing on account of floating mines. When I presented him with the map he said, "Where are you going?" I said, "To the Island of South Uist in the Outer Hebrides." I had to point it out for him. After studying the map and markings he said, "I can't make anything of this but it's clear you cannot be back on time after your leave. Report back as soon as possible."

We got the steamer from Dublin to Glasgow where I met my brother Peter and acquaintances from the Merchant Navy. I stayed in Glasgow that day and made for Oban the next. Sailing was cancelled on account of mines in our course to the Minch. However, the boat left late and stayed in Tobermory that night. We left in daylight for Tiree, where a floating mine was bobbing up and down near the pier. The sea was calm with an onshore light wind. The ship we were travelling on had a gun mounted on the stern and a naval crew to man it. As soon as we were away from the pier and a short distance from the mine, the naval ratings with small arms

74

were ordered to fire in an attempt to blow it up. I was standing by, and when they failed to hit it, the rating in charge asked if I would have a go at it. I said, "I have a rifle but no ammunition." He said, "I'll supply that." The first shot was short, the next was very near, the third was a hit, but nothing happened, not even after hitting it several times, which was lucky as the mine was a large one and would surely have destroyed the pier, according to the information I learned later on.

We crossed over to Barra without another incident and reached Lochboisdale in daylight where she tied up for the night, and I left for home. The boat only called twice a week. Before the next would call, and in order to have 36 clear hours at home, it was evident that I could not be back in time. It was the month of December, cold but not stormy. I spent my leave quietly at home, and waited two days for the boat. I gave them some of the money I had. The parting this time was sadder, perhaps with the thought of third time unlucky.

On arriving in Glasgow my brother's ship had already sailed. I spent the day in the city before I enquired about sailings to Ireland. There were none as that part of the channel was closed to shipping, but Holyhead was open. I got a stamped slip to that effect from the shipping agent. It would perhaps help to explain why I was so late in reporting back. On the train to Holyhead I got acquainted with a North Uist navy man who, like myself, was adrift for several days on account of the existing transport problem. There were no sailings that day, this time it was submarines in the channel. We had money and spent the rest of the day in pubs, mainly those I had been in not so long ago.

Before boarding the steamer we made sure that we had something to show for this delay. The slip said, 'Port closed due to enemy action'. The ship left as soon as it was dark and reached Dublin safely. We stayed at the Y.M.C.A. that night, as we were late for the train. I had a first cousin married in Dublin whom I had not seen since I was a boy. As I had her address we called on her, and when I explained who I was we both received a very warm welcome and spent part of the day with her, the rest in the pubs and window-shopping.

Our way took us to Sackville Street and the Post Office where the main part of the 1916 Easter killing took place. My mind went back to that time, to where I was in the trenches in the front line on the left of Hulluch, where our battalion was breaking in a raw Irish regiment that had never been under fire. I can't remember which, the Enniskillens or the Dublin Fusiliers. In the front line, we were told to keep an eye on those of them amongst us to see that they obeyed orders. We did not know then there was any trouble in Ireland, I think because of the strict watch the officers kept. On one very dark foggy night, visibility was only a few yards. In the morning when the fog cleared up, a poster was seen a few yards from our barbed wire. Written on it was 'You Irishmen are foolish fighting for England while English soldiers are murdering your fathers and brothers, raping your mothers, sisters and sweethearts while you are doing their fighting. Throw away your rifles and come over to our side, you will be safe'. At first we were edgy not knowing what the Irish might do. We need not have been, for the Irish willingly took part in the German destruction, and we had to restrain them from going over the top to attack them in broad daylight. I was told the Camerons on our left, doing the same as us, were not able to hold them back, and the result was almost total annihilation for the poor Irish who, to my own experience, had always been great fighters.

In the evening we left for Cork where the North Uist lad was to join his ship. Our money was getting low. Much of the time was spent sightseeing and walking, till at last the sailor thought he was sober enough to report to his ship. We said goodbye and good luck and I never saw him again. In the paper I bought at the station, to read on the train to Kinsale, there was reported much enemy action in the Irish Sea and Channel. Many ships were sunk and ports closed. I think that on account of this, and the two slips I had, was the reason I had no difficulties in explaining to the company commander how it was impossible for me to be back sooner. He looked at the map, and islands the boat was supposed to call at, and seemed satisfied.

5   More Horrors, Beers and Some Excitement

The draft I was going to France with was gone days before then. I was at once warned that my name was top of the list for the next draft, which was in a few days. We went the same way from Dublin to Holyhead and then overland to Southampton, landing there on Christmas Day. We did not get extra rations in spite of our requests. When we embarked at night, the troop ship was not so crowded as before. We landed at Calais with no alarms and stayed there for two days, when we were sent up the line again in cattle trucks to reinforce this time the 7th Argyll's, 51st Division with whom I stayed till the end of the war. They were out of the line after the Battle of Belleau Wood where they suffered heavy losses. The weather was very cold but dry, and apart from bombing raids, that section of the line for the time being was quiet. The trenches were made much wider at the top to prevent tanks from getting past. The ground was so churned up after the long Battle of the Somme that tanks could not operate, and when the rain and thaw came the area for miles was a quagmire. We used duckboards to walk on up to the trenches, that were, in many cases waterlogged.

I think the worst experience I had in that condition was when we were in that sector of the line for ten days and nights. The trenches were dry but frozen. We learned later that it was the same all over Europe. It was called the 'Big Freeze'. One morning when we were due to

First World War Trenches **(Pròisect Muinntir nan Eilean, An Cogadh Mòr: 1914 – 1918)**

return from our rest, it started to rain and with it came the thaw, which lasted all day. We were soaked many times over before we reached the communication trench at dusk. In places the water was more than a foot deep.

77

With the movement of wading through the water it was soon turned into thick slush, which was hard to drag the feet through. Sometime during that day a large number of hip high gum boots were sent for our use. How to wear them with the kilt was another problem. Even with trousers it would be impossible to wade through the mud in them. I tried on a pair over my boots and became stuck. I managed to draw my feet out and left them.

In the part of the trench where I was posted to, the water was above my knees. While standing, part of my kilt was in the water. There was no way of getting a hot meal. After the first night and day in that condition, the feet began to swell till wearing the boots became unbearable. Many became so weak, hardly able to stand and, fearing drowning, they were led out by the stronger ones. On the second day, when only another lad and myself were left in that part, an officer and a sergeant, carrying a large jar of whale oil, came round. You were ordered to lean against the wall of the trench, raise one foot out of the water, take off the sand bag, and hold both hands out to form a cup while the sergeant poured the oil in them. You rubbed the feet first, finishing off at the groin, replaced the wet sand bag and did the same with the other. No doubt it helped to keep the cold out.

The water in the trench I compared with the water when gutting and curing herring at a pier. The offal and guts were flung into the sea, which turned many colours. It brought a thought of nostalgia. When my partner gave up, the place was lonely, there was not a shot fired from either side. The rifles were choked full of mud and of no use. As it was flat ground with no way for the water to run out, the enemy must have been as badly off as us. With no rifle or shell firing, it seemed as if the war had ended. I kept moving to keep the circulation going.

I discovered a short trench, which led off the main. It had a small dugout with about six foot of earth on the top, but it was also full of water to the level of that in the trench. I came on two empty petrol tins and was to use one that was already cut open to bale out at least some of the water in the dugout. But at first a break wall of sand bags had to be made across the mouth. That stamped down, I started to bale, throwing the water over the top and as far away as I could, thinking it would turn that way. Instead, it flowed back. I then got a shovel, thinking if I dug a large hole and by filling the mud inside it, would make sure the dam was watertight. After a long time I got the water level down to where placing both two-gallon tins, one standing on the other flat across, I was able to sit with my bottom just out of the water. I had a lighter and was able to light my wet pipe.

I was enjoying that wet smoke and hoping that I would be relieved soon, when I heard moans and a cry for help. I went outside and heard the cry again. Going along the trench I made out that it was coming from the top. There was no danger from rifle or machine gun fire, there was none. I tried to climb out but on account of the height and the deep soft mud, I was not able to. I got some discarded rifles and anything solid to put under my feet. With that aid, I made it to the young soldier now stuck fast in the mud up to his hips. I tried to pull him out, but the more I pulled, the deeper I sank myself and, fearing for both, I took his equipment and jammed it under my feet. With that I was able to drag him clear and into the trench where I scraped the mud off us both. As he was very weak, I took him down the line and left him with others. I made my way back to the dugout and found that the water there had risen.

After a rest and some hard biscuits, I had another go at baling. This time I found it stayed out. I kept at it till I had it down to about six inches deep. I took a rest with my bottom well clear of the water. I got the pipe going again and was enjoying it. I happened to look at the back wall of the dugout and noticed there was a large bulge forming which was not there before. The bulge

78

was growing bigger and I knew what was behind it and wondered how long I could safely stay there. When I was considering leaving, there was only time to take a salmon leap over the dam with water cascading after me. I landed flat in water now nearly two feet deep and before I could get up, I got the full force of what was following me. It went over my head for a moment. I could not be wetter but thankfully I escaped drowning.

Occasionally the sergeant who was still able would come splashing along the trench to see if I was still there and on my feet. I could hear him long before he arrived. It had stopped raining but the level of the water remained the same. At last word was passed to me that the relief was on its way up. My feet were not greatly in pain, just numb. I tested the swelling and thought I could get the boots on without socks. I found the boots floating in a corner, one had no laces and the other was in bits, I think due to the swelling. After taking the bags off I got them on with much effort. I drew the discarded bags over them with an equipment belt to tie them on. Although very awkward, it had to do.

Those of us that were left were in that condition for three and a half days. I think it was in mild terms the most miserable time of my life. We had only one casualty through enemy action and that one was doubtful. And yet with all that wet and cold and lack of sleep, I came out of that lot without a slight cold, I think due to my hard rearing, when I would think nothing of going out swimming in the winter and pushing the ice in front of me. Before we came out of the trenches the engineers had pumped out some of the water and our way back was much easier. After a hot meal and a good wash, we were given new kit and some days rest. After that to a dry sector of the line where there was more action, none of it to anyone's liking.

It was an old part of the line, which for years was at a standstill. There were many deep dugouts and if you were lucky to be near one, life was much better. We were taking over that part of the line. I was the last to be allotted to the deep shelter, and when my turn came there was no room for me. There was an unused dark hole in the side of the trench, last used as a storage place for hand bombs and grenades. The officer said I was to go there. In order to get in I had to go on my knees on a bag at the entrance. I knew well what that bag contained. After crawling in I found there was not enough headroom to sit up straight. After I got a bit of candlelight and saw where I was, I felt a shudder pass through me. The stench was made worse because I had already touched the decaying body, which was partly uncovered with his face turned from me.

My first reaction was to clear out of this corruption, but where to, there was no other place I could lay down. I was very tired after the long march from our rest camp and why should I have any fear of him that was half buried beside me so long as I did not touch him again and raise more stench. I reasoned it was better for me to stay than to lie down in the wet and muddy trench. I had to stay. The floor was on a slope and where my stretched feet would be was wet and muddy. The higher end where the boxes of ammunition, old papers and rubbish were was dry. I got my waterproof sheet under me, took my water bottle out of the straps and laid it flat near my head. I stuck the inch of candle, all that I had, on the top.

For a long time, and especially in the trenches, I had a habit of reading at least a part of the Mass from my simple soldier's prayer book. This time to save the candle and lying on my back with the great coat over me, covering my nose and mouth to keep part of the stench out, my intentions were to read only a short part. Trying to keep my eyes open I fell asleep and in a clear dream I saw myself in an attack about to clash with the enemy and I was making for one that was very near me. It was then that I heard a voice behind me. I knew the voice so well; I ought to, although the owner was dead for years. The voice said, "Look out for the one on the right of you Donald." I did from the corner of my eye and I saw that he was much further away than the one

79

in front of me. I got very angry saying loudly, "You" and naming the person I was sure it was "must know that if I make for him the one in front will be on the top of me." At that moment I got a hard slap to the face that woke me. The place was full of smoke with the flame from the rubbish then licking the ammunition boxes. I used my overcoat to put it out and when doing that, I still felt the pain from the slap on my face and for a while rubbed it to take the sting out, which I knew was not caused by the fire or imagination, and had I not been wakened in time, it is easy to imagine what would have happened. The fumes from the rubbish and the stench from the dead made the place impossible to stay in. I spent the rest of that night walking up and down the short trench, taking in mouthfuls of fresh air. There were some casualties and the next day I got a place in the deep shelter.

There was another occasion, which showed I was not brave, although at times others would differ. On a very misty day when visibility was almost nil, another lad and myself were on sentry duty standing on the firing step, one at each end watching and listening. We could not see our own barbed wire a few yards away. Highly keyed up in that condition, after two hours we had nothing to report, all was quiet and we were relieved. Chetty, as we called him, was a very quiet lad, well liked; he came from Rosyth. He was ahead of me in the dugout. I lay down beside him at the foot of the steps. I was dozing off to sleep when we heard a commotion above. A moment later a hand bomb came hurtling down the stairway. It landed beside me. I got as far up in the sitting position, expecting every moment to be my last. I opened my mouth to let out a horrifying cry but no sound would come out. I was struck dumb, unable to move.

Chetty got up, picked up the bomb and ran up the stairs with it before the rest of us gathered our wits. Rushing up the stair we heard the explosion and when we saw the damage Chetty was standing there laughing and saying, "I got him, I got him." The two who had recently relieved us were lying slumped with their heads smashed. The raider, or parts of him, was hanging on our barbed wire. In the thick fog he had found a hole in the wire and surprised the not wide-awake sentries. With a club he put them out of action, and flung the bomb at us but, in his hurry to get away, he had forgotten to pull the pin. That is the reason I am here to tell this tale. He got it himself from brave Chetty. The sentries I think would survive, but double sentries were posted till the fog lifted.

No concrete reason has yet been put forward for these lucky escapes with which the majority of the fighting forces were familiar. Some would say if your number was on a certain shell, you were to get it or part of it. All that doesn't make any sense to me. Fate, if we know what it means, seems nearer yet lacking in explanation. I myself hold the belief that everything is ordained, even before you are conceived, and what is ordained for you, you cannot escape. To think you are master of your own destiny is only false and misleading. Without knowing why, you are following the dictation of that ordination. Perhaps that is the meaning of the word 'fate'. Many times I had indications of the truth of that thought.

On one occasion, in a quiet sector of the front line, a battery of heavy guns were at the back of us. There was a small canteen which sold beer and tasty biscuits, and at night when bringing up the rations, those who went to collect them and had money, always called. It was a real treat and everyone looked forward to his turn. When mine came, I was delighted. It was not long past my birthday when I had been flat broke with not even a smoke to celebrate. Now, with five francs in my pocket, I intended to do that. Three of us were to go. Shortly before we were due to leave, a friend of mine approached and asked as a favour if I would let him go in my place. I said no, definitely not. He begged me and said he would give me five francs and bring me up as much beer as he could get. Still I said no, "Why don't you try the other two?" He said he would. Soon after that he came and said, "None of them would let me go." He also said, "It's not for the beer I want to go down, I had a letter from home today telling me that my brother, who was out in Egypt, was now somewhere in France. I know that is the battery he is in. It is three years since I saw him last, that is why I am asking this favour of you." I thought deeply, putting myself in his place, how would I expect a friend worthy of the name to react? I said I would let him go, providing he would do the same for me when his turn came. He said he would, gladly. They were not long gone when some shells came over. We thought nothing of it, but after allowing for time at the canteen, there was no sign of them coming back. A search party went out. They searched down to where the rations were left, without finding them. They took the rations back and another party went out. They found them all three dead in a gun pit that we had dug the night before which, without a direct hit, was quite safe. I was at the time sorry for my friend who came from Dundee. I wondered then, had I not given him my place, would that be the end of me too. Somehow, no, because there was so many other things waiting that were destined for me to go through.

We stayed in that sector till March. One day after coming out of the line, the sergeant asked if I knew anything about horses and farming. I said I did, that I was a farmer's son. "Let me see your pay book." I did and there it was – Occupation, Farmer. "You are the very man I am looking for, report to the Army Service Corps" which I did, with three others, one from each regiment in the Brigade. The job, we were told, was to spread manure on a forty-acre field where they were going to plant forty tons of potatoes. We worked at that, there were no parades or rifle inspection, and the rations were good and plentiful. There were forty tons of potato seed in a hut waiting for the ground to be prepared.

We had started the ploughing and, as I had no knowledge of ploughing, I left that to the others who were well used to it. I kept on spreading the dung and that went on for over a week. Next morning, on the 21st March, we were to start planting. Instead, we were wakened before dawn by a terrific bombardment, which kept on all morning. We went to the field to work but the shelling was getting nearer, and before we had gone further the field was under very heavy shellfire. We saw the hut getting a direct hit with a shower of potatoes spreading in every direction. We made a hasty retreat, everything abandoned. The Germans had broken through on our left on a wide front throwing everything they had in their last attempt to capture the channel ports. As far as I can remember we retired fast for a day before we were ordered back to our regiment, which was then retiring and fighting a rear guard action, either that or be surrounded. In fact some of us were retiring among the Germans advancing, who thought of us as prisoners and did not greatly mind us, and when it became dark many would get through.

The shelling of the roads so that no reinforcements could get up was continuous, but wherever possible, ammunition was left for us to pick up, the same with rations. After days of that we finally held them. I think because of the wet ground being so churned up they found it impossible to move their artillery to follow us. We were relieved at last by the Australians who held them, and what was left of us moved back for rest and reinforcement. When we three were at the spring work they gave us trousers and we handed in our kilts. I was still wearing them and had to go through all the fighting until I joined up with the regiment. One day early in the morning they took us to a field outside a fair sized village. With others, I lay down beside a hedge. I had two francs on me. I thought I would sneak out to the village, which was about 300 yards away. Perhaps wearing trousers would make it easy. When I came to the sentry at the open gate, he only looked at me. Before I reached the Estaminet a Seaforth Highlander caught up with me. He asked, "Are you going for a beer?" "Yes, where are you going?" "The same, how much have you got?" "Two francs, we can't stay long they might be on the move again."

We went to the nearest Estaminet, and we were the only customers. Our money did not last long and we were on the point of leaving when an English Tommy came in carrying in his hand a large parcel wrapped in cloth. He went to the bar and ordered a bottle of the best, then looked at us and said, "What are you drinking boys?" We thanked him and said we were broke and were just leaving. Walking to our table with the bundle he said, "Forget about that" and laying the parcel on the table said, "Take a look at this." The parcel was crammed full of franc notes, some of high denomination. "Where did you steal this lot from?" we asked. "I did not steal any of it, I could have a lot more if there was time. We were passing a British Expeditionary Force canteen in full retreat, the Germans were close behind us, we were told we could take anything we wanted except drink, as the enemy would have it very soon."

After many drinks from him and no matter what notes were passed over to the barmaid he would not accept any change back. We were still the only customers and we wondered why. We left the Englishman behind with Madame, I imagine, thinking him a very profitable customer. Outside was quiet and peaceful, no signs of war. I was about 25 yards ahead, walking as steady as I could, wondering if the same sentry was on duty. Looking to my left I saw a stream of mounted horses galloping wildly, and then on the road in front of me and towards me, a crowd of men running in disorder. When we met them I tried to find out the meaning of it. By then I was sure it was not what I drank that was making me see things. They did not stop and I could not make out what they were talking about. I kept on till I met our chaplain who was walking fast. I asked him why they were all running. He said, "Don't you know, the Germans have broken through, armoured cars are on the roads, and their cavalry, the Ulans, are sweeping the countryside. We are nearly surrounded and we are ordered to retire with everyone for himself." He did not need to tell me twice.

When I looked back I saw and heard the Seaforth chap waving and shouting, "Come back you bloody fool." He waited for me and we made straight for the Estaminet that we had so recently left. There was no one there, all had fled including the Englishman and his bundle. We shouted but no answer came. My pal pulled out the till. It was full. We took out all the paper notes and left the heavy silver and crammed it in our overcoat pockets and left in a hurry, not touching the tempting bottles on the shelves. Outside was in disorder with everyone running one way.

While deciding which offered the best means of escape, the road or the countryside, we saw a light ambulance coming down fast. I tried to jump on it but the next thing I knew I was on my bottom on the sidewalk. How I missed going under the car I have no way of knowing. There was no damage, it only sobered me, and when we saw another one coming more slowly, I grabbed the tailgate, he grabbed my coat and the ambulance was nearly brought to a stop. The vehicle picked up a little speed and then stopped. The driver said, "The axle is broken, all out, we can't leave it to block the road, we will capsize it in the ditch." At that time the big trucks which had been behind us, began to move and we got in one which was crowded with getaways, one a piper with his pipes and when he spoke saying that the pipes was the last thing he would throw away, I knew then that he was a highlander. I asked where he came from. He said, "South Uist, a place called Howbeag." I said I knew it and that I came from Locheynort. He said, "You must be one of the new people there or I would know you." His name was Seonaidh Beag Bowie. I met him again long after the war, but we never had the chance to talk about this retreat.

The truck went about another mile when there was another hold up. This time my pal and I decided to get out and take to the country, thinking we would have a better chance to evade the enemy. After leaving the road and walking fast, as we had neither rifle nor equipment, only our gas mask and overcoat, walking was easy across the farmland until we got hungry and thirsty. We saw a house ahead and made for it. On knocking, a young girl came out. We asked for rum, she shook her head; the same for beer; for coffee she nodded. We could only talk a few words of polite French, however we got the coffee and two slices of white bread and fresh butter. We asked for more and got it. We gave her five francs each. She smiled but did not refuse it.

Outside was very peaceful. We saw in the distance some ploughing in the fields. We decided to make for a road which we could see in the distance. When we reached it, there was a light truck there with two Frenchmen loading it with scrap iron. We waited till they had her loaded and jumped in. One of them was trying to push me out. At once my pal picked up a bar of iron and held it over his head. The Frenchman at once let go and with the iron threatening him, he took his seat in front. My pal Jim still held the bar over them. They drove away and did not stop until we were on the outskirts of a large town. We got out and had they been nicer to us we would have given them the price of a drink.

We were desperate, and moving in the dark things about the town seemed to be normal with many soldiers about, but none that we could see of our kilted kind. We went to a cafe and had a good meal. Not having had a wash and shave for days we looked, and were, very dirty. The gas masks slung over the topcoats made us look more conspicuous. After the meal we went to a large Estaminet which was crowded, mostly with troops. Not joining anyone, we stood at the bar drinking and listening for any information that would tell us where our regiments were as by now we were beginning to doubt the wisdom of leaving the road. We did not want to get involved by asking questions. Beside us stood two Tommies who were feeling merry, and one of them passed a remark for us to hear, "Look at those two dirty Jocks." "Yes," said the other, "I don't think they have had a wash since the war started, keep away from them." They both laughed. Jim was older than I was, not tall but broad and no doubt strong. I said, "Don't start a fight, there are too many of them." Regardless, he said, "They are going to get it." And with that he hauled off at the nearest, who went down with Jim on the top of him. He was getting up when the other chap hit him. I thought it was time to step in. The fight was between the four of us and going well our way, even with our topcoats on, then they got help and we were then getting the worst of it. Then some took our side and the fight was spreading with everyone joining in, chairs and tables were smashed, lights went out. Whistles began to blast hard. Before the police came in, some got away. We did not and were arrested with the rest.

Two red caps took us away. One said, "We have been looking for you, let me see your pay books." We did. He said, "I am taking you in front of the Mayor." We thought a firing party for us, and we wondered why. They took us to a large building. There was no sentry at the gate. In the centre of the room they took us to a table on which they told us to empty our pockets. We did so but not our topcoats. A man in civilian clothes came in and began to question us, "Where did you leave your regiment and why. Where have you been since and who did you talk with and what did you tell them? We told him everything except our going to the Estaminet where we went first and the taking of the money. "Since you came to this town," he said, "did anyone ask you about anything?" We said no. "Why did you start fighting in the Estaminet?" We said it was not our fault, someone said the Jocks were a dirty lot and no good as fighters. We did not like being called that and a fight began. "Will you promise to stay in this room and not try to get out till tomorrow when an escort will take you back to your regiment." We said we would. "Alright, pick up your belongings, food and blankets will be sent to you in about an hour. Are you hungry?" We said no, and with that, the three of them left. We came out of the fight with only a few bruises.

We began to take stock of our situation and concluded that it did not look good. We would never be able to spend all the money we had, or any of it now. Looking for the toilet where they told us, we saw a window was partly open; it was on the ground floor. We looked at each other and listened for sound but there was none. It was very easy to get out and away. We put our topcoats on and slung our gas masks on under them and then looked much like the rest.

We went to a café that sold food and drink. We had a good feed and planned what we should do next and how to gather more information. I think we were there more than an hour when two red caps came in, the very pair who arrested us not so long ago. They both walked over. "So this is where you are, enjoying your drink. You're quite right, it will probably be your last. Where did you get the money? You did not have much when you turned your pockets out." We said a soldier that we did not know had left us this drink. "On your feet." I put my hand out to finish the rest of the good wine, but he grabbed my hand and spilt it, saying, "You are under arrest now." We said, "We got very hungry in the room waiting for the food we were promised and went out to get some. We were just leaving to return there when you came in. We have committed no crime and don't understand why we are arrested." "You will know that soon, in the meantime we are making sure this will be your last one."

They took us to an ordinary tent with a sentry with rifle and bayonet fixed standing in front. "In there you go" and turning to the sentry he said, "These two men are dangerous, keep a good eye on them, and if they try to escape, open fire on them, walk round the tent and see that your rifle is loaded." We had no way of knowing how much of this talk was for our benefit. The tent was bare of everything save a wooden floor, which was dry. We lay down using the gas masks as a pillow. The sentry started his endless walk around the tent. We talked in whispers, planning how we could get a drink in. Jim was silent for a while and then said, "I think I have a plan; how much do you think we should offer the sentry as a bribe?" I said, "Try him first with ten francs." This did the trick, and by Jim saying he needed to be escorted to the latrine, he managed to get two bottles, one of the best wines, the other cognac from the nearby Estaminet, which we opened. We invited the sentry in for a quick one and passed the bottle round, warning him to go easy. When his relief came, they brought us two blankets and when we asked for rations, they said our breakfast would be taken to us. The sentry left saying goodbye and good luck. We needed it. Jim got the blankets and spread one under us. We had another go at the bottles, lay down and I fell asleep.

In the morning we awoke to much slapping on the tent with cries of 'show a leg there' and at once it reminded me that I was still in the army. They brought us a bucket of water and soap but no towel. When we asked why, they said no one would lend theirs. We took our jackets and shirts off and tossed for who would get the bucket first. I lost, and like myself, Jim was very dirty. I managed to scoop off the thick scum and did my best to wash. We dried with our shirts. The breakfast was fairly good and we ate it all. After that we drank more, with no intention of leaving any. Soon our escort arrived, armed with rifles but no fixed bayonets. They took us to the building we had left. The Mayor was there to welcome us. He said, "You broke your promise, why?" We said, "We were very hungry and just went to get some food, intending to return as soon as we got it, but were arrested before we could do that." He said, "That's not a bad story, I am not going to put in a bad report against you." Beside him in the room was a chaplain "You will be in this officer's charge, he will take you back to your regiments." The chaplain didn't ask our names, just said, "Let's go boys."

We had walked for some time before he asked what regiment we belonged to. We told him and asked if we had far to walk. He said, "A good bit, I'll stop the first car for a lift and when we get there, I'll put in a good word for you." Little else was said before a truck came along and he stopped it. The truck was a water tank. There was no room in front for the three of us, so Jim and I climbed on the top. There was a place that we could hold on with care. The water kept splashing back and forward and making much noise as we went along. We thought we were on the same road as we were when in the French truck and when we came to the scrap iron dump we were sure of it. Also that it was not far to where we first began our retreat and coming to that village, the truck climbing a brae, was slowing down. Jim said, "Let's get off, they won't hear us in this sloshing. I think we will have a better chance reporting back on our own. Those we just passed were some of the artillery, our lot can't be far away." We crawled to the back and Jim slipped off with me following him. We went in the ditch and watched the truck going out of sight and then made for the nearest Estaminet.

A crowd of soldiers were there but none of our kilted kind. We did not ask any questions or pay any attention to them, but listened to every word they said. There was plenty of talk. One of them, laughing, said to a man standing beside us, "How far did you get?" To which the other replied, laughing "Must have been fifteen kilometres or more before we were turned back and told it was a false alarm. I never ran so fast in my life, and whoever started it, there would be a firing party for him." the other said "I heard that some of the jocks are not yet back, but of course they can run faster in the kilt." I saw Jim making a fist so I called him aside saying, "It's not wise to start a fight here, we will only make things worse for us." "Well, all the same, I would like to knock his teeth in." Quietly, I asked him what he thought of what we heard, "It's very strange we have not heard any gunfire since we left here. Everything indicates that what he was saying about it being a false alarm seems to be true. And if it is, then we have nothing to worry about, we were ordered to retire, we obeyed that order, perhaps we will know soon why, let's have another drink and get out of here. If we are caught, we are in more trouble."

We had the drink and I said I was leaving, he said he was not in any hurry. I replied, "It's best to leave while we are still sober." I bade him goodbye and good luck. I never saw him again. I passed the Estaminet where we met the English lad with the big bundle. I did not fancy going in to trade with Madam what was rightly hers. In a short while I met a kilted lad of my own regiment. I said, "Do you know where the Argylls are?" "Yes, in that field ahead of you on the left of the road, you can't miss it." I said, "Were you in that retreat?" "Sure, I only got back this morning, some are still out." "Did they put a crime against you?" "No, but I hear there's an investigation going on, it certainly was not our fault." "Where are you going now, is the village out of bounds?" "Yes, but I have a pass, I am an officer's batman." I gave him two francs to buy himself a drink. He thanked me and said he was broke. The sentry at the gate asked for my pass and I said I had none, "Then report to the N.C.O. in that tent." I did. They took my name and number and asked why I was wearing trousers and where was my kilt. I told them about the kit,

85

and about the order to retire and leave everything. "Well you go and look for your kit, it will probably be where you left it, and report yourself to your company sergeant."

I found my kit beside the hedge where I had left it, rifle and all, unharmed but wet. I shook them and put them on and went to find the sergeant, and when I did find him he said, "Ah, here comes the farmer, when do we dig the spuds?" I said, "The Germans have already dug them, they did not give them much time to grow. "Where is your kilt?" I told him that the Army Service Corps took them off us in exchange for trousers and we did not get them back. We were sent up to join the battalion, which I did, while they were retiring. "Yes" he said, "I saw you in that mad scramble, when did you eat last?" "Yesterday." "Go to the cooks for something. Tell them I sent you. Wash and report to me for guard duty, I am a man short." "Do I need a kilt?" "No, if you can't borrow one." I got a good feed and wash but did not borrow a kilt. I reported to the sergeant who sent me to the guard tent, where at once I was sent to relieve the sentry who had let me in so recently.

While I was on duty, more than twenty stragglers came in to report back. All, like myself, were expecting to be severely dealt with. I could only tell them to report in the tent to have their names taken. All this time I was trying to get information of how it first started. Not all had the same answer and most were reluctant to talk about it, feeling that it was a come-down for such as them, the famous division, the 51st Highland Division. Some may be sceptical of the truth of this event and not believe that it could happen. What I do know is that it did happen, and the reason that it did was the result of spies, dressed up in high-ranking staff uniform, spreading orders firstly at Brigade Headquarters and the battalions, who in turn spread them to us in the ranks. It was easy for the spies with their credentials to pass though the retreating troops on our left and make their way to where we were. It seemed that instant communication with those in front of us had broken down, so they were able for a short time to convince those in command that the order was genuine. When communication was established, they were soon caught to face the firing party. Some said there were three of them. I only saw one and not only did the Australians hold the line but they attacked and pushed the Germans back in that sector. The reason why Jim and I were kept prisoners in the tent, apart from the rest, was so that we could not spread talk of what we had known and seen.

I heard no more of our break away from the chaplain. I think all were back that evening, including our transport. They had gathered all the horses, and the camp was back to normal. We joked about it and called it the 'Retreat from Montenescourt', for that was the name of the village. Afterwards when we asked a newcomer "Were you at the 'Montenescourt?' he would say, "I never heard of it." For myself, I would rather have it that way.

In the evening I was relieved of guard duty and warned that we were leaving early in the morning, which we did, and marched the whole of that day. When night came we were taken into billets to rest. Long before that we could hear the roar of the big guns. We knew what lay ahead for us tomorrow, and when dusk came, we moved forward. The Germans had advanced before they were halted in their last bid for the Channel ports. There were no trenches on either side, so that when we took over our new sector in front of a deserted village, there was not much protection. Our task in the dark was watching and manning listening in posts in No-Man's-Land for the enemy attack, the rest at the back digging a trench as hard as they could. It was a low lying area and before it was dug to three feet, they came on water but kept on till near daybreak when those in listening posts were called into the new trench.

In the one I was in, there were nine of us. It was narrow and no room to walk. The morning was very misty, overhead a low ceiling but clear below. We saw a plane coming in low.

We thought it was ours till we saw the black cross then we fired with our rifles. He kept coming and raked us with machine gun fire and away. Not one of us was hit. If we hit him, it seemed we did no damage. He got our range and position, for soon our small area was strafed with whiz-bangs, many of which did not explode I think on account of the soft ground. We lay as flat as we could at the bottom of the trench. One actually hit a few feet in front of me, passed close over our back and entered the other side and never exploded. It was a close call and in spite of all the shelling, which lasted about a quarter of an hour, none of us were hit.

Next morning at dawn they attacked us in force but not on a wide front. We had been standing to and expecting them and when they advanced to the point where we could clearly see them we opened fire with Lewis guns and rifles. The slaughter was terrible and yet they came over the wounded and dead bodies of their comrades. We did not leave the trench for a bayonet charge and none got nearer than 30 yards from us, then they broke off the attack. There must have been very few who got back according to what we could see in front of us. Their losses must have been great. No one who saw them in action can in truth say that the Germans are not good fighters.

Next day we were running short of small arms ammunition. Another lad and I were picked out to get it from about a mile back. We had to go through the deserted village, which was being shelled, but not too heavily. On the outskirts we had to cross a bridge that the Germans were interested in. When we came to it, there was a lull in the shelling. We crossed it running. When we came to our destination at our transport dump, two saddled up packhorses with two boxes of small arms ammunition hung on them waited. We asked the cooks for something to eat and got some soup and hard biscuits. We started back leading the beasts. They appeared well used to pack saddles and were easily led. Before we came to the bridge, the shelling began and we were held up for a time. The firing was not accurate, and when we came to the bridge it was still there.

A lull came. It was time for us to move and fast. The other lad leading, we trotted the horses across. They seemed to know what was expected of them. There was a lot of telephone wire lying on the road. My horse got his two hind hoofs caught in it. I tried to free him, but with his restlessness he was getting more tangled and when the shelling was coming near, I had to leave him. I felt sorry leaving him tied up. I ran for shelter and when the shelling eased, I went to him, expecting to find him dead or wounded. He was neither. He had the shoe of one hoof off. The other was hanging on by two nails with the wire twisted round it. I got my jack knife and managed to cut and break the nails, and he was free, and except for the loss of two shoes, unharmed. I did not go far when the heavy shelling began in the direction I was going. When I saw a large haystack just off the road, I took the horse for shelter close behind it. I thought he would like the hay. He tasted it, no good, and began cropping on the young grass as far as the reins I was holding would allow him, and when he had that space eaten, I took about 12 feet of rope off the hay stacks and tied it on to the reins. He had that stretched out and was eating, standing broadside to me, when I heard the roar of this shell. In a split second I knew that it would hit the haystack, or very near it. It landed between me and the horse, ploughed under his belly, went at least four yards past, entered the ground deep and did not explode. I am sure the horse did not move because his hind legs were on one side of the furrow while his front legs were on the other, still eating as if nothing had happened. It was an amazing sight and a lucky escape for both of us.

Unfortunately he was not to keep that luck for long. We left when the Germans stopped strafing the village. Perhaps it was their way of getting their own back after the rough handling we gave them the day before. I found where I was to deliver the ammunition and they unloaded the horse. I went to draw my rations. Shelling began and one landed near the horse and exploded. The poor horse got most of it and had to be shot. I was ordered back to where I came from in that short trench now a little beyond. The house about 50 yards at our back was still standing and intact, so two of us crawled over and found that it had a well stocked cellar. We did not have an officer with us so discipline was easy with only a lance corporal. Bottles were brought back, everyone taking care not to get too merry. One overdid it. After tanking up in the cellar, he went upstairs to sleep it off and refused to leave. When the shelling was resumed, the house had a direct hit and it caved in. When the shelling ended, the lance corporal sent two men over to get his identification disc and bury him. They found the bed upside down among the rubble on the ground floor and him under, still drunk and not a scratch on him. Things like that don't happen often.

After many other near misses, one would be inclined to think that there was no more fear in you, that the more action you took part in, the more fearless you became. In reality, it is the very opposite and I think that was true of everyone there. Like everything, the nerve wears out and only peace and quietness will restore it. When a shell fell near or you came under fire of any kind, your first instinct always, no matter where you were, was to throw yourself down flat. We had a sergeant with much service who was at first considered brave. One day in a trench on sentry duty with a witty Irish man, an officer came up and asked did we see Sergeant Brown? We said "No, Sir." "Has he been round here lately?" The Irishman bent down and looked closely at the bottom of the trench and said, "No Sir, there is no button marks in the mud there." The officer just laughed. A shell had landed close not long before then. We went from there after some fighting, mostly raids to the Arras area where there were better trenches, old but full of rats, very tame, sometimes you had to kick them away from you. In the front line we used to gather any scraps of food and scatter it in front of a Lewis gun already in place, wait till a large crowd would gather and press the trigger, the squealing was a good laugh and many would get away.

In our platoon we had a chap, his name was MacDonald, and never in my life did I hear a man snore like him. All avoided lying beside him and many a cursing and slap he got. He would often come to my side for protection, which sometimes he got. He was not a highlander. One night, after digging a jumping-out trench that we were to occupy before dawn for a raid, we crawled back to a deep dug-out for a few hours sleep and though it was dark inside, I felt sure that MacDonald was not beside me. We were all very tired and looking forward to those very few hours of sleep. For many it was going to be their last. I was half wakened by crying which I took to be snoring. I thought it was MacDonald. I got very angry and in complete darkness I hauled off and connected. I then came to my senses to discover that I had hit my pal. I said "What's wrong with you?" He said, "I have been hit on the head." I said, "Will someone light a candle." They did. It showed blood streaming down his face and a large round patch with no hair on and a flap of skin with long hair attached hanging from it. We put it back in place but some was missing. We bandaged him then he went to the First Aid. We looked where he lay down beside me to find his head had been blocking a rat hole. I was very sorry for what I had done to him and wished that MacDonald would start snoring.

6   Trench Warfare and Some Horsy Business

Shortly after that I was posted to our trench mortar battery. There were six of us, three men on the gun when in action. It was a strange gun called Stokes. A muzzle loader and very fast depending on the loaders. The shell was 3 inches in diameter and about 18 inches long. With a fast crew it was possible to have thirteen shells in the air before the first one hit the ground. They travelled slowly, you could plainly see them in the sky and their longest range was 400 yards. They were very destructive, much more than ordinary shells. We in the front line hated to have one of them near us as the enemy guns were always searching for them. While on this gun I was wounded for the third time. I am not going to say unfortunately or unluckily, anything to be out of that hell. I got it in the back and it just missed the spine and vital internal organs. It was not bad and when the piece of shrapnel, the size of my fingertip, was extracted, it only required eight stitches. I got down as far as a hospital on the coast.

Stokes Gun

On the second day waiting my turn for the operation, we talked in the ward about operations. One chap said that the way to take in chloroform was to inhale it through your nose only. They will tell you to breathe in through your mouth and nose, don't do it because you will be very sick when you come out. But it will take longer for you to go off. I had experienced this sickness already and decided to take his advice. When my turn came on the table with the usual mask clamped on my face, a nurse with a long row of war ribbons on her breast said, "Breathe in through your mouth and nose." I used the nose only. They had a large rubber sheet, which seemed to be moving out of place. They evidently thought I had gone off, for they took the mask off and stuck a large safety pin through the rubber and through my shoulder. I got up with a cry of "What the hell do you think you're doing?" Two of them grabbed me and stretched me down clamping the mask on again, giving me a ticking off for not breathing in through my mouth.

I don't know which caused it, the telling off, the pin or the double intake that made me angry but I began to dream, seeing myself on board a ship and looking down the fo'c'sle I could see the nurse with the many ribbons. The dream faded and after I came to in the ward, an orderly, the only one for many wards, came over to my bed and said, "Are you a sailor?" "No" I said, "I am a soldier, why?" "Well I never heard such bad language in my life, what you gave Lady Dudley while she was operating on you, it would make a tart blush, you called her everything bad." I said, "I don't believe you, I don't remember anything." He said, "It's true but forget it." I felt very much ashamed and could not forget about it for a while. The next day I saw her coming up the ward, and I expected at least a telling off, but no, she just smiled without stopping.

The hospital was built of corrugated iron elephant huts laid out end to end with a short closed-in passage between each, made into a ward. Sister Baird had three of them to look after, alone. She was nearly run off her feet. After I had been an 'up' patient for a day, she came to me and said, "MacDonald, I have a very bad case in the next ward. I was wondering if you could give me a hand with the dressings. All I want is someone to hand me the bandages, do you think you could do it? He is one of the worst cases I have had to handle." I said, "Yes Sister, I am sure he can't be worse than what I have seen many times." I followed her to the ward. There I saw a young boy stretched on a bed, stretched because his feet had weights on, his right arm stretched along the side of the hut, only his eyes, nose and mouth were showing, the rest of him in bandages. She started on his chest. Firstly the stench of the burnt flesh was awful; it was not long before I began to feel dizzy and sick. It was well that the Sister was keeping an eye on me and thankfully she caught me before I fainted on top of him. I woke up in bed and did not feel so brave. The Sister told me afterwards he was a lad aged eighteen and while going up the line with a load of shells in a wagon drawn by two horses with him on the top, a shell landed under it and exploded and he was found a distance from the road burned to that state. Of the driver, horses and wagon, there were only bits. Not only did he have to suffer all that but again he was wounded in the stretched arm by a piece of a bomb that came through the hut when we had an air raid in which nurses were killed and wounded.

In that ward I made two friends, both from London, one whose name was Smyth, just a common ordinary lad like myself but a little older. Trevelen was different. He claimed that his way of life was stealing, especially from the aristocrats. When I asked why them, he said that he was a bastard son of an aristocratic father who had denounced his mother, and when he grew old enough to understand, he began his revenge on that class of society. "If you don't believe me, here is the proof." He took out a wallet and from it he took a newspaper cutting with his photo. Under it was a long list of crimes he was wanted for and believed to be in the Navy. When I said, "Why the navy?" he said, "I got a friend to arrange it and to keep one jump ahead of them, I joined the army. I robbed the officer's mess and was caught. I was doing time in the glasshouse, where I volunteered for France. After three weeks in the trenches I was wounded and got as far as this. I don't ever want to go there again. To bluff the doctor, I developed a heart condition myself. Every morning as soon as he begins his visiting round, I swallow a piece of soap, it makes your heart beat fast and by the time he examines me, my heart is racing like an engine. When he leaves, I make for the toilet to vomit it up and the clock slows down. For a while there is a bad taste and bubbles come up!"

I was to see more of his tricks in the convalescence camp when we went there together. Three days after my stitches had been taken out, I was feeling much stronger than on the day of the dressing failure. Smyth and I went to the cliff top at the back of the hospital, watching the high waves splashing up on the sand. There had been an onshore gale the night before. All the red flag danger signals were up which meant no bathing as long as they were there. After watching and seeing the cliffs of Dover on the other side, and fondly wishing to be there, Smyth said, "Can you swim Donald?" I said, "Yes, but not that far." He said, "It would have to be a good swimmer that would go out here." "I don't know, it doesn't look that bad to me." "I'll bet you couldn't do it." "How much?" I asked. "Five francs." "If I had that, I would take you on." "Alright, it's worth that to see you try, you'll never get off the beach." We descended the cliff and I saw the height of the waves and regretted my harsh bet. However, I would try and off came the hospital clothes. There was a man about 100 yards away trying without success to swim out. I waded out to meet the first wave. It carried me back to the beach like a cork and left me there with Smyth laughing his head off and shouting, "Come in and get your clothes on, I'll give you the five francs. I don't want to see you drown." I said, "I would earn them first" and went for another try.

This time I waded out and when I met the oncoming wave, I dived under it. Emerging, I was in shallow water and able to wade further out to face the next. Under I went. When I came up I was past my depth and kept on swimming and going under as they came till I turned for the shore and only making slow progress, I began to see the folly of my dare, but did not panic. Struggling as hard as I could, I tried if I could to touch the bottom. I did and it gave me extra courage. I filled my lungs and dived to meet the cascading wall of the merciless sea and when I saw daylight at its back, there was only about two feet of water. I put on all the strength I had and on my hands and knees, I managed to hold on till Smyth grabbed me.

I dried myself and began putting my clothes on. As I was doing so, I saw the other would-be swimmer coming towards us. He stopped and we saw that he was an officer, a doctor with a scowl on his face. I knew that it was not to congratulate me that he came over. Seeing my hair wet, he said, "What's your name?" "George MacKay, Sir." "Which hospital are you in?" "No. 54". "What is wrong with you?" "I was wounded." "Where?" "At Arras." "I don't mean that, what part of your body?" "In the back, Sir." "Take off your jacket and shirt." I did. "When were these stitches taken out?" "Three days ago." He wrote in his notebook everything I said and closed it saying, "If you are fit enough to go swimming in that sea, hospital is not the place you should be in. If not, you are retarding your treatment. You will soon hear about this, put on your clothes." "The jealous bastard" said Smyth "just because he failed to swim out." I said that he was stupid enough not to ask for my rank and regiment and if by chance there is a George MacKay in that hospital, he will have a lot of explaining to do. In the end I think the not so nice officer will be made to look foolish. "I think I'd better go back to the ward and tell Sister Baird I am not feeling well. She will order me to bed and you keep your eyes and ears open for any sign of an identification parade in the other hospital ground."

The Sister ordered me to bed and said she would take my temperature after she attended an urgent case, and after a long while, she took it and said it was normal. She also said there was a lot of searching going on across the road. I asked why. "They're looking for a patient who went swimming." "Was he drowned? Why look for him there?" "I don't know, an orderly asked me if I had a patient by the name of George MacKay in my wards, which I have not. How do you feel now?" I said, "Much better Sister." The search was fruitless. I head no more about it.

On the staff of that hospital there were nuns, but I didn't know which order they belonged to. They sometimes helped Sister Baird with the dressings, and during air raids, they carried the

91

bad cases on their backs down the cliff for protection. One of them came to my bed with a small cross in her hand. She said, "Would you like to have this little cross?" I said that I would. Looking on it, it did not have the figure of Christ on the cross, only an inscription in Latin on the back. She asked if I knew what it meant. I did not. She said it was 'In this sign, thou shall conquer'. I asked, "Is there any special prayer to be said?" "None at all. Keep it around your neck." I grew very attached to it but lost it in the trenches many times through the breaking of the tape that was rotten by much sweat and dirt. Someone would find it; they all knew who it belonged to, and many a time I was asked for it, especially when going into action. I would never part with it, and finally when the war ended, the next day at a small stream running with a trickle of water, I took towel and soap for a good wash. There was a small pool less than a foot across, about eight inches deep. I took off my jacket and shirt. With the towel I laid them on one side of the pool I was standing over. I placed the cross on the other side of the frozen ground where I could reach it on bending down. After I had dried myself I reached for the cross but it was not there. How could it leave that spot? I wondered if it was possible that somehow it slipped into the pool. With that thought I dammed the stream. When the pool was dry, there was no cross there. I had to give the search up, but I returned to it many times. I never saw it again. I was perfectly sure that I had put it in that spot and that no man or beast was near. I missed it, and often wondered why it had vanished; perhaps its work was done. Many of the boys carried religious articles and charms about them for their protection.

When in that hospital it was the time the Asian 'flu was raging in France and taking its toll there. Perhaps that was why the Doctor on the beach was so keen on getting those mended back up the line again. I did not take this 'flu but I did get German Measles while in a trench not more than 200 yards away from the Germans. After doing sixteen days in the line, we were due for rest that night. In the early morning with three others in the dugout after we had some breakfast, I began to feel ill with cold sweat. After a while I felt better and when the Sergeant came round to see if any of us wanted to report sick, no one did. Shortly afterwards I began to get worse and regretted I did not report sick.

It was not long before the Sergeant came round to turn us out for work. I said I wanted to report sick. He said there was nothing wrong with me 10 minutes ago and what was wrong with me now? I replied, "I don't know Sergeant." He replied "I know you are trying to get out of this working party, there is nothing wrong with you." "I want to see the doctor, Sergeant."

"Alright, we'll take you to him and if he gives you medicine and duty, we will put a crime against you for malingering." The first aid post was only 50 yards away. The doctor was not there, the sick parade was over. When the doctor came he asked what was wrong with that man? The Sergeant said "Nothing, Sir, he is just swinging the lead. I am putting a crime against him." The doctor took a few steps towards me, then turned to the Sergeant and said, "What dug-out is this man in? Have it isolated at once, this man has got measles." The Sergeant ran, a stretcher was found, my temperature taken, I was past the danger point. I woke up in Isolation in hospital, where I was kept for eight days. I was broke, as usual. Patients there often gave me tobacco and an occasional bottle of beer.

The Regiment, after their eight days rest, had gone back to the trenches, my company to the front line. I had to walk there although still very weak and felt that I owed the measles nothing. This event happened some time before I was admitted to the hospital where I was helping Sister Beatrice with the dressing, a chore she asked me to do. "It might keep you from the eye of the doctor who most likely is under pressure himself to empty his wards as quickly as possible. Keep at the back of me with the bucket of swabs." Although I did not like the idea of hiding behind a woman's skirt, still if it gained me time there, I was all for it. I was only a few days doing it when, at the end of the rounds, the doctor looked at me, and turned to the Sister and said, "What about him? I think he is fit enough for convalescence." The Sister said "He is very useful here, but just as you say Doctor." I was marked out the next day along with Smyth and Trevelen. The convalescent camp was some two miles away and we walked to it. It was in a hollow on the outskirts of the village in tents. We reported and were shown to our tents, Smyth and I in one and Trevelen to another. It was a near starvation camp with the patients queuing up for food long before it was mealtime.

It was a fairly large camp with enough nationalities fighting on our side including Americans. We were only a few hungry days there before Trevelen got himself a job in the dining hall where his stealing habit came in very useful. He would steal from the cooks and bring the best food to our tent. We in that tent were well fed and besides that, at night with one of us on watch, he would take the best articles left drying on a clothes line to the dining hall and press and iron them. Usually the Americans bought them. Stuff easily hidden on us, we sold in the village. It kept us in wine and beer. It was a mean thing to do but then almost everything is mean and rotten in war but those responsible in the first place should bear the blame.

Sentries were always parading round the camp and no one was allowed out without a pass. With Trevelen's skill the date was changed until it was worn out. From the sale of stolen articles we had a little money but were unable to spend it and no sentry would allow us out. Trevelen said "Let's try the sentry at the far end", which we did. He was a young soldier, not fit for the trenches. When he asked if we had a pass we said we were not going out, just having a stroll round. We began talking to him, after a while Trevelen said, "That's not the kind of rifle we use at the front, is it loaded?" "Yes, I have orders to fire on anyone who refuses to halt when challenged." "Is it heavy? Let's see." The young sentry handed the rifle over to Trevelen who put it to his shoulder and said, "It's much lighter than ours. How does the bolt work?" and began ejecting the shells onto the ground. "Pick them up Donald." I was thinking he was going to put them in the gun again. I handed him the five shells. He laid the rifle down and flung the shells as far as he could among the sand and tall grass. Turning to the sentry he said, "Never part with your rifle on duty and don't say anything about this or you will be in bad trouble. Come on Donald, before he finds any of these bullets we will be out of range." We spent our time and money in the small town and no one asked for our pass on coming back. We explained to another sentry how we had lost it. We only tried that trick once.

After we had been in that camp nearly two weeks those in charge and the staff got up a boxing tournament, I think more for their own entertainment than ours. The conditions were anyone taking part would be allowed to stay in the camp for three weeks extra, two weeks for training, one week to cover the contest. Not all were accepted. I put in my name, was examined and accepted but although I had been in many fights, I had never been in the ring and it was not for any reward that I put my name down. It was because of the three weeks stay there instead of them being in the trenches, and if by chance I did get killed I would at least be afforded a decent burial and my people would be officially notified that I was killed in action. The training started off easy with short runs and lectures, which gradually increased to sparring. We had the then famous Bryan Carpenter, at one time world holder of the title. He used to come round fairly often to give hints to our instructors. He never talked to us. The training grew tougher every day, many were dropping out and they were marked out to join their regiments.

I managed to hold on although at times, after a long spell punching the bag, with my arms ready to drop off, I doubted the wisdom of my decision. Never was a Sergeant Major as hard as that instructor. The day for the first contest came. There was a large audience in the open air. It was a warm sunny evening. I was matched with a chap about the same height and weight. It was to be a three round of three minutes contest. We were the second to go into the ring and when called, we dashed to the centre and after a few words of introduction from the referee, we started boxing, or rather slogging with no thought of what the instructor taught us. Standing toe to toe the first round was bloody, to the delight of the spectators. When the bell rang, I think we were even.

After sponging the blood off our faces the bell rang. I thought it was less than a minute since the last one. We got up and this time did a little sparring, and within seconds I ran into a haymaker. I got it on the nose and the blood ran like a river filling my mouth. I spat it into his face, which was then decorated. The referee checked me, but said box on. I did not do it for spite only to get rid of it and his face was the most direct target. I think that the onlookers would say that we were slowing down, although still toe-to-toe, and were thus slapping each other when the bell rang and the referee had to pull us apart. I felt rightly or wrongly I had the edge on him. Round 3 was the hardest, not from the fighting but by the efforts to keep standing. We could not be bloodier and I think the spectators got their money's worth, if not for boxing at least for blood shed. I was declared winner on points. That night I was a sore man and did not know where the hurt started or ended, it was spread all over. I was then in the finals. Win or lose I would get a medal.

The next fight was to be in two days time but that night the doctor had to be called to me. He ordered me to a hospital with a strained heart where I stayed on my back for three days and missed the next contest. I would have nothing to show for the battering I got. I heard that my final contest was to be against Smyth. I knew he would give me a hammering, as it was known he had a good knowledge of boxing. At least I escaped that.

Trevelen had stolen a new overcoat off the Americans, which we sold to a Frenchman. We three had a good spree on that. Besides his many other gifts, good and bad, Trevelen had the gift of the gab, and with it he made himself indispensable to the Officers in charge of that camp and when his time for leaving came, he was kept on the staff. He said he was giving up soap swallowing and also that we were mugs fighting for nothing. A few days after the tournament, Smyth and I were marked out. We said goodbye to Trevelen and thanked him for the many thick pieces of tasty roast, etc. he snatched for us. We made our way in the small cattle truck towards the front, each to a different section. We parted and I have never seen or heard of them again. When I joined with the battalion they were out of the trenches after a hard battle in which they had lost many and were now being re-enforced.

The next day we marched to what was supposed to be a rest at the back of a Portuguese regiment then holding the front line. It was a quiet sector with a canal at the back between us. I was on guard and just before dawn the S.O.S. signal flares went up in a long stretch of the front line. I reported that and the camp was turned out for action and forced march towards the line. The Germans had attacked. The Portuguese could not hold them. Instead they retreated in disorder and by the time we met them, most had disposed of their gear. Their uniforms were almost the same colour as the Germans, dark blue. The only way, if you had time to tell friend from foe, was that the enemy always had their rifles, but not so with the others who passed through us as we attacked the Germans, stopped them and pushed them back to their original position with heavy losses on both sides. We were relieved that night by more reinforcements.

The next day I read the headlines in the *'Daily Record'*, which was then printed in France. It said that the 51st Division again covered itself with glory. I don't know what the Portuguese thought of it, because when, on entering an Estaminet, I saw them walking out, I don't know if it was fear or disgust. In our platoon we had a butcher to trade. He said if you catch me a pig, he'd slaughter it. There were many of them about. We dare not shoot or it would be heard. Our chap in his kilt got hold of a loose horse left by the Portuguese; with his rifle with fixed bayonet he began chasing a pig. After much laughter he speared it through and then fell off the horse frightened by the squealing of the pig.

We were then in the flying column. Anywhere trouble broke out we would be sent there. Our transport had suffered some losses. Another lad and myself were sent as replacements. I felt I was again lucky and hoped that although I did not know much about horses I would bluff my way through. I was given the task of looking after a bay mare. She was the Colonel's ride and was wounded in the flank where a large scar was not yet completely healed. I had to groom her twice a day. She was a quiet beast and when we moved to another part of the line, I was put on the mess cart in place of its driver who was going on leave. In a way it was considered to be the best job on the transport, because every day when drawing the Officers' rations and drinks from the expeditionary force canteen, the corporal along with you always drew an extra bottle of whisky, which he shared with the driver. You were expected to take them to the Battalion's headquarters, if they were in the line, and you went through heavy shellfire on most of those trips.

On this occasion the headquarters were in a sunken road. It was very narrow, no room for two wagons to pass. We started off ahead of our transport, which was bringing up the supplies for our men in the trenches and before we were half way the shelling began. It was accurate, not surprising as they themselves had held that area a month before. The corporal asked if I wanted to turn back. I said "No, the next one might not land so near." "Well" he said, "we'd better have another drink." We carried on. The horse was willing and when the next one came, it was not so near, but the one after was. We nearly got hit ourselves and I think being so close to it was what saved us. The fragments went over our heads and when the mud came down, we and the horse were covered with it. When we checked on the horse there was no sign of her being hit. We needed another drink and regretted we had nothing to give to the brave horse that did not bolt. The near shelling ended and when we reached our destination they were not expecting us. After the stuff was unloaded in the dark, an officer asked me if I had my rum issue. I said, "No, Sir." He went into the dugout and came out with a mug half-full of rum. I managed to climb into the cart before it took effect. The corporal climbed somewhat more steadily than me. We let the horse make her own way.

When we came to a shell hole in the road the horse would stop and smell it. If it was safe on either side, she would carry on. If not, she would stand still. We would get out and with the shovel we always carried, we would fill the hole enough to get through. I liked that horse and whenever I had the opportunity I stole something for her. On the way back I asked Corporal Mitchell if the officers would ever know about his fiddling with their whisky. "No" he said, "I know the orderly, he can always water the other bottles down." I said, "The other driver will soon be back from leave. He will most likely be taking this job again." "He may, but not after tonight's work, if I can help it. I know he would not risk going out through the road tonight." When the other driver did return in a few days, he was given his old job back, which I thought was fair enough. I still had the rider to look after and any other chores the sergeant could find for me.

The other chap, Joe Laverty from Edinburgh, who came with me was also just holding on. The transport was in tents on the outskirts of a small village. During the day and at night when they were not needed, the horses were tied, head to head on each side of a rope that stretched between two poles. Watch was being kept on them, especially at night. It was Laverty's and my turn for picket lines. We took over at 8.00 pm till midnight, when we were to be relieved. There was an old haystack where the horses were tied. We dug into it for shelter and gave the horses the best of it. For some reason they did not like it much but they were quiet.

The night was quiet with very little shelling between us and the front going on, and although the village was put out of bounds to us, we thought there was little risk of being caught in the dark. We counted the money we had between us. It was enough for a few drinks and to be back at our post before the next watch came on. It was not more than 400 yards to the house we took to be a café. We thought Madam was closing early and when we knocked she was not keen to let us in. Laverty, who could talk a little French, said we won't stay long and so she let us in. There were no other customers and only a small bar with Madam and a young girl in attendance. We were on our third drink and counting our pennies when the door was knocked. Madam grew agitated and came over to our table and said, "Drink, drink, police." We drank. She took us to another room and closed the door. By that time there was loud banging on the door. Madam went to argue with them, about what, we could not understand. Just at that time, two long-range shells landed and exploded with a heavy crunch on the outside of the village. The police, fearing the village was in for a bombardment, left the shelter. We wanted to leave because we thought the shells had landed not far from the horses and anyway, our money was finished.

I said to Laverty, "What do we do now?" We stayed for a while in case the police came back and then said goodbye and vanished in the darkness to find our way to where we left the horses. We found the haystack first and then the two poles with one horse standing and tied to the rope. All the rest were gone and no one was on guard. We were sunk. It was Laverty's turn to say, "What will we do now?" I said, "First I want to know if it's the Colonel's horse that's left and if where they were tied it is much churned and then we will look for a new shell hole within a radius of say 100 yards before we go searching for them. Our story must be that we went after them but lost sight of them in the darkness. Now we better start looking for hoof marks to find out which direction they went." In the declining moon our search began and it was not long before we found their tracks. They were not hard to follow and so we walked faster and soon heard the clatter of trotting. We waited to let the horses pass but saw that four men were driving them. We asked, "Where did you find them? We have been looking for them since they bolted." A voice I recognised as the Sergeant's said, "Was it you that was on watch?" We said, "Yes." "Why did you not raise the alarm when they broke loose?" "We thought we could catch them without any help. We caught one but he had no halter on and got away again." "Is that you Macdonald?" "Yes, Sergeant. Did you get all the horses?" "No, there are two missing. The Colonel's ride and another and you better get them. We last saw them about two kilometres back on the right of the road, in a field just past the first house you come to on the right. Report to me when you come back."

As expected he did not sound too happy. We kept on, and past the house by some 300 yards, in the dim light we made out a bunch of horses tied the same way as ours. We began to inspect them knowing it was easy to tell the horse by the scar, the others not so easy, and when we caught a loose one, regardless of the identity, we held on to him. Of the Colonel's horse there was no trace. Daylight was coming fast and we had to get away. There was one light horse tied on the rope. It resembled that horse to us but we could not be sure in the dark of the exact colour. I untied him and he seemed to be quite happy to be led away.

In daylight we reached our camp leading the horses thinking that no one except the guard would be out of bed. We had just passed the Sergeant's tent when we heard a shout behind us. "Where the hell did you get these animals? They are not ours." We said "In a field after we had left you, they were together and looked the same as ours in the darkness." "Do you still say they are ours?" "Yes, they are very like them." "Rubbish, tie them and report at the Officer's tent at 10.00 am."

We got them tied. The two on watch began to laugh saying, "They're not our horses, you're in for it, the Sergeant is very angry." "Why?" "Because you did not report it when they broke loose." We felt sure nobody knew we had left our post for if they had, their talk would have been different. We washed, had something to eat and at 10.00 am reported to the Officer's tent to find the Sergeant was there before us. We did not have an escort and the Officer was sitting at a table inside the tent. We two were outside with the Sergeant who ordered us to attention. The Officer asked, "What is the charge, Sergeant?" "The charge, Sir, is neglect of duty. These two men were on duty guarding the horses when two long-range shells landed near them. The frightened animals broke their halters and ran. These two men went after them. They neglected to report this matter first to raise the warning. I visited the post shortly after the shelling and all but one horse was gone. I had the camp alerted and a search party was sent out. We found them all but two, the Colonel's horse and another. We also found the two accused on a road about two kilometres from where we found the horses. I ordered them to search for them. They came back leading two horses which are not ours."

The Officer addressed himself to me seeing that I was the oldest soldier with a red and three blue chevrons on my sleeve. He said, "What have you to say for yourself?" I told him our story. "Sergeant" said the Officer "I have never had a case like this before me, are they good men?" "No sir, they are both absolutely useless." "What punishment can we give them, can we make them pay for the lost horses?" The Sergeant said, "I hope to God the war will not last till they are paid for." "Do you know what they are like in the line?" "The reports are that they are good and reliable." "Send them back to the Battalion with no charge against them."

We were free and, although we lost a fairly safe job, we considered ourselves lucky that deserting our post on active service was not found out. The Sergeant said, "Be ready with your kit to leave here after dinner." When we joined the transport they gave us trousers, which we wore, and packed our kilts, as they did not take them from us. Then we got more rations from the cook.

We were on our way, walking towards the Battalion and as it was very warm, we rested in front of an Estaminet with nothing in our pockets. "I wish," said Laverty "That we had something to sell." "How about our kilts, we are not wearing them? We might be able to sell them, one at a time." "Alright" I said, "Let's toss to see which one first." We did with a button and I lost. "How much will we ask?" "Fifteen francs at least." We went in and took our packs off, sat at a corner table and took the kilt out. It was a good kilt, fairly new and clean, worth much more than we intended to ask. A young girl was hovering about and came over. I showed the kilt and said "Twenty francs." She took it and held it against her, smiled and said "Bon, bon." I again said "Twenty francs." She shook her head. I said "Fifteen." She hesitated, looked at it and went over to the till. We ordered Vin Rouge and a meal and talked over our escape. We were lucky to be here instead of being tied to the wheels of a gun carriage doing our punishment, which was common and worse for crimes like that.

I and many others have seen prisoners tied to the wheel while the gun was in action. That had been changed and none were allowed to be tied when in action. Also changed was the rule that a soldier could be shot without trial. My only experience of such a case was when we first went into battle at La Bassee, which I have already partly recorded. Before we came under fire, marching along the road in semi-darkness, an old soldier that I did not know came staggering along. It was easy to see that he was drunk but not falling about. The Sergeant was on my right. I was in the second last file of four. The Colonel on horseback came up and saw the staggering man. In a loud voice he asked the Sergeant "What's the matter with that man?" The Sergeant said that he was drunk. The Colonel said, "I am ordering that man to be shot at once. Take a file of four and see that it is done." I felt a strange weakness passing through me and I recall bending my knees to make myself as small as possible so as not to be called for the firing party. The Sergeant took the file of fours behind us and I at least was greatly relieved the march was not halted. We heard the volley and that's all I know of it. To say that discipline in those days was strict would be an understatement. I have already spoken of the senseless stupidity of seeing a company of what was left of the Scots Guards having to mark time under heavy machine gun and rifle fire, waiting for those still standing and running to join them.

After our long rest, we left the Estaminet in good spirits. We still had a few kilometres to go and, on account of our trousers, did not want to be there before sunset and when we came to the last café we felt we had time and some money to spend. Laverty tried to sell his kilt but Madam was more particular. She said in good English, "It is far too lousy" and would not buy it even at five francs. I said I had enough to last us, as we didn't want to report back unsteady.

We met a few from the Battalion in that café. They told us where they were and also that they heard they were moving up the line at dawn. We left before the rest as we belonged to different companies. I did not see Laverty again. On enquiring about him. I learned that he was wounded the next day and with luck the war would be over as far as fighting was concerned for him. I reported first to the guard on duty then to Sergeant Brown, still in charge of No. 7 Platoon. He said, "You are late." I said, "The transport is a long way behind the line." "Where is your kilt? You are improperly dressed." "When we joined the transport they took the kilt off us and gave us trousers. We did not get them back when we left." "Well we are going up the line at dawn, see that you get a kilt or there will be a crime against you."

98

7   Gas, a Lewis Gun and Court Martial Threat

We did not go at dawn but we did the following night and, except for snipers, the line was quiet. The task for our platoon that night was digging gun pits at our back and another man and I were picked out for an all-night sentry duty on the firing step while the rest were at the digging with a young officer in charge. They had been gone more than an hour when the shelling began. The shells were going well over our heads and landing, we thought, in the area of the digging.

Gas mask and Lewis gun

The shelling was not heavy and some of them, we thought, were not exploding. One fell near us but did no damage. After a short while, my partner said, "Do you smell anything strange Donald?" I said, "No, do you?" "Yes, it's faintly like lilac. I am not taking any chances. I am putting my gas mask on." I did the same and after a short while, we sniffed again. I could smell it then. We kept our masks on longer and tested it at intervals till we felt it was safe to take them off.

The night was very dark, calm and warm. We took turns to allow the other an hour's sleep in corners of the firing step if no one was around. We kept on like that till the diggers came at dawn. None of them were hit and no mention was made of gas. The Sergeant said "These men worked hard all night, you had it easy. You will stay on sentry duty. One of you draw the breakfast. See that everyone gets his turn. Every one out shortly after sunrise, then you will be relieved. Is that clear?" "Yes Sergeant" When all this was done and breakfast eaten, very shortly afterwards the diggers began to be sick and vomit, and as the sun was rising higher and stronger they began going blind and it was not long till all were nearly completely sightless.

We had to lead them to the first aid post, one touching the other. It was a pitiful sight. All because of a stupid Officer who would not listen to an experienced private who claimed it was a new kind of gas. When he put on his mask, the Officer said he was only imagining it and there was no need for it. "We must get this done tonight. It can't be done wearing gas masks."

Sergeant Brown was not one of the casualties and outside of the gassing, we had no losses. It was mustard gas and, apart from blinding, it was very sore on those wearing a kilt. We were re-enforced and the platoon was brought up to strength again that night and we attacked at dawn under a creeping barrage. This was a new method of attack. The big guns opened up on the enemy's front line and back for five minutes. While this was going on, our own barbed wire had to be cut at the end of a given time. The big guns would lower their sights allowing the shells to land forty yards in front of us. We went over the top and advanced, keeping our distance as our gunners gradually raised their sights and, if these shells fell short, we cursed them. If everything went according to plan, our objective was easy to take and our losses would be small. Our losses were not small but we took our objective and held and consolidated it.

After 48 hours we were released for more reinforcements. Corporal Binnie was promoted to Sergeant and again I was offered promotion. Again I refused with the old excuse. We also got a new young Officer. I did not get a kilt as those that I had looked over were far too bloody, but when we came out of the line, Sergeant Binnie got me one from the Quarter Master. He also told me that I was to be S.L.B. the next time. S.L.B. meant 'some left behind.' Going into action one man from every platoon was left, so that if the platoon had the misfortune to be wiped out, there was still one man left to build upon. It happened very seldom. In a few days some reported back from the gas affair. I had now, after passing a test, been a Lewis gunner for some time.

Sergeant Binnie was due leave and left leaving orders that I was to be S.L.B. It was near the end of October and the war had taken on a different character. We had Germans on the run except where they, for some reason, made a last stand, leaving many of the villages without taking the civilians with them. We came to one such village at night for a twenty-four hour rest, our platoon being billeted in a large cellar.

Early next morning, I went to see what the village was like. It looked large and not a soul in sight, and except for the broken windows it didn't look damaged. I stood in the square for a while thinking there was no one left in the village when I saw heads peeping through the broken windows. I waited thinking maybe they would come out. In a few moments I saw a crowd, evidently afraid to come out because I don't think the Germans would have told them anything good about us.

I was about to leave when a single piper came and began to play beside me. The crowd in the close mouth was becoming larger, some being pushed to the street but they would at once try to push back to the safety of the house. As I stood watching and listening to the pipes, a teenage girl dressed in a white blouse and black skirt and holding a large bunch of flowers, came over and walked towards the piper, put her arms around his neck and began kissing him. Needless to say, he responded. When the crowd of spectators saw that no harm was done, there was a general rush to circle the piper who was by this time, was joined by another piper and a crowd of soldiers. Someone called out for a Scottish Reel. There was no shortage of partners or sparks from the cobblestones. This jolly time lasted for more than a half-hour when the familiar gas alarm went. This was by striking a piece of iron on an empty shell case. The Colonel came on the scene. "Attention everyone! Word has just come through to me that this town will be bombarded with gas shells within an hour unless all the civilian population is moved out." This was impossible, since no one had yet been interrogated. "Go back to your billets. Everyone must wear his gas mask and this French interpreter will advise all civilians what to do." We made for the cellar with a crowd of Frenchmen who had no gas masks, following us.

It was a large cellar under a brewery, with many empty casks. We donned our masks and got two blankets and hung them double across the entrance and with buckets of water, kept them soaked. The gas shelling began and I felt sorry for the Frenchmen. There were no small children among them. One of our lads thought he would be gallant and removed his mask and placed it on a teenage girl. An officer came in and saw that he had no mask on. When asked where it was, the boy pointed to the girl. The officer said, "Take that mask off at once and put it on yourself. Sergeant, take this man's name for disobeying an order and for endangering his life." The girl did not cry when he took it off her and I don't know if he faced that charge.

We moved up the line for another battle that day and many did not come back. We gave the civilians some of our rations. They were very hungry and all we had would not satisfy them, but they were grateful and did not appear to have caught any of the gas. I think the plugging of the holes and wet blankets kept it out. As soon as the long-range shelling ended, we moved forward. I don't know how the rest of the population fared.

We rested in an area waiting for nightfall. It was understood that I was the one to be left behind there. Many would say, "You lucky bugger." At dusk they formed up. I stood at the back wishing that they would leave at once and feeling a tinge of sorrow knowing that many would not return. Our platoon was waiting for the order to quick march when a young lad fell forward in a faint. Despite anything they could do, he was still out and so they carried him away on a stretcher. Scarcely had the fallen boy been taken away than another fell forward in the same manner. The Officer called MacLachlan said, "My God, is that you MacDonald? Surely you are not staying behind." I got very angry and having nothing to lose I said, "No Sir, a MacDonald will go anywhere a MacLachlan will." At least I had the satisfaction of hearing the old boys saying "Good old Mac."

The trenches at that time were left behind us. It was open warfare except when you met with stiff resistance when you dug in with your entrenching tool to make cover as best as you could. I was put on a Lewis gun, No. 3 on the gun. We advanced in the open to where we took over from what was left of the Naval Division. The battle for this large area began in the afternoon. Headquarters thought that the Germans were leaving and began attacking with a squadron of cavalry, none of which got anywhere near it. The Naval Division then attacked without any success but with great losses. We were next to try. 'A' company attacked as it was getting dark, more with the smoke of the battle than the time of the day.

On account of the civilian population there, the town was not shelled, making it impossible for us to capture it. The enemy had machine guns posted at every point of advantage, so that they could put up almost a wall of bullets against us. Their gun was so near that they could throw a hand grenade at us in a shell hole, but still they missed hitting us. No. 1 mounted the gun and kept firing at them and after a while he was hit in the arm and useless. He began to make his way back and I don't know if he made it. No. 2, William Binnie, replaced him. He was from Falkirk.

Before going into that battle, as always, an Officer was taking our names, home addresses and next of kin. Binnie was next to me in line. The Officer asked me my name. I told him, next of kin, father's name and address in South Uist, thinking if it was to be bad news, it would take much longer to trace the full address, thereby lessening sorrow because it happened some time ago. When he asked Binnie his next of kin, he said he did not have any, not even aunts and uncles. At that moment I felt sorry for him, then it struck me why should I be, he was not causing grief for anyone, while with me, there would be many. Binnie was a steady soldier under fire and he kept blazing at them, at least in their direction, until word was passed to us to retire to our original position.

When it became darker we began to crawl back, missing shells as they fell around us. We were lying flat beside each other, waiting for the next chance to move, when a shell came and landed not many feet in front of us. It went deep in the ground before exploding, covering us all with mud. I got a big lump of it on the head but the steel helmet saved me. Apart from that and a little shock, I was unharmed. Being so near and lying down, the stuff went over us.

Kilt march

Binnie, when my senses came back, was moaning. I said, "Are you hit?" "Yes, my leg is blown off." I began to get the small bandage I had, thinking it would not do much. I started on one leg and found there was no blood and the other was the same. I said, "You legs are alright." "It's not my legs" he said, "It's my arm." I tried both arms. There was no blood anywhere on him. As I was telling him that he got up, swearing and cursing that he would fight the whole German army alone. With that, he took off running, leaving the gun behind him. I knew then that he was out of his head and so I ran after him. After a struggle and a few hard punches, I was able to drag him to where those that got back were.

There was our Officer and a few others; there were no N.C.O.s left. Binnie was then raving. The Officer sent a man down with him to the first aid post. The man was Bob Campbell from Islay and when I asked him afterwards if Binnie was alright he said laughing "After the struggle I had getting him down, the poor soul went and shot himself." At that moment a shell landed. There was no time to ask if he had killed himself. Shell shock was common in a battle or in a long bombardment. We had a man in our Platoon named Hill. He was having spells of insanity and during these he would cry, sing and curse in turn, sometimes to the danger of giving our position away to the enemy. At such times, he was persuaded to report to the first aid station. This was one of these spells.

When I got back with the Lewis gun from where I left it to take Binnie back, the Officer said, "Mount it and keep a sharp look out." This was the Officer I did not think much of. He was in a hole by himself, some 15 feet from us. Except for bursts of machine gun fire at that moment all was quiet. There was a village on fire a long way at the back of the German line, and in its glow, any moving object could be seen. About seven of us were in that short shallow trench, watching and waiting for our relief to come. We already thought there was no one but the enemy in front of us but with the aid of the glow, made out objects advancing slowing towards us. The Officer said, "Have you got the gun ready trained on them MacDonald?" I said, "Yes Sir." "Open fire when I tell you."

The party was getting nearer and we could see more of them at short intervals as they propped themselves on the ground. Whenever a Verey Light shone above them, I thought they numbered from 12 to 15. I was still uncertain if they were friend or foe. At this moment they would be about 25 yards away. Next time they rose the Officer ordered me to open fire on them. I knew I could not miss and felt sure none could come out alive. Again, "Open fire MacDonald, what are you waiting for?" I said, "They might be our own men." "No they are not, I have already told you there is nothing but the enemy in front of us. Open fire." I said, "I am still not sure." He said "Then open fire men. You will be court marshalled for this MacDonald." I said, "Don't fire boys till I tell you." "MacDonald, I have my revolver out, I am entitled to shoot you." I said, "I am the only one left that can fire this gun. My finger is on the trigger. When I know for certain they are Germans, I will annihilate them." At that moment Private Hill, the mad man, jumped in among us, and whether he was listening to what was going on, or not, I do not know. He could not contain himself. With fixed bayonet he climbed out and charged those in front, who nearly all at once shouted, "'A' Company, for God's sake don't shoot." I felt a shudder of relief passing through me. There was no room in our small trench for them. The Officer asked if there were any more of our men out there. They said they did not see any. "Alright, carry on down. The relief is on its way." He then turned to me and said, "You are a brave man MacDonald. Will you volunteer to go out between the lines and report any movement

103

of the enemy? You can take anyone you want with you." I said, "No Sir, I will not volunteer but I will go anywhere I am sent." "Alright, take your rifle and whoever you like and go out there." I said, as if testing him "Of course, you will come out yourself to show us where." "Yes I will. There is no N.C.O. left."

The three of us crawled out to about 40 yards when he left us. I wondered why he did not ask me to take the Lewis gun. I was sure that none of them knew how to fire it but perhaps he could do that himself. We lay down in an old furrow for cover, watching and waiting for perhaps half an hour, when we both saw a movement on our left as a star shell lit up the ground. It could be a wounded man trying to get back or there could be many waiting to attack. The object was slowly drawing near to us, slowly because of the short time between the lights in the sky. We made out that there was only one man and when he came within 15 yards, the boy beside me raised his rifle saying, "I'll get him." At once I pushed his rifle to the ground and told him to keep it down, that I would do the shooting. I covered him and let him come. At about 12 feet, I challenged him. He answered, "'A' Company." "Who the hell are you? Advance to be recognised." He did. I asked, "What are you doing out here?" He said he was looking for his pal who was wounded but could not find him. I said "A bunch of 'A' Company got in at our trench a good while ago, you better make for our lines and keep calling "'A' Company. You are still lucky."

The Canadians relieved us that night. They attacked the large village, Lieu-Saint-Amand at dawn and surrounded it with hardly any casualties. The Germans had fled that night leaving only a few men behind to be taken prisoners. They also left all the civilians. I had a chum in 'A' Company, and when we got back I enquired and went to see him. He was safe and I asked if he was in the lot that stayed behind in 'no mans land'? He said no, but that he heard they were very lucky. He also said that he heard of a Gordon who was due to go on leave to be decorated with a high Order Medal, was killed by his own men while trying to get back to them. I felt then and many other times, thankful to God that I was not to carry any scar of remorse in connection with the affair with 'A' Company. Nevertheless, later on I used to ponder why and at what point did I make the decision not to press the trigger that would send these men to eternity.

Of one thing I feel sure; that I was not brave beyond the ordinary. The Officer was acting on the information he had, backed by the army's regulations. On active service, in the face of the enemy in those circumstances, he was entitled, without blame, to shoot me. Why did he not do it? The reason must be because I was ordained for other things and it could not happen. Those in possession of the gift of second sight reveal a glimmer of that, but it still doesn't fully answer why. In trying to capture that town we suffered very heavy casualties and were out of the line for days for re-enforcement. It was plain that the young and inexperienced suffered most under the same conditions.

Before the unit went up the line again, Sergeant Binnie was back from leave and he made sure that I was left behind. On our second day out, the company was inspected by a young Officer who had just joined us, and when passing he put his hand on my face. "Do you have a razor?"

"Yes, Sir." "Use it then. Take his name Sergeant." He did and four of us were up for the same crime. We got three days' punishment. Next day, a windy day, the Corporal took us to a field in full marching order, with a blanket strapped over the top of our packs. He tested the weight and added three more bricks to it and then ordered us round the park at the double. The day was warm, with him shouting if we slowed down. When we got back after less than ten minutes, the sweat pouring off us like a river, we were to stand at ease for five minutes. During that time a long-range shell landed in the field. The not so brave Corporal said, "Alright boys, let's get out of here. As far as I am concerned you have done your punishment." Apart from that, and being caught for the joke on the minister on church parade before the war, it was the only punishment I received in all of my nearly six years in the army. Regardless of the many crimes committed, some very serious as already recorded, I was just very lucky.

Reinforced, the Battalion went up the line. Their objective was another village, which they captured after heavy losses. I regret many of my pals did not come back. I heard it was due to an over brave and stupid Officer who sent them forward in daylight without any cover, with their canteens exposed, shining on their backs, and when lying down they were an easy target for a machine gun to mow them down. It was sad after coming through so much. When the survivors came back for rest, and more reinforcements, we were billeted in a small village outside the large town of Cambrai. We were in an upstairs room large enough to accommodate the whole platoon. We were to be there for a few days. I think it was on the second day we were told that we were to go back up the line again next day. They issued us with extra ammunition and hand grenades, also extra rations. We knew without being told that it was going to be a big battle. All our mail was written and collected for censoring. I had a letter returned to me with much of what I said scored out. I foolishly told them at home that we were going soon into a big battle. I got a row for it but no more.

At dawn and into the morning of the 11th November 1918 we could hear the usual booming of the big guns and thought they were getting things ready for us. At that time my pal was David Lohans who was much older than me. Towards the evening of the 11th I came across the Bulletin Board for orders. I saw written on it, "Catholics wishing to go to confession may do so from 3.30 to 4.30" and naming a nearby place. I went and found the confessional. The Priest was there. I went in and began my confession. I was given absolution, got off my knees and, while in the act of turning away the Priest said, "Are you long out in France?" I said, "I came to France in 1914. I have been wounded three times. I got home twice. I have been out this time since last year." "Are you going up the line tomorrow?" "Yes Father. We are leaving here before dawn going up the line." "You are not leaving here tomorrow my boy. The war is over." "But that is impossible Father. I wish to God it was true." "It is true. Did nobody tell you that?" "No Father, all we know is that we are carrying more ammunition than usual and are all ready to move at dawn." "Well you are not going. The war ended at 11.00 o'clock this morning."

I left the confessional in a daze and feeling very sorry for the poor priest who I thought was off his head. I walked slowly towards the billet, thinking about what I had just heard, and wondering why was the priest allowed to perform such an important duty. I could not tell there was anything wrong with him, till he said the war was over and the convincing way he said it. What was I to believe? True, I did not notice any gunfire in the afternoon but I thought it was because our troops had advanced so far that we could not hear them. Would a Priest in the confessional spring a joke like that? No, never if he was sane. I thought there was nothing wrong with him and yet as I slowly walked, the doubting Thomas stayed with me. I climbed the stairway to see the others lying down and heard David shouting "Where have you been Donald? I have been waiting for you. Take off your kilt to put under us." We always did that when out of the line, kilts under and coats on the top.

There was a big fire in a pot-bellied stove with a trestle in front. I said I had been on a walk and now I was going to make tea or drum up. "What, at this time? Give me your kilt." I got my canteen and my emergency rations of tea and sugar out, filled the canteen with water from my water bottle and put it on the stove. David said, "Is there anything wrong with you Donald, you are acting very queer? You know, we are leaving here at dawn, you better get some sleep, you'll be alright in the morning, put your emergency rations back or you might get caught. Throw me over your kilt, I want to lie down." The rest were lying down, not a word was said amongst them. I was sitting on the bench waiting for the water to boil. "Boys" I said "I have great news for you, you are not going up the line tomorrow, the war is all over." "Yes" said someone "all over France." I said, "That is not what I mean. The war has ended." Then someone said, "What latrine did that rumour come from? Throw a boot at him." And he did. It missed the canteen. I said, "Do that again and I'll knock every tooth down your throat." They knew well that I was able to do it. Nothing else came my way. David again asked me for my kilt, saying again "Is there anything wrong?" I said, "No, I got the news from a high authority, you can believe it David." I gave him my kilt and he put it down without being, as far as I could see, impressed. When I said, "How about a bit of the cake you got from home?" He said, "We'll have it before we leave in the morning." "We are not going David." But I knew he was not convinced, while I myself was hopeful. We were in that state of mind when we heard the bagpipes playing. Someone said, "What is that drunken piper doing at this time of the night, where did he get the rum? Maybe they are giving out some for this battle tomorrow."

First World War Pipers

Then we made out there was more than one piper. With only my tunic on, I dived for the stairs and the road in front. It was packed with troops, shouting, singing and yelling. I asked a chap what was it all about? He did not know, he was just following the crowd. I saw an Officer whom I knew. I asked him, he said "Don't you know?" "Know what Sir?" "Well boy, the war is over." I waited for no more, but dived back for my kilt and yelled to the rest upstairs. I met them on the stairway coming down in a bunch and there was no way of getting past so I was carried down with them to join the mob outside. Like myself, many were without kilts, only jacket, shirt and boots. The moonlit night was calm, but pressing hard we walked, sang and yelled as an uncontrolled mob behind the pipers.

It was good and fortunate that we were many miles from any drink. It was snowing before we got back at daylight. No one minded. I did not catch even a slight cold on its account. After a long sleep we had breakfast and it was do as you like that day. That is there were no parades. There was no bathroom attached to the billet, so I took my towel and soap to a small burn nearby which was still running, for a good wash. I took my crucifix off, which said, 'In this sign thou shall conquer' and as already recorded on a previous page, I could not find it although quite sure of where I had laid it beside me. Many other times I searched in vain for it, as I was very much attached to it. I could only conclude that its work was done. In the billet that night I saw men that I knew well as brave and steady under fire, now crying uncontrollably and when asked what was wrong, some would say "My mother died, I have not seen her for so many years." Others would say "My brother was killed early in the war." Others, a sister had died without him seeing her for a long time. I was amazed, knowing that they would face any dangers without showing it at other times. I expect it was the reaction to all the other events.

For myself I had no feeling of remorse. There was no cause for it. I do not know why we were not told of the great news long before we heard it, but I can well understand the havoc it would have caused among armed men, going mad with joy and the armistice being uncertain to hold for that next night. I saw in our billet men with their Lewis guns mounted in the windows, blasting thousands of rounds of ammunition at an imaginary target in the darkness. Many bullets were hitting our roof and walls, let off by some other fools. Luckily we had no casualties. Through the grapevine I learned others did not escape. These would be put down as killed in action, as would be those in other cases.

After a few days doing nothing but guard duty and a little P.T. training, we began to attend lectures and classes. I enrolled in forestry for a week before my name came out in orders for leave next day. I was given a clean rigout and a pass for fourteen days, also 1600 francs. There were six of us going. We walked back to as far as the railway came. The station had a roof on but no sides or any other buildings and there was no sign of a train. There was a group waiting and we asked our N.C.O. when the train was coming in. He said, "Some time tonight if we are lucky." We were very tired after the long walk carrying our equipment, except the ammunition, which was taken off us. But with me I had 86 rounds sewn into a belt and worn under my shirt. If I was found out, my leave would be cancelled and my rifle, which I intended to leave at home, would be taken from me.

We lay down near each other on the open platform. The night was calm and not yet freezing. I fell asleep and was wakened by the train coming in. Gathering my gear I found that my haversack was gone, although I had it tied on me. It contained, besides my rations for the journey to the boat, small souvenirs picked up on the battlefields. No gold watches or rings. I would never touch them. A square of embroidered silk which I exchanged a new shirt for. Luckily I had two wallets on me, one with the 1600 francs, and the other just small items. I was the only one robbed in the crowd. They shared their food with me as we went along. It was cattle trucks again and into one we went. There was plenty of room with only six of us. I have seen many times over 40 packed in. There was no straw on the floor. If there was, it was sure to be lousy. We slept before it pulled out. Daylight was coming through the cracks. It was very cold and frosty. The speed was slow with many stops, letting more important trains pass.

It was a single track. We were just a 'leave train'. We came to a halt outside a large town, not far away. We saw three French soldiers warming themselves at a large brazier. We said they are lucky, as we were shivering, and wondered when we would get moving. Whatever was their reason, the Frenchmen left the fire and we saw them going into a building. The train was due to start any time. Three of us dashed to the fire and inserted a bar of iron through the holes at the top of the brazier, and ran back with it. One of us carried a large bag of charcoal. When all was on board, we pushed the sliding door shut. There was no sign of the Frenchmen coming back. If they did, a shower of red cinders was waiting. We set the fire in the centre, away from the door, on the wooden floor. As soon as the train started, there was a real danger of it toppling over. We got our bayonets out and with a rifle butt, hammered them in the floor for support. It worked and we were cosy, in fact, too warm at times. When the door was slid open there was very little smoke. Things were then going fine until the floor under the brazier started to smoke and caught fire.

We emptied our water bottles on it. That helped for a time, then some would say, "Throw the bugger out." Others said no, we have a long way to go. Some that could, urinated on it, with little results. Being obliged to open the door to let the smoke out only made things worse and we wondered what were our chances to hide the smoke when we came to a station, which we soon did. We began with our overcoats from both ends, to coax the smoke out or as much as possible before we closed the door tight.

We worked on that till we were within 300 yards of the station. The door was closed with one man standing by to open it if it became unbearable. Except for the one at the door, we lay on the floor under the gathering smoke, hoping that our wait was a short one and indeed it was the shortest we had. If there was any smoke showing we did not hear of it but were very glad when it was safe to open the door, relieving much coughing and sore eyes.

The brazier had another fill of charcoal, which it should not have had although there was plenty left. By this time it had burned itself deep into the floor and needed no support. We pulled two of the bayonets out. They were useless and with much draught from the bottom, sparks began to fly. We were glad there was no straw on the floor. The train was going too fast to risk jumping out. We were trapped by our own foolishness. Fortunately the brazier and bayonets went through the hole, throwing up a shower of sparks. We were watching and expecting it to happen and so were prepared. The door was now wide open. We dashed for both ends of the truck. Most of the shower of sparks was carried by the draught through the door. We got busy with rifles and bayonets slicing round the burning hole till we had it out and safe to partly close the door. When we arrived at Calais in the evening, we were told that we had missed the boat crossing and were taken to a hostel, a large building used for looking after travelling servicemen and women.

After a wash, we were given a meal. In all my life I have never seen so many signs and posters warning of pickpockets. I was pre-warned by the haversack affair. Now I would be pre-armed. The bunks of mesh wire were in double tiers and I was allotted a top one. In full view of everyone there, making plenty of noise, I loaded my rifle from the belt round my middle, with a round in the firing chamber and five in the magazine with the safety catch off. My bayonet bare on one side of the bed, the loaded rifle on the other, I took off my tunic and placed it under me. With a blanket and my overcoat over me, in that position with the money I had, I felt safe as the Bank of England. Lying on my back with a hand gripping my rifle, the other on the bayonet, I thought, God help anyone trying to rob me. I was thus going to sleep when I heard a voice saying "Place all your money and valuables with the office downstairs." I felt warm and safe enough to ignore him, and tired after the long journey in the cattle truck.

I slept like a log and did not wake till I heard someone calling to show a leg for breakfast. I felt the lump of the jacket and to make sure, I felt the first pocket. There was nothing in it and before I tried the other, I felt for the rifle and bayonet. They were where I put them apparently untouched. I had little hope of the other pocket containing anything. My shock turned to joy when I found that a wallet was still there. I knew it was the one with the money I counted it in the open, knowing that with the rifle beside me, no one would dare to come near me. It was all there. The other wallet contained nothing of value to other persons and I wondered what the thief was feeling at risking his life for so little. I reported the matter only to be told, as expected, why did you not deposit your valuables as advised? I said that I didn't think there were so many clever thieves in the building here. He said, "We get complaints of stealing everything but your toenails." I felt glad to be clear of that hive of robbers. A large number of us were paraded in front and marched to the steamer that took us to Dover, where we got a meal.

The next stop was London. In Euston Station we changed our French money and for the 1600 francs I had I got £16.00. We got another meal and were separated onto different tracks. Mine went via Edinburgh. A meal ticket was supplied for any station that we stopped at. There was a long stay in Edinburgh. I went to the Radio Telegraph Office about extending my leave. I saw an officer there with the badge H.D. (Highland Division) on his shoulders. He was a Seaforth Highlander. He asked me where I left the Division. I told him, saying I wanted to apply for an extension to my leave, he gave me a week. We talked about the Brigade and many battles. He asked me if I had been to Teachers for my bottle of whisky or did I know about it? I said, "No, Sir." "Well they are giving a present of one bottle of Teachers Highland Cream to soldiers coming home on leave from France. I will show you where to go." I went and got two bottles, one free, and the other at reduced price, which I think was 7/6d. Real good stuff!

I got the train to Oban where I stayed at a boarding house on the High Street; it was crowded with people going to the islands next day. There were many girls boarding for the night, going home from the herring-gutting season. I gave them all a dram. The single glass used was still the custom and each girl only put her lips to it and shook her head. Only the landlady made any impression on the full glass and a sailor finished it. It would now take a half gallon to do what the one glass did then, and yet there was more laughter and sing song there that night than a gallon could produce in this age. The calm sea journey across the Minch to Barra was made very pleasant by the singsongs and laughter of those herring girls. My father and brother with the boat met me at Lochboisdale and gave me a warm welcome, and the same with much kissing from my sisters when we got home. I then felt as if tons of weight was mysteriously lifted off me and I

109

was young again, although I was not yet 21 years old. So much for war and the things related to it.

No one can know how horrible war is except those who have been through it, no matter how educated or clever the person is. How to punish those responsible for such carnage and grief? No human mind is capable, nor is it able to invent any form of torture that has not already been used, often on defenceless, innocent people. The mind gets bogged down at the thought of where to begin. I think it is best to leave it to Him who sees all and knows all.

In the morning of the next day at home, a neighbour's wife came to the house enquiring if I had any news of her son Ewen. I had never met this boy because we were away from home a lot. She told me the regiment he was in but I did not know the battalion. I said that I could not say anything without knowing the number of his battalion. She had his last letter with the number I wanted and the date it was written. I was able to tell her that this battalion was in our brigade and was not in any battle since the date in the letter. She told me how long he was in France. I said he would most likely be due leave and with luck he would be home in a few days. She put her arms around me and kissed me, a thing unheard of at other times. Her cup was full when Ewen, without notice, came home the next day.

It was time I had a look and stroll on my beloved hills, particularly on the one above our home and at the path of heather that was always lush and full of life. I had no need then to chew and eat it for satisfaction, but there were times, many of them, when I would gladly welcome it in exchange for my leather straps which, no matter how long being chewed, failed to give any satisfaction. I remained in that spot long in contemplation, thinking how fortunate and thankful the people on this land should feel that the war had left no scars, at least on the land.

I was greatly enjoying my leave with a good rifle and plenty to shoot at. Anyone wanting a seal for its oil he had only to say so, but I would never hurt them for any other purpose. I wanted to leave the rifle at home and before going on leave I paid a chum five francs to have one for me when I returned, which he did. When the time for my departure came, I said to my father that I was going to leave the rifle at home. He would not hear of it saying he could not sleep with it being on the croft. I tried others but it was the same with them. I was only allowed to leave my steel helmet, which could not have killed anyone. I was obliged to take it back with me.

When my enjoyable leave ended, I did not ask for an extension knowing it would not be long before I would return and when saying goodbye all eyes but my sisters were dry. Ewen and I left together and as it happened we were stationed less than a mile apart in Belgium. Our passes were for different routes crossing the channel. Ewen's via Folkstone, mine via Southampton. Anyway, we did not miss a pub wherever there was one.

The train was late arriving at Buchanan Street Station in Glasgow. With full equipment, we ran to the pub opposite. It was closing with the customers being pushed out. We both put our backs to the door and whoever was at the back was forced to give way. We went to the bar, there was no one behind it, and a man said, "What do you boys want?" "A drink. The Oban train was late." "Where are you going?" "France, back from leave." After we had several drinks, the barman said, we had better leave or we would miss our train, and, although we had plenty of money, he would not take any. We left and got the southbound train in time. We had to change trains in Euston Station. I went along with Ewen to the Folkstone train, thinking I could bluff them. My argument was no good and they escorted me to the Southampton train, warning me if I did not stay there a charge would be put against me. I stayed, as I would have much to lose given I was still in the army. I went to see Ewen after a few days in Belgium and we had a jolly afternoon. I rejoined the battalion, but in a different and better billet with a good stove, which was kept red hot after every bit of fuel was examined for detonators and booby traps left behind and planted by the Germans. These and time bombs went off frequently, sometimes with much damage.

One day I was detailed for guard duty. After we were inspected, I was picked out as being the tidiest and cleanest man of the Guard, which meant in army terms, that whoever it was, he got the stick and did not have to stand guard. It was the first and only time that I got that honour. The duties attached were running messages between battalion and company headquarters, always carrying a stick instead of a rifle. One time coming back from a message, I saw a damaged building and in the rubble was an exposed large bottle of wine that I took to be Vin Rouge. It was tempting to investigate it but there were many people about. I would have to wait till the way was clear to remove it for if I got caught, I would be charged with looting. I had passed several times close to it and had found a place to hide it, but every time as I came near, someone would appear. I would walk past to return with stronger resolution, only to be thwarted by the appearance of yet another person. This time at my furthest point from it as I turned round a blast went off, shattering the building and had I been a little nearer, I would have at least had some of it. The bottle and whatever there was connected with it were gone. If that was luck I know I did my best to prevent it. That was the last incident of German treachery that I was involved in, the first being in 1914 when the trench was mined.

The Officers sometimes held drinking parties. Those of us who wanted to volunteer to guard the drinking place were given a small drink and a sandwich. Four of us volunteered and we got a bottle of beer and a sandwich and when we asked for more, it was refused. We told the Mess Sergeant we were leaving. He then gave us a little more. Making the same request, he told us that that was all we would get. We told him to do his own guarding and left. Outside we saw a large 50-gallon hogshead full of beer. There was no one around but plenty of merriment inside. The circumstances were enticing. We quietly rolled the hogshead to the road and away with it. No one was following us.

On the downhill road, we were making good speed to the billet and about a mile away, we intended to open and hide it. There was a pale moon, which enabled us to steer her clear of shell holes in the road. We took turns rolling, two at a time and were nearly halfway home, when we heard shouts and running behind us. We were in no doubt as to who it was. "What the hell is the meaning of this stealing the Officers beer?" said the Sergeant. We said that we just found it lying at the side of the road and thought it was empty and did not belong to anyone. We were going to make firewood of it, as we have no coal. "I don't think you are as stupid as that", he said. "You got it at the door of the Officers Mess and stealing it will mean prison for you." We started to walk away and leave him with the hogshead. "Come back, I know you all. I'll tell you what I will do. Roll it back to where you got it and I will not put a crime against you." "Can we have your word for it?" He said, "yes." And so began the task of rolling it back uphill and what one could do easy coming down, it took three pushing hard to make any headway going up. With the Sergeant laughing at us, I think all agreed that we were punished enough before we got it exactly where he wanted it. When we asked him for a drink, he said no and that we were lucky getting off so easily. It was near daylight before we got back to the billet, tired and angry.

A few days after that a notice appeared on the bulletin board, "Catholics wishing to go on a pilgrimage to Lourdes to hand your name in at the Orderly Room." They were to leave within a week and I gave in my name and was issued with new kit. I was very much looking forward to it, as everything was free. Unfortunately, the day before we were due to leave, my name came out in orders for demobilisation. The next day I found it hard which one to choose. If I went to Lourdes I would miss my turn for demobilisation and no saying when my turn would come again. I cancelled my trip to Lourdes, which I have regretted ever since.

That day I was taken before the Medical Officer. The Adjutant was there. He turned to the doctor and said, "This man is A.1 and quite fit." The doctor ignored him and began examining me. Seeing the scars on my body he said, "Have you got any claim against the Government?" Before I had time to say "Yes sir", the Adjutant chimed in again saying, "This man has been in and out of the trenches with the rest for more than a year. He is quite fit." The doctor again ignored him and asked me when did I get the wound in my back? I told him less than five months ago. I also have two pieces of shell in my body, one in the leg and one in the shoulder. He had a look and when I said, "They don't bother a lot", he said, "They will if not taken out. I would not be doing my duty if I passed you as fit and I don't want to be involved with this case again." He was an American. I saw the Adjutant's face turning red and whatever he had to gain as a result of this examination, I was awarded the handsome sum of eight shillings a week pension, better than nothing.

At the desk I collected my Discharge Papers, which the clerk was making out, and turning over the papers he said, "You require a reference for the time you were in the army. I will make it out according to these papers." He wrote on the form, "Clean, sober and trustworthy and has proved himself a very reliable soldier." In honesty, I could only claim some of it as true. The next day our batch left. That day I turned my back on France with no regrets and my face towards a land fit for heroes to live in. The first example of that was my meagre award of eight shillings pension.

8   Home, the Dole and Diamonds

I think we took the shortest route from Calais to Dover and eventually landed at Kinross where we handed in our equipment. We were allowed to keep our topcoats and kilts and given a suit of civvies and a pound note. I took the train to Oban and stayed for the night with the same people on High Street. There were no herring girls this time as the season was over. I arrived home to the usual welcome, nevertheless a changed man whose spirits were very much dampened and not knowing where to begin to live again. No longer did I want to enjoy playing tricks on anyone or enjoy minor jokes. I pitied those city dwellers who could not go out into the hills to converse with nature, thereby restoring the mind and healing the hidden scars.

There was no work to be had, regardless of the many things that were urgently required. The long look forward to the land fit for heroes to live in was a land of neglect and poverty. The state of affairs then is unbelievable to the present generation. I was not as badly off as most. I had the small pension and there was the dole of 29 shillings, which, if I had known about, I could have had as soon as I came home unemployed. As it was, I only got three weeks of it. When it ended, I was not in the least worried as I had survived under worse conditions. It was near Christmas and the family had every reason to be happy and to celebrate, which the whole township did at both Christmas and New Year.

There was no work to be had on the island and so I toyed with the idea of going back to sea again. The family was against that, saying that after what I had already gone through I needed a long rest. I could understand and feel the wisdom of their advice. Apart from going out herring fishing some nights with my Father, that was all I did.

One night I won't forget was in late January when we set out in a 16 foot sailboat, with no engine and with nets. The wind had eased after days of a strong northeast wind. We had a pot of peat fire. The sea was very heavy at the mouth of the loch so that when the boat went into the trough, the tops of the high hills were out of sight. There was hardly any wind. We shot the big nets and placed the fire pot on the stone ballast, as there was no other shelter. It helped to keep the frost away. With the rolling and diving of the boat, it had to be well supported with ballast stones. There were no boats or lights visible round us. We had none except the glare from the pot when it lit into flame.

My father was sitting in the stern keeping watch around us and when we tried the nets there were signs of a good catch. It was then that father said in anger "I saw a flash of light not far away, like someone lighting his pipe. Get a large cinder out of the pot and blow on it." I was doing my best to stick my knife in a likely cinder and blow, but on raising it up it gave a weak flash and toppled into the sea. A large dark object was nearly then on top of us. My father said "I never saw you doing anything right. Raise that pot." As I was doing that, I heard a loud voice coming from the dark object saying in Gaelic, "Did you see anything there, Archie?" "Yes, I think there are a few crans in them." To me he said, "Ach, it's only an Eriskay boat." Had we known it, we were in no danger of being run down. With their height, they could see us a long way off. The catch amounted to over three crans of good quality herring. We cured much of it for the house and sold the rest to those in need of it. Due to the lack of wind, we had to row all the way back against a strong current, no need for the pot to keep us warm.

Not long after that, on a Sunday at church after mass, the priest who always talked to the people outside, said to me, "Stay behind Donald, I want to talk to you. Go to the house for a cup of tea, I'll be with you shortly." I said to myself, I expect he wants more seal oil. When he came in and we had our cup of tea he said, "Donald, how would you like to learn a trade?" I at once had visions of a joiner or a stonemason. I said "That would be fine Father. What kind of a trade?" He said, "Diamond cutting." I said I had never heard of it. "Well, recently I had a letter from the Ministry of Pensions asking me to submit the name of an ex-service man requiring and wishing to learn the light work trade of diamond cutting. I thought of you and if you want to try it, I will write away tomorrow with your name and my recommendations. Have you got a reference from the Army?" I said "Yes, at home. It is short and I remember every word of it." He wrote it down and said it should be good enough for anyone.

Walking home with my head high I was thinking of what I knew about a diamond. I heard that it was the best thing for cutting glass. I even saw a joiner once cutting a pane of glass with it and noted how careful he was when finished with the diamond as he put it in a small case. That was all the knowledge I had. Never held one in my hand. Anyway, I did not think my name would be accepted among so many. The only thing I could do was wait and hope.

All that week I was anxiously waiting and watching for the postman and when he did not call, I thought that was the end of it. To confirm that, the priest did not say anything to me the next Sunday, although I felt sure he saw me. Perhaps he had not written or had forgotten to post it. Towards the middle of the next week, the postman called with, I noticed at once, a fat large letter from the Ministry of Pensions. It contained a letter stating that the Ministry of Pensions accepted me for training in diamond cutting, and while in training I would be granted a full pension.

The travelling warrant enclosed would take me to Fort William where I was to report at the Highland Hotel to the manager of the diamond works. There were also other papers I had to sign and post including a J.P.'s reference. The Priest, Fr. John MacIntosh, was one himself. Also in the letter it said that my board, lodgings and laundry in the Highland Hotel were free during my training period.

That night I walked to the Bornish manse to thank the priest for what he had done for me, knowing full well that I was not the only one to benefit from his help, regardless of creed. Not many are aware that, through his actions and connections with certain people on the mainland, the Alginate factory in North Boisdale came into being and became a profitable concern for the Island. The people of Bornish and Ormiclate are indebted to him for his stand against those managing the Estate. When it was broken into crofts, the Estate was trying to prevent the crofters from cultivating the machair, particularly for potatoes, claiming that it ruined the game life. In the Spring of 1915, the crofters began preparing the machair for the potato crop. Soon after the factor, supported by a high-ranking member of the church, came to put a stop to them, saying if they did not they would be in danger of losing their crofts or, at least, action would be taken against them. Some did not stop whilst others went to Father John for advice. He told them to carry on with the work they were doing, that he would make sure they were not interfered with. The crofters did as he told them. Next day the factor and the other man approached Father John, angrily demanding to know who gave him the authority to advise these crofters to break the law by breaking up land they were not entitled to. "I don't need any authority; they are responsible people. The land is theirs by law and they are entitled to cultivate it as they see fit. No law is being broken."

When they left in anger promising he would hear more about this, he was not sure of his position and so he wrote out a long telegram to the South Uist Department of St. Andrews House, Edinburgh, explaining the case and what he had done. He got a return wire at once to thank him for the interest he had taken in this case and assuring him that the Department felt he had done the right thing and would welcome any complaint in this regard. Many a potato has grown on the machair since then. All the people who were then involved have gone to their rest long ago. Father John bade me farewell with his blessing, saying that I would be the only one in the islands with any knowledge of diamond cutting, and indeed, apart from four boys from Lewis, I was.

I left for Fort William that week. I had visions of being employed sweeping the floor for the first few weeks and not allowed to touch a diamond. But that is not the way it was. Diamond cutting was not done in Britain. Before the war all our diamonds from Africa and elsewhere were sent for cutting into gems to Belgium and Holland. With so many disabled ex-servicemen the Ministry of Pensions began training some almost at once. With real diamonds, any mistakes or waste caused was made good by the government through the Ministry of Pensions.

I was introduced to my instructor, Harry Garland, from Birmingham. I made sure that I would pay more attention to listening than I did to my schoolmaster, Mr. Rea, from the same city. After four days on marble training, I was given a real diamond to begin my training in cross work, which meant to cut or polish four facets on the table and four on the collet. That was the first part to begin on. It was polished down to near the girdle, before the facets were put on, the first at a certain angle and across the grain to near the girdle. The second facet was parallel and made to the same gauge and depth, the same on both ends which had to be a perfect square. It is called 'the table'. We had three instructors, one on the finished diamond, one on the eights and one looking after six of us on cross work. There were twenty four of us working in a partly glass building that was connected to the Hotel.

Everything was strange with so much to learn. Only another diamond ground down to powder can cut or polish one. That powder comes from stones not worth cutting into gems on account of flaws and knots inside them. The powder is of the finest and is the colour of snuff or coffee and has to be mixed with olive oil into a very soft paste. There is little or no machinery except electrical power involved rotating the disc or mill on which the diamond is being worked. It is surprising how few mechanical tools are used. The mill is about the size of a large gramophone record and is a half inch thick, case hardened, with very fine grain or saw lines and spins it round at more than 5000 revs a minute. The only other tools used are two gauges, one for the table and one for the collet.

When you got a diamond to work on, you signed for it and kept working the same diamond till that stage was finished. At the end of the day, whether finished or not, it was handed in at the office to be resumed the next day. When you got an issue of a diamond, you were constantly under the watchful eye of the instructor in case you made irreparable mistakes, rendering the stone only fit for diamond dust. These were seldom made because of the watch kept over us.

Every diamond, although not visible to the naked eye, has a grain in it and a magnifying glass is used to see it. Sometimes, even with a glass, the grain is not visible and has to be searched for to find the direction it runs as no work can be done on it unless it is across the grain. The grain is named according to its direction, 4 point, 3 and 2 points, with the 4-point easiest to work on and the 3-point the hardest. It was a very intricate trade to learn but most enjoyable.

Fort William was a very nice place to live and work in. My room-mate was John Flett from the Isle of Flotta in Orkney. We were in the same class and we got on well together, and although he had a leg off, below the knee, which happened at the Battle of Loos, he was otherwise very strong and fit. He told me, and showed me his papers to prove, that after he had a foot fitted, on leaving hospital and a spell discharged from the army at home, he thought as a joke he would try and pass for the Navy. With that in mind, he went to see a doctor who did not know him. He had already hidden the shoulder straps that held up the dummy leg. With his shirt off the doctor examined him, finding him in good health and he was passed for the trawler section of the Navy. To continue the joke he went to the Base Commander with his medical papers and was told what ship he was joining.

He then told the Commander who certainly did not believe that he had only one foot and part of a leg, but pulling up his trousers, proved it. The Commander in anger said, "Was that fool who passed you fit drunk and blind? What do you want to do since you have got this far?" "I am fed up doing nothing. At first I did not think I would get past the medical officer. Now that I have, I am sure I can do something useful afloat." "I admire your spirit and will phone the Admiral of the Base as to what to do with you." The reply was that if he has two good eyes, he could join a trawler and so he did. His main concern was how to get in and out of the hammock at sea. He was a fisherman and well used to trawlers' ways. In the foc'sle the first night, with most of the crew there, being a newcomer all questions were directed to him. He told them that he was a minister's son and that he intended to follow ministry and hoped some day he would do that. When the sailors heard all this, swearing and teasing was the order of the day with him listening and pretending that he was in a state of shock. Not one of them suspected his condition.

One of the sailors took out his sheath knife and began playing with it in a disguised attempt to frighten Flett, who then said, "I know you boys have gone through a lot of hard training on how to stop the flow of blood from wounds you are likely to get in the war, when bandaging is not possible, something like stab wounds. Let me see your knife and I'll show you what I mean. It's a little tricky but fine if you can stand the pain. Give me the knife and be ready to pull it out when I tell you so that I can stop the blood at once. Do you want to stab me yourself?" "No indeed I do not." By this time there were no jokes and everyone was tense. Flett took the knife and stuck it hard in his calf with a loud crack and yell that he had struck the bone, would someone pull it out. Nobody would. Instead they rushed to the door in case they got the blame for stabbing him.

One man did put his head in the door and when he saw Flett struggling with the knife, now hidden to the hilt, he said in alarm, "I'll go and get the shore doctor at once." "No you don't, I promise it will be alright in the morning." With this he was content to tell his mates that Flett was in no danger of bleeding to death. Before they had time to come back he had the knife out and a scarf wrapped round his leg. When they did, all spoke sympathetically and hoped it would not fester. Flett was doing his best to keep a straight face and when he came to turn in he was concerned about the hammock. It would look odd to lie there with one shoe on. He knew all eyes were on him and when he removed one shoe and vaulted on top of the hammock, he took off one trouser leg and the other followed with the wooden leg clattering on the floor. Everyone was in awe of the stump below the knee and one of them in haste said, "He has cut it off." There was much laughter at the way he played on them. He told them everything and was accepted as one of them and given much help when in need of it. He served eighteen months on that trawler.

Bernard Oppenheimer

From Wikipedia, the free encyclopedia

Sir Bernard Oppenheimer, 1st Baronet (13 February 1866–13 June 1921) was a South African-British diamond merchant and philanthropist.

Oppenheimer was chairman of Pniel's Ltd, the New Vaal River Diamond & Exploration Company, and Blaauwbosch Diamonds Ltd, and managing director of Lewis & Marks Ltd of Holborn. His brother, Sir Ernest Oppenheimer, was also heavily involved in the diamond industry.

In July 1917, Oppenheimer established a scheme for training disabled soldiers in diamond cutting at Brighton, England. The Bernard Oppenheimer Diamond Works (National Diamond Factories Ltd) opened on Lewes Road on 1 April 1918. It was mainly paid for by Oppenheimer himself and by Lewis & Marks. In 1920 it also opened branches in Cambridge, Wrexham and Fort William. By 1921 the works employed about 2,000 men who were referred to it by the Ministry of Labour. New men received six months training, during which they were paid a maintenance allowance by the government, and were then virtually guaranteed employment at a good wage. The factory had a well-equipped clinic to provide ongoing care for the employees, many of whom were amputees or otherwise severely disabled. The business did not do well and closed in 1923, but reopened later the same year. It finally went into receivership in 1924.

For his work with the disabled, Oppenheimer was created a baronet in the 1921 New Year Honours. He died suddenly six months later at the age of 55.

References

- Obituary, *The Times*, 14 June 1921

External links

- Old Diamond Works, Brighton (http://www.mybrightonandhove.org.uk/page_id_5954.aspx)

Baronetage of the United Kingdom		
Preceded by **New creation**	**Baronet** (of Stoke Poges) 1921	Succeeded by **Michael Oppenheimer**

Retrieved from "http://en.wikipedia.org/w/index.php?title=Bernard_Oppenheimer&oldid=618300664"

Categories: 1866 births | 1921 deaths | Diamond | British Jews | British businesspeople | British philanthropists | South African Jews | South African businesspeople | South African philanthropists | Baronets in the Baronetage of the United Kingdom | Oppenheimer family | African business biography stubs | South African people stubs

His pension from the army and his pay as Able Seaman amounted to more than the skipper was getting. Twice he failed to attend a medical board but at last they traced him and he had to leave the ship. He showed me his discharge. He was a strong good looking man with rosy cheeks and laughing, sparkling eyes, and full of humour. When he lay on his back on the floor stretched out, hands palms up with my twelve stone odd standing on them, he would raise me up with ease to his arms length many times without a break, not an easy feat.

Life was very pleasant in Fort William in those days, long before it was industrialised by the Hydro scheme. There was only one small farmhouse between the Nevis Bridge and the Canal at Inverlochy. Almost all the people in the town knew each other and it was a habit for every male to nod and raise his hat or doff his cap to every female that passed him, and they in turn would nod and smile. Most of the time, males also showed that consideration to one another, it engendered friendship. I learned that it was the diamond cutters that started the habit, and before we left it was the accepted thing. Many years after that, I had an occasion to pass through that town. There were only a few landmarks left that I knew, and when I asked an old man if the nice custom of raising hats and caps was still in use, he said it died long ago.

Flett and I went on long walks up the glen and as far up Ben Nevis as he could manage, beautiful scenery all round that one never got tired of. I did go up to the top of the Ben once with three other able bodies. After a rest and playing in the July snow, we began the descent, skylarking and rolling stones. Dodging these was dangerous but fun. I have known two of our boys going to the top with both legs off at the hip, using their artificial legs. We had an Irishman who wanted to see the sun rise from the top. One day after the pubs closed, he started off alone with a bottle of whisky. He climbed Cow Hill and descended to the glen in the dark. When he came to the cemetery he went in and rested with his back to a tombstone and had a long refreshing drink which led to another and by the time the third was taking effect, he was dozing off to sleep, which he did stretched on the grave. When he woke, shivering, the sun was up so he decided there no point in going further. When asked afterwards if he had slept well, he said, "I have never slept better in my life. You see, I was full of spirit and there were spirits all round me."

During this time I was making good progress in my training. I had received a rise in wages for accuracy and a bonus for output. With growing confidence, my trips to the instructor were growing less till at last I was entrusted to finish the part I would be working on totally on my own. No longer was I afraid that I would spoil the stone through being careless. I began to dream of the future as a diamond cutter and the riches that were in store for me, how I would see to it that my father got a new boat, that I would build a new house for him with the money earned. It did not seem unreasonable but there would be a few years before that could happen.

Fishing was then very good for sport on Loch Linnhe. The water was clean, the grounds good and the weather was suitable. We hired a small boat and those fit and keen spent enjoyable evenings there and nearly always took back a good catch of codlings and whiting. These were given away on the shore. Once we persuaded the cook to prepare them for us. People wanted them done in so many different ways that the cook in anger boiled the lot, saying she would have no more to do with it. After that, those on the shore got it all. With my knowledge of boats, I was always put in charge and when taking the legless on board for a sail one had to be careful.

One day there were five of us in the boat, three on crutches without their own legs, and another chap on one leg, so we promised the boat hirer that we would stay within sight.

After pointing out how easy it was to capsize the small boat, we set off as far as the beautiful small islands opposite Corpach. The village looked very enticing because it was a warm day and the pubs were open. After taking all aspects into consideration, we decided that two drinks would be the safe limit as the tide was high. I got the boat alongside the pier and tied it tight, the legless grabbing the pier and being helped, crawled ashore. The next task was to get them up on the crutches. I then moored the boat and we made for the pub with me hoping they would keep to the two drams. Only one broke that pledge. We did not stay long and I cannot say I enjoyed it.

When we returned to the boat, I got her alongside and made her fast as before and began loading, which was trickier I think on account of the whisky. I got them all but one on board and this one had taken extra and wanted to show he could do it without any help and before I could stop him, he leaped on his crutches into the boat and landed on her planking, his crutches going through as far as they could go. The sea began gushing in fast. Two began to panic and I managed to lift them ashore first. The other was heavy and I had to get a rope round him, pulling and pushing until we got him ashore safely. The last man with the one leg was of much help and got ashore on his own.

Crutches were passed ashore except the pair still stuck through her bottom and when I pried these out, the boat was nearly water logged. I was the only one that got wet when pulling her to a nearby slip. We saw a motor launch coming our way and knew it was the owner. He gave us a row first for coming so far, then asked what happened to the boat. The one who did the damage owned up and said he was standing in the boat on his crutches and they went through the wood. He said nothing about the leap. The boatman said he did not think the wood was that rotten. I helped to get her on the slip and when the water ran out and he examined her, we asked how much he charged for the damage. He said 30 shillings would cover it. We thought it cheap and paid him. He did not offer to take us back in his boat. For that we had to hire a car which cost us more than the repairs and when the story got around, I was not allowed to take out anyone on crutches.

Flett and I, alone in our room at night, usually after hoisting a few in the Ben Nevis talked much about religion, a subject neither of us knew much about, only that he was a Protestant and I a Catholic. We respected each other's beliefs, no arguments; he also told me he was a Thirty Second Degree Mason, a society I did not know anything about, only that I heard it was against the Catholic Church and what it taught. Nevertheless I did not find anything disagreeable in work or deed in Flett's company, and when he asked me if I thought that Catholics were better than Protestants I said, "If you look at it on the religious side everyone is bound to stand by his own beliefs. On the material side, take the man as you find him. You can never tell who your enemy is in your hour of need and the same holds true with your friends, be they Catholics or Protestants."

When the day of the Oban Games came round, we were given a day off and many went by boat; Flett and I did the same. It was a very enjoyable run down to Oban on that windless sunny day. Flett said, "You better get the tickets" as it was not easy for him to manage the stairway. He gave me his money and I got both our tickets and gave him his. We got to Oban. The first port of call was the first pub and then we continued sampling them as we went towards the games. Before we reached them, many were making heavy weather of it, especially those on crutches, and when we did arrive, the games were performing the last event. We began our trek back to the boat, hoping we would catch her, and fortunately by then the pubs were closed. We heard the ship's whistle and when we came in sight we saw them preparing to let go her ropes. The captain on the bridge must have seen us and delayed the order to let go, as those on crutches needed the help of the crew up the gangway. We got back without anyone being hurt or charged.

Preparing to leave the ship I discovered that I had lost my return ticket. I told Flett this fact and he said, "Stay to the last, he will let you through when all passengers have been passed." I approached the officer and told him that I had lost my return ticket, "All right" he said, "get another one from the purser." "Do I have to pay for it?" I argued that I had already paid for my return ticket and refused to pay again. Flett was standing at the bottom of the gangway laughing. He walked up and looked at the officer and then at me saying "Come on Donald, the Ben Nevis is open now." I looked at the officer who, without a smile said, "Off you go." On the pier I said, "You must know that man well John." "No I never met him." "How then were you able to get me ashore without paying a second time, a thing I could not do myself?" "Well Donald, I have already told you that I am a free mason and after giving the officer a certain sign, I knew he was one. I vouched for you and he accepted that." That is the one and only time that free masonry did anything for me.

John consumed a large amount of whisky without showing the effects and when I taxed him for spending so much, he said he could spend it and that it was not his wages. I challenged him saying, "I think you must be very rich then." "No, not very rich but I have some which I got fairly easy. You remember when the German navy was scuttled in Scapa Flow? Well I was at home then. I could see them from our house and when all the personnel cleared off, there was no watch kept on them, some bottoms up, some sunk, some water logged, some with their superstructure showing at low tide. Another lad and I, with a small boat in the moonlight, boarded where we could and removed much brass, copper, lead and any other valuable gear we could handle, caged it inland to be stowed in herring barrels for shipping to Glasgow where we had a broker that would take anything we could send him. It took the Receiver of Wrecks a good while to wake up and some were caught and imprisoned while plundering at night. When things got too hot, we stopped sending away. Some is still buried deep in peat bogs, although what was taken out was nothing compared with what was left."

"Well John" I said "I don't now feel guilty in enjoying the fruits of your plundering, I certainly don't look upon it as stealing" to which he replied, "I never gave it a thought." There seemed to be something else bothering John but what it was I had no way of knowing and if he chose to tell me that was up to him, I would respect in confidence his secret. It happened one night over a quiet drink in the room. John said, "Were you long in the war Donald?" "Yes, almost from the start to finish, with spells in hospitals, why?" "Have you been in many battles?" "Yes, more than I care to remember, why?" "In these battles were there any incidents that you don't want to remember but keep coming back as if accusing you?" "No John, when the war ended, I wiped the slate of that memory clean, and if something persists, I take comfort in the true saying 'kill or be killed'. "Kill or be killed" he said and repeated it.

After a while he said, "That's what I had to do." I said, "There's nothing strange about that you know, we were all doing it." "Yes, but this man was my own pal at the battle of Loos in 1915. We were in a shell hole in no man's land, very near the Germans. He was badly wounded and shell-shocked. There was nothing I could do for him, he went raving mad dying from loss of blood and his raving brought a machine gun on us. I had to kill him and shortly after that I got

120

this leg off and had to stay with him till a stretcher bearer found me in the dark." "That was" I said "another example of 'kill or be killed'" "Yes, but what if I had waited until he had died." I said "It might have been yourself before then." I don't know if it was on account of our long talk that I detected more brightness in John. Anyway the subject was never brought up again.

The working hours in the small factory were from 9.00 am to 4.00 pm with one hour for dinner in a dining hall. If people thought that pilfering was going on, there was none, each being responsible for his own diamonds and time. Often when a stone leaped out of its cup, all work ceased and everyone began looking, some sweeping the floor, till it was found. Only one stone went missing all the time we were there. It was a valuable, nearly finished stone, and I heard that while they were dismantling the building, a workman found it on a beam. There was no suspicion regarding the man who was working on it. Christmas was drawing near, there was talk that production was to be cut and that before long we would be on a three-day week. The reason they gave was that the Russians had flooded the market with diamonds stolen and commandeered from the Tsar and other states during the time of the Revolution and were selling them at less than cost price. De Beers, who held the bulk of the world's raw diamonds, stopped cutting them in order to keep the price up.

As time went on it was becoming more apparent that before long the factory would be closing down. John said to me "What shall we do?" "I think" said I "that I will go to sea, that is, unless something comes of what the old American was telling me." "Have you heard from him since he went to the Hebrides?" "No, he called on his way back, I was not in. He left me a message saying he would write me on his arrival and arrange everything if I was still willing to go. I have not heard from him. I am wondering if he was genuine or not." I met this old American gentleman one day sitting on a bench near the Hostel. He was tall and well dressed in clothing not of this country's make. I sat near him. Turning to me he said, "Have you got the Gaelic?" I said, "Yes, more than English." "That's good, mine's not so good but I understand it. Well, I am here on a little business on my way to the Hebrides to an island near Benbecula called Flodda." I said that I was from South Uist and that I was working here. He said, "I have been nearly all my life in the southern States of America, and am back to trace any relations alive there. The name is MacDermot and the family went to the Carolinas and settled there a long time ago. Thanks to the Free Church we had some education and we prospered. I had two brothers, one became a banker and finally owned it, the other was a famous doctor and I, with less education, took to ranching. The banker and the doctor died during the 1914 war. None of us married and both left a lot of money to which I want to add some of my own. That is why I am trying to trace any relations that I may have. Better them getting a good share than Uncle Sam taking it all.

"My business here is with the manager of the diamond works. Many valuable stones like diamonds have been found on one of my ranches and I want first-hand information about them. I have discovered that the diamond cutters are not working today" and when I said, "No we are not" he asked, "Are you one of them?" "Yes, I work there." "On real diamonds?" "Yes, I've been training here for the last two years." He said, "Then you will know something about a diamond." "Yes I can make that claim." "I have here some of the stones that I am going to show to your manager, perhaps you would like to look at them." "Yes I would but I can't be the judge, I have no magnifying glass on me and the mill to test them for hardness." I had a look and they appeared nice but there was much hidden that without a glass, I could not make out and I doubted that they would stand the speed our mills were running. I told him what I thought and added, "If they are not suitable for our gear, the manager may know some other place where they can be polished."

Next morning at 11.00 am, with the manager, he came in. They made for my bench. The boss said, "Can I have your mill MacDonald? I want to do a little testing." I got up and stood by. The instructor Garland came over and began testing first with his glass to locate the grain. There was no problem in what direction it would cut but when it came in contact with the speeding mill, it began to slowly melt, and regardless of efforts, refused to take on any polish. It was plain to see our gear was too fast for it. Further tests were not necessary.

The manager took old MacDermot aside and talked to him for a while. Afterwards the old man came over to me and said he would like to see me again, tomorrow at his hotel if I was free, and named the time. I kept that appointment and when seated, I said that I was sorry for his disappointment. He said, "That's alright, all is not lost yet. I had a long talk with the manager who told me these stones could be worked on leather into a very attractive stone that would command a good market. I wanted to talk to you to find out if you would be interested in joining me in America to work on these stones if this place closes down, as I hear it is going to do." I said that it would be a good opportunity but that I was not a qualified cutter yet and had another year's training to do. He said, "I talked to the manager about you and he thinks you have enough for the work required on that kind of stone." I said, "I don't have the amount of money to pay you for my fare and expenses for such a long journey." He said, "If I did decide, you would not have to pay a cent, everything will be taken care of, I am not asking you to answer today. I will call on you on my way back in a week or ten days".

"When he did call I was not in and would not be that day, and all I know, John, is what I have already told you. Sometimes I wonder if he was pulling my leg." John said he didn't look the kind to him and that I may hear from him yet. I did not and it was seventeen years later that I was to learn why. Regardless of my efforts, it came about in an unexpected way. Not very long after I had met MacDermot, I was at home and had to attend a Medical Board in Inverness. On the boat I met a strapping young man going to join the Police Force in Inverness. He was from the Benbecula area. It was over seventeen years later that I was to meet him again at Lochboisdale as a Sergeant stationed there. In the conversation I asked if he remembered about the time he joined the force of a man, an American named MacDermot, and old man, looking for relations on the Island of Flodda. After a moment he said, "Yes, I was talking to him, he was a nice man. He managed to trace one old woman who was distantly related to him. He was supposed to have given her a lot of money with more to come but sadly he died on the ship two days before it arrived at New York and was buried at sea, why? Did you know him?" I said yes and told him the whole story. To that he said, "If things had gone as the old man thought, then you would be well off today instead of fishing lobsters." Well at least I am glad that he was what he had led me to believe and not a fake. At that moment I wished I had a way to tell John the reason I did not hear from that old gentleman.

Once when staying with a friend in Detroit, he told me he was getting engaged and that he and his girlfriend had selected a beautiful diamond ring. I congratulated him and asked, "Do you know much about these rings?" He said, "No, not a thing, but this one really looks nice. Helen is delighted and I think longing to see it on her finger. The man behind the counter told me it was a perfect stone and he could not keep it for more than two days for me. I am paying for it tonight. We are having a small party, you are invited and hope you will join us." I said, "I would like to but first I would like to see that perfect stone of yours before you pay for it, in case you have been taken to the cleaners." He said, "Do you know something about them?" I said that I had worked and did some training in that line and if he did not believe me I had my reference in my case to prove it. He asked, "Then will you come with me to have a look at it?" I did and brought my own glass.

He introduced me as his friend and said he wanted me to look at the stone he intended to buy. "Of course he can, it is a beautiful perfect stone and I recommend it as such." He handed me the stone but not the glass. I said, "Can I have your glass?" He said, "Yes if it will help you." I put them both to my eye and saw much that I did not like. I took out my own glass and saw more. I said, "Do you claim this stone to be perfect" "Yes I do, I examined it myself." "Then you must be blind, as you don't know what you are talking about." "What" he said "Are you calling me a liar?" I said "No, but the stone is poor workmanship. It is anything but perfect. It has a knot in the centre that would render it less than a third class gem and as such, can only have a very low value."

He got really angry and in turn called me a liar and that I was interfering with his business and he was going to call the police and have me arrested. I said, "Go ahead. I can prove that I know what I am talking about and if arrested, the police will be obliged to hold that stone for evidence that will prove my statement. Besides, you will have to answer to the case of you misrepresenting this stone as perfect. Consider that and do as you like." He then said, "I may have been conned about this stone. I bought it in good faith. I admit I don't know everything about diamonds and you appear to know more otherwise you would not go this far. Choose another stone for your friend and I will put a price on it." "I will, if he wants to, but remember, I am also knowledgeable about prices". I did pick one a shade smaller with more brilliance, and much cheaper. My friend and his love were well pleased. This happened long after I had left Fort William.

Towards the end of my stay there I went home for the Christmas holidays. My return fare was paid. Arriving at Mallaig at noon, I put my kit on board the steamer. She was leaving at 1 pm going via the north route, Kyle and Harris. It was a long route and would be midnight before she could make Lochboisdale and it was Christmas Eve. To pass my time in Mallaig, I went to the hotel for a beer. There were only two fishermen in the bar so when I ordered my beer, I asked what they would like to drink. The older one said, "I know your father well. What are you doing here?" When I told him he said I should go with them, they were going straight to Lochboisdale and leaving soon. The skipper was Angus MacKinnon, nicknamed 'Stormer' because of his daring manner, the other was his son Neil, and the boat was called 'Virgin'. We left on full sail intending to be in Lochboisdale in less than seven hours.

Although two small engines powered her, one was out of order and under repair by the engineer. Masts and sails in such boats at that time were cut down by two reefs and by the time we passed the Point of Sleat, the wind was up to gale force and we had to take in a reef. It was evident that we would have to put in at Canna and when we made the sheltered harbour of that island, the wind appeared to have calmed to a light breeze. We made tea. There was another boat at anchor ahead of us. She was the *St. Patrick* going home like us. She was longer but had no engine. After tea, they decided while there was still daylight to try again. We passed the headland about a mile into the Minch. The sea was very rough and we were taking in so much water, the pump could not cope with it. The skipper said he was turning back and to get ready to lower the sail and take the other reefs in and soon we were back in the harbour again as was the 'St Patrick'.

The fishing boats in those days did not have a wheelhouse and so there was no shelter from wind and spray for the man at the helm. In the cabin we had a substantial meal, after which the sail was got ready, the anchor was heaved in and we were on our way again. The other boat was following and soon passed us because she was in better trim and had a larger sail; there was plenty of wind and no propellers to hold her back. Leaving the headland behind, we knew the wind had gone down some but the sail was kept at three reefs. The moon was climbing steadily behind us, casting its shimmering light in the troubled sea and we were nearing mid-way when the wind went down to nothing and darkness fell. A solid greenish-blue wall appeared to windward and was fast approaching. With the small engine Angus headed the *Virgin* into it, at the same time he ordered the crew to stand by the sail and let go when he told them. We were not long kept in suspense when the blast hit us before they had time to let go. Over her beam end she went, gunnel well under but   fortunately for us the sail was torn off her and she came up to near even keel. Our peril was far from being over. The small engine was powerless to keep her head into the wind and on her beam end again, one of the forty-gallon paraffin drums that was lashed down in the hold broke loose, threatening to stave in her timbers with every roll. Although I could not stand to give them a hand on deck, I was very useful in the hold, fighting with the loose drum, which I managed to lash down.

With his superb seamanship, Angus managed to get her stern into the wind, Neil having crawled out with a piece of rope and lashed his father to the seat he was on. The first wave that came over him was not so bad and he just shook his head and the sea from his eyes. I had a bottle of whisky in my case and thought he could do with a good dram. I crawled to him and asked if he would take one. "No, no" he said, "I won't touch it, it's too dangerous." The sea frequently splashing over the stern was covering Angus.

It was obvious that running for Skye was impossible. The engineer all this time was doing his best to bring the dead engine to life when suddenly it started and kept going sweetly. Again with the old man's expert handling, her head was brought up. With the two engines, she was making good progress, and when we passed Calvay lighthouse, I knew they were not calling at Lochboisdale but heading for Eriskay. I did not care as I was never ashore in Eriskay and it would be another adventure. When we arrived in the harbour in bright moonlight, the *St. Patrick* was there at the harbour. Her crew had already left for home. The islanders saw us coming in when far off in the moonlight and were relieved we got back safely. Donald invited me to stay the night as they had plenty of room. We all went to midnight mass and on our return there was a large feast waiting, more than plenty of everything including whisky. We all slept soundly that night.

After saying goodbye to the household and thanking them I caught the post boat to South Uist. The boatman had one other passenger who had wired a chap called Harris to meet her at Polochar. Harris was an Englishman. He had an old model T Sedan and as it was almost the only car in the district he was often in demand for his services. The roads were very bad, untarred and full of potholes. The result was very hard on the tyres and when they split open, they were packed tight with old hay or heather. Heather was best because of its buoyancy and was plentiful and near the road.

124

When we got to Locheynort I put the heavy suitcase on my back and hoofed the three miles home. Coming in view of the house, I saw someone standing outside. I was a hundred yards away when my sister ran towards me and threw her arms around my sweaty neck and kissed me fondly, saying "We thought all the time it was the packman Murphy or we would have met you long ago." Murphy was an old Irish worthy who came round with his pack as long as I can remember, selling his wares, safety pins, needles, combs, clay pipes, ribbons, scissors, sometimes small clocks and other small items. If money was short, as it generally was, he would take rabbit skins in exchange, always saying there was not much demand for them. Between them and the cup of tea he was sure to get, he would never be out of pocket even if we thought he had done us. His Irish jokes more than made up for the loss. We had a very enjoyable Christmas and New Year, well worth all the discomfort I had to endure on the passage from Mallaig. It was to be our last together.

CPR LINER The Metagama

When I got back to Fort William we were still on three days with no further prospects, just waiting for the end that we felt would soon come. With that in mind, John asked me one day would I like to go to America. I said, "Fine, what part?" "Any part, let's write to the American Consul in Glasgow for an application form to emigrate." We did. I said, "I haven't enough to pay for the passage." "That won't keep you back, I'll pay for your passage and keep you until we are in work."

We were waiting for a reply and dreaming of life in America when it came. It was a disappointing moment for in the form it said, "Under no condition will limbless ex-service men or women be admitted to the United States." I said to John, "You can't bluff them this time." "No, but if you want to go, I will still pay your passage and give you some money besides. You can pay me back when you become very rich." "No, I won't go now, let's make an application for Australia." We did and before we left Fort William, his came through, mine did not. I was at home before I got it and when I did, my mind was set on a westward journey.

A few weeks later, the manager told us the factory was closing down and since I had another month to go, for that part of my training, I could go to Brighton to finish it, and then I would be discharged. That was no consolation and I told him I would rather leave with the rest.

He gave me a good enough reference, it said, "The bearer, D.MacDonald, has trained in diamond cutting with this firm and afterwards was employed as a diamond cutter. During this time, we found him honest, sober and a skilful craftsman. We feel sure that in whatever category, he will be entirely trustworthy. He leaves on the closing of this branch. Signed H.E.White, Manager."

In the spring of 1922 I said goodbye to John and the rest of the boys. John was making for Glasgow, I for home without any prospects in view. I think I was there over a month when an agent for the Canadian Pacific Railway arrived on the island. He showed us pictures and, lecturing on life on the Canadian farms, he was looking for immigrants to enrol. Everywhere on the slides looked pretty, and easy to live there, and there was a free passage and a well paid job waiting. His name was Macdonell, an ex-Canadian war chaplain with the Military Cross. I liked him, many did not, as he did not keep his promise to some who found they were stranded in Alberta. He claimed that the C.P.R. did not keep their bargain. I went to one of his meetings and decided to emigrate. I also wrote to John to inform him of that decision. When he replied, he was in a job in Glasgow and that was the last I heard of him.

Understandably, there was much talk about who was going to emigrate. Was all Macdonell said true and what would life be like over there? If there was a map of that part of the world available, it was well read, concluding that it was a very large country and the expanse of sea between us was also huge. At home they were much against me going, saying they would never see me again, to which I would reply "I will send for you all when I make my fortune." That seemed to give them some hope. Only five of us enlisted at that time. One drew back at the last moment. The rush came next year when there was full-scale emigration. The four of us left in mid-April to Glasgow where we joined the C.P.R. liner *Metagama*. We called at Liverpool where she took on more emigrants. Judging by their suitcases and attire, they were no better off than we were.

The passage across the Atlantic was fairly smooth. There was plenty of entertainment helping to lessen the sadness of our recent parting. The food was good, a big change from the too often potatoes and herring that we had left behind. We were assigned to the same table in three relays. Ours was the second relay. The four of us sat at the same table, always talking in Gaelic, confusing the steward who would look annoyed, knowing or thinking the talk was referring to him. Most of it was. Every day a sweepstake was drawn by a steward on the westward progress of the ship, tickets one shilling. There would be three good prizes. We never won any of them. Also there was a second-class bar where we went but not often, unconvinced that money was easy to get once ashore.

It gradually became colder as we neared the Newfoundland banks, with a thick cold fog which often slowed down the ship. Once she was stopped for nearly a day with extra look-outs, and the fog horn blaring at an ear splitting level, not only to protect us from the danger of other ships, but also from icebergs of which we saw plenty when the fog cleared. Radar was not yet invented and when one of these large ones appeared in the ship's path, the ship would steer close for the benefit of the passengers in daytime. We often saw large bears swimming ashore, I expect catching a free ride to better fishing grounds. We were nearing the mouth of the St. Lawrence River and had not seen another ship in many days. We wondered if our delay in the fog would prevent the captain from receiving the silk hat, which he would get if his ship was the first to enter the Port of Quebec that year. It's a longstanding custom from the time of the sailing ships.

My first memory of the name St. Lawrence River was from old Roderick Macleod in 1912. He was then approaching eighty and was in sailing ships all his working days. I used to swallow every word he said of his adventures. Once he told us that he was on a three-masted, square-rigged barque from Greenock, going to Quebec. They had gales most of the voyage across and the food was running out but they had plenty of fresh water. The food was cut down after a month at sea before they were halfway across, but they ran into calm windless weather and with no rain showers to fill their casks, water was also cut down. They drifted back with the current for nearly a week, when a headwind storm broke out. They could only run before it and before they had the sails off, many had been torn to ribbons. With what sails that still held, they got her head to the wind and began tacking.

It took them three weeks to gain what they had lost and they caught no rain in that time so food and water was again cut. At last the wind slackened and changed direction. They put more sail on her and would have put more on but the crew was too weak to bend and hoist them. As it was they had already lost three men overboard because they were too weak to hold on. In the storm, their navigation instruments were smashed, leaving them with only a vague idea of where they were. Although the master was a good seaman, he had nothing to guide him in fog and starless nights and was only keeping going by guesswork. Their last stock of food was down to a small basket of potatoes. The last drop of water was issued the day before, with a stern warning from the captain not to drink seawater or they would go raving mad. Anyone going like that would have to be tied up and as no one could be spared to take care of them, they would have to be put over the side.

In the morning, the ablest amongst them managed to climb the mast to the crow's nest. He was only a short time there when he saw a sail on the skyline and sang out with this welcome news that was greeted with cheers. "Keep your eyes on her and sing out every minute." After a while he made out she was making towards them with the fresh wind on their beam. In an hour they would be near the passing point. The watchers were called in to get the ship ready to hove to and run up the distress signal. The other vessel saw them and the lookout had reported seeing her throwing more sails on when she evidently saw the distress signal. In a short time she was on them and moved to within hailing distance using her megaphone "Ship ahoy, what is your trouble?" "Starvation and lack of fresh water. We have been on short rations for a month, our fresh water ran out yesterday. We are not sure of our position, can you help?" "Yes, glad to. We will send the small boat over with provisions. You can help yourselves to fresh water. There is plenty of it around you." No sooner said, a bucket went over hauling up the life preserving precious liquid. The captain was given his position with the offer of a good sextant if he needed it. "If this wind holds up, you should make landfall tomorrow." They thanked them warmly and both ships were on course. I think all of them had been up that river before but the error nearly cost them their lives and happened not through any fault of their captain, but by bad weather and faulty navigational instruments. It took them over two months to cross over. It is well known now that fresh water in the St. Lawrence River flows far out to sea, not so then. I asked if anyone was put over board and he said no, but that many were ill by drinking too much water at once.

After our long voyage we docked in Quebec, and preparations for disembarking began. The *Metagama* did not earn the coveted silk hat for her Captain. We were told there would be a short medical inspection and another one ashore both of which took place without any problems. We disembarked and were warmly welcomed by Mr Macdonell. He took us to the train and had a trolley of sandwiches and coffee taken to us. After a while he came into our carriage and told us that he had found a place for each of us with farmers near Chatham, Ontario. The farmers, on account of having not sold all their wheat, were obliged to lower the wages. The best he could get out of them was $30.00 a month, board and laundry and that, he said, is better than wages in the old country. We had to be content with that. He said "I am taking you today as far as Toronto where the four of you will stay overnight with a native of South Uist, a John Mackay." At the end of the long journey, we were made welcome in real Highland style. The house was crowded with people, all keen to hear news of their people and the old country, as they called it. John came to Canada many years before and now had a general store of his own, and was prospering.

In the morning we left for Chatham, a fairly large town. We were taken to the town hall to meet our masters, the farmers, to whom Macdonell had already engaged some of us over the phone. The rest were hired at $30.00 a month, I expected that included me. In the buggy we rode the eight miles to Wilson's place and he was at the gate to meet us. We all got out of the buggy and Wilson looked at us and said, "Which one is mine?" Before anyone could say anything, he said, "I'll take him" pointing to Donald MacInnes who was about three inches taller than me at five foot, nine. The other farmer said, "You can't have him, he is already hired to me" to which Wilson replied, "I'll swap." "No you don't." Donald spoke up, "You are getting the best bargain." "I don't think so" said Wilson, "You come from a small country compared to Canada." "Small in that sense, "Donald replied "It is much larger than Canada in culture and knowledge. Canada is still in the dark ages in comparison." Seeing that he was not gaining anything, Wilson said, turning to me, "Well come into the house anyway." I felt it was not a friendly welcome. He introduced me to his wife and daughter, and the lady of the house asked if I cared for a wash before my meal. I said I would and was shown to my room where I had a wash.

The table was set when I came down the stairs; Wilson began saying grace, I with the sign of the cross said mine in silence. The meal was good and plentiful, eaten in silence. When finished the farmer said, "Do you know much about farming? I was not there when the hiring was done. I wanted a man with plenty of experience in farming. Have you been doing this kind of work before?" I said, "No, I don't know much about big farms." "What other work did you do?" When I said fishing I thought I saw a change in his face. He only said that they don't have much in common. "As you don't seem to know the work, what wages are you asking me to pay to teach you?" "All the rest have been hired out at $30.00 a month and I expect to get the same." "I cannot pay you that amount. I would be wasting a lot of my time showing you what to do." I said "I don't think I will take long to learn." He said, "I have been at it all my life, I am still learning."

Further talk was, I thought, useless. I got up without excusing myself and went for my bags. They were still at the table when I came down with them. Wilson said, "Where are you going?" "It is evident I am not wanted here. Canada being as vast as what you have said, surely I can find work somewhere." "Sit down, and let's talk this thing over." I did because I was dog tired, due to the change of climate. He said, "I did not hire you but since you are here, I'll agree to take you for a week on trial. At the end of the week if I find I can use you, I'll keep you."

Donald and his pals on the farm

130

I thought it over and decided to stay on condition that he would pay me for that week at the rate of $30.00 a month and if he decided to keep me further, it will be at the same rate. After a pause, he said, "Alright, have it your own way." I took my bags to the room and, although there was plenty of daylight, I did not leave the room, as I was tired and disillusioned. Never before had I been employed on trial. I wondered if that was common practice in Canada, but my immediate need was to enquire where the bathroom was. Before going down, for no reason in particular, I happened to look under the bed. I was surprised to see a chamber pot there.

I went downstairs and asked Mrs. Wilson where the bathroom was. She said, "We have not got one in the house, we are getting one in the fall. The out-house." she said with a smile "is round the corner of the house." I remembered it was the first smile given to me since I had arrived. I found the out-house to discover there was no running water and the only improvement from our way of such things was the catalogue hanging behind the door. A long way to go before the scented toilet paper would arrive.

Going back to the house I met Wilson who said, "I am sending some cattle to the market tomorrow morning Donald, I want you to help." There was no more said. I expect he thought he was getting the worst of the bargain. At six o'clock I was awakened by a loud knock on the door. Bob and the other two had already gone to gather the cattle for shipping. I put on my working clothes and came down the stairs, Mrs Wilson gave me a pair of gumboots and told me to keep them clean.

Donald came and handed me a stout stick saying, "Use this when you have to." He must have thought me very stupid if I did not know that much. The other two hired men were at the pens waiting. By way of introduction he said, "Meet Donald, the Scotsman. These are my two men Frank and George". Already they had the loading ramp against the rail wagon. Each took his place to drive the cattle in. I was given the least important task. George was to drive the steer up the ramp hoping the rest would follow. When he had it nearly in, it turned on him. I could see that George was giving way and in danger. I rushed in to help him getting hold of its tail and putting in many twists and managed to hold and turn it, not sparing the stick. I told George to get out of the way. He did quite gladly I think, but held that against me saying he could manage himself. The rest knew better and said so. From that day on George never missed an opportunity to deride me and he had plenty of those. The loading was done and finished in less time than they used to take. I thought I made a good impression for a start.

The next job before breakfast was repairing a snake fence, all new to me. They had nothing to do with snakes, only the name because it was erected in a zigzag line. It was all made of timber split into ten-foot long pieces, held erect by posts driven into the ground supported by lean-to stakes at every angle. It was very strong and very wasteful of land and wood but when it was first used, there were plenty of both. That was long before the iron fence came into use. The trees that were cleared off the land to bring it into agricultural use were then split and made into these snake fences. They were easy to erect once you saw it done, and before long I could do it like the other two. George however found fault with my work although Frank said it was good. Frank was a French Canadian, I got on well with him, he was the leader on that farm. George was half Indian and Canadian. Later I found out that Wilson didn't trust him. He said, "He is a good enough worker, but if I am working in the fields, he can creep up behind me; that makes me jump. I just don't like his style."

131

Next day at breakfast, Wilson said that Frank was well pleased with the way I worked at the fence but George was not too happy. "Don't pay much attention to him, but he knows his work." When the meal was over, Mrs. Wilson said, "Bob, the windmill has stopped some time ago. There is not much pressure." This was how they got their water supply from the ground. Bob said he could not climb that high. I said I could. It only required a few knocks and grease. He was pleased to see that done.

They had only twelve cows to milk, which they both did. Surprisingly, I had never done it before. When I began, I was quite useless but kept at it until my wrists were numb. I used to roll a long piece of string tight around them. That helped, and in a week I was near as fast as the rest and then would leave them behind. The milk was put through the cream separator every day and that too was new to me. One morning, while Mrs Wilson was showing me all these new machines and praising their use, I was watching closely and wondering what to say. I said, thinking of my tired wrists "It's a wonder they have not yet invented a milking machine!"

"They have, we tried it, but it did not work. It was drawing blood and useless. Some day they may get it right. This," pointing to another gadget,, "is the churn. It is also fast and saves much labour, only needing the button pressed. I will show you the old one we have been using until recently. We will do the churning there today." She scalded it clean. It was a small barrel holding about five gallons resting on a trestle with a hand crank attached on one side, one end held fast by a latch. It tumbled end ways as you cranked. At home it was the plunger type and I sometimes gave my sisters a hand. On a small scale it took about twenty minutes. When I had it turning merrily, Mrs. Wilson said, "You can spin it as fast as you can Donald, the faster the better." I don't know if that was the reason why the latch worked itself loose. The end sprung open and the remaining cream and dollops of butter splashed over the cement floor. I was highly embarrassed. When she saw this, and looking at the mess, she only said, "It's no use crying over split milk, Donald." With anyone else I would be laughing. "We will mop it up and give it to the pigs. It's really my fault for not remembering the latch would be dry." The pigs got a good feed of it and very likely hoped the same thing would happen often. After the evening meal when Bob came home, the incident was not mentioned. I thought that was the end of it but it wasn't.

I had two days of my week's trial to go. After the meal I went to my room and wrote a letter home telling them I was well and working on a farm. I did not say I was on trial or they would think I had committed some terrible crime. I omitted putting a cloverleaf in the envelope as I promised an old man when I was saying farewell. The clover present was to be the sign to prove and believe that all of what the good priest said was indeed true about Canada. I could not in all honesty go along with it and so closed the letter without mentioning the leaf.

The next day Bob told me to harness a horse in the stable and hitch it to the roller and roll the field near Frank's house. By trial and error, I managed to get the harness to stay on its back. When I got to the field with the roller, Frank was there. He saw me coming and said, "Who harnessed that horse?" I said "I did, is there anything wrong with it?" "Yes, the only thing right is the collar, but the harness is upside down. I'll show you how to do it and hitch it to the roller." He did and showed me how to work it doing two rolls, telling me they had to be overlapping. I took over and thought it was easy, not paying much attention to Frank's instructions. When finished, even to me it did not look right. When the boss came round much later he condemned the lot and told me to go all over it again, this time crossways. He inspected it again and said it would do.

Next day I was at it again, did better and finished it. George and Frank were cutting the hay. I was told to take a look at a small field of potatoes he had planted before I came. I did and reported the plants were at least three inches above ground and that I thought they were doing very well. He was not satisfied and had a look himself. He said that they should be better than that, and to harness the grubber and rake them all out, the seed was not suitable for the heavy soil. He would go to town and get different seed and would be back before I had it all clean. I thought he had gone crazy, but a week after planting the new seed, I could see how right he was. It was virgin soil and required no manuring.

The two scares I got since arriving on the farm are maybe perhaps worth recording. The first on that roller. The day was clear and warm, but towards evening, it became hot and close. The sky darkened with a dark blue cloud creeping towards me. I stopped rolling and was going to try for the shelter at a nearby tree when it burst, reminding me of the Battle of the Somme, with its zigzag long tails of forked lightning, coming near me. The rain, or rather water pouring down, the likes of which I had never seen before, nor do I remember since. I wondered what the end would be, electrocution or drowning. I began to run, then thought of the poor horse tied to the roller. Strangely I thought of another horse caught by his shoes by telephone wire on a shell swept bridge in France. I turned back and released the frightened horse and led him down a lane to the barn come stable. The lane was flooded to many inches, and where the hot weather had split the soil deep in many places, the water came bubbling up when full. Before we reached the end, the lane was dry with much steam rising. My dungarees, shirt and sand shoes were also dry and hot, with not a cloud in the sky and a very hot sun. I thought of turning back to the roller and then remembered it was the last day of my trial on which nothing yet had been said. I continued to the stable and stalled the horse that had quietened down. I was rubbing him down when Wilson came in. "You got caught in that blast, Donald, you did well to take the horse in there, they get very nervous in heavy thunder. Seldom have I seen a worse cloud burst. "A fine day I have chosen to start on the hay." I said "I could see them cutting when I was in the lane, which they would not be doing if that burst of water came their way." Wilson said, "Well, it does sometimes happen like that. I have seen fields ready for harvesting, ruined by hailstones, while others were left untouched. You can take the horse back to the field as I think he is alright and then come in as it's past quitting time."

I did and washed and made sure to stow in a good meal as it might be my last one there. I went upstairs, packed and dressed in a going away suit, took my cases downstairs and stood. "Where do you think you're going, Donald?" said Bob. I said, "I am not sure, today is the end of my week's trial and I want to know whether I am to go or not." "Sit down, Donald, let's talk this over. I forgot that you are here a week. When I hired you I did not like the week's trial, I was forced to it on account of a countryman of yours. He was here for three days and made no attempt to work or lend a hand. I guessed you to be the same. Now I have seen what you are capable of, I want to hire you on 6 months terms at $30.00 a month. I will employ you all winter at a little less, if you stay. Are you satisfied here?" I said, "Yes, I am learning something every day, but I will not stay unless it's on monthly terms." "Well, we will leave it at that." He offered his hand to seal our bargain. He paid me for the week, my first pay in dollars. Like all foreign money, I did not think anything of it and left it on my dressing table, although I had a purse with still many pound notes in, which no one but the bank would accept. I took my bags upstairs the second time, wondering how long they would stay this time.

Next day I was put in charge of the pigs and their litters of which there were many. There were a number of them forever running about and I had difficulty counting them correctly. Wilson had his own grinding mill. I half filled a long trough of meal, mostly maize, milk and other stuff and fed them well. The piglets left their mothers towards the end of that week. He said he had not seen them looking so well. "Tomorrow I am going to the pig sale at Toronto. I want you to pick two of the best piglets, as we have to show them." I did and he got first and second prize. It was only luck, as I knew nothing about pig rearing. Before he left he told me to feed the boar that was locked in a shed beside the house. "Be sure and keep the bottom half of the door closed when feeding him. Take a nearly full basket of corn ears and throw them to him. He is fed every three days. I always feed him myself, you can do it now." I had not seen the beast before and only very few of its kind at a distance. I took his feed to the shed, which was about 14 foot long, 7 foot wide and 8 foot high. The door was in two halves, with strong hinges on both. I opened the top half and there he was, a huge beast on his side at the far end. I threw him an ear but it did not reach him and another went fairly close to his large head but he only looked at it. I thought he was sick but might eat out of my hand. Without considering what I was about to do, I opened the bottom half and went in, closed and bolted it, picked up an ear of corn and walked slowly towards him, the ear in my extended hand. Fortunately for me, his head was not facing me. Turning towards me and opening his mouth wide, he let out a loud grunt. It was time for me to get out if I could. The distance to the door was short but it was closed and bolted on the outside, and before I could open it, he could have easily had me. I felt that was his intention. In life one encounters moments, that even to oneself, one cannot explain how they are overcome.

In the short distance and time allotted to me to escape being eaten alive, I had to overcome the closed door with the angry boar on its feet and coming towards me fast. I put every ounce I had in me into a salmon leap. I cleared the bottom half and landed flat outside in the mud, the boar snuffling and grunting and trying to climb out. I was not hurt but badly shaken and dared not go near the door to close the top half. I made my way to the barn to arm myself with a pitch- fork and if I saw Wilson I would tell him what I thought of him for not telling me that beast was wild. I did not care what the consequence would be. However, I did not see him but met Frank coming up the lane. He looked at me and said, "What's wrong Donald, you look very pale, are you ill?" I told him what happened, he said, "Well, Donald, you were indeed foolish and crazy to do that and are lucky to get out alive as that animal is wild. He is tame with Bob as he has been feeding him since he was very young and thinks it should be the same with everyone. Never go inside that hut or trust him again." I returned to the shed with the pitchfork and tumbled the rest of his feed over the door and closed the top, take it or leave it.

When finished that chore, I made my way to the field where Frank and George were working, horse raking the hay, which they had cut 24 hours before. Frank showed me how to work the horse rake and when to pull the lever to drop the load in line with the rest. It was important to leave it in a straight line as the loader, when working, straddled it. The drill was connected to the loader also on wheels, by a chain from the rear hub of the wagon to the hub of the loader, which then travelled at the same speed. This chain had slightly bent forward prongs about a foot long and as they made contact with the hay, it was carried to the top where it fell into the wagon. A man with a pitchfork received and stowed it high, after which it was conveyed to the barn for storage. The large timber barn was about 80 ft. long and 40 ft. wide. It was built on stilts about 3 ft above the ground with two storeys. The animals were below and the hay above.

The barn was constructed with a rail running along and bolted to each top crossbeam. A small under trolley was held suspended from the groove in the rail, which extended to some 7 ft. past the open gable with a buffer to stop the trolley. An arm on the buffer when the trolley came into contact threw a lever that put a brake on the trolley. One end of a long strong rope was made fast to a fork assembly, the other was passed through sheaves or pulleys with the end being attached to the harness of a horse, and its job was to pull on the load till the trolley moved along the rail until tripped, when its load was tipped out and stored. I thought the thing was well rigged and labour saving.

Next day Wilson announced that the field was ready to be taken in and if everything went well we should be able to finish it that day. Everything did not go well. On the third load before reaching the trolley, the rope broke. The load fell back into the wagon and the other end of the rope sprang through the trolley before the drawing horse was stopped. Wilson said, "The rope was put in new last year and something must have chafed or cut it." He found that that part had been tampered with and partly cut. He thought a rat was responsible. "Now, I will have to buy a new rope." I said, "The rest of the rope may be sound. It could be spliced." George looked at me and said, "It could, but it would not pass through the pulleys." I said, "Are you sure?" "Of course I am sure, how do you expect a double rope to go through a pulley meant for a single? If you are thinking of putting a knot in it, you are very silly." I knew he was after a chance to make a fool of me. "Well" I said "if Mr. Wilson wants me, I can put that rope together in working order as there is a good length spare at the horse's end. If that is long enough, we can use it in place of the short broken part, if not I'll put in a splice that will go through the pulleys." We then brought the two broken ends of the rope together and I put in a fisherman's bend with whipping.

Now I said, "We will test the whole rope." "How?" George said. I said, "If you get some pieces of short heavy wood, or anything heavy that stays on the load while we hoist it, if it can take twice its weight, it should be a good test. Do you approve of that Mr. Wilson?" "Yes, Donald, I think that will be more than enough." I made the rope to the animal fast, they put the desired weight on the load and all was ready for the test. Bob was to lead the horse and I said "I'll raise my hand when you are to stop." We three stood clear, the horse took the strain and the load began to rise till I raised my hand and told him to back the horse slowly. We did that three times until everyone was satisfied, and then the load was lowered onto the wagon and the extra weight removed. Frank and George went to the field for another load and Bob invited me to the house for a cup of tea. Over it he said, "Well Donald you earned your wages today!" I said, "That's what I am here for." We finished the field that day and George surprisingly made no comment.

A few days before then, Bob asked me to help him to plant a fifty-acre field with corn using a special planter on two wheels with a long narrow box which contained the seed. A strong light pole, about 8 feet in length, extended from the side with a disc at the end. This acted as a rudder. A wire was stretched from one end of the field to the other with a knot every four feet along its length. This wire ran through a gear on the planter and when the knot came into contact with a lever, it opened a slot long enough for three seeds to drop into a 3 inch deep hole already made by a down and up movement of a 3 inch rod that came down again after the seed had been dropped to cover the hole leaving the next four feet blank when the process was repeated.

135

The planter was drawn by a steady horse and when it came to the end of the field, the stake in the ground was moved four feet onward after the wire attached was disconnected. The planter was turned round and the wire replaced ready for the next row, making sure that it was the same length as the first. With the help of the rudder, it would hold a parallel line to the cutter. When the first stake was moved 4 feet onwards, the field was planted and every stalk grew 4 ft. apart. The ears were taken off the stalks when fully grown and were ground and blown into a silo for silage.

Wilson also had a small flock of sheep, Suffolks I think they were. They were at least twice the size of our black-faced breed. One day he said, "Do you know anything about sheep shearing Donald, you saw them in the field with their lambs?" "I can shear but I am not very good at it." "That's alright, if you can do it, no one here knows how. I bought them in the spring to see how they would turn out. If we gather them into a pen, will you start on them today?" I said, "Yes" and with shears, a large bag and a bit of rope in case they would be wild and needing tying I set off. I tied the first one by its three legs but found it very tame, more so than the black face. The rest I did without tying. They would be glad to get that warm heavy load off their backs. The shears were good and I made better time than I had expected. Bob arrived before I was finished and was pleased with my work. "Donald, I am going to Toronto, I want you to pick out two lambs, male and female, to take with me." I said, as if I was an authority, "Are they to be for show, or the butchers?" "The show first" he said. I went in among the flock. I was successful with the piglets, would the same blind luck hold with the lambs with which I was more acquainted? I picked the two largest, finished the shearing and drove the sheep back to the field and packed the wool. It was near quitting time so I rode back with Bob and his two lambs to the barn.

The rope was as we left it, I said, "That rope should be taken inside, if it is not to be used soon." "No it won't be Donald, not until that field of alfalfa is ready, that kind of hay takes much longer to cure and dry." "In that case" I said, "The part of the rope outside the barn should be taken inside, the hot sun is not good for it. I will undo the knot and pull it through the ground block. Do you want me to put a long splice in that part? It would save time when using it again." He said, "How long would it have taken you to rig the whole thing if we had to put a new rope in?" "Well" I said, "It would be unwise to put in a new rope from the coil without it first being conditioned and that meant two days stretched in the sun to remove the danger of kinks forming. In this kind of rigging I think a quarter of an hour should do to put it through blocks and sheaves and the tying at both ends." Next day I got Frank to help me with the long splice as it is best to have two involved in the operation which is an art in itself but being a fisherman, I was adept at this process. With Frank's assistance we soon had the task completed and when done, it was hard to tell where it began or ended. Frank was very impressed and as George happened to be in the barn he called him over saying, "That's your splice in." "Where, I don't see a splice there, it's the same rope, nothing added to it, you can't fool me." Frank just laughed. George turned away still thinking he was right.

Bob came back the next day looking happy because he got first prize for the female and nothing for the male, which he sold to the butcher and got a good price. That evening Bob said he intended to buy more piglets as he heard that a boy, who an old Frenchman, a nearby farmer, brought up, was selling off all his pigs and piglets, below market price. The story went around that the old Frenchman came to Canada as a young man, married and took up farming, intending going back to his native France where it was understood he had a younger sister. This was known through Gordon from the store-cum-post office, from where the old man sent a substantial money draft to her every Christmas. They had no family and later decided to adopt an orphaned boy from a home. He was about ten and, although at first hard to control, later they were well pleased with him. They saw that he wanted for nothing and things were going very well. Their small farm was paid for and life was good, till his wife took ill and died. The boy was nearing manhood. On the promise that the place would be his when the old man retired, a will to that effect was made but unknown to the boy, it was not signed for some reason. The boy stayed on and they were making a fair living. The Frenchman, getting old, was seldom seen, so no one was surprised when they heard that the old Frenchman had gone back to France.

Wilson did not get the chance to buy the piglets, instead, news of a tragic nature got round fast. It happened when a customer was buying the last of the piglets. The price was agreed on and paid. The small pigs were in a safe enclosure but as they loaded them into a small truck and as the farmer was ready to pull out, one of the piglets jumped out and ran under the barn before they could catch him in the darkness. The boy said, "I will give you back what you paid for him, besides, you will only get your clothes dirty crawling under the barn. He will come out when he is hungry and I will catch it and if you still want him, I'll see to that." Regardless of protests and excuses from the boy, the farmer went to the barn and crawled under where, in darkness, he could hear the piglet grunting and so he quietly made in that direction and in darkness he touched it, but it jumped and got free to begin grunting a short distance away. It was while he was crawling in this space that his hand touched a thing that gave him a shock, and a great fright. He backed away in haste and crawled out from under the barn.

The boy was standing where he had left him, smiling. "You did not catch him, I am glad of that." "No, but there is a body of a man lying there and we will have to report it to the police at once. You better stay here till the police come." When they did come with torches, the boy was not there. They dragged the body of an old man out. He had a length of rope tied around his neck and one of the officers was sure it was the body of the old Frenchman. A warrant was issued for the boy who was caught at the borders to the States and admitted doing the foul deed. I heard afterwards that for his cruel greed, he was imprisoned for life. It was said that the poor Frenchman was indeed planning to go back and had already transferred most of his money to France. The farmhouse and stock he was leaving to the misled, misguided boy who, if he had stayed his hand for another few days, everything or nearly so would have been his. He had planned to dig a grave under the barn when all the pigs were sold, and no one was coming round.

One evening after tea, Bob began to question me regarding my character. He began after an unusual silence, by saying, "Donald, early in the spring the farmers around here who require hired help are invited to attend a meeting with a C.P.R. agent taking emigrants from Scotland to hire to Ontario farmers requiring help. They are all supposed to be of good character and as you know, I am engaged as agent for all the farmers around here and when I sell their stock, I bring a lot of money home with me which is kept here unguarded overnight and I don't sleep till it is off my hands. Do you happen to have any references from where you have been working before you came here?" "In the circumstances" I said, "It is reasonable for you to feel that way. I have no farming reference and have never worked for a farmer but I have one from the army, the merchant navy and from the last place I worked," and when he read them he said, "There was no need for me to be worried."

137

Although this had passed, I did not forget his declared poor opinion of me when I spilled his cream, which I wrongly thought was not spoken of again. Soon after the event, it seems Wilson was in Gordon's store, which at the time was crowded, and when asked by Gordon how his new man was doing said, "Well the one I have, I only took him for a week and yesterday the stupid fool went and spilt six gallons of my fresh cream. What I intended to give him for a week's trial will not cover that loss. I expect they are all the same." There was general laughter at this statement, and more laughter from Gordon, as it was his way of getting his own back on me because I had had angry words with him the second day after I arrived over his refusal to accept a Scottish pound note in payment for items I had bought. He said it was useless to him, like toilet paper. I got really angry at this ungentlemanly remark and with that, I left. It was on account of that incident that he was pleased at my downfall. I learned this information from a Barra man, Donald MacDougal, who was with a farmer nearby who was in Gordon's store when Wilson told his story. We used to see each other often. It made me very angry and I intended to take Wilson to task, but thinking it over, that would have involved his wife and I would come off second best. I decided, unless it cropped up again, I would forget all about it, but still that was not the end.

Wilson needed the roof of his barn mended and hired a carpenter. He asked me if I would help him, as he had no head for heights himself. I said I would. The repair was taking off old shingles and replacing them with new ones. I wanted to learn how to do it. The carpenter told me he was an ex-service man, Canadian army, and when we compared times, places and battles, we were both there at the same time. Because of this we became friends and he invited me to his home but I never had the opportunity to go. He showed me how shingles should be laid which I soon grasped. The job was finished much sooner and more cheaply than was expected and that pleased Bob.

It would not be true to say that I was unhappy working on that farm. They were good people to work for and they showed me respect and kindness and I was to have every Sunday off to go to mass. On the eve of my first Sunday, Bob and I were walking home down the lane. There were cattle in the field beside us. Bob pointed to two cows and said they would calve tonight or tomorrow, but they would be alright. On the first Sunday after coming home from mass, and a meal, I took a walk up to see how the two cows were doing. Wilson knew his business and when I got up there, the two cows had their calves beside them. They looked strong and I got near enough to know that one was male and one female.

Although not unhappy there, I was not earning much money, while my friends who had left their farm houses for a job in the city, were by all accounts doing so much better and why should I not do the same? These thoughts often came to me so when letters came telling me of the good time and wages they had in the city, I did not stop to consider what would be involved in getting such high wages that were to come.

It was on one such day when these thoughts were more overpowering that things began to happen. I was alone in a field cutting thistles. It was a very hot day and I sat down after a spell for a smoke. After a short while, I saw Wilson coming towards me. I did not get up. I decided then and there to quit. He asked, "Is there anything wrong Donald?" I said, "No." "Then you better start cutting the thistles instead of lying there." I said, "I am leaving you. I want my wages today." "What! What's wrong with you?" "Nothing, I am just leaving today." "Well, that's a dirty trick, when I am at the busiest time of the year and after what I have done for you this is the thanks I get. When you spilt my cream, I did not keep it off your wages or say anything about it." I said, "Not to me. It would have been more honourable of you if you had, but instead you ran to Gordon's store with your story of how that stupid ignorant Scottish fool that you took on trial, spilt all your cream, and that you thought all the emigrants that Father Macdonell brought over were useless and should be sent back to where they came from, causing everyone there much laughter as if in agreement. Someone said you were of Scottish descent yourself. It doesn't look like that as you would have been very proud of that fact." "Who the hell told you all this?" "Stover's man who was in the store at the time and heard every word you said about me, branding me stupid and ignorant, while all the time I take it, you knew it was accidental, and so with a reputation like that it would be pointless for me to look for work in this area."

We were standing some five yards apart both with a hoe in our hands, when he said, "I'll show you that you can't talk like that to me. I'll knock hell out of you." With the hoe, he began walking towards me. It was time I was at the on-guard position. "Mr. Wilson, I want to warn you that, if you intend to attack me with that weapon, I have been in many a fight, in a tight corner, and come out the best. I advise you to calm down or you are going to get badly hurt." To my surprise at the rage he was in, he stopped and said, "You're thinking of the war?" "Yes, and what could be worse?" "I guess you are right. I talked too much, but there is one thing I want to say. I am stuck. Will you do me a favour?" I said, "I don't think I am the kind of man who would refuse that to a man in need, what is this favour you ask?" "That you stay with me till I get someone in your place." "How long will that be?" "As soon as I can." "Alright, I'll stay for two weeks, that should give you plenty of time. I am not that important, but should you get someone before then, I shall leave here that day. I would advise you not to hire a man on trial, it is dishonourable and degrading."

During that week and working as before, there was nothing said about my quitting and I wondered if he had made an effort to get himself a man. I did not tell the rest I was leaving. One evening I went to see MacDougal who I knew was not too happy with his lot. When I told him I was quitting he said, "Is it over the cream racket?" "No, I don't think I'll ever make a farmer." I told Donald of my understanding with Wilson and that I had two more days to do to keep my promise. He said, "Then I will give Stover my notice and leave with you." I said, "Okay if a man comes to replace me before then I'll let you know. Meet me tomorrow at the usual place."

Next day, sitting on the veranda when all the chores were done for the day, Wilson said, "Are you leaving Donald?" "Yes, tomorrow, it's the end of the two weeks I promised to stay. I hope you got a better man to take my place." "I have a man in view but I can put him off, if you will stay with me I know that you can do things outside of fieldwork and if you stay with me till you want to get a place for yourself in this area, I promise I will give you all the help I can. I think it's a good offer. What do you think, do you accept?" "I think it's a good and generous offer to anyone who is interested and I thank you for it, but as I have already told you, my interest is not in farming. I don't think I could make a living out of it I would not be happy or content so I am sorry I cannot accept your fine offer."

10   Border Problems, Deportation and Renewing Friendships

Next day, Donald and I left with another Barra chap who had a brother in Windsor, Ontario, on the U.S. border, and we went there instead of going to Toronto where my friends were. We found the brother's house and were welcomed, but there was only one small spare room for the three of us. We learned that work was hard to get. Hector the brother, got us a small job however and we were to report at a certain lumberyard. We did and found the job to be emptying two large railway trucks of timber. The man in charge of the yard told us it was piecework and for removing the wood from the two trucks and piling it on the top of three railway sleepers, the price was ten dollars. "Do you know how to pile lumber?" he asked and we said yes, thinking anyone can pile wood in a tidy heap. He left after pointing out the rail sleepers. They were not far from the wagon and we thought it was going to be easy money.

We began pitching from the wagon and soon discovered that we should be wearing gloves, as our hands were full of slivers. However, we kept at it. The pile was mounting high with the lumber thrown in every direction. We had finished the first wagon when the same man came round. He stood looking at the huge heap and at us, picking slivers from our hands and rather pleased with ourselves for fast and tidy work. He began laughing, and when he got his breath, he said, "I thought you told me you knew how to pile timber or wood of any kind and if you had told me at first that you knew nothing about it, I would have shown you how. If you still want to earn the ten dollars one of you go to the store and buy three pairs of gloves and then start clearing that heap. I'll be back to show you what to do as it's got to be done right." The gloves were good protection and when the boss returned he showed how the wood should be stacked and he stayed with us till he could trust us to do it correctly. We did that pile to the height of 6 feet and began the other wagon. The next wagon was easy since we now knew how, and when the man came he paid us the ten dollars and said, "I don't think there is any more work for you here." With the pain in our hands, we were not disappointed and went home with three hard-earned dollars and thirty-three cents each.

Outside my work on the farm, it was my inclination to work in Canada although I had not yet discovered the land of milk and honey promised to us immigrants. It was not our intention to stay in Windsor but to cross over to Detroit, a matter of five minutes in the ferry, which meant facing a battle of immigration officers who questioned you closely as to where you were born, the reason you were entering the U.S.A, where you came from, did you pay your head tax and if so, where? We knew from Hector these were the main questions likely to be asked and in our old country clothes it was easy to spot us.

Donald MacDougal, on his own next day in town, met a man who after conversation said he could get him first papers. These were papers you applied for after being legally in the States for two years. Donald paid him three dollars and felt safe to enter. The next day we boarded the ferry, trying to remember what we had to say. John was to go first in the queue and I was to follow. Donald armed with his first papers felt confident. When the Immigration Officer asked John, "Where are you from?" he said, "Windsor, going back tonight." "Alright, pass on." He said the same to me. We walked on a piece waiting for Donald. We saw the Officer examining his papers and after a while, we saw them both coming towards us.

We stood there and heard the Officer saying, "Is that them?" and heard Donald saying, "Yes." The officer said, "All of you come back with me." He took us to an office where he first began to question Donald asking where did he get the papers and how much did he pay? He could not remember and did not know the man but that he had paid three dollars and thought they were all right. "No, they are not, they are false. I could jail you for trying to enter the country with false papers. You are all to be deported back to Canada for a year and a day. If you are caught again before then, you will not get off so easy." With that he led us to the return ferry.

I noticed there were three queues with an officer for each. When we got to the Canadian side, another ferry was loading. I said, "Let's try it again and go to a different man." The others thought it was too risky. The first man might spot us. I said I would try. I went to a different queue where he only asked where I was from. "Windsor. I am coming back today." "Alright pass on." I went uptown and had a look around. It was at that time Ford, who had been working on an assembly line or conveyor, for the Model T car, was paying five dollars a day for eight hours work to all his employees, including the floor sweepers. All industrials were up in arms saying he would go broke in less than a year. I could get a job there but the question of how to get my suitcase across with a year's deportation order against me was not easy to solve and impossible without a friend there. I had none.

Even then, the car traffic in Detroit was greater than anywhere. Traffic lights had not yet been installed so there was much delay before you could risk crossing a street if a policeman was not on duty there. Coming back, I had to cross such a street with a crowd on each side waiting for their chance. I saw a policeman standing at the curb, also waiting. I saw a gap and made a dash. I escaped by a small margin and landed against the officer who grabbed me and gave me a sound telling off for trying to kill myself. He said, "You better go back to Ireland where you come from, you're safer there." I told him I was going to Windsor. "Alright, stay there till you are wiser." I decided on the ferry and returned to Canada. I would try Toronto. At least I had friends there. Before going to Hector's house, I enquired about trains and found I could get one that evening. I told the other two of my decision but they decided not to go.

Friends in Canada

I arrived in Toronto and made my way to King Street West, No. 341. In that vicinity and looking for that number, I saw an old man sitting on a veranda. I asked him where 341 would be. He said, "Are you looking for John MacKay's house?" I said that I was. "Well you are near it," and pointing to a store, he said, "That's it." I received a warm welcome in the MacKay household. I had stayed there one night on our way to the farms, I was not a stranger. John's house was always an open house to the Highlanders and more so to those from the Uists. It was always a cheery house, full at nights, with much of the conversation about the islands in the old country and, of course, newcomers were the target for questions and expected to know all the answers. My two friends Donald and Angus that I was in correspondence with while on the farm were home from work. After the usual greeting I told them that I had been to Windsor and Detroit, and that work was not easy to get there. It was easy to get past the emigration officers if you didn't have a suitcase, but since I knew no one there, and without my case, I couldn't stay. "Well" Donald said, "If I had known you intended going there, I could have given you an address as I have a sister married there. I have not seen her for a long, long time but I am sure she would welcome you, in fact, I think I will make my way there myself soon!"

"Well, I think I'll try Toronto for a spell as I have been deported from America to Canada for a year and a day so I don't want to risk it too soon. How are times here?" Donald said "No, come along with us tomorrow, I know the foreman well and he will give you a slip for the employment office then you can start right away." I was hired the next morning and was sent to Donald's department. He took over and showed me what I was supposed to do, which was to remove by hand truck small boxes and packages that were already packed and stencilled for shipping. Until I got used to it, it was best to ask advice which I often did. I was never asked to move faster and I thought it was an easy job. Massey Harris was the name of the firm, known worldwide for its expert knowledge in building and inventing farm equipment.

Their building was on Front Street, stretching, I have been told, to nearly one mile long. I worked in most of its departments as a labourer. They employed many thousands, mostly Europeans, Poles and Hungarians. The wages were low, 34½ cents per hour, although some were on piecework and were a little better off. I was on day work and at the end of a month in that department I was no better off in money terms than I would have been had I stayed on the farm. I learned nothing useful and thinking I could do better, I went to the Blacksmith and Engineering Department. I was put to work as a blacksmith's helper. After some weeks, and only making slow progress, I decided I had had enough of it. At the employment office they told me if I would stay, they would give me a better job in the foundry, as winter was upon us. I took the job as outside jobs were declining.

The job was attending to moulders, bringing them the required frames, which were of iron or wood for light castings. Also feeding the furnace with pig iron, scrap iron, coke and sand, all taken up on a lift and dumped on the boiling crucible of molten iron. At first I thought it unbelievable that when I threw a large lump of iron in, it would float like wood, only to be boiled down to liquid form in a minute. The crucible or furnace was the first I had ever seen. It was built of firebrick, about 15 feet high and 6 feet in diameter. The molten iron went through a hole in the wall, slightly above the level of the bottom. That sump held back unmelted impurities covering the bottom, keeping it from melting. When the iron stopped running, the winch outside pulled on the chain, which pulled the prop from under the bottom. A cloud of ash and smoke would rise to the top.

The molten liquid was in pots suspended from an overhead rail, with a swivel to turn it around. It carried a load of two tons of liquid iron, and the overhead rail ran from the furnace to the centre of the building, pushed along with handles by a man. This was known as running the hot pot and was not part of my job, and I did not envy the Pole who had it, even if it did pay a little more.

One day the foreman asked me if I would run the pot as the Pole was off work. I said I would for the day. The job involved pushing the pot when full along to the moulders. Once it started it carried on by its own momentum and, when nearing the first moulder, it was slowed down by letting your feet slide along with it. The moulder was waiting with a long ladle which would hold about half a gallon of the hot stuff. You then tilted the pot and gave him all the iron he needed before continuing to the next man, who would be a few yards further on. Great care was taken that nothing wet was left lying around for the least small drop of moisture touching the boiling iron would cause explosions worse than rifle fire. One day I remarked to an old man there that I was puzzled with how the pig iron floated in the furnace. He told me the reason and also strictly advised me not to go too near the edge. A man doing the same work as I did had fallen in. After the iron cooled, they buried him with a crane outside. I was extra careful after that.

The day I was asked to run the iron there was one pot on the rail ahead of me. The Irish foreman was at a switch that was closed to allow that pot to go on the main rails. He opened the switch and went down to attend to something else. When my pot was full, I began to push it,

Donald in Highland Dress

knowing nothing about the switch being open. The distance to it would be about 50 feet. I had got it moving fast when I heard above the noise of popping moulds and crackling wood on fire, loud cries of "For God's sake stop the pot!" Instinct made me aware there was something wrong.

I began sliding with the pot, trying with all my strength to stop it but I couldn't and with the smoke now thick, I could not see the switch. I saw the Irishman running towards where I thought it was, shouting, "For God's sake, Scotty, hold her!" He never reached the pot; instead he turned back, running for his life. The rest of the workers in that area had already scattered. By then I knew that the crying and shouting was meant for me and also knew my only chance to save my life was by holding the pot back. I put into it more than I thought I was capable of doing and the pot with its deadly load came to a stop three feet before the plunge that would have destroyed many lives, and if the explosion had struck the furnace, only 50 feet away, a major disaster could have happened. When the workers saw that the pot was stopped and on the rails they began creeping back.

The Irish foreman came up to me half crying and said, "I am real sorry about this Scottie, I hope you will forgive me." "Forgive you", I said after I had closed the switch "For trying to kill the lot of us and yourself. You didn't have the guts to keep running to the switch. You could have made it before I stopped the pot." He said, "Are you going to report me? You have every right to. I know I will be sacked and perhaps a jail sentence. I have a young large family and they will suffer. I will do anything that is possible if you will not report me." I said, "You can take my notice." I ran the pot that day, as if nothing happened, only with many congratulations from the moulders. Conroy, my Irish foreman had already put in my notice and my time in full for that day. He gave me a good reference. The manager said they would employ me any time I wanted a job. I did not learn anything in Massey Harris that was useful to me in later life.

It was the beginning of April 1923. The weather was getting warmer every day. In dollars, I was still no better off than if I had stayed with the farmer. Work outside was fairly easy to get. I thought I would try the Canadian Pacific Railway goods station, and after testing if I could read and write English, I was hired and the pay was better. The job was transporting goods from one rail wagon to another, with a hand truck. I was put to work with three others under a checker or boss whose job was to check off from the manifest every item in the wagon and dispatch them to their respective destinations. Each wagon, all closed, had its own number clearly marked in chalk outside.

Inside the wagon with the checker was a loader, whose job was to call out the town to where each item was going, so that the checker could check them off his manifest. He marked off the last item loaded by writing in figures the number of the wagon they were going in, along with your works number below it, so that if the goods were put in the wrong wagon it was easy to check back to ascertain who made that mistake. This would mean dismissal or a black mark on your record. A mistake meant a loss to the railway and a long delay to the customer before the goods were returned to the dispatching station. As an incentive to avoid mistakes, the railway gave a free travel pass for two months service free of mistakes. You could travel free in Ontario for six clear months, and a once a year concession for the whole of Canada with a pass to travel on C.P. railways and steamers to any port in Europe that the ship called and returned from. After I was there two months, I received a slip in my pay packet to that effect. I never used it as I left there shortly afterwards. Many of the old-timers used it for their annual holiday to the old country and on making the trip so often, it gave the impression that they had struck it rich! After this I had a job working for the city and helping as a labourer to plumbers who were adding in lead piping in readiness for new houses to be built and connected to the water main. It was about this time that John Mackay, the householder, took very ill from appendicitis and, although removed to hospital at once, developed peritonitis from which he died. He was a man well thought of. His house was always full at weekends and not a word but Gaelic was spoken, and nearly always about olden times in the Islands. I found it very amusing listening to the things that amused them and brought back happy memories. His death caused a deep gloom in that house. Although the widow was a fine lady, bearing her loss with Christian fortitude, gone was the mirth and laughter. Although born in Canada, she learned much about Uist from her mother, who was born in the south-end of the island. I met an older sister of hers in Glenella, Canada, who learned much about Uist from her mother. The conversation was all in Gaelic, asking me if I knew of the many places she mentioned. I knew the area well because that's where I went to school. I was greatly surprised to hear how well she remembered the names of those places and where they were. I said, "You must have been well up in your teens when you left there to remember it so well." "No" she said, "I have never seen them. I was born here. Our mother talked about them often when we were children." Actually, she could tell more about the place than I, and I felt ashamed, as I had herded cattle in that area. She would be nearly eighty and was related to the O'Henleys in Garrynamonie.

About this time my two friends, Donald and Angus, had left Massey Harris for a job in Altona, U.S.A., to join a pipe band there. They were both good pipers. The job however was disappointing and they went to Detroit from where they kept in touch with me. The building trade in Toronto got slack. I was laid off with a promise I would be sent for when things picked up.

My next job was on a construction site, shovelling metal into a wheelbarrow which, as soon as one was loaded, another took its place. There was never a break of one minute between them, with more often than not no time to stretch your back. By the end of the day almost all of the casual workers had quit although I had lasted the day. The foreman came over and patted me and said, "Well done Scottie, you have outlasted our six Canadians." Knowing I was ready to quit, he said, "Come in tomorrow and I will get you a better job." "If that's a promise, I will consider it but it will have to be much better." "Alright, I'll do the best I can."

I did come in the next day and the job two of us were put to was carrying iron rods up three flights of staging to the third floor where they were used for re-enforcing concrete. Once again I lasted the day. However by the end I had had enough and told the foreman to have my time ready in the morning, which he did. After that I had a few labouring jobs until one day I learned there was a cargo boat coming in.

I went down to the docks, hoping for a berth as an able seaman, for which I was certified, but before I reached her a man stopped me and said, "Are you looking for a job?" I said, "Yes." He said, "I have a job unloading this ship if you want to take it." He told me the rate of pay and the conditions including free meals and a ten-dollar bonus when finished. I said I would take the job. He asked if I had done any trucking before?" "Yes, in the C.P.R. Goods Station." "Well, it's the same here and you can start now."

We talked for a moment in Gaelic before I picked up a truck and took it to join the line of others going for their load. There were two lines, one for the aft cargo hold on the ship, which was discharging with her derricks, not shore cranes. The load was landed on each truck with a sling holding it together and left where it was put. That routine was followed throughout the operation. After my experience with the C.P.R I found the trucking easy while towards noon some were showing signs of fatigue. At 5.00 pm a few did quit.

We worked throughout that night with only a few breaks and after a meal at 6am we started back. At the end of that day, many had quit, and those that were still there sticking it out, looked like zombies. When I finished, I sat with my back to the shed wall with a mug of coffee beside me but, before I tasted it, I fell asleep. The next thing I knew was someone trying to waken me, saying, "You are sacked for sleeping on the job." When I got to my senses, the Highland boss was there. He said, "No he is not, his truck was the last for loading. There was nothing for him to do. I would hire him any time he wants work here." I was paid in full with the bonus and they made me drink a lot of black coffee before letting me go home on my own. I was in no condition to observe how the few that were left got on.

145

When I got home that night weary, I thought I would sleep for days. Instead, I found it impossible and later the people in the house told me they were alarmed when they heard me talking a lot of nonsense. It took me the best part of a week to recover. And the extra money I made was certainly not worth it. I took the rest of the week off and with two friends went by a small passage steamer to see the wonder of the Niagara Falls. They were absolutely awesome, and the beauty of it left you spell bound. There are two falls, the Canadian Horse Shoe and the American, joining into one before going over the fall about twenty or more yards wide. Looking down in the basin of alluring water you saw a ship called 'The Maid of the Mist' which was very appropriate, as she was always in it. She was then coal burning, carried a small crew and took about a dozen passengers, who were given oilskins for the trip around the pool for which they paid 50 cents. We had a very enjoyable day there and had our photos taken with the falls in the background.

At that time I was able to send some money home. My younger brother, John, was intending to buy a boat. I told him to use part of the money for such, part for repairs to the house and to erect a head stone at Mother's grave. He didn't buy the boat but repaired the house and erected the headstone before going to sea, trading between Leith and Montreal where I went to see him. I had hoped to persuade him to leave the ship there and that we would go west and take up land there. To that plan he was agreed, providing that father agreed and gave him permission. He would write home. The answer he would get on his return to Leith and would write to me from there. A letter from home awaited him but father was against him staying in Canada. He wrote from Leith with this information, saying it was to be his last trip to Montreal and would consider

our plan later on. I didn't get his letter in time to meet him again and sadly, he was lost overboard on his homeward bound trip to Leith, in the Straits of Bell Isle off Newfoundland. Although a good sailor and a good swimmer, and despite the ship searching for him, they did not find him. Much later I found out from one of the crew members that the job he was doing when the accident happened was lashing down the cover of a lifeboat which they found unfinished. He was a first class seaman and well liked by the crew. I did not get this sad news from home till much later after I had left Toronto for Detroit.

Donald and his
brother John

A letter from John

Extract of ship's log announcing the death of Donald's brother John

Being aware that a quota of emigrants to Canada was to be allowed to enter the U.S.A. legally, I left Toronto for Windsor hoping to cross the border with no bother. However, when I enquired at Windsor, I was a week too soon. I took a room there and would look for a week's work the next day. The room looked clean, at a charge of one dollar for the night, however I turned down the bed to make sure. I went to bed early and soon after, the bed became alive with an army of bed bugs. It was my first experience of them on a large scale and so I got up and shook them all off, or what I thought was all, lying down again after much scratching. The same happened again until I was forced to retire to the floor, wrapped in a clean sheet. I managed to get an uneasy sleep there. In the morning I complained to the Italian owner who said, "They don't touch us" I left in anger and hoped that the cases escaped the bugs.

That morning, with my bags, I crossed the dividing line to face the Immigration Officers. I told them that I wanted to enter the U.S.A. and with their permission to pay my head tax. I was told to go into the office where they questioned me and asked was I willing to have my fingerprints taken and why did I want to enter the United States? I answered all these questions to their satisfaction, had my bags passed and my fingerprints taken. I was allowed to pay my head tax of $8.25, which entitled me to go and work anywhere in the U.S.A. If there was a record kept in the same office of the year and a day deportation order, it was not mentioned. Perhaps it was only to scare me in the first place. They even wished me the best of luck. I was now legally admitted to the land of the almighty dollar to seek the fortune I failed to find in Canada.

I took the tramcar up Woodward Avenue to where my friend Donald was staying. I recognised the resemblance in the lady and received a warm welcome. She had left her native land many years before, married a man from Dundee and they had one child. During a meal and much talk of the old country, she told me Donald was out working and would be home about 6.00 pm.

After a while, to pass the time, I went out sightseeing, making sure I stayed on the same side of the wide street, as the traffic was heavy. I had never seen so many cars without accidents happening. Traffic lights were not yet thought of and Traffic Directors could not be everywhere at the same time. It was risky for pedestrians to cross over. My sight seeing walk brought me to a large square. Standing there, propped up, were many coffin lids, some of them were in groups of three and four, some single. Cars were still able to wind their way through, few slowed down in reverence. I thought what an odd cemetery. I later found out from Donald who said, "When one buys a car here, he is not obliged to take a driving test, the result being many deaths through bad driving aided by strong home-made whisky." The coffin lids were meant to act as a deterrent. However the City Council finally admitted that they were the cause of many deaths and took them all off the street, and replaced them by sentencing offenders to 90 days in the house of correction, no fine accepted. There was a marked improvement that lasted until traffic lights were brought in which allowed one to cross with safety.

Donald was working for a firm called Fisher Body on the finishing line. The prospects for a beginner there were not good but the operation on which a good friend of his worked was better, and he was sure I would be taken on the next day. Donald, his friend and I, went that night for a dram to a speakeasy where they were known, but left there and found an Irish bar where the hooch was much better. Frequented mostly by Nova Scotians and Scottish Highlanders, madam kept an orderly respectable house, but strictly against the law. Although Irish herself, she did not readily welcome the Irish because she said their love of a fight could mean her house might be raided. It never was while I was in that city, proving that she was paying heavy protection money. They made a lot of money and when prohibition ended, she and her husband went back to Ireland and bought a large hotel.

Donald's friend did talk to the foreman on my behalf and I was given a job in the car factory. I was put to work on a slow moving conveyor, in the charge of a man who had the task of teaching or, breaking us in, as they called it. The purpose and aim of this operation was that

148

after many coats of rough paint were sprayed and dried on the cheaper car bodies they were rubbed with rough wet sandpaper. On the more expensive ones, the operation was done with fine sand stone cut up in small segments, held together by a wad of wet cotton and tape, and after much rubbing with this disjointed stone, the removed paint was washed off by a wet sponge. The next operation was to go over the same area with a pumice stone, after which the work was inspected by an expert, who used white chalk, and by holding and drawing the chalk flat any scratch or pit would show. If there were none, the job was marked okay. If there was, the flaw was marked with an 'X' and you were called down the line to repair it while you were working on your next job. The conveyor was moving all the time and any delay in repairing meant you were losing your place in the space allotted to finish your work.

At that time it was all colour varnish that we used, and eighteen coats of paint were used from start to finish, brushed on or sprayed before polishing. That was done by mixing fine cut horse hair with special paste and again well rubbed with a ball made from cloth rags until, finally, being wiped clean with a wad of white cotton. You could then see your reflection in your work. The job that I was doing was making the foundation for that effect. It was considered hard work and many could not stand the beginning of using muscles that had never been used in that way before, but after a week or so they got used to it. You were provided with a hot and cold communal shower at the end of the day's work.

I was there a week when I was promoted to one of the fast lines. I was making good money, the most yet. My boss however objected to a beginner making so much, and he began marking my work after the inspector had passed it, with many remarks saying it was not done properly. I knew it was and also that he knew. He kept that up for a while, I was tired of working hard to keep up with the rest. There was no one I could appeal to and there was no union. At last he said, "Put on your clothes, you are finished. You are turning in too much money." There was no point in saying that I had worked for every cent of it. In the long run I would gain nothing by saying what I thought of him. He said, "You will get your money tomorrow and let that be a lesson to you."

I called across the street to the bar and had a small drink before my friends came. When they did I was buying them a drink when in came the man who had sacked me less than an hour ago. I said, "I am buying a drink, will you have one with us?" "I don't mind if I do." Having drunk some of it, he turned to me saying, "Hey, I have seen you somewhere before." "You did, I am the man you sacked a little over an hour ago." He told me that he was called to the office on account of the money I was making and that he got a row from the boss. He was sorry he acted the way he did, as there was nothing wrong with my work. He said to come in tomorrow and everything will be alright, but to be careful in future not to overdo it. I did not believe him, as there was another man I knew who was turning in more than I had and he was not sacked. I wondered if he was giving part of his wages to the foreman. I knew he was on the point of leaving to join the police force. I had no proof of any of this but I was quite sure I would never give part of what I earned in order to retain my job.

I went to work next morning as usual. My time card was in the right place so I punched it and went to work as if nothing had happened. If the rest of my team was surprised, they didn't show it, and strangely only once that day was I called out to repair my job. As I have said, after work, we showered together before dressing. One day when Jimmy was passing, like myself naked, he said, "Where did you get those scars?" "In the war in France." "Did you get them all at one time?" "No, if I had, I don't think I would have lived. I was three times wounded in 1914, 1916 and 1918." "Did you see many Americans, were they good fighters?" "Yes, I saw many thousands of them, they were good fighters, second to none." "Well I had a young brother killed there, I shall never forget him." When he told me what part of France, I knew it well, and although it was only a name then, I had good reasons to remember it. Many times he would talk of it. I don't know, and never will, if that was the reason why, every time during my eight years working there, whenever a lay off for any reason was taking place, Jimmy, with a list of those he had to lay off, on coming to my team, would call out loud for all to hear him. "Macdonald, you are a married man with a large family. I can't lay you off yet." He knew as well as I did that that was not true. I knew of no reason whatever for this attitude towards me unless he saw me in the image of his younger brother and daily, as we took a shower together, that image was renewed.

Fisher Body was a good firm to work for, the best I ever did. They were three brothers whose father was a coachbuilder, and when car bodies began to be built, they began building them as a family concern and long before I left, they had 35 plants working to full capacity. Such was their worldwide reputation for workmanship, they paid top wages and there was no union. Once when a new job came on the line, we wanted a higher price for the work. They refused; we walked out, only to come in the next morning and start work as if nothing happened. Next day

Fisher Body Plant

they gave us twice the amount we asked for. I don't remember the year General Motors took the firm over but when the take-over came, our wages were slashed. The conveyor went faster and we had to work much harder to make a day's pay. Still it was better there than in most places.

I think that it was about this time that the talk went round that our foreman Jimmy was held up and robbed of his month's wages. Everyone was sorry for that, more so, because he had a young, large family. The boss was easy going so at once a subscription list was made up to which we all donated handsomely, making up more than what his pay check called for. If he

150

acknowledged that generosity I never heard of it, but thought nothing of it. Things were going on as usual when, at the end of the month, word went round that Jimmy was held-up and robbed again, and my sympathy and others was extended, for although it looked rather odd, there were many hold-ups at the time.

Although it looked odd that the boss was held up twice within a month, it was quite possible. I knew a man that was held up three times in a week. Nothing was taken from him because he had nothing. That was during the Depression. When I enquired from an inspector friend of mine, where was the hold-up and when the collection was to be, he said, "Well, the son of a bitch was never held-up, he lost his pay playing poker and I know what I am talking about because I was playing with him both times and won a good part of his money and that is true or I wouldn't be telling you". I said, "In that case, the donation will be called off." "Like hell it will, he'll get it replaced and more." "Not from me" I said, "not a red cent. I will not be held to ransom by any man. Are you going to donate?" "Well if I do, it will be part of his own money. I would advise you Scotty to put a little in as there is a lay-off coming." I said, "No, never, in these circumstances." The next day an old man, a sailor friend of mine, came round with the subscription list and said, "How much will I put you down for Scotty?" I said, "Not a cent from me, do you know that he was never held up? This is becoming a habit of his." "Yes, I know now, but I am an old man, it will be hard to find another job, You know there is a lay-off coming, put in something." I said, "No." "Alright, for old times sake, I'll put in $5.00 for you, myself. That will ease your pride." "No, you won't Red. I would rather lose my job than keep it by donation."

A few days later, Jimmy came down the line with the list of those he was laying off. When he came to my team, he said, "You are a single man, Scotty, I have to lay you off." I said, "I know." He just looked at me and said nothing. Although I worked there for nearly eight years, and had some shares in the firm, I was never able to find employment there again. I never knew exactly why, but sadly, not long after that, Jimmy was drowned along with our superintendent while out for a day's fishing. When I heard that a fund to keep his widow and young children was got up, I and I am sure the old hands donated, as in general he was well liked.

At that time I was in my second winter attending a technical college, aspiring to become an aero-mechanic, and gathering speed quite well. Prior to starting college, the applicants were given sums in decimals and fractions to work out. I knew nothing about that and failed the test. However, a professor who had been marking the papers, spoke to me and said I was good at writing and advised me to go to school for a term before reapplying. I took his advice and passed that term with an A1 grade.

Unfortunately my then place of work closed down and I had to leave the city for employment elsewhere, and my dream of becoming a first class aero mechanic faded. I did learn something if only a little. My employment elsewhere was to be in Toledo, Ohio, some one hundred miles from Detroit. Four of us arrived there on a very cold night. We didn't know anyone or where to go. In 15 degrees below, we began searching for a place to live. There were single rooms but we wanted to be together since that town had a bad reputation. At last we found a transient hotel that, after many questions, took us in. We wanted an apartment with two bedrooms and cooking facilities. They had that, and also would provide us with a maid who would do all the cleaning and washing dishes. All we had to do was bring in the food. One of the boys was a good cook and we lived well and cheaply. Everything was spick and span and we spent most of our time at work and never saw the maid.

After a month or more like that, a tall well-dressed man came to talk to us. Casually he said, "Where are you boys from?" We told him. "Where are you working?" We asked him why he wanted to know. At that he turned up the lapel of his coat and said, "I am a police officer, a special detective. I am investigating two bank hold-ups and I have been keeping an eye on you. Tell me, why are you staying in that immoral house? That's the most notorious house in town." We said we didn't know that and he advised us to get away from the house of shame as they now had the evidence to raid it. We left and found new digs, and nearly a week after moving in I read in the papers that the transient hotel was raided by the federals. Many gangsters and their prostitutes were taken in. Some escaped but were followed, and two were captured in Detroit where they were held for bank robbery. I never found out what happened to them. We were glad we took the officer's advice.

11   The Great Lakes and Slavery

I left Toledo to see what life was like sailing on the Great Lakes. First I had to pass a test for my lifeboat certificate, which I didn't have. A Coast Guard U.S. naval ship was tied alongside and that was where these tests were undertaken. I went on board her and enquired for the chief petty officer and told him what I wanted and where I was from. He tested me and I was given the certificate and, as far as I know, only once did being the holder of that certificate do me any good. That was when a choice for a job was being made. I got it on that account.

After I got that official piece of paper I left for Ashtabula, a shipping port on Lake Erie, and on registering at the shipping office there, I was told that prospects for a job were not good. The lake carrier's hall was half full of hopeful sailors and I was asked would I take a deck hand's job if one came up? I said yes. Standing at the corner near the dock that evening, I saw a man approaching. I knew him. His ship had just docked and he was on his way to the hall to look for a deck hand. He asked me if I was on a ship. I told him how things were and he said, "Come along with me to the shipping master, he will have to sign you on. I am the chief officer on that ship." Everything was in order with the shipping master and I was signed on as a deck hand.

The ship was empty and only called in for stores and then set off to load coal at another port. She was a small old ship, about 700 tons, called the *Norton*, with heavy wooden hatches which all had to be manhandled. Nearly everything was new to me and being the lowest rating, my mistakes with a curse were overlooked. But keeping my eyes open and by acting ignorant, I soon caught on, knowing well there is a huge difference between the working on deck of a ship on the lakes and that of one on the high seas. First the construction is different. On the lake boats there are no derricks for handling cargo, in or out. It is done from the dock by large cranes. Navigation was by flashing lights according to where they were placed for bearings. A sextant was seldom used unless caught in fog and when clear land was not visible.

In some of the rivers you could be making your way all night at reduced speed, without any navigational aids but your own judgement, in order to take each sharp and long bend. When we were loaded with 700 tons of coal, it was to one of these rivers that we were bound. The river was so narrow that only daylight sailing was possible. Even at that, we sometimes scraped the overhanging branches. Once I heard the Captain swearing loudly, "Why the hell don't they cut these damn trees down, to let my ship through?" This was on the bridge after his cap had been knocked off. My friend John was from Barra. He was a superb wheelman and he took her safely up. We were told that we were the largest vessel ever to make these bends. The village was small supported by a sawmill which the coal was for. It was mostly French in the North Bay territory, near where the Dionne quintuplets were born near Callander, Ontario. As soon as we tied up, they began the unloading with the one crane and grab. Sometimes it was changed for a large bucket when much dross accumulated.

It was their intention to unload us that day with enough daylight left for us to clear the river. However, with the large amount of dross and the time it took to shovel it, with arguments for more money for the dross shovelling, the unloading was not finished in time for us to leave that night. John and I went ashore. We were for the last six hours on watch. There was little to be seen in the village. It had a poolroom and no other entertainment. We played pool for a while. John asked a likely young chap if he knew of anywhere we could buy a drink. He said he only knew of one place where the whisky was good. "Scotch whisky, very dear, they only sell it by the bottle." "How much?" "$5.00 a bottle." "Alright," I said "come and show us where." "No" he said, "I must go alone as the place is sometimes watched for strangers and the whisky must be

Great Lakes map

154

paid for before it's handed over." "Well, here is $10.00 for two bottles, how long will you be?" "About a quarter of an hour." Outside in the dark we waited, half an hour, an hour, then we said goodbye to the $10.00. It would not have been so bad if we had been cheated in a large city. It was aggravating to be taken for a ride in a one-horse town. To go to the police, if there were any, would be far worse for us as it was prohibition time, and with the ship leaving at daylight he could feel quite safe with the $10.00 knowing there was nothing we could do. I was however cheated in a different way while on another ship in Duluth. I was off watch and went ashore and decided I would go for a drink. The nation was still dry and I was on my own, and not knowing any speakeasies, I got a taxi. The driver knew one and would vouch for me. He did. The five minutes ride was a standard price of 25 cents. He rang the doorbell and said that I was a friend. I asked him in for a drink. He came in and I began buying the drink and then a meal for us both. When my money was getting low, in fact, finished, I said it was time I was getting on board and asked if he would drive me back. That's when he looked at the meter and told me that I owed him $6.35. I said, "Are you joking? I paid the 25 cents fare to the joint you took me to, it's no further than that to the ship." He said "No, but you did not tell me before we went inside to turn the meter off so I thought you wanted me to stay with you." I said "I will pay you for the fare to the ship and nothing more." He said, "Alright, I can easy get it from the Captain and charge extra for my trouble." Now I had a reason for not getting involved with the Master as he was the last

Great Lakes steamship

155

man I wanted to see, knowing well that he was looking for a reason to fire me, and times were bad. Two of my shipmates, going ashore, appeared. McGarry, our second mate asked, "What's going on Donald?" I told them. McGarry took me aside and said, "I think it's best for you to pay up as the old man is in a bad mood today. Most of the crew are drunk and you know you are not his favourite. If you have not got the money, I'll let you have it." "Alright" I said, "but it's damn humiliating."

Subsequently however we got our own back on the driver by sending a long distance call to the office of the taxi company, to have that driver go to a certain hospital in Fort William to pick up a patient there and take him to the *Altona*, a ship berthed ahead of us. Later, the Bosun heard from his friend on the *Altona* that the driver turned up demanding that the Captain pay him $20.00 for the hire. The captain threw him off the ship and we considered we had got our own back.

We left Duluth, and after coming down the narrow river we were busy hosing her down to remove the coal dust, of which there was plenty, before scrubbing her for painting. After that there was very little to be done in deck work. She had no working gear, no paint, a little wire and no rope. We were told she was only taken out of mothballs, hoping that trade would pick up. If not, she was to be laid up again. They did not want to spend any more money on her. Until that was decided, I think it was the laziest ship I was ever on as a crewmember. They even stopped scrubbing the white paint for fear of taking too much off. When we arrived at the Detroit marine river, post office workers were waiting for the old man to tie her up in Sandusky, a port on Lake Erie. When that was done, we were all out of a job. Although a short trip, I learned all I needed for an Able Seaman on the lake boats.

John and I made our way back to Ashtabula. Things there had not improved. The hall was full of hopeful sailors with very few ships coming in. We passed the time playing games in the hall and bathing on a nearby clean beach where we could watch any ship coming in. Things began to get better and some were signed on. John shipped out as a wheelman the next day. I had to wait two more days sitting in the hall when the *Negaunee* came in and was looking for a watchman, I was signed on there and then. I hurried for my gear and boarded the *Negaunee*, which was a small vessel of about 2000 tons. She went up small rivers and creeks with coal and iron ore down from the upper ports. After settling down, I found the deck crew to my liking. I also got on well with the chief officer, I think because he too was a saltwater sailor, at one time a master who lost his ticket for some reason that I don't know about. He was now sailing as mate. Many were the stories we told of different ports we had sailed into throughout the world. Before we left Ashtabula, a member of the crew told me that the old man and the mate did not get on well but the rest of the gang were alright.

I was sent to relieve the wheelman, and at that time there was only the mate on the bridge with the old man in his room. I was given the course to steer but did not know what port we were going to. It was none of my concern, but when I saw many rocks straight ahead, I said, "Where does this course take us to?" He replied, "To those rocks you see ahead of you." We were about a half a mile away. As we were fast drawing near, I said, "Are you going to change the course?" "No, this is the course the old man told us to keep and not to change it without his orders," and here I was standing at the wheel on a bright afternoon, steering her to the rocks.

The situation was tense. Who would give in first. I knew it was a test to see if the mate would ask his permission to change course. If not, how near would he risk the ship to those rocks? It was the old man that broke; he came rushing up the steps and shouted, "Change that course to two points to starboard, let her come round fast." Long before completing his order, I had the wheel hard over and not too soon. When she was on course, he looked at the mate without saying a word, and went downstairs to his room. I said to myself 'what a stubborn pair' but I am sure the mate would have acted if the old man had not come up then. Because it was a near thing, if anything did happen, both were finished. I made many trips up and down the Great Lakes and creeks on that boat.

The Chief Engineer, whose name was Brown, spent much time on the bridge, He was for ever talking of engineering, what he could, and had done, with engines. It was easy, as we knew nothing in that line. At first we listened eagerly till we were fed up, when we christened him 'Bullshit Brown'. To his back he was always known by that name. Once in Buffalo we shipped a young man as third engineer, who seemed to have hit on hard times. For gear he had only the clothes he stood up in and that was dungarees. The engineers and firemen thought, another hobo, bluffing his way to the lakes. When he went on his first watch in the engine room he took a look around and then Brown told him what he wanted done. The Chief Engineer said afterwards he did his work better than any of his other two engineers could do, yet he hardly spoke a word. We were bound for Falado, for coal dross, a small port on Lake Michigan, to a sawmill that was run by a new turbine engine. The coal had to be very finely pulverised for blowing it into the furnace. Loading even on a windless day was a very dirty operation, even the cook was complaining, saying that he could not open the galley door without a cloud of coal dust coming in. His dishes and food were covered with it. It took us a long time before we had the ship spick and span again. I never had a load as bad as that before. The same drill was waiting for us when discharging.

We arrived at this port late on Saturday. Unloading began at once but did not finish that day. The Chief Engineer went ashore to see this new engine and got permission to take a party of us through the powerhouse. That port did not work on Sundays so most of us, including this Third Engineer, went on this sightseeing tour. The powerhouse was near the ship. We left with the Chief leading us. Except for maintenance, the plant was not working and a manager admitted us. First he showed us a very large dynamo, driven by the new turbine engine, which had not many years before then come on the market. After praising the engine and saying that it was built in the U.K. Brown took over. By his way he knew far more about it than the manger did! We believed him.

The would-be Third Engineer was listening to what Brown had to say, and plainly was not impressed. He walked away to look at another engine of the same kind, but smaller. After going round it a few times, he bent down and began doing something. As we were warned not to touch anything, the manager went over to him quickly and said, "What are you doing?" "I was just trying to remember the number. I know the engine. I assembled and commissioned it for an engineering firm in New York." "Well" said the Manager "is that not strange. That's just where we got it. It worked without any trouble till the engineer looking after it left the firm. His replacement claimed he knew how to run it but evidently not. It's been like that for over a month and we have sent to Detroit for an engineer to check on it. The Third Engineer said "I remember the number now, it's 1x68, look if that's correct."

The Manager said, "I don't have to, I wrote it down often enough." The manager went over with our new engineer and we went with him and left Brown talking to himself. We had

157

heard the talk regarding the idle engine and looked on our new engineer in a different light. He asked the manager if he could have a better look and when he did, he asked permission to do a little adjustment and worked on it for about five minutes and then asked permission to start it. "Yes, go ahead, if you can." He could and he did. Slowly steam rose and then it came to life. After a few minutes, he turned it off, saying it needed better timing. The Manager asked him if he could do the work given it was Sunday, and he agreed and we left them there and returned to the ship. We never found out what the young engineer got for doing the job and he left the ship at the end of the trip. As far as I know, some said he knew too much for the Chief and was asked to leave. He was from Greenock where he trained and where that engine was built.

Tied up at our stern was a small ship loading copper ingots. She was all the way from Norway and it was fascinating to see an ocean-going ship so far up on fresh water. They claimed that it did not cost them anything to collect such a cargo for Norway, as the copper had much silver in it and when it was re-melted, the extracted silver paid for the voyage. From that port I took away with me bits of raw copper with much silver embedded. We also found two respectable speak-easies where the beer was good. It was a German community. They knew how to make a good brew. We left for Ashland to load ore, which only took us an hour. No one got ashore.

The trip back to Erie was short, and as she was a small ship loading and unloading, did not take long, hardly time for us to go ashore. She was a pleasant ship, the same crew stayed on, and the food was good and plentiful. The bad feeling between the skipper and mate was always there, but we had nothing to do with that.

I only made one more trip on the *Negaunee* and then she was tied up due to no orders. The season was nearly over. I went to Detroit to work ashore where I soon started in the Hupmobile Factory, in the paint shop, but before I begin to relate events there, believe it or not I was three times on board a convict ship, but not as a crewmember. About that time we read in the papers that a strange ship entered and tied up at Detroit. A long queue of sightseers was waiting to board her. Her name was the *Success* and, with many others, I went on board her and what I saw there did not make me proud to be British, the very reverse. Her history was written in a pamphlet given when you paid 50 cents. It was a long description. I can only remember part of it. She was built I would say at least 100 years before, and was used for transporting prisoners to Botany Bay, and when that dreadful voyage ended there, those who survived were put ashore to join the other slaves.

The ship was taken out of sight to anchor, and to stay a long time until someone thought he would make lots of money out of her. Nobody wanted her. Americans bought her cheaply and towed her to Sydney Harbour. There they formed a company to put her in order as a showpiece, to take her round all the Australian seaports. However the venture failed and it was decided to tow her out to deep water and sink her. This they did and she lay on the seabed for some time. Subsequently an American syndicate asked permission to raise her and were given the go ahead. Following her re-floating she left Australia and arrived in the U.K. Following a refit she was again sailed across the Atlantic to America about 1914, where she was exhibited as a convict museum with statues of the prisoners placed in their cells, with a poster outside naming their crime and punishment with a short history of every criminal.

There, and at all the eastern ports of the U.S.A., she was a showpiece and the talk of every city and town. She did not miss a creek before being towed up the St. Lawrence to Detroit where I went on board her. Entry was 50 cents, the pamphlet was free. Before then I read much about her in the daily papers; none of it made nice reading. Like the rest, I was curious to see her. There was a long queue. In small crowds we were allowed on-board with a guard, because many would, I am sure, want to destroy most of what they saw. On deck at the gangway, stood the iron maiden. A most hellish contraption. She stood 6 ft. high. What made it so different was the fact that it was split from top to bottom on hinges to form a door, held closed by a strong clasp. Inside the hollow form spikes were driven in back and front leaving a small space for a human being to stand free of the spikes In truth the poster said, only one person was ever made to enter, for when they were releasing him they had to use crowbars on the door. He was impaled on the spikes and long dead. The agony of that unfortunate man, with the ship rolling, can barely be imagined.

Next, we were taken to see the guard area where the hanging took place. The plank beside it extended some 6 feet over the side, giving the victim the choice of hanging or walking the plank, which was on hinges. The hanging was always carried out when in shark infested waters, and when the sea turned red hanging was preferred. The rest of the prisoners, men and women, were made to view all of this punishment, regardless of their condition. Some of the women were pregnant and only that saved them from being put on the rack and whipped, before throwing them in a large tank of seawater that had a large quantity of extra salt stirred in. The men were thrown in after much lashing and blood spilling. This rusty tank was to be seen at the fo'c'sle head and it was claimed to be the one used. Neither that nor the hanging and plank were for crimes committed ashore but for small crimes on-board. The cells were on each side below the deck with life-size statues of the in-mates within. Their crime and history were written on a board above them. The condemned cell, about 4 ft. wide and 5 ft. long, sloped down to only 2 ft. On the floor were two large iron balls with a chain and ankle cuffs attached and there was no door.

In one cell stood the statue of a young girl, I would say in her teens, with the card of history of her crime hanging above her. She was from Nairn and was an only child. Her parents had the post office there. One day the postmaster came to inspect the books and money and found that sixpence was short in the till. The office holder denied taking the money or any knowledge of it. His wife and daughter did the same but he said that he would replace the sixpence himself. That was not good enough for the postmaster. He had to do his duty whenever he found anything wrong. and whatever the head officer did was not his concern. The head officer was as hard-hearted as himself. The man was put on trial. Before the sentence was passed, the daughter broke down crying and confessed that it was she who took the sixpence from the till and she could prove it by things she bought. Her father, with no crimes against him, was released. She, having been found to be the thief, regardless of her tender age, was ordered to be transported to Botany Bay, to a colony of slaves for ten years.

The convict ship was a vessel of about 300 tons. The reason why I had gone onboard her three times was because of the short time that they allowed us to see the exhibits thereby making more money out of her. It was said in the press that, after many failures, she became a gold mine, and it is good to know and remember that today our laws and methods of punishment are second to none and civilisation is thankfully changing for the better.

As I said, I began work for another company, Hupmobile, a small plant that did work for other firms. There was no conveyor. It was high-class work. Many of the cars were custom built and went to a Rajah in India with parts of them gold plated. In those I saw the first wireless installed. As we worked on them, we used to turn the wireless on. It was the first music while you work I ever heard. I thought of it when I saw one of my sons with a transistor, cutting peats on the bog. How times have changed. There was only a small crowd of workers and when slack times came, more and more were laid off until there was only an Irishman and myself left. Even the foreman was laid off as there was no work for him, and it was the head foreman who kept an eye on us.

Sometime later I answered an ad in the papers wanting men in my line of work, and when I attended the office I took a seat along with six other hopefuls. At last my turn for interview came. The man in that office asked me a lot of what I thought were unnecessary questions and I wondered what he was getting at, and eventually I said, "Do I get the job?" "Well" he said, "I am prepared to hire you." He then explained that they were an organisation paid by most firms. "We hire men and the firms we place them with don't know anything about them, and never will. Their pay goes direct to us and there is nothing dishonest in the arrangement. The firms are glad to pay us, since they know we are a protection. What we want you to do is to stay in your present job, keep your eyes and ears open for anything that you see done or hear that, in your estimation, is likely to harm your firm through neglect or carelessness, from your foreman, inspectors and work mates. Anything that you think is wrong, get the name or names and, if possible, the badge number, and write me a letter every night regarding what you have seen and heard. Do you agree that there is a need for such organisation as ours?"

I said, "I agree with you that there is a need for that kind of watch and also the pay is good, but that would be spying on my fellow man. I hope I shall never sink to that depth. I can't take the job." "Alright" he said, "we have them in almost every city in the U.S. and Canada. One may well be keeping an eye on you." I said, "Let him." I never knew before then that an industrial organisation of that kind existed.

It was the start of the Lakes season and I soon joined a ship as deck hand, the lowest rank, rather than be idle. Unknown to me my old friend John Mackay was on her. Loading coal in Toledo, as a deck hand, I was on the dock handling the lines. The wind was strong with the river running fast and the ship had to use the engines to leave the dock. After taking her out in the river, the old man had to put her full astern causing her to back fast near the dock. I began to shout as loud as I could to the engineer, who was looking through an open port hole, to put her full steam ahead or he was going to smash the propeller and wreck the dock. He acted as fast as he could and slowly she came to a stop a few feet from the wharf. John was at the wheel. He told me afterwards all about it. It seemed the old man was drunk, but the jolt he got by the engine going full ahead without his command, sobered him enough to do what was required.

I was called to the bridge once the ship moored. I fully expected the sack for interfering, yet I knew it was time for someone to act and if I was sacked, I would not feel guilty. When I got to the bridge the Captain was still there. He said, "How far was she from the dock?" "Less than six feet." "Are you sure we didn't touch it?" "Yes, quite sure." "Alright, go and attend to your work." I did, knowing I still had a job.

In a short while, the mate came and said, "MacDonald, you are promoted to watchman."
I said, "Who is leaving?" He told me whom he had let go and that I was taking his place. I said,
"I don't want to take anyone's job from him. I would rather not take it." "Well, that's the orders I
got from the Captain, you better take it." I stayed on that ship for seven seasons. She was 11,000
tonnes, always coal up the lake with grain or iron ore down. At first it was two watches, six on
and six off. Then we got three watches, four on and eight off. Times then were easy. The food
was the best but very little time ashore. One took an hour and a half to load 11,000 tones and
three and a quarter hours to unload.

Most of the after crew of our ship were German/Americans, one indeed I had fought
against in the war and we compared notes on some of the battles we had been in. Regardless of
that, we became good friends and many's a dram we drank together. The Chief Engineer was
German/American, a hard man to get along with. He had sore eyes and wore steel rim glasses
that made him look more crabbit than he really was. Being so long on that ship, the mate used to
give me jobs that had nothing to do with my work as a sailor, more a jack-of-all-trades. Often the
chief would come round and say, "What are you trying to do, Scotty?" I would tell him. "You
are making a mess of it. Go down to the engine room and bring me up my toolbox." When the
Chief did the job it was perfect.

Our steward was also of German origin, a first class cook in middle age. We had 32 crew
and that kept him busy with the help of a pantry boy, from 4.00 a.m. until 8.00 pm when a table
was laid out with three kinds of meat, beef, pork and mutton all roasted, with all the trimmings
for those on night watch. There were more leftovers that would keep a large family.

The rest of that trip was uneventful, except for a small incident. I used to bank part of my
wages at the head of the lakes. The last few trips I did not get ashore and had that money in my
suitcase, locked. I had lost the key. I had not needed to force it open. It was a good bag and I
intended to take it ashore for a new key. Two days before we got into port, a down and out that
we had shipped came to me for a loan of $2.00 I said I would let him have that but my suitcase
was locked and I had lost the key. It was an old country case and might be hard to find a key to
fit. "Well" he said "I can open it for you any time you want." He had a look at it. "It's British
made." He got a small piece of wire, gave it some twists and inserted it. The lock sprang open as
if it was its own key. I said, "Will $5.00 do you?" "Two will be fine, I only want to buy
dungarees and a few smokes." I said, "Are you out of smokes? You should have told me; here is
a carton. I smoke a pipe." He thanked me and said he would pay me back when he got paid. I
kept the homemade key and did not need another. I was afraid he might take the rest of the
money before I could bank it. He did not touch it and when he got his pay, he offered me a
dollar extra, which I would not take. I got a lot of pleasure out of helping him. It was his first
time on a ship. I thought him well educated and whatever his story was, he never told me. He
got off as soon as he was paid, perhaps keeping one step ahead of the law.

Some time after that, when loading grain in Port Arthur, Canada, the mate said to me,
"Donald, there is a rivet missing in the bulkhead leading to the dark hole. Get me one of your
men to plug it up." This dark hole was only used for ballast water, when required. The man I told
to do the job forgot about it, and when the level of grain came up to the rivet hole, much was
going through. The mate, looking for any other hole, saw this one with a stream of grain gushing
out, with about 4 tonnes of grain already wasted on the wet and rusty floor. He used a rag torn
off his coat to plug it and came up angrily searching for me. "Why the hell was the rivet hole I

161

told you about not plugged?" I said, "I don't know. I gave the order to close it. I thought that was done." "Then, go yourself and see that it's well plugged at once."

After that dressing down, when making my way on deck, I hit my head on a beam. That did not put me in a good mood. As I was passing the grain, an Inspector with his stick and small cup on the end was pushing it into the stream of grain and then into a small bag. For no reason, except that I was angry, I said in Gaelic, not thinking that it would be understood, "Whoever the devil is paying you for playing with that stick and mug should have his head tested." He turned round and said in good clear Gaelic, "Do you think so, boy?" I could have dropped in shame. I said, "I am sorry, I did not mean what I said. I beg your pardon for that remark." "That's alright", and seeing my embarrassment he began to laugh. "Are there other Gaelic speakers on this ship?" I said "One" "Where are you both from?" "Uist and Barra, the Hebrides." He said he was from Lewis. We cordially shook hands and talked. "Is this your first time loading grain?" "No, we took several loads already this year." "Then you must have seen a man doing the same as I am doing?" "Yes, and wondered if he was just someone taking grain home for his hens without paying for it." At that he had a good laugh. That hatch was nearly full. "Reach down" he said "and take up a handful." I did. "Open it." I did. "How many different kinds of grain can you make out in your hand?" I began to look and sort it out. After a while I said that there were two kinds. He said, "I'm afraid you would never pass an Inspector's test. To pass you would have to make 16 kinds, each with its own name. I am a Government Inspector. Also I am the man who grants the ship permission to land after I have inspected her for cleanliness, and if she were not to my satisfaction, I would order her to tie-up elsewhere to be cleaned. I could make a lot of extra work for you if the mate tries to hide anything from me."

He invited both of us to go ashore with him at 6.00 pm when we stopped loading, but I had to say I couldn't go as I was on watch then. He spoke to the mate and I was allowed to go. He drove us to his beautiful home where we met his wife and three pretty young daughters. It was all Gaelic songs and stories, high-class food and plenty of drinks. It was a wonderful night, which we greatly enjoyed. Next morning he drove us to the ship fairly sober. I had to stand watch for the next six hours, no mercy from the mate. We called there again near the end of the season. We were then using tarpaulins, which the same man was passing for sea-worthiness. Some he didn't pass and there were none to be had in that port. It meant a wait of several days. Rather than that, the old man sneaked out at night. When we got to Sault St. Marie, he was ordered to tie her up before being allowed through the lock. He had to wait for a set of new tarpaulins and fined for thinking he could bluff the Lewisman.

If there was only a day or so from unloading coal to the next port for grain, we had to work non-stop with hot water hoses, brooms and rags as the ship's hold had to be as clean as a dining room table, and every time we went to the port for grain the mate would ask me, "Is your friend still there Donald? Have a talk with him before he comes on board to inspect us" and when I did, he would take my word for it. I would never try to hide anything. It saved us time and labour when in port.

From September on we had to have tarpaulins on the hatches, and towards the middle of October the weather got really bad with wind and ice. On the last load there was always the danger of being frozen in until the next April. On such a trip going to Duluth, with coal up and hopefully grain down, we ran into much frost and strong winds on Lake Superior. As the waves splashed on-board, they froze almost solid. We had to keep the hot water and hammer chipping

162

going. Nearing port we began to thaw the melted ice around the hatches and tarpaulins. There were 28 hatches to deal with. We would do six, enough to loosen them from the clamps, and then back to the first with the 100 pounds hot water pressure that would enable us to slide the tarpaulin off the hatch, but not to fold it. Much hot water was hosed on before they could be dragged to above the stoke hole to thaw out.

It was my job to man the hot water hose. It was quite warm and as we were entering port I was called to the lookout on the bridge. I had a load of clothes on with two pairs of gloves. I stood in the same place for perhaps 5 minutes when the old man arrived and said, "Go down Donald and bring me up a cup of coffee." I started to move but could not as my clothes were frozen stiff although I was not cold. "What's the matter Donald, did you hear me?" "Yes sir, but I can't move. I am frozen solid." They felt me. I was like a board. Two men had to carry me to the galley to thaw out. I lay stretched there, dripping for some time, before I could bend. Regardless of all that, I did not even catch a slight cold. It took us much longer to load as the grain moved so slowly down the chute. Once loaded and before leaving, all hatches had to be fastened down as this load was for storage, with a double layer of tar paper first then double tarpaulins, all this tucked in and fastened all round. In every cleat there was an iron wedge with a butterfly screw to hold it fast, which was turned with a key. It was a very cold job and if you touched the bar of iron, all your skin would come off. We wore double pairs of gloves.

My roommate, a Dane, was ashore and brought back a large flask of whisky. I was soon to go on watch. He said that it was really cold outside, "Donald you better drink as much as you can from that bottle. It's good stuff and you need it out there." I drank as much as I could hold and went on deck to work, putting on the tarpaulins and screwing the wedges in like the rest. The mate was there too, working like the rest. After a while he saw that I was far ahead and called out, "None of that kind of work here Scotsman. Come back and do your work properly." I said, "What do you think is wrong with my work?" He said, "You are not screwing these wedges in far enough." "Alright" I said "I'll bet anyone here, including you, my trip's pay against yours or anyone here, that he cannot get another half-turn on what I have done." He tried with no results and turning to me said, "What the hell kind of hands have you got, you are doing more work than the 6 of us. I said, "That's the Scotch in me." I did not say whisky or he might catch on. I was not afraid of the smell, as he would not be aware of that in that cold. Anyway, I was feeling sober. It was the last trip and I could afford to be out-spoken. The rest were as able as I was in normal conditions but I was 'full of spirits' and they were not. Only the Dane knew anything about it and said afterwards that it was the longest drink he had ever seen taken. "I thought you drank it thinking it was water." "Well, you told me to take a long one." "Yes, and I was sorry for it."

We were glad when everything was made ready for sailing. We were lucky because that port had been closed by ice for two days. On the way to Sault St. Marie we had snow and ice and had to tie-up before entering the lock to remove most of it. The captain took a liking to John and myself, and whenever we came to a Canadian port the immigration people would come on-board to question if we were Americans or legal in the country. Fearing that we were not, he would take us to the emigration officer and say we were his own two boys and he would vouch for us. Often he would advise us to study for our ticket. He himself was on the board of examiners and had been appointed inspector of hulls and boilers for the Great Lakes and sea border and knew we would pass. He said "All you have to do now is make your application, come up before me, name where the lighthouses are and their flashing, and as for the rest, you have been with me for years and I know what you are well able to do." It was a good opportunity, but first one had to become an American citizen and that to me was a horse of a different colour.

The reason for my saying that is that on the last ship but this one we had a Polish mate whom no one liked. He was a near giant of a man and feared by all, except an Irish fireman. This Polish guy, on payday, used to come round with a large tin can and rattle it in front of the deck hands saying "My baby needs new shoes." The implication was clear. If they didn't donate, they were finished. He tried it on me once and I just laughed at him. He passed with a comment "scum tight Scotchman." I tried to put a stop to them giving him anything. Some did and were then only waiting for the heave. He tried me again in a different way. Alone one day, on the bridge, he said to me "Scotty, how much is your job worth to you?" I said, "My job is worth to me exactly what I am paid for doing and not a cent more. Why are you asking?" "Well forget it, I was just wondering" and that's all he would say. I knew my time on that ship was going to be short. I only made one more trip before I got the heave. I heard afterwards that the Pole had to give up the Lakes on account of the bad name he had. Since there was no union or anyone to appeal to when suffering any injustice, I could see the force and wisdom of the informers' association I have already written about, whose aim was to protect employer and employee alike.

There was an old saying in America, 'two more payments and the baby is our own', which I found to be quite true. I used to visit a pal who had married, and whose wife had to go off to hospital for her confinement. Some days after that I asked him if all was well. He said, "Yes, it's a boy. I am expecting the wife and baby home in a few days' time." I congratulated him. About a week or more later, I said to him, "You will be quite happy now that you have your wife and baby home with you." He said, "The wife is at home but the baby is still in hospital." I said, "I am sorry, is there much wrong with him?" "No, nothing." "Then why are they keeping him there?" "Because they won't let us have him till all payments are made. We still have two to make, that's why I am trying to get as much overtime as I can." I have never heard of any case like that in the U.K. There, then, it was the accepted thing.

12   The Great Depression, Eucharistic Congress and Car Factories

The depression of the late thirties hit the Detroit area sooner than most places because of its car building. I was sailing at the time and some of the lake ports we went to had no money. They were using tokens made of hard wood instead of money, and these were of different shapes and numbered according to their value. They were always got rid of before leaving that port, as no other town would take them. Each town that was broke had its own form of exchange. Most of the ships were tied up with no orders, while all the grain elevators at the head of the Lakes were full, waiting for ships to move the grain. Banks were closed, shipping companies had their money lost or frozen, and were unable to pay for their running expenses. The same thing applied to ore and coal. On account of ours being a small ship, we got loads of coal for small rivers and creeks, wherever there was a sawmill, enough to keep the place alive. We always got our pay in dollars and everything we bought was very cheap.

Long before the season ended due to bad weather, the ship had to be tied up with so much work needing done on her and no money to pay for it. I made for Detroit, which was my hometown. Most of the people I knew were idle. There were daily hints in the press that all the small banks would have to close. The Bank of Detroit, where I had my deposit, was one of these. The First National, the second largest in America, I thought would be the safest, so with what I had saved on the Lakes and all but a little of what I had in the Bank of Detroit I put in the First National. In a few days I got a job ashore and over a week, while going to work and passing that branch of the bank it was business as usual. Shortly afterwards I saw a large sign above the door 'This Bank is closed by Federal Order, until further notice. Depositors need not apply for their money'. There were angry queues of depositors, swearing and shaking fists, which was all they could do. With police trying to control and disperse the mob, many took the hard way in the river or from high bridges. Many of these were patrolled to try to prevent these acts. Myself, although far from being happy, felt that I had been many times worse off. I was single, and no one depended on me. I had a job, which might at least last a while; if not, things could not be as bad as I had already been through.

Casting my mind back to the times in the war when I had nothing to eat or drink for days, surrounded by death and desolation with not even a blade of grass to chew on, how thankful I would have been then for a handful of heather to fill my belly, rather than crawling about searching the haversacks of the dead for any crumbs of bread that they might contain, regardless of their blood-soaked condition. When a tin of meat was discovered, it was much better than a fortune. Although these events are now far back in my memory, I still remember them as if it was yesterday, as many others do. How little did I have to complain about compared to then. Even if what little money I had ran out, I would not go hungry. What was vexing me most was what I had invested in real estate, stocks and shares, denying myself the pleasures of life, in order to meet the required payments. I spent very little money on my friends and myself, and acquaintances would say that I was the meanest man in town. I would rather walk three miles than hire a taxi. All my endeavours in regards to real estate had come to nothing. After years, the First National Bank paid out in full with an 8% interest.

When working in the Dodge plant my teammate, a farmer's son, took a day off to go to a bank for a closing sale of stock and implements. Next day I enquired how it went. He said, "If you had $20.00 in cash, you could buy enough stock and implements to start a good sized farm." The sale only lasted an hour. The law governing the sale was that after three bids with no other response coming, the article had to be sold. A team of young working horses, after three bids, fetched 50 cents. Seeing how things were going, the bank put a stop to the sale and cancelled the foreclosure notes, telling the farmers no interest would be charged until times got better. This was not the first sale of that kind. For those who were first, the prices were reasonable till the farmers put their heads together in what to bid. In the end, the owner got what he was obliged to sell, back for next to nothing. There were cut prices at first and not all who took advantage of these forced sales benefited on that account. A few houses from where I stayed, a black doctor got a nearly new high priced car for $4.00. He parked it in front of his house. That night, the car and his house were set on fire. The last owner was found to be blameless.

Countless were the tricks that were tried to raise money or to sell property, such as the farmer who had already gone broke on account of these forced sales. He worked out a plan on how to sell his small farm that no one wanted. Long before Christmas, he bought a flock of geese and turkeys, which he was rearing for that season. When all preparations were done, with what money he had, and what he could borrow, he bought gold nuggets, as much as he could. He would feed them to the birds marked for dealers the next day. It was sure to be a winner and no one would ever find out. He used to say, "How do you know there is no gold on my land? Gold is anywhere you find it." It first appeared in a small column in the local paper, where a local housewife found a gold nugget in the crop of a turkey she was preparing for Christmas. Next day, two reports of the same nature made the headlines in two different papers. The ball was rolling. Tracing where the birds came from was easy. The farmer, seeing that much publicity had already been obtained, cut down on the feeding, and at night began depositing some nuggets here and there on his land for him to find, pretending that he was prospecting. Offers to buy his land were pouring in. He would not allow anyone to prospect on it, till a stranger by chance reported finding a gold nugget far from the farmhouse, causing more publicity and increasing the value enough to pay off his collaborators. He made more money than he required and after selling his farm he disappeared. It took a long time for the law to catch up with him, and according to the press it was going to take a long time, if ever, to convict him. I never heard if he was convicted

I myself was made to part with some of my hard earned cash. Prohibition was not long ended and a very large brewery was built not far from me. It was, as expected, a profitable concern doubling its output from time to time. The President and Directors and higher-up officials were all Jews and everything seemingly was going well. They contrived and caused it to go broke, and in the hands of the receivers the shareholders, after the employees were paid, got nothing. Shortly afterwards it started up again under a different name, still managed by the same people. Much the same thing happened in a building society. Who are you going to believe or trust?

Sitting in a tavern about that time with my sailor friend Angus, drinking palatable beer, a well-dressed party of four, two young men and two women, sat at a table near us. One stood up and ordered four beers, naming the brand. This was the new brand from the brewery that went broke. The barman came over and said, "I am sorry, we don't sell that kind." The other three began showing their disappointment, saying they thought that all the good taverns in town had it on tap. It was so popular they would never dream of drinking any other kind. They all got up and walked out. I turned to the barman and said, "Don't fall for what they said, they are promoters for a beer company and very few people like that brand." I saw them again in other pubs, with the same story.

In hot weather, three of us used to drive to a small lake, some forty miles out of the city, for fishing and bathing at the weekends. We hired a boat with fishing tackle and bait. We always took with us cases of beer which, to keep cool, we anchored in the lake. One of the boys was a good cook. We had a fire at the edge of the lake, and were kept supplied with good fish and cool beer. There was a carryout restaurant nearby where we could buy anything we wanted in the food line. We ate well, drank well and slept well in the open air, too hot for playing anything other than cards, and swimming.

Donald and pals swimming in Detroit

I went for a long swim and when I got back the others were cooking a meal and playing cards with many empty bottles around. They said that they didn't realise I had gone for a swim. I was to remember that lake by being careless and getting severely sun burned, near naked, playing cards and drinking beer. My shoulders, arms and back were in a sore mess. After a sleepless night, I managed to go to work in a silk shirt. My work-mate remarked, "You are well dressed today Donald, where is the wedding?" "Don't touch me, I am burning." Badly sun burned I worked in near agony that day, and had to take the next day off before the pain subsided and I could return to work.

I used to go bathing to a man-made bathing beach in Detroit along with another friend, John, who was from Dundee, a real nice guy who first got me started in Detroit. The area where this bathing beach was situated was where International Boat Racing was held in a mile and a half stretch of water, between the island and the mainland, a distance of about half a mile. Both on the island and the mainland, the shore was crowded with spectators, giving all a splendid view of the race. Kaye Don, in a fast boat, was representing Great Britain, and when the French, Germans and Belgians were left far behind, only Garfield Wood and Kaye Don were left in the race. They were even and the next race would decide who would win the trophy. Wood was a sporting millionaire boat builder. He held the trophy. For a long time, as a sportsman, he was not held in high esteem as most of his wins were achieved by bluffing his opponent. No doubt he always had a fast boat but was considered sometimes as taking unnecessary risks, causing the other to slow down to avoid a collision.

On this deciding heat, as always, they started their engines to warm them up before coming to the starting line a hundred yards or so away. They were a short distance apart, each timing their speed to be on the starting line when the gun was fired. Shortly before then, a matter of seconds, Wood gave his engine full throttle. There was a loud roar and the boat leaped ahead only to be throttled back at once to a much slower speed. When Kaye Don heard all this, although not quite on the line, he thought that the starting gun had been fired and so gave his engine full throttle and crossed the line without knowing his mistake. Wood crossed over the line less than a second after the gun went off, following Kaye Don at a distance with no apparent speed to catch him, knowing that he already had the race in the bag. When Kaye Don crossed the finishing line, he was given a deafening ovation from both sides of that lagoon. When Wood came in shortly behind, only a short burst of cheers went up. The press that night was very critical of the race with some headlines stating 'Wood won the international boat race but Kaye Don won the hearts of the spectators'.

In Chicago in June 1926, I attended the 28th Eucharistic Congress with my old pal Angus from the First War days who came from Gerinish, South Uist, and for this purpose we took a week off work. Chicago then had the worst crime record in all the U.S.A. Al Capone, with his murdering, robbing gangsters, was nearly in control of the city. Adding to the population of over two million, another million invaded the city for this Congress which was to last a week. We found a room. The opening was to be an open-air mass at 10 am, the next day, at Lake Mundelein, a small lake 40 miles outside the city. For two years roads, railways and buildings of many kinds had been erected in order to accommodate the million or more that were expected to come around this lake, a mammoth task to accomplish. We were fortunate. We got an empty taxi and had not gone far when we passed two nuns walking. We asked the driver if he would take them along. He agreed and so we gave them a lift for which they were grateful. We arrived at our destination long before 4 a.m. The taxi took us as near to the church as he could get, which was about 300 yards. That area round the church was crowded, with people lying down, sitting and sleeping, waiting for the 10 a.m. mass and the procession after it. We joined them on the ground, and while many had rugs, we had nothing but a dustcoat that I had bought before leaving and we put it over us. Both of us were well used to sleeping in the open.

There was a pious spirit manifest throughout that week of devotion. Not only Catholics were taking part but also most other churches had their own spiritual exercise. Later, the chief of police gave out a press statement, saying that during the week of the Eucharistic Congress, the city, with its estimated million extra people, was free from crime. Unbelievable but there it was. Reciting the rosary and singing hymns, we waited for the 10am mass. Once it was over, the loud

168

speaker announced that, for want of space, only the clergy would be allowed in the procession that would start from the church, go round the lake anti-clockwise, and finish at the church. To see only a little of it, we made our way back, walking fast and running as best we could, till we came to where we could see it approaching some 300 yards away. Tents away from the road were busy selling sandwiches, coffee and milk, which we needed.

At that time a dark blue cloud appeared, low in the northeast, fast approaching us. The sky darkened and I wondered if it would pass over us. The procession then was about 100 yards away from us. Leading were the cardinals, with one of them holding the host in front of him, under a canopy carried by four bearers. I thought what a pity if the cloud burst, as indeed it did. The first drops were already falling on us and were larger than I had ever seen before. In a very short time, everyone was drenched with drops larger than a man's finger tip and still the rain came, almost straight down. Soon the area where we stood was flooded and the culverts in the road were unable to cope. Tents that were full of food collapsed, and anything that was flooded was carried towards the culverts that were still open. It was a strange sight. Moments before, what was dry land was now submerged, covered with floating sandwiches and anything else that would float. Even if one wanted to, there was no place to shelter. The procession, six abreast, sang hymns and never faltered like the guards on parade, with spectators doing the same along the route. I had with me the dustcoat. I used it as shelter for some small girls who were standing near me. It was a little better than nothing. The atmosphere of calm, fervent devotion and friendship was amazing. In front of me were two fairly old ladies, seemingly unknown to each other. The youngest put her arm around the other, kissing her and saying, "I am so sorry my dear, you are getting so wet." The other said, "Thank you. I'm alright. I don't mind it. I don't feel it." No one could say who was the wettest. Scenes like these, one comforting the other, were common. Nowhere did I hear protesting words or bad language.

The shower was over in a very few minutes and the sunshine became very hot, so that it looked as if all were having a Turkish bath, so dense was the vapour. I think with the light clothes people were wearing, everything was bone dry within twenty minutes but it was the straw hats that suffered most, as none held their original shape, causing much laughter, but on account of the hot sun, they simply had to be worn. They were an endless source of laughter for both women and men.

Much was written about that event all over the world, as indeed the people forming that massive crowd were from every part of the world. The way round the lake was said to be two miles and the circle was completed long before the rear had moved. Everyone was dry long before then. When parting with the nuns we told them we would take them back if we could find them. When it was over, we did search but it was like looking for the proverbial needle in the haystack. We left in the direction where the loaded trains were still coming in, hoping at least to see some of the Congress. They unloaded quickly and we got a welcome seat. We arrived back, tired, grimy, hungry and thirsty and made for the nearest place to quench it. Wearing the Congress badge, we entered a small saloon. Only a few were there. A large man sitting at the bar spotted us and said, "Are you back from the Procession?" We said, "Yes." whereupon he ordered the barman to give us the best he had. We ordered beer and asked him if he would have one and he joined us. After quenching our thirst, we left for a clean up then a meal, as it was a long time since we had had a proper one.

The Eucharistic Congress

That evening I went to confession and Holy Communion, which I received in front of a Cardinal who in later years became the Pope. To me, personally, that was significant, nevertheless it was no more sacred than receiving it from a newly ordained priest. The host cannot be more sacred no matter who administers it. Mass that night was to be one of the largest in the world. It took two years to build the high altar with its dome, and children occupied many acres of floor space. Each school in the city had its own coloured dress, so arranged to blend into a beautiful field like flowers. It was called the 'Mass of the Angels'. The stadium was situated in front of the city on the shores of Lake Michigan. Besides the vast multitudes inside, a great many thousands flowed around it, unable to get in. We were there early and got a seat high up on the sloping arena. Near the centre of the field was the high altar from where the celebration of the mass was relayed through loud speakers.

Before the sun went down, each person was given a candle, and as dusk was falling, boys with lighted tapers went up and down the many aisles, giving a light to the person at the end of the row who, in turn, gave it to the one beside him and so on, until the whole mass of candles was lit. There was not a breath of wind, so that the area looked like the sky on a clear dark starry night. It was a never-to-be forgotten sight, with the beam of a searchlight shining on the field of children below us. A sight never seen before, according to the press. The celebration of the mass, assisted by 23 Cardinals, was so far away from us that we could only see it in the distance. The host was not given out to the multitude, as that would have been impossible. When it was over,

170

the clearing of the arena began, as far as we could see, in an orderly manner with no rushing about, pushing, or no unkind words spoken. I don't know how long that took. We walked through the dense crowd till we could get transport. After seeing all that we wanted of that city, we left with a feeling of contentment from our experience at the congress, and regret knowing how different life was in the world outside.

Back in Detroit, life and work was as usual. During the depression, I cannot complain in not getting my share of the work going. In fact, I had three jobs for a time. These were for three, two and one hours a day, from firms that I had already worked for and who could not afford more labour. The reason I think I was getting those jobs was because our 'phone was not yet cut off and I was easily contacted. Whatever wages I got were used to keep the household from being hungry, or going to the soup kitchen or a penny an item meal. One day I went in the queue to see what I could buy for a penny. A long table was covered with dishes of good clean warm food of every kind. You took these to a table and had a satisfactory meal. Those that did not have the penny went to the soup line. No one, if he was able to get to these charitable places, needed to be hungry. I think it was going on non-stop. It was those who were housebound who suffered, as there were no meals-on-wheels that I knew of. There was no shortage of food in the land, even though every kind of food was being destroyed, burned and buried, trying to keep the farming prices up. All that was paid at a reasonable price by the state.

There was plenty of gold in Fort Knox, but at that time no one seemed to know how to make it work. At that time the word 'technology' was much used in the press but only the learned knew what it meant. I quit the one-hour job as it was on the outskirts of the city and the fare almost ate up my wages. The Dodge plant was one of the others, and it was in the process of being taken over by Chrysler, which occurred a short time after I had been there although the name did not change. We built and sold products under the Dodge name, which was then world famous. We were told that every new engine had to pass a three-year test on the proving ground before it was installed in standard cars. Those that were left of the Dodge brothers and their families, sued Chrysler for using their name on their products. While the trial was going on, the press came out with the question of what's in a name?

At that time there was much bootlegging going on, crossing the river from Canada. I did a little of it, never being caught. One time I took over for a friend a set of bagpipes in their case, in which I had a large flat bottle of whisky under the bag. When I came to the Customs man, he said, "Anything to declare in that bag?" I said, "Only a set of bagpipes" and moved to open the case. "Can you play them?" I asked "No" he said. "I don't like the damn things, pass on." I did, but not in too much of a hurry. A lady who used to visit my landlady told us she was in that game. Her method was to use a long rubber tube, wrapped loosely round her naked body, filled to the desired level with whisky. She then put her outsize clothes on top and had no bother passing the Customs with gallons of the stuff wrapped round her. There were many of these incidents, far too many to relate.

I turned down the next job I was offered because of the risk involved. Although the pay was high, three times what I normally earned, the health risk was correspondingly high. I was not afraid of any danger regarding the work involved, which was preparing to build a bridge, almost a mile long. A friend of mine who was working there told me, if I was interested, he could get me started any time I wanted. I was interested in the money and up till then we had only read in the press about this new kind of work.

171

The workers were called 'sand hogs' and worked under air pressure, which changed according to the depth the work was being done. My Canadian friend Donald O'Henly, fifth generation from Garrynamonie, gave me first-hand information as to what to expect. If I took the

Donald and friends in Detroit

job. Having seen him a few weeks before then, I was surprised at the change in him, although he said he was quite well. He said the medical inspection was fairly strict but that I would pass no bother. The next morning he introduced me to his foreman who told me that he would take me on if I passed the medical. He would take me to the doctor after he had a look at those coming off shift, out of the decompression chamber. "If the doctor okays you, report for work in the morning."

At this stage the 'sand hogs' were working under 45 pounds of pressure, to keep the water out and the large hole from caving in. There was a lot involved in this work, especially as they were operating in a 'sealed' area, which was under air pressure with no other support. This meant that at the end of their shift they had to enter a de-compression chamber and remain there for several hours. At that stage Donald told me they could only work for a short space of time, and to go down, or come out in less time, you were in great danger of getting the bends caused by air forced into the blood stream causing bubbles, very painful and fatal if not attended to quickly. Each 'sand hog' had to display a badge stating his name, religion, address and where to

172

take him if found in distress. Being the first kind in that area, there was much talk about it, from which I learned most of this.

Before committing myself, I wanted to see those coming off the shift out of the decompression chamber, and talk to them, before seeing the doctor. Watching the door I thought there would be a mad rush. There was none. The first man came out with extended arms, as if to defend himself, and instead of making his way forward, went to the side of the hut, leaning against it. The next did the same as if trying to adjust to the outside world. I thought both had too much to drink. The third was steady on his feet. When he was passing me, hoping he would stop for a chat, I said, "How much is the whisky in this joint?" He stopped and looked at me and said, "There is no such thing here and our condition is the effect of being down below. If you are looking for a job, think about it first." I did and, for better or worse, when the foreman came my way, I took cold feet. So, although I later drove over and sailed under her, I had nothing to do with the building of that bridge. Donald worked there till he was obliged to return to the farm, hoping to recuperate. When I saw him again, after I had done a season sailing on the Lakes, he was only a shadow of the man I knew. I had no regrets for not taking that job.

My next job came as a surprise, not knowing there was work of that kind in that city. I saw an ad in the papers, 'a diamond cutter wanted to work on industrial diamond cutting', and where to apply. I read it over a few times. My only knowledge of these diamonds was during my training, as stones spoiled through careless or bad work were used for industrial work. It cannot be as particular as working on gems. On them I had a good enough reference and felt that if the job was not already filled, I had a chance. Early next morning, dressed in my best suit with collar and tie, no dungarees for digging this time, I made my way to where to apply, expecting a long queue to be ahead of me. I found the place. It was a small new building on its own with a display in large letters above the door 'Industrial Diamonds.' The door was closed, no queue and no one about.

It was then nearing eight o'clock, which was likely the starting time, as indeed it was. At 7.55 am the first man arrived and with a short glance at me, he unlocked the door and walked in and left it open. Others followed and still no queue. I thought it was time and went in. The man inside asked what I wanted and I told him I had come in response to their ad in the press for a diamond cutter, and would like an interview with the employment manager. "Well" he said, "I am he. Are you an industrial diamond cutter?" I said, "I have not worked on them. My training was in gems, and with the training that I have had, I feel sure that given the chance I can also work on industrial diamonds, to your satisfaction." He seemed a very pleasant man and asked if I had any proof that I was what I claimed to be. I gave him my reference in that regard, which he read at least three times over and said, "If you are what this paper claims you are, you should have no difficulty working here. Where have you been working for the last four years?" I told him and he noted my full name and address and phone number. I left feeling that the prospects were good, and if they enquired about me, they would find nothing wrong.

In less than two days the phone rang and I was to report for work the next day at 8.00 a.m. which I did, and was given a diamond and shown my place to work. The mill was in motion all the year round. All the gear that I well remembered was on the bench, except the magnifying glass, which I was then given together with diamond dust, and my job was to cut and polish that stone to a needlepoint. Working on industrial diamonds was easy compared to gems and I got on very well. The first day, by chance, the stone I was given had all four points true and so no time was wasted to find the grain. I finished four stones, which they said were correct and good.

With me was another cutter who was employed full time. He told me he had trained on gems in New York where his father had a small diamond cutting business. Also there was a Pole who spoke very poor English, and I found it hard to understand him, which made things worse because I sensed that he had some authority. He did short spells of cutting on a side mill and spent much time looking at raw stones and sorting them. I often felt that he was keeping an eye on me. However, at the end of the first day I felt I had given a good enough account of myself. The pay was good for a small firm, but not nearly as good as the sand job I had turned down. The next day, I increased my output by one and continued that rate to the end of the week, when I was ahead of the other chap. I knew that was because he had been working on stones that had cross grain and were hard to move and follow. I knew he was faster than I was up till now, and I was just lucky in the stones I was getting. The next week, without asking, they gave me a rise in my pay, not a big one, but still something.

When I would be well established, I would expect more. I liked the working conditions and the people there, all except the Pole, and I had the feeling that he felt the same about me. He began to find faults, small but yet touching on my work, on which, being the inspector, he had to pass or reject at the end of the day. When I had the chance, I talked to my mate in this regard who knew the way the Pole was acting and warned me to be careful. "He has a lot of power here," he said, "not so much for his know-how, but for the large sum of money he has invested here. His knowledge of working diamonds is not as good as yours. I don't like working under him but I am staying till I have saved enough to start on my own, and if you want to come with me, I will be very glad to take you. Think it over." I said I would but would rather stay and put up with him as long as I could.

I was trying to please the Pole, at least to be on guard, but I felt for some unknown reason he wanted to get rid of me. My output dropped, I didn't get my expected rise and my issue of diamond dust and olive oil was cut. One day I was working on a very slow moving stone due to a knot in the centre and I thought it was not worth the effort. I pointed that out to the Pole who, after looking at it said, "There is nothing wrong with it. You are not using enough dust on the mill." I said, "I am not getting enough of that for the work I am doing." He said, "You are wasting far too much, that's valuable stuff." I replied, "I know, but no-one can work on any stone without it." He said, "Don't tell me what is needed, just carry on with your work." I finished that troublesome stone and two more that day. In the circumstances I thought I had done well. Next day, with better stones, I doubled my output, all of which were correct and there were no complaints from the Pole. I was now in my third month there and with Christmas near, it was cold outside and the ground was frozen. Inside was cosy and clean, and as long as you were seen to be working, no one bothered you.

I was beginning to think that my troubles with the Pole were over, since he was now more critical of my mate's work. I wondered how long he would suffer it as I thought he was a skilful worker. I asked him what he thought the Pole had against us as our work seemed to be okay. He said that his guess was that he is not very sure of his job and that the money he had invested in the company was his strong arm. He said that soon he would be ready to head back to New York and if I wished to come with him he was sure we could make a go of it. I told him if he did pack it in to keep in touch. He left the following week and I never heard any more from him.

In a few days the ad in the papers brought his replacement, a Frenchman, older than me, a good craftsman. He told me he did his training in gems in Antwerp, Belgium. When we compared time, he knew and remembered my old instructor, Harry Garland, from Birmingham, who the Ministry of Pensions engaged to teach us in Fort William. For the time being, the Pole left him strictly alone. I was again at the receiving end, although for a while things were going quite well. I had increased my output and expected another rise, which I received. From then on, there were awkward times with the Pole who seemed to watch me constantly. One morning, soon after I had begun work, I saw him and the boss at a table looking at some stones and looking my way. I thought nothing of it until they both came over. The boss spoke, "MacDonald, we have a stone here that broke when it was not under full pressure and has been traced as your work. Mr. Protosky here claims that the point was not in the centre, resulting in it breaking." I said, "I am really sorry about that" and asked to see the stone. On examination, I remembered it as I had worked on it. I said, "There was a knot in the centre, a very hard stone to finish on that account, the way the grain was running." The Pole said, "We are not concerned with the way of the grain, but why the stone broke under light pressure. It can only be because the point was not in the centre as it should be." I said that I understood that all the stones when finished were examined by Mr. Protosky and he never mentioned anything being wrong. The Pole was not asked if he had examined and passed it, and I wondered why as that would be me off the hook.

Later, I could see the Pole and the boss were having a long talk, and I knew by their glances it was about me; also that my fate was to be decided there and then. Towards noon, the boss came over and said politely, "MacDonald, I want to talk to you. It has been brought to my notice that you and Protosky don't get along very well. The success of any firm depends on harmony in its work force. Mr. Protosky has been with us much longer than you and we are quite happy with him and regret this feeling between you. We don't want to lose him, therefore I am prepared to offer you another job on tool making for our products, which we will teach you. The pay is a little lower than your present rate."

I had an hour to decide. It was not hard. I already thought that as long as the Pole was there, my future under him would not be a happy one. I told the boss I was not interested in his offer and thanked him. He said that was the best he could do, that I could call for my pay next day and if they could use me again, they would let me know. This was the second time I was forced to give up a job on account of a Pole but I do not condemn that nation. There is good and bad everywhere.

It was between Christmas and New Year, and I had no great reason to celebrate, having lost my job. I decided to try Fords, who were taking on men for their new model at the Rouge plant. When I got there, on a very cold morning, there was a long queue outside. No one was allowed to smoke. Not being quite used to this cold and only yet halfway to the gate when the snow began to fall heavily, I said to hell with it. Many of the rest of the hopefuls stayed in line. I thought they must be broke or had a large family. It snowed all day and night, bringing the city almost to a standstill. Next day, in sunshine, an army of shovellers was clearing it from the centre of the main streets and sidewalks. Only once before did I see a heavier snowfall and that was in Milwaukee.

When the snow was cleared enough to get around, I again tried my luck at Ford's. This time I was lucky in so far as I got what I was looking for, but after working there for a week I would not call it luck, more like being sentenced to hard labour. I worked on a fast moving conveyor that ran alongside a hot drying kiln. The Ford car was cheap compared to others that I worked on, Cadillacs, Packards, Buicks, Chryslers and Lincolns, all built in the Detroit area. The conveyor moved so fast that you either kept up with it or quit. It was not your foreman you had to be wary of, but the time and study man standing a short distance behind you with a pad, pen and stop watch, timing every move you made. If that was not in line with production the conveyor was speeded up accordingly, so that Ford lost nothing.

Henry Ford was a trained engineer who began to make cheap watches, but that did not prove successful. He then thought of manufacturing a pill that had enough nourishment to do away with eating and the waste of time preparing food. I don't think that nonsense got off the drawing board. When his fertile mind turned to combustion power, as the whole world knows he made a success of that, far beyond his cherished dreams; however it must not be assumed that his was the only brain involved. He made enough money at the start to buy the rest out, and in 1922 I was in Canada when he put in the conveyor system in his Highland Park plant, and announced the mass production of the model T. The wages of the workers were to be $5.00 for eight hours' work for semi-skilled labourers and for floor sweepers. Besides this unheard of wage, which before then was from $2.50 to $3.00, he opened a grocery and clothing store where, on showing the Ford badge, his employees could buy their food and clothing at half price. No wonder the badge changed hands often. The store was open from 6.00 a.m. till midnight and was unable to cope with customers from a wide area. Perhaps that gave him the idea of selling his produce cheap and fast. However he was forced to close these stores because merchants complained that they were unable to pay their rates on account of his cut prices. The other car makers, using cheap skilled labour, resorted to press articles predicting that, in order to keep their best workers, Ford would be broke within six months. Instead, Ford was going ahead like wildfire, while many of them were going to the wall.

There was no union in any of the Detroit car plants at that time, hence the management doing as they pleased with their workers. Ford was the last to give in to unions, and only then because of the pleading of his wife to avoid bloodshed. Regardless of the safety rules of a kind, many were being hurt, and even with bandaged hands or being on crutches, provided they could place items on or take them off the fast moving conveyer belt, they remained employed. Wages were as before. Seeing so many bandaged and crippled men coming off the shift, reminded me of battles in France. There was no dole or sickness benefit as Ford did not believe in such, maintaining that he was paying a wage that should support bad times. So many stories were told about Ford's efficiency. One story was when he was out for a walk he caught up with a funeral, and saw that the badge worn by those carrying the coffin showed that they were his own workers. He called the man in charge over and asked how many men did he have on that job? "Six", was the reply. "Well, five can be laid off, and put two wheels on the coffin, it will go faster."

Only once while I was working there was I called to the carpet. I always signed important papers with 'Mac'. However on one occasion when signing my pay stub I signed 'Mc'. One day, the slip with my time card said 'call at the employment office on your way out tonight.' I could not think of anything I had done wrong. In the office a man asked me if my name was

MacDonald and I said, "Yes." He had my pay stub beside him and accused me of drawing two men's wages by signing a different name. I told him that I was only trying to save myself time with no thought of fraud and with the Lakes season about to begin, I did not mind being sarcastic. I think he got my meaning because he said, "We'll let you off this time. Go back to your work and don't spare that pencil." I did hear of men drawing two men's pay, but cannot confirm that.

I was on a different shift when the cyanide poison case happened. I knew the place very well because near it was where I used to sit when eating my lunch. Nearby in a corner stood a small furnace for case hardening gears used in the cars. Cyanide poison was used for that purpose. A fairly large box of that white and dangerous stuff stood beside it with a lid clasp and padlock, attended by one man. No other was allowed near it. This man, whenever he wanted a scoop of poison, had to unlock the box with the key that was always kept on a belt around his waist. If he needed the toilet, another man replaced him. With this safety precaution, everything was thought safe, but not so in the wicked mind of a strange, revengeful man.

Ford had provided a lunch wagon from where sandwiches of every kind, with coffee and milk, could be bought. Lunchtime was 12 noon. The wagon moved slowly till the bell rang and no one was allowed to go near it till then. It always stopped at the same place when the bell rang, and everyone formed a queue. Only half an hour was allowed for dinner and if last in the line, you had to chew fast! Where the wagon always stopped, two men worked a few paces away. They were always first in line for their coffee and the usual sandwiches of cheese and lettuce, which were always on the top. This day, it was routine. The two men got what they wanted, carried it to their usual sitting-down place and began eating. The first man chewed and swallowed. The second did not like the taste and spat it out. He looked at his mate and saw him topple over dead. Both were rushed to hospital, where a post mortem on the dead man showed he died of cyanide poison. The other was, after attention, let home. The almost untouched food was taken care of.

Investigation began first with the man in charge of the cyanide, who claimed he had never left his post unless relieved, and did not think it possible that any of his stock of cyanide was used. All the food left on the floor by the two men was tested. The coffee was normal but the sandwiches were saturated with the white cyanide poison. How did it get there and why? Outside investigation proved fruitless. It had to be an inside job. The police and detectives, who did not gain any useful information, closely questioned everyone in that department and on that shift. Work was going on as before, only the lunch wagon stopped coming. On the third day, a man was taken away for questioning. This was because of some information that one of the workers, a toolmaker, had held back, thinking at the time it was not worthwhile to mention when questioned with the rest. Now and again what he had seen was growing clearer in his mind, and so the next morning he saw the head foreman and explained that about four days ago he looked in the direction of the furnace and noticed there was no one there. A man was walking towards it who he thought at first was going to the toilet. He was then about six feet from the fire. A moment later he saw the same man walking away and thought it suspicious.

The toolmaker was not long at his job when he was called to an office. There, two plain clothed men stood. One asked him to take a seat. One of them said, "What's your name?" He told them. "This morning you told a story to your foreman. Do you remember it?" "Of course I do." "Is Karl the name of the man you are talking about?" "Yes." "Alright, go back to your work

177

and thank you for your information." Not long after that talk he saw the same two plainclothes men take Karl away, He did not come back. In the evening news it was stated that a man was detained and charged with murdering, by poison, a workmate in Fords. He stood trial and admitted that he had committed the crime and that no one else was involved. He said that he was sorry and did not mean to kill anyone, only to make them sick, and that he did not know the stuff was poison.

His dislike of these two men was because they were ahead of him at the lunch wagon every day, no matter what effort he made to be there first, and for that reason he planned to try to get some of the white stuff in the box to place on their sandwiches. His plan fell into place when it happened that the furnace man took very bad stomach pains, and as a result was constantly running back and forward to the toilet, each time pushing the bell for his relief to take over, but before the relief arrived Karl was able to get some of the powder. Strangely, none of the workers reported seeing this happen. Had it not been for the short glance this toolmaker had of Karl, this crime may never have been solved. That night Karl prepared sandwiches just as he knew his victims liked, but added the white powder, and the next day he managed to plant them on the top of the lunch wagon without being seen. That was the gist of the story he told, and for his foul crime he was sentenced to life imprisonment. Capital punishment was not in practice in that state.

It was then nearing the time for the ships to be laid-up for the winter, and to be fitted out with gear for the coming season as soon as the ice melted. I made an application to join one of Ford's ships, although I did not like the thought of being compelled to show the Ford badge on my breast when on-board, regardless of the pay being a little better. These things had a military or naval smell, but if one kept one's nose clean, life on-board was as good as on other ships. The last ship I was on was tied up in Buffalo, full of storage grain. I was expected to join her there in later spring. The main advantage of being on a Ford ship was when she tied-up for the winter, if your record was good enough, you were given a job in the plant ashore till next spring, when you could join your ship again. It was all very good if you could swallow the discipline. I had enough to last me a lifetime of that in the army.

Henry Ford 11

178

13   More Great Lakes and Back to the Old Country

When I arrived home from work one night, there was a letter waiting for me, post marked 'Buffalo'. It was an offer to join the *Henry Ford II* the day after tomorrow. I had been on this ship for the last seven seasons and liked the ship and the crew who stayed on her. I got my wages the next day, and the day after I made tracks for Buffalo and began to help fitting out the ship, as there was much work to do. Getting gear ready, stripping hatches, getting victuals on board, moving ship with a skeleton crew, when steam was up, to an elevator to discharge her cargo of grain, and paint as much as we could of her outside hull. For that I was paid extra. The rest of the crew joined the next day and we left for Sandusky to load coal for Port Arthur, Canada. We thought it would be grain again, which meant hard work cleaning the ship's holds from coal to grain. However, the orders were iron ore from Superior down, an easy trip, and we had no holds to clean.

On the way up it was very cold with large patches of ice still on the water, and when the ship hit these at full speed, she shuddered from stem to stern. If on watch, after hitting one of these hard, I would be sent down to the foredeck to report the damage and how much water was coming in. Once she did hit very hard. In that small space, the bang and vibration reminded me of when, at the bottom fore part of a troopship during the war, we were fearful of being struck by a torpedo and subsequent death, but after all it was only letting go both anchors safely back in port, after evading the torpedoes. I found the damage not bad but with a lot of water coming in. The pumps were able to cope and speed was not reduced. Double lookout was kept at night on Lake Superior. It was not pleasant to be down there alone with only one torch. No doubt the old man had his orders to drive her to get ahead of the other fellows heading for the same port.

The rat race began on the Lakes long before ship to shore 'phone was possible. Leaving the head of the Lakes, the master often did not know his destination. At the office block, he was informed if it was to be any of the Lake Michigan ports. If not there, his next information was through the marine post office on the Detroit River, as to which port of Lake Erie he was to go. That information was timed to get him there with no other ship ahead of him. A quick turn round meant much to the firm. We arrived carrying tons of iron ore. To unload that lot, our time was always three hours and a quarter, which was far off being a record. Also at that time, on some ships, the course you were steering was traced in red on a chart, showing if you went off course, how much and for how long. You signed that chart at the end of your watch. It was sent to the office so that not only the officer beside you kept his eye on your steering, the office boy could also have you fired for wasting time and fuel. Only when you were asleep were you free. I have written of much of my time on that ship, and every time we went for grain the chief officer would ask, "Is your inspector cousin still here Donald? Have a talk with him."

Our Second Mate, Raymond McGarry, was a first class navigating officer. In deck work he was not so good because he only spent one season as a wheelman before being made an officer. As wheelman he had very little to do with the deck work. His father was a retired captain of some distinction. After doing one season steering on the Lakes, Raymond went that winter to navigation school, passed, and his father's influence got him the job of second mate. He was a fine fellow and did not mind being corrected. When doing deck work, on that account, I didn't mind making suggestions, most of which he would take, but would never thank me. I liked him better for that but if I met him ashore, there would be frequent showers of the hard stuff.

CANADIAN PACIFIC LINER "DUCHESS OF RICHMOND" 20,000 TONS

When we reached Fort William there were no ships ahead of us at the elevator. The ship was ready for loading and my inspector friend was not there. We had a fast loading and only a short time in that port. We were bound for Cleveland, and when the emigration officers came on board the old man, as usual, took John, the Barra chap, and myself before them, saying these are my own two boys, they are alright and are good Americans. We would not be questioned. It usually took a day to suck the grain out of her, and then to another port for coal and sometimes, a deck cargo of cars for the head of the Lakes. The Welland Canal was not built then, so that we only went down as far as Buffalo. The round trip took about nine days.

At the end of that season, or before, I began thinking about making a trip to the old country to see my people, the hills, the rocks and the lochs before I would settle in America. For that I took out a re-entry permit, good for three months, if I cared to stay that long. After leaving the ship, I worked in Chrysler's for a month and then booked my passage on the CPR liner *Duchess of Richmond* from St. John's Halifax to Southampton. My reason for that route was that

I had two sisters, both nuns, one in Chatham, the other in Newport, and I wanted to see them before going home.

I left Detroit early in December by train. It took 35 hours to reach St. John's. It was very cold there, I thought worse than the upper lakes. I was glad to be on board in a warm cabin to myself. She left the next morning on a southerly crossing. When two days out, the weather was much warmer for strolling on deck and getting acquainted. I did not know anyone on the ship but soon made friends. It took me a little while to get used to not working on board and having so much attention. The food was good but no better than on the Lakes' boats. The *Duchess of Richmond* carried 1st and 2nd class passengers, mostly 2nd class, of which I was one. Except for the accommodation, there was not much difference between. Everyone was allowed to roam on the decks as they pleased. I think it is the best way to get acquainted with fellow men. Not all of them were rich, coming from the land of the almighty dollar. In fact, many were poor and not able to spend any time in the bar.

The day we were disembarking a man, middle-aged, approached me. He said, "You are a Scotsman, yes? Well, I want to speak to you. I wonder if you would let me borrow half a crown from you? I saw you going into the bar sometimes and perhaps you have some money." I said, "What do you want the money for? Come on in and I'll stand you a drink." "No, no, I would rather not. My fare is paid to London and then I am flat broke. That half crown, if I had it, would pay for the fare to my sister's place. I should be alright then. I had a little over my fare from Manitoba but I used it on tips on the railway. It was a long journey." "Well" I said, thinking of the policeman who helped me when I was drugged there in London, "A half dollar won't do much for you, you will need a meal, 10 shillings or a pound would tide you over better." "No, I had a good breakfast. All I need is half a crown and your address so that I can pay you back." I said, "Don't bother about the address, half a crown is nothing." "It's a lot," he said, "if you haven't got it." "Alright, have it your way." He insisted on the address. He told me how he was doing well farming in Manitoba till the depression came and he lost everything but a lot of machinery, left rusting, to which some day he hoped to come back to. His name was Charlie.

After a month at home, I got his unexpected letter to thank me, along with a postal order for 2/6d. saying his sister staked him for a comeback. He was leaving soon for the wide-open spaces. I mentally wished him the best of luck. It is always nice to meet an honest man, be he broke or in the money.

Another man I often talk about was an English-American. After general conversation one day, he asked me what I was doing in the land we had recently left. I told him truthfully and then I asked him what he did. He said he was at the moment a kind of engineer, if you could call it that. He could see that I wanted more information. He said, "I am part of an enterprising company, dealing with scientific projects. We believe that it will yet be possible to send an image or picture through the air, the same as we can do with talk or voice. Now at present, we can send dots on to a screen a distance of 25 feet, where you can make out the dots clearly. We know there is a man in Scotland, near Glasgow, working on the same thing. He can put these dots out 50 feet. He is that far ahead of us. I expect it will take many years before we can master it. I would advise you if you have money that you can afford to forget about for the next four years, you would do well to invest in this company. The shares are 50 cents each." I thought of the hard earned money I invested in real estate and not likely to see any of it. I said, "I will think about it" but with no intention of buying. If I did, it went no further. Later, doing some business in the bank at home, the manager asked me if I knew of good shares to buy. I told him of those.

181

He laughed and said, "They will never be able to do it." Like me, he was too much a Doubting Thomas. Nevertheless, had I invested as advised in what I now know to be television as invented by John Logie Baird in Helensburgh, Scotland, the course of my life may have taken a completely different direction. This is maybe a suitable point to mention that, when I arrived home, and for many years afterwards, people thought I was wealthy and used to call me 'Dòmhnall an Oir' – Gaelic for 'Donald of the Gold.'

Although a long voyage, it seemed to pass quite quickly I think because of the number of interesting people I met. We docked at Southampton and passing the emigration and customs did not take long. I was soon reunited with my trunk, last seen in Detroit. I would see it again when claiming it in London, which was the end of the fare. I did not have long to wait for my train to Newport where I hoped to see my two sisters. The journey there in that train was cold and uncomfortable. I was surprised the carriage was so long out of date, worse than those on the West Highland line that I remembered from 15 years before; just plain wooden seats. It was snowing heavily in Newport where I found a small hotel. After a wash and a meal, I went to the bar, not expecting to see anyone I knew. The proprietor was a talkative old man and when the bar closed, he invited me to a back room that had a blazing fire, with a kettle of hot water beside it. We added that to the rum and sugar and he refilled his glass as often as I did. When I told him why I was in Newport, he thought I had better 'phone the convent in case my sister was not there. "You know, they sometimes go to other places, this way they will be expecting you. It's not far uphill; I'll show you tomorrow. I am not a Catholic myself but I know most of them. They are good people." I used the 'phone and said who I was. The voice said they would be delighted to see me tomorrow, especially Annie, who was not professed and given another name yet. After a few more words, I rang off, fearing the rum would make me too talkative. Tomorrow I would have to use more manners when facing a community of nuns.

Once in a hospital in France a nun came to my bedside and said, "How are your feet?" I looked at her and said, "There is nothing wrong with my feet, it's my back that's got shell pieces in it." "I just want to have a look at your feet." I said, "Go ahead if you want to." Her mission was evidently to look after that end of the body. When she saw them she said, "Oh, dear" and went to get her tools of the trade. These she found quite useless to deal with what she hoped to do. The scales and corns refused to be removed in spite of all her effort, till at last she said, "I can't do anything with them. How did you get them in such a state?" I said, "I'm not sure, but I am certain that it was not done by any running away." She looked at me and went away with her instruments. In a short time she was back with a small object in her hand. She said, "Would you like to have this small cross and wear round your neck?" I looked at it and saw that the figure of Christ was not on it, only some Latin words which I did not understand. She said they meant that, in this sign you will conquer. Of this particular medal I have written already and how I wore and lost it many times. At the end of that war, it vanished without me being able, in the circumstances, to offer any clue or reason.

Next morning the old man directed me to the convent on Stow Hill. I pressed the bell. The old nun who welcomed me seemed to know me without me telling her. It made me feel I was in the presence of someone special, as indeed I was. Someone greatly loved by all. She led me to a room. At once I noticed the complete silence. I said to myself that it must be near eleven, nobody but the old lady and my sister entered. I nodded to the nun, embraced my sister and fondly kissed her. The old nun left us. I said to Annie, "Are you the only two out of bed?" She began to laugh. I said, "What's wrong?" "Nothing, this is our silent hour. I am excused because you are here. Soon they will be coming out, then you will hear plenty." As indeed I did, reminding me of my young days at the herring gutting and curing station in Uist, where at least forty young and not so young girls would be working, some laughing, some singing, others talking, none in particular listening. They left the two of us alone till the bell rang for dinner, in which time we talked mostly of home and those that had departed since I left, including our father and John, our brother, and all the others we both knew. I loved Annie more than my other two sisters, I think that was because she was the youngest in the family. I found it easy to persuade her to watch where father put his tobacco and she would cut a piece out for me. I was then learning how to smoke a clay pipe. If I was suspected, she always took my side.

I remembered one day playing with her jumping off a rock. I fell and cut my knee and pretended I was dead. Poor Annie began to cry, and when I did not show any signs of life, she ran for father and mother. They came running. Lying on the ground I could see them coming, puffing, out of breath until, at 3 yards away, I jumped up and ran for my life. My father said, "That devil is doing his usual mischief." And turning to my mother, "You look after him and don't spare the heather broom when you catch him." She never did, but I don't think I ever got as much as I deserved. In spite of the many tricks I used to play, she was very fond of me and I of her, always. I said to Annie, "Are you sorry that you entered the convent? You are still training, you can leave any time you want." "I don't want to Donald. I am quite sure I am far happier here than I could be outside. I don't find any task I am doing disagreeable, or distasteful. Discipline as far as I am concerned is easy. Others don't find it so. With me, most of my training was already done in my hard rearing at home. Everything we do, we do it for the love of God and find joy in doing whatever act that is, but of course, without the vocation for that, I don't think one would find life in the convent so joyful." "Are there many pressures to stay put on anyone who decides to leave?" "No, all are free to go. Very few do, after they are professed."

I spent two very happy days there. The food and attention were of the best. I left for Chatham where my reception was just as good. I was happy to spend more than a day with my other sister Mary, known as Sister Paschal, going over the old times. She asked if I remembered the time when I was leaving home to join the army, I had to get my hair cut. She told the so-called barber that I was just running away and to stop cutting, and I left with only one side of my hair done. The recruiting sergeant finished it. I put the same questions to her as I did to Annie. It was easy to see they were both happy and would not change for any other life. Since that was so, what right had I to wish for more of their company? Sister Paschal was a very special person. She was obliged to leave school early because of mother's health, to look after the rest of us children, and when mother died, she took over that burden regardless of times being hard. She did her task well and when the family was in a position to look after themselves, she joined the convent, the order of St. Joseph, where she spent the rest of her life. She died at the age of eighty-four on the 23rd February 1977 much loved in her order and by all who came in contact with her. Many people, not of our faith, told me that in her presence they felt they were in the presence of a saint. If it's hard work, care and devotion to the love of God that is required, it was plain she had all that in a large measure. While her departure saddened us, we were happy that she deserved to be loved as much.

After my visit, I made my way to London for my train connection to Oban. It was Christmas Day and few were standing to travel north. For a long way I had the carriage to myself till two men boarded. When they settled down they began talking to each other. One said to the other in Gaelic "I think we should have a dram, it's a long time since we had one." The other agreed they should and produced a large bottle, uncorked it, and gave it to his mate who took a long swig. A glass was not involved. When that round between them was finished, one of them said, "Don't offer him any, you never know who he might be." I was reading a book and pretending not to be concerned when in fact I was doing my best to keep a straight face. By that time I knew where they were from. A Lewis man seldom loses his accent.

I learned they had left the ship at Southampton and were on their way home on leave. We would be fellow passengers for a long time and I too had a bottle in my case. To produce it now and offer it would almost amount to an insult, to do without and sit like a dummy was not the best way either. I had to get acquainted. The carriage window was too wide open. I felt it and did not like it. I said in Gaelic, "Is this window too far open for you boys?" With their mouths wide open, they looked at me. That moment passed and one said, "We had no idea you could talk Gaelic. Where are you from?" I began to tell them. The other went for the bottle. I told them that I had met a lot of Lewis people. They asked if I was off some ship and going home like them. "No, but in a way I am. I came from the States. I spent a few days in the south here. I am now on my way home." The one opening the bottle said, "Where is that?" "South Uist, I was born in a place called South Lochboisdale." The one with the bottle kept looking at me as if a bell was ringing and said, "We know a man from there out in New Zealand. We always go to his house. His name is Jack Campbell, he is harbour master in Oamaru, South Island." "Yes" I said, "I know him well, he is a first cousin of mine. His name is John not Jack." He pushed the bottle over saying "If you are a cousin of his, you are a friend of ours. We have known him for years. His home is a home from home to all Hebridean island sailors calling at that port. We will be calling there on our next voyage. What's your name?" I told them.

What I first thought would be a long dreary journey was, instead, very jolly. They were both good singers. I enquired about John Montgomery but with no luck. We parted at Glasgow and they went Inverness way, I to Oban. The journey from Chatham was long but nothing like Detroit to St. John's. At Oban my other sister, Sarah, was not expecting me. I had to ask my way before I located her house, and when she answered the bell she got a big surprise. Her husband Iain was still at work and three of her five boys at school. I spent a very enjoyable week with them before heading for the Minch and home, where the only one of the family, my eldest brother Peter, was living, and if it had not been that I wanted to see him so much, and the hills where as a small boy I used to play, I think I would have turned and headed for the Americas again. I well knew that I was leaving behind a standard of living that I would have to forget if I was to spend my time in Uist. I wondered how far the standard had advanced in Uist, since I left more than fifteen years ago.

Before the depression in the States, I read that they were then 100 years ahead of all the working class standard of living in the U.K. I know that the islands got their share of the misfortune because a fund was set up in Detroit where I was, to keep them. Needless to say I helped that cause as much as was reasonable. I learned afterwards that my father and another man didn't get anything. The reason was they were not badly in need. I heard my father saying he would rather not get anything and let them think he was well off, which of course was far from the truth. I did remember sometimes the home I left, although not as often as I should have.

I made my goodbyes to my sister and family and said that I would likely be back in a week or so. I boarded the 'Lochiel'. There were few going to the islands and I didn't know any. I found a fairly comfortable quarter and began dreaming of the future, seeing the same old places on the ship reminding me of other times long ago. One in particularly was when, during the First

War, with a naval rating friend, we were on this ship going to Oban, I to France and the trenches, him to Grantham and minesweeping. At Castlebay they took boxes of fresh herring for Oban. Of the small number of passengers was a man escorting a mental patient to Craig Dunain. We knew him well. He was the Truant Officer in our school days and we helped to keep him in steady employment. It was a bad night and when the cook went to bed, we asked the escort if he would like fresh herring. He said no. We asked the patient, and he said yes and any man that did not like herring fried must surely be crazy. The escort looked at him with silence. The boxes were stowed open in a corner, a tarpaulin about them. We picked out more than a dozen of the best and made our way to the galley. There was a good fire on and the cook was likely snoring by now. Everything was shipshape, even his apron was hanging up, but we did not use it, not then. We split and cleaned the fish and looked for where he kept his oatmeal, found it and gave each herring a good dressing.

While one was doing that the other was attending to the stove and a large frying pan left ready for use in the corner. Lightly fried herring would be the menu of the morning. We were not great cooks but we knew when the herring turned brown on both sides, it was then ready for devouring. The large pan had room for ten herring and when these were ready, we looked and found one of his enamel ashets and loaded it. Going to the steerage past the bridge, there was no danger of being seen. The deck was in complete darkness, wartime rules in case a submarine was in the area, lights were put out in any room on deck before opening to leave. The same applied to the galley. We also dipped into the cook's stores for tea, sugar and milk and one loaf of bread. We found only one large mug and a fair sized kettle. We put the lot in a clean bucket, put out the light and were glad to be in the fresh air again.

The steerage was as we left it, some dozing to sleep. We poured the tea. I already had the bread out. There were two middle-aged ladies, the escort and his charge and an old man. I gave them a slice of bread and herring. The ladies would not take any, although one said she would like tea. We gave her the first shot of the mug. I gave the mental patient two herrings for a start. If there was anything wrong with his head, his appetite was sound enough. After the rest was served to capacity, there was one left. He also demolished that and the one mug went from lip to lip. We took the ashet, kettle and bucket back to the galley. Everything was as we left it. Alistair said, "I think we should fry these two, somebody will eat them." I said, "Alright, put the pan on. I'll get them ready." The fire was going good, too good. The pan was sizzling hot, it had far too much fat in it and Alex threw the first herring on. There was a splash that set the pan on fire. I quickly pulled it off and put it on the floor. It was by then much alight. I grabbed the apron off the peg and covered the pan. That, for a moment, kept the flame down till the greasy apron caught on. I then used the jacket that was hanging on another peg and that put the flame out. The galley was soon full of smoke and hard on the eyes and much coughing. I am not sure if it was that or the racket made when, in the smoke and dim light, a pan was knocked down that woke the cook. He came in a hurry without his pants. "What the hell is going on here? You have set my galley on fire. I am going to get the Captain."

Without seeing that everything was safe, he left us. In a few moments they came, but much of the smoke was gone by then. As we held the light out and the door open, the captain, when he saw there was no fire said, "What's the meaning of this? Did you two start a fire here?" "No, sir, we were only frying herring that we brought from home with us when the pan caught fire. Just a little flame, we put it out at once, no damage done." He and the cook went in, closed the door, put the light on and saw what was left of the apron and jacket that we had had no time to get rid of. They came out and the captain said, "Are you sure you did not get this herring in Castlebay?" "Yes sir, we got it in Lochboisdale." "Well, it's hard to tell the difference but be sure you don't touch them lobsters in the boxes up there." We said we wouldn't. Turning away he said, "Where are you going?" I said, "To the trenches, my chum to a mine sweeper." Looking at us he said, "Good luck boys" and turned away. The cook had no time to suggest what should be done to us. Perhaps the captain thought it was a good way to get rid of the greasy outfit. Captains do sometimes have weak stomachs. Regardless of the cook's threat to report us at Invergarry, he did nothing about it.

Many of the passengers using these ships in the winter, crossing the Minch, would have a story to tell of a rough crossing and no comfort, not one, but many. In my memory of these ships, the *Plover* was the worst. She did not have steerage accommodation for her third class passengers and very few from the islands could afford any better at that time. She had a large horse stall where a little shelter could be had. If there were no horses on board, wooden benches were taken to sit on. The wide front part was open to any sea or spray coming over the bow. In bad weather one could not stay and had to find shelter wherever one could. I don't remember the fare then, I always went with an army warrant, but the fare from Glasgow to Lochboisdale was 7/6d. She took three days doing it. Another of the boats was the *Dunara Castle*, which called in nearly every port and island between Glasgow and anywhere south of Lewis. On most islands she anchored off to wait for small boats and her arrival timetable was when she arrived. At least in two places that I know of, if it was daylight, her arrival was made known by large columns of black smoke announcing that the *Dunara Castle* was at the port where the smoke was. If it was a windless day, old and not so old carts could be heard for miles rattling their way on the uneven road to where the smoke was. The smoke signal was for those living on the west side of the island. For us, if we had not seen her coming, we got word through the grapevine and collected the township stuff by boat when suitable. She called, weather permitting, every ten days. Going away on her, you had of necessity to take with you enough food to last to your destination. That was a good supply of potatoes and salt herring, tea, sugar, milk and oat bread, a cup without a handle that you could throw away when finished, along with the small enamel plate. To save cutlery, the bread was buttered before you left, knowing that the knife would go with the cup over the side. You were allowed to cook your own. Of course, there was plenty of food of every kind served in the dining room, with a steward attending, a four-course meal with wine or whisky, costing 2/6. That kind of money to spend on one meal could only be found among the very rich.

Among the ships that I know trading to this island, the *Plover* was the only one that had the distinction of being attacked by a submarine. While heading for Barra, the sub came up, ordered them to the lifeboats and to abandon ship. While doing so he began shelling them. The distance was said to be about a quarter of a mile but no hits were made. One lady from our township was hit on her arm, only a slight wound. Those that took to the lifeboats rowed away. When shelling ceased, the sub went under without firing a torpedo. Whether the ship was worth it or he was afraid of giving his own position away, was not apparent. What it was, in fact, was that the sub's commander was a very humane man. He could have easily hit and sunk her at that distance. Most of the lifeboats returned to the ship and carried on as before, landing ahead of those that did not turn back. I know of only one person living that was on her at the time. Lady Pollen from Gloucestershire, a very dear person. Of her I shall have more to say when I am at the time when I met her family.

In my memory lingers yet another time crossing the Minch from Oban, on hospital leave. The day was fine leaving. Walking the deck was a nice looking woman and a younger girl who I took to be her daughter. They never paid any attention to me. Besides, I was on a sunny seat most of the time, enjoying reading one of Zane Gray's books.

After we had left Tiree behind, the weather was different, heavy seas and strong winds, and when I went down below I found them huddled in a corner, holding onto a rail, both very seasick. As soon as I saw them sitting on that up-turned fish box, I made for them. I said, "I am so sorry that you are so ill. I will try and help you. It won't be long before we are out of this rolling." I helped them both to get cleaned up, and by the time I finished attending to the mother the child was sleeping and had stopped being sick. The sea also had gone down a lot.

I made my way to the galley and told the cook of the two very ill passengers, a mother and her daughter. I asked what would he suggest and he told me to go and get a large glass of brandy from the steward, which he mixed with Bovril and said, "I think it might help." He asked where I was from and when I told him Lochboisdale he said, "Do you know an old sailor from there called Peter MacDonald? I was along with him on my first trip to sea in the *Loch Torridon* a three-masted square-rigger, and he was boatswain who worked us hard but I liked him. Many a time he saved my bacon." I said, "He is a cousin of mine known as Patrick Mor, very old now, but still living." I then took the pick-me-up, which was in a large mug, and gave the mother and child the drink and watched for an improvement, which I saw coming slowly. I went back to the steward who by then had made some soup for them, which I gave them and having finished the soup they felt much better and the spark had returned to their eyes. I returned the dishes, thanked him for the lovely soup and asked if he was on the ship when the sub attacked her and did he leave in the lifeboat. He said he was and stayed on her. The steward left and when the sub went down, he had a good spree on his whisky. He went from this to his young days on the *Loch Torridon* sailing and competing with the other ships in the wool trade between Brisbane and Falmouth. He had much to say about Patrick Mor. I would have stayed longer talking to him but for all I knew about the ladies, Castlebay might well be their destination, so I went to check on them. They were both sitting up, fully recovered, and so I introduced myself to discover they were heading for Lochmaddy to visit relations and for a short holiday. I said, "You will be in smooth, sheltered water to Lochmaddy and you'll be alright. The worst part of the journey, crossing the Minch, is over, and many a hardened sailor has suffered the same plight as you on that journey." We parted at Lochboisdale, I never saw or heard of them again.

My brother Peter met me at Lochboisdale with a hired car and he had a small boat waiting at the road end to get us home. My father and young brother John were dead years before, and all my sisters were away, but for all that I received a warm welcome. I soon discovered that the place had not changed much since I left and not for the better. The footpath they were building when I left had now disintegrated into a path of deep mud, so that when one went to mass, or anywhere on the west side to the main road, one had to carry two pairs of footwear, one Wellingtons, one shoes. The wellies were left at the end of the mud path to be used on the return journey. When the area was divided into crofts, late in 1914, the crofters were promised a footpath. This path called for a six-inch stone bottom, with six inches of gravel on top with a two-foot verge, at two shillings and ten pence a yard completed on contract. The first to take it on went to the war, the second, a neighbour and my father, both good workers, worked at it for a few days and found that it was impossible to complete a yard in a long day. They went on strike for more pay. Unknown to them, three others from the same township took the job at the same rate. They completed the path with little stone bottoming. There was no blasting used and about three inches of gravel spread on the mud centre, a foot verge, a foot deep drain on either side and that was the path finished and passed by a man from the Department made half drunk with whisky before he set foot on it. The only tools ever used in the construction of that school path on both sides of the loch, a distance of over six miles, were a few spades, shovels, sledgehammers and wheelbarrows. Where barrows could not be used, gravel was carried in sacks on their backs. When the cattle began to use it, very soon the heaviest got bogged down till long stretches of it were made impassable for man or beast. It was to remain so until the second war, when a labour government gave us a twelve-foot wide road. By then most of those that suffered the hardship of not having a good road to their homes had gone to their rest.

In bad weather, when boats were unable to go to Lochboisdale for food and materials, all that had to be carried on our backs from the main road, a distance of over two miles across the moor and away from the path that was unusable. Supplies had to be collected from a grocer's van that came to Bayhead at any hour or day that suited him. Having stayed on and endured these hard conditions for over a month, it was not surprising that the locals began to murmur among themselves "Why is he staying here? What's keeping him here? He must be hiding after committing some terrible crimes. No one in his senses, after being so long in the land of milk and honey, would stay in a place like this unless afraid to leave." This came to me often through the grapevine but it was not like that. I was free and welcome to go back to the States whenever I wished, yet I could not answer their whys, not even to myself, except that I liked the place and the people. I am a great believer that one must follow the path of life regardless of how we like it, and I had to follow the path that was ordained for me. To partially explain my meaning my neighbour, in whom I had every trust, told me many times that he saw me and knew me walking about the croft years before I occupied it, and yet while in the States I had no intentions of coming back and only once in a while thought of home. This man had the gift of second sight and could see into the future. It is hard to believe it if you haven't got it yourself.

I am told those who have that gift would rather not have it. I don't regret not having that sight myself, which I think is less talked about than it was in my young days. The commonest was that someone with second sight would see a funeral procession and recognise the people or

Permit to re-enter USA

house concerned, long before it ever happened. One man told me he walked into a thing like that, and what puzzled him was there were two coffins in the procession. Some years afterwards there was a drowning tragedy in our township in which my boat was involved in saving one man, and yet there were two coffins in the funeral procession. When I asked him if he knew anyone he would not commit himself. I did not press him.

Time was passing with me not yet setting a definite date for my departure, one part of me urging me to go, the other urging me to stay. Undecided like that, and not sure of what was keeping me, I let my re-entry permit run out. To renew it meant applying to the U.S. consul again and, if accepted, it would take a long time before being granted. I had to make a living of some sort. What I had saved from bank closure and bad investments in the States could not keep me very long without work, and that was not to be obtained as most were on the dole, if they had enough employment stamps. If not, they were on the means test, and what they got from that infamous test barely kept them alive. My brother was on it after giving most of his life in the Merchant Navy. For himself and wife, he was getting eleven shillings weekly. Those on the dole fared better. Stamps to fill your employment book could be bought at the post office, but you had to have an employer before you could lodge it.

Some took the chance of being an employer, although they had nothing to show they needed to hire anyone. In our neighbourhood township was one of these, an old man who took over the croft of a man who had emigrated to Canada. The dwellings, having been left to him, this old man made it known that he intended to re-build the house and steading, and anyone who required an employer went to see him. He never refused his consent. Of course there was no work done. When any officials were on the prowl, the old man would knock down part of the old wall. If the man from the employment exchange asked where were his workers, were they here? He would say, "Today is a Holiday of Obligation." When the old man reported the progress, his office accepted it. It appears they turned a blind eye, knowing there was no other way round it. I did not apply, perhaps on grounds of conscience.

Since my brother did not have a suitable boat, we talked of getting one between us. I wrote to boatyards on the east coast for a second-hand one. No luck. One man said he would build me one at so much per foot. We liked the idea and gave him an order to be built to our specifications with a Kelvin diesel engine. He wrote by return saying that a boat with the measurements I gave him would have to be three inches longer, and that he wanted half the cost before he laid down the keel. I told Peter that I would pay for the boat myself and wired away what the builder wanted. I did this for two reasons. Firstly, that Peter did not have that kind of money to share and secondly, I thought it best, if possible, that a boat of that kind should be the responsibility of one man and one owner. I have seen boats neglected by having more than one owner. In the meantime, spring was here. I was at where I left off 15 years before. While I knew what should be done, I was not good at doing it. Peter would sometimes laugh and say, "Was it pigs that they used in Canada to turn up the soil Donald? Strange the crops grow so well there." He would redo the part I had done and quietly explain why nothing much would grow there. I was very willing to learn from him. He was easy to get along with.

He had so many stories to tell from local and many parts of the world where his ship called. He was a big man, over six feet and built in proportion, very strong. Many people claimed that in his prime he was the strongest on the island. As an example, he thought nothing of carrying two 140 lb bolts of meal over 100 yards of rocky seaweed shore to the small boat.

189

Firstly, he would pick one up from the flat ground by the lug and throw it under his left arm, holding it there, the other he would throw on his right shoulder and walk away with them. Often when out fishing, if a dogfish got tangled in the net, he would catch it alive, one hand by the head, the other the body and twist it; in a moment the head came off as if cut with a knife. I have never seen anyone else do the same thing. I am very sure that his strength saved us many times when we should not have been to sea. I got word from the builder that the boat would be ready in June and ordered a new engine for him to install.

About that time my war wounds began to bother me, more so the two that still had bits of shell in them. It was arranged, through the British Legion, for me to go to Edenhall Hospital for treatment. I arrived there and was put on heat ray. When I told them of the iron still in my leg and shoulder, they would not believe me but would soon find out. I was marked for X-ray and that day I had on a dressing gown belonging to the hospital, the kind held closed by a cord. The man doing the X-rays said, "Are there any buttons on that dressing gown?" I said, "No, just a cord." He checked it and said, "You can keep it on." He took a picture of my shoulder and leg and found the shrapnel that I knew was there. "Now" he said, "I'll take one of your stomach, they want it." He did but before showing it to me, he said, "Do you remember ever swallowing a button, a large one?" "No" I said, "I don't think I ever did." "You must have, there it is lying there on your spine, a large one. Buttons don't grow in a person. See it for yourself." I did but could not offer an explanation. "Let's have another look at that dressing gown you are wearing. Take it off." I did and again he found nothing. "It's alright, put it on again. I'll have to take another picture" which he did and the button was still there. He grew angrier, accused me of having been drunk at some time, swallowing the button without remembering, and so he took a further picture without the dressing gown. This time there was no button showing. He made a rush for the discarded gown, and on further examination found that the gown had a small belt sewn on the back with a button hidden underneath it. Without feeling that spot, no one could tell it was there. He was very angry and said how much that button cost the hospital and after he finished the tearing and swearing there was very little left of the dressing gown.

My main purpose for applying for admittance to that hospital was to impress the doctors there that I was entitled to a war pension in regard to my disability. I needed to develop a limp in order to prove my entitlement, and maintain it while in hospital. A few days after I had been X-rayed, I was examined by two doctors who had my X-rays with them. After looking me over, the ward doctor said to take a walk down the ward. I did with the not too bad limp. Sitting down again he said, "I am not sure what is causing that limp. I don't think the piece of shell in your leg is the reason. Are you right or left handed?" I said, "Right handed." "That" he said, "is quite obvious. Look at the muscles on that arm. It must have taken a lot of hard work to develop it to that extent. Does that small piece of shell there ever bother you?" "Yes, it certainly does, very painful, but not all the time." "Well we could take both out for you, but I must tell you that to do that would require much cutting and digging, and in the end your shoulder and leg would not be any better than what they are now. If you want to risk that, we will operate and take them out for you. It is up to you to allow us to do that. Let us know what you decide within a week." I said, "I was renewing my claim for the pension that was taken off me. Would my refusing that operation affect my claim in any way?" "No" he said, "I don't think so. It will be for the Pension Board to decide. We only assess the degree of your disability and report it to them." I knew I could not bluff him nor could I expect any sympathy.

At that time, the Ministry of Pensions was divided into two sections, the southern and northern command. At the head of these were two eminent doctors, Sir John Mackenzie and Sir Angus MacEwen. They both used to visit Edenhall Hospital fairly often. I was allowed outside after the doctor was finished with his ward rounds, and used to go for a walk in the hospital grounds or sit on a bench and read. When walking, and if anyone else was around, especially doctors or nurses, I had to make sure I remembered to limp. There did not seem to be any hurry for one to leave and I was allowed out to the town of Musselburgh. Still, since the treatment I was on was not doing me any good, I saw no point in staying. I told the ward doctor I wanted to be discharged and that I was taking his advice to leave the bits of shell in. He said, "I did not advise you, what I said was we would take it out for you if you wanted us to. Do you now say that you don't want us to?" "Since you have said that removing it would not make me any better I see no point in taking it out at this time, but I feel the disability that I have entitles me to a war pension." "Well" he said, "We will put you before a board in a few days." They did and it was one of the top doctors. He asked me why I was discharging myself from the hospital. I told him and asked if, due to the fact that I still had pieces of shell in my body that gave me trouble, would he recommend that my pension be re-instated. He said he would but that it was the Pension Board that had the last say and they were in England. I didn't get a cent.

The day before I left was a Sunday. I went to mass early and at the church I met another patient. We talked of the long past war in which he was in the Royal Scots. He said, "Since there is plenty of time before mass, I think I'll go to confession. It's a long time since I have been. Anyway, it will be different from the one I had in the Dardanelles." I said, "What was so different about that one?" "Well, we were under the cliff on the beach, no shells could reach near us, all falling in the sea about two hundred yards out, and between that and the shore, crowds of us went bathing. One day I was out when a man swimming near me came over and asked if I was a Catholic? I said I was. He said, "I am a priest, I can hear your confession here if you want, just swim out along with me." I did and began my confession swimming out from the rest. There was a lull in the shelling. We swam to the safety line and shells began to fall near us. We dived under and swam back to safety, where he gave me absolution and said that was the strangest confession he had ever heard.

I returned home in no better condition than when leaving, as my developed limp did not do me any good. I gave Peter a hand with the remaining spring work and then began making preparations for lobster and herring fishing. Before that was done the new boat had arrived. We were very pleased with her and we named her the *St. Theresa*. Peter knew a little about the engine. I beached her and began the chore of painting and tarring her. In doing the inside of a new boat, the best method of curing the wood is by using warm Archangel tar, very hard to get. I was lucky to get two gallons of it from an old store. It penetrates the wood and gives it a lifetime endurance of nearly a century, if done properly. It was no good under the water line. I used mid-green paint above the water line outside and bitumastic paint under. I got a fleet of nets and great lines. Peter and I took her out on her first day ever fishing. Another man asked if he could come along and so the three of us began fishing with a line each. The other man said, "Let's see who will take the first fish on board. I hope it will be her owner." as indeed it was. I caught it, although it was a small one.

That day, before we came back, we had caught nearly a boatload. After giving much away, we salted and dried the rest, barrels of it, for lobster bait. It proved the best I have ever tried. Shortly afterwards we tried the herring nets and got four crabs and sixteen boxes of good quality herring in Corradale. As there was no market at Lochboisdale we had to go to Castlebay, a long distance for an open small boat. It took us five hours to get there. Some Eriskay boats were in and they gave us a hand to put our catch ashore and we got top price for it. We had a good meal on one of the boats and then put fuel on board before going for a dram. It turned out that the barman and owner knew our father very well and that he was a pal of his long ago. He was sorry when we told him that our father had died many years before. We had a few drams with him, all the time talking of his young days in Uist where he belonged. We did not stay long, but as we were leaving he pushed a flask over the bar saying, "Take this, you'll need it on your long journey."

As the boat was not loaded we made better time on the return journey to Locheynort and, although we intended to shoot the nets again that night, tiredness and possibly the effects of the drams prevented that. Together we had many narrow escapes in that boat out in weather that we should not have been. During the first season from July till March, we only missed a day from going to sea. That could not be said of much larger boats. Peter was a superb seaman, much better than I was, and more experienced at sea, and yet in bad weather he depended on me for handling the boat, knowing that I could do it better. When we began lobster fishing he had some years experience at it, while I had only a month at the most and yet I was the skipper of the boat. I had sense enough to learn from him and go by his decisions, which I willingly did and we got on very well in that arrangement. All the time I was gaining knowledge of the shore and its bottom ground, and he often remarked that I was getting on better. I was keen to learn. I liked the gamble and the expectation of the work better than any I had done before. Whatever happened you were always in a state of anticipation, which you would not be on a weekly wage, regardless of how sure you were of it. We caught a lot of lobsters that season but the price we got, if they had reached Billingsgate alive, was miserable. Death was due to bad, slow or too hot, transportation.

I recall sending a consignment of 288 prime lobsters to Billingsgate. In return we got a postal order for 7/6, or about 35 pence in today's money, with a letter warning us of the consequences of sending shell fish to the market that were not fit for human consumption. The last thing we would do was to pack a weak lobster that we had any doubt of it reaching the market alive, knowing that if it died most of the rest would also. When our lobsters reached the salesman, he could tell us anything about their condition and he could then pay us whatever he liked. Some salesmen were honest; most were not. Trying to fool them we often sent consignments of the same kind in different names. That revealed how crooked they were. We could do nothing to change that. Thankfully things have now changed and the salesman comes to you and pays a fair price, which does away with the need for boxing and transportation. When I think of the amount that I have caught at today's prices, I should have been very rich.

Herring fishing then was different, forgetting all the aids there are today to guide you. At that time your guide was the movement of birds, seagulls and gannets and how they were acting. There was also plankton and its movements which few took any notice to study. I knew of an old man who did. He was not a native of the island but was considered a very lucky fisherman, so much so, that many boats would follow him to wherever he went because it was rare to see him come back empty. Very often, boats fishing with him in the same ground would come back with a light catch while he would have a heavy one, leading some to whisper that he was in league with the devil, although it did not stop them from following him. One night, an Eriskay boat, having shot their nets before dawn, were taking them onboard with no fish in them. The old man's boat came near and hailed, "Did you see any herring boys?" "Yes" was the reply. "We have at least 15 crans" they lied. At that the old man ordered the nets out. The Eriskay boat made for Lochboisdale, tied up and they went to bed sure that the other boat would for once not catch any fish. In the morning the other boat was tied up next to them, the crew were busy cleaning their nets from a big catch of herring. They watched them shaking the herring out of the nets with envy and one said to the other, "What did I tell you, he must be in league with the devil." The other said, "No doubt about it." One man called to those working the nets and said, "Where did you catch all that herring?" The reply was, "This is the herring you left behind when you hauled in your nets blank and took off to an easy bed at Lochboisdale." It was like adding insult to injury but there it was. The truth of the matter was the devil or his work had nothing at all to do with it. What had to do with it was plankton on which herring feed, very small organisms which swim at different depths at certain times of the year, and if a shoal of herring found its track, that's where you generally would catch them. But first you need to have a good idea of what that depth might be. Sometimes in daylight you can see it in minute form near the surface, at other times there is more depth, so that if your nets were not let down far enough, or too far, you caught only strays or none. This man, in all his long years of herring fishing, kept a log on where he was fishing, the date, the depth, the state of the tide and any other relevant information concerning that area. From those places he would choose where he thought best. Although not always 100% accurate because of circumstances such as whales, sharks and dogfish attacking and scattering the shoal, it was much better than going out blind and trusting to luck.

It is not easy to recall the many escapades that Peter and I had while out fishing. One day, when out from Uisinish Lighthouse, partly lost in fog, Peter was at the stern trying to see land or hear the sea breaking on the shore. The boat was slowing down when all of a sudden, without warning, a whale jumped out of the water, I thought about six foot high across our bow, missing us by a few yards. Because of the nearness and the splash it made, much water had come on-board and we had to bale fast. It disappeared in the fog. We were glad when Peter spotted land. I have a healthy respect for these mammals but it's fascinating watching them swim round and under you. I was never hit by any. Once in a small boat we were kept for at least two hours in a small bay by a fairly large one. I felt sure she was playing some kind of game with us, yet I thought it unwise in a ten foot boat to go near enough to push her with an oar to get out of our way. She kept a distance of about 15 feet, sometimes less, and every time we made to leave that small bay, she kept us hemmed in by keeping that distance and moving beside us at our speed. At the end of the bay she would put on more speed and stop about the same distance across our bow, we would backwater in a hurry and make for the other end. She would turn over and follow on the surface to be there again in front of us. We tried that many times. It was no use. We dare not go too near as one swing of the tail would smash or capsize us. We stopped in the middle of the bay looking at the high cliffs above, wondering if we could climb and let the boat drift. There was no way we could haul her up. We had nothing to anchor her. We thought that to tie her to the rocks would smash her. All this time the whale remained at the same place with only an occasional flip of the tail as if to say, come on let's have more fun. If it was fun for her, it was certainly not for us. We waited, hugging the shore, with nothing happening. We did keep on trying our oar just away from the rocks, hoping she was asleep or had lost interest. We quietly got past her, or so we thought. She began to move and so did we, to the shore, fast. Before we hit the rocks, we saw that she was not following us, instead her head was pointing seawards. We drew a sigh of relief thanking God for the escape from another harmless whale.

Another brush I had, happened in another bay, the area would be less than three acres of land space. In that space I counted 35 whales and basking sharks, not counting the many seen

194

outside that space. Another man and I were lifting our creels along the bay's shore, when they began coming in from the open sea. The day was sunny with very little wind. They kept their distance at least 30 yards from us. A dark cloud was building up in the south west, and the nearer it came the blacker it got, blocking out the sun, leaving us in semi-darkness. None of us had seen anything like it before. We thought of leaving but where to? The whales and sharks were almost packed between us and the open sea, and to venture out in that light would be madness. We had finished lifting and the catch was stowed away. The creels we pitched out anywhere so that the boat would be in trim to face whatever was coming. The extra dark and black cloud was now nearer and much lower; there was still no wind, and when it reached the hill top it burst with a crash of thunder and lightning and the rain came straight down in buckets. The whales in the bay went mad with either fear or joy, diving and leaping high in the air splashing waves off to the shore.

We had to row the boat out, as there was too much water in her to start the engine. We stopped a short distance out and baled her dry. As a result of the heavy rain, many rivers formed and were rushing down the mountainside carrying with them large chunks of earth, some still having long heather sticking out, which floated out among the whales. I wish I could draw for you a clear picture of what happened. A very large whale, perhaps touching the earth and smelling the heather crashed dived, surfaced some yards away, leapt high and made at high speed for the open seas as if in terror. Many put on a display of jumping, pushing and diving, all very amusing since by now we felt safe enough. That downpour lasted more than a quarter of an hour, in which time we had to bale the boat out three times. When it did pass over us, the sun broke through shining on that curtain of heavy rain. The picture indeed was long remembered and talked about. A good camera at the time would have been invaluable. We followed them out of that bay and turned right into Locheynort; still no wind and the tide was long on the ebb. We were met with small and large chunks of earth resembling islets or rocks. A stranger following his chart would hesitate to enter. A local boat fishing south of the loch, about three miles from us, said they had no rain but saw and heard the black cloud when it burst. They thought the wind was past gale force where we were. We saw none of that. It was not a profitable day for us, the lobsters we thought safely covered over, were flooded by the rainwater in the boat. We nursed them in a separate float but most died. Next day those creels we had in the bay of the whales had nothing in them, not even crabs that we always got too many of. We blamed it on that thunder and bolt of lightning.

Peter and I worked at the lobsters well into March. It was not a profitable season in spite of having fished well. Prices were low and death rates were high. After clearing expenses there was little left. Nevertheless, I gained a lot of experience. By then I knew almost every yard of the sea floor along the coast from Lochboisdale to Uisinish, having fished up and down so many times. The good and bad patches became well recorded in my memory. I think it is wise to remember the old Gaelic saying, "The sea always invites you to call on her, what she has to offer it's for you to search."

Towards the end of March we began spring work again and making preparations for the next season. We had lost a good part of our gear that had to be replaced. One would think that it doesn't take much time or labour getting a lobster pot ready for sea. It may surprise you that in order to complete one of the old type, 2 feet x 14 inches with one eye, any man who could do that work in a long day was considered a top man. Not many could. This type of creel is useless today. I do not know when lobster fishing first began on our island. It was claimed by old men that it was during the Napoleonic wars, when doctors found it of great value as food, sustaining the wounded and restoring them to health. Before then, it was not used for human food. Perhaps, like in my own time, when we caught a large prawn in the creel, we threw it overboard as no use. Old men told tales of their fathers and grandfathers catching whales along the coast here, following them in a 14-foot boat, with a homemade harpoon made by the local blacksmith. The rope attached was made from the mane and tails of horses. The same thing applied when we, in later years, made casts for haddock hooks. Any crofter who had a foal with a long silvery tail had to watch it. A clipped tail meant reduction in price, which he often suffered. The reason why these tails were so desired is that they blended in colour with the sandy bottom, would not rot and, if properly made, would not kink. It was very time consuming and quite an art in preparing the tail for use, but time during the long winter nights was what they had.

Stories say that the men in the rowing boat continued to follow the whale, as evidently they were plentiful, following shoals of herring left undisturbed along the shores. The inhabitants had not yet nets to fish with, and they depended on crude walls built across narrow bays at low tide, the incoming tide bringing many kinds of fish to be left stranded if they stayed until the level of the water was below the wall top. Salmon were caught, and when the ground officer got to know of it the wall was knocked down, and restoring it meant your miserable patch of land was taken off you and you were perhaps transported abroad.

When the whalers saw a stationary whale, they approached it with care. The men on the oars backed the boat near enough for the strong harpooner to plunge his crude weapon in the place where he wanted, with one end of the hair rope made fast to the harpoon, the other in the boat made fast to an air-tight hogshead cask that was put over the side when a strike was made. The men rowed hard to get away from the whale, which usually crash-dived and swam away from them, but there was no guarantee that it would not turn on them, as sometimes it did. Then it was a case of trying to dodge it. When it reached the length of the rope, the hogshead took over and acted as a brake. Perhaps thinking that was the enemy, it often turned on it while the boat kept well away, watching it careering in every direction, submerging and taking the cask down with it. After some time, and when the cask surfaced with the whale towing it, they followed, judging the speed and the remaining strength of the whale. If it slowed down and headed in the right direction, they took in part of the rope on board but not yet the cask. They took an easy slip turn at the stern and let her tow the boat and cask, which acted as a sea anchor, wearing her down. That depended on how much blood and energy she had lost. Sometimes she put on an extra spurt to get away. That was when the turn on the stern was thrown off and she was let go where she wanted, taking the hogshead with her. That play could go on for a day, and when there was no more fight left the task of towing her began, depending on current and tide. When the whale was considered harmless, two half hitches were put on the tail making towing easier, keeping to shallow water to where it was anchored before it turned against you. They said, if lucky, it took three days to get the whale to the place you wanted. At very low tide I saw evidence of large bones in such a place. It is still called the Port of the Whale where they were skinned, the blubber taken off and rendered into oil that was used for light and given to cattle that were not thriving well, and sold at a penny a bottle. Only once have I seen that oil used in the raw state. That was on myself when in a flooded front line trench, with water and mud past the knees for days, and boots not useable through swollen feet that were wrapped in sand bags.

196

About the end of April 1937, I took over one of Peter's crofts. There was a small thatched low wall house on it. I liked the croft and the view from where the house was. The house itself was not long built. After much thought and doubt, I decided to build my own home. I took the roof off and cleared the stance. I got the stonemason who first built it, he was my neighbour and known as Seonaidh a'Clachair, I asked his opinion on the wall and the size of the house that could be built. He said he could not build a better wall. All that was needed was to build it higher to give space for an upstairs accommodation, as building a large house would be foolish. I could see his point. He did not, of course, mention it, but I was getting old and not yet married, not even a girlfriend on which I could build hope, and the fishing so far did not make my bank roll much better. However, I made a start quarrying stone whenever I found time between getting fishing gear ready and peat cutting. One day, doing that for a cousin across the loch, I met a girl, Mary Ann, who was visiting Morag, her married sister. I liked her and we talked much. There was a dance that night and I asked her if she cared to go. She did and we met at the arranged place and walked to the dance. It was very enjoyable and the more I saw of her, the better I liked her. She promised to write as she was going home the next day to Taobh a' Chaolais (East Kilbride), about 12 miles south of Locheynort. She kept that promise till eventually she became my dear wife.

Much water went over the dam before that happened. We lived far apart and seldom saw each other but correspondence was regular. With that moral support, it made my hard work a joy since I firmly decided this time I would drop the anchor for good. When I thought I had enough stones quarried to build a castle, I consulted the mason. He said I would need at least three times that amount. I had to believe him knowing of the many houses he had built. Peter and I took another man to crew with us, as the boat was heavy to work. He was a man with much experience in that line. We fished well but again, prices were low and the death rate was high. We also fished for herring and sold it locally.

While out one night just before Christmas, we were involved in a drowning tragedy in which two men lost their lives. As we came into the loch from the North, we saw a good place to set out nets, but decided to go further in the loch to a sheltered place. When we got there, another boat was there and they had already set their nets and had gone to the shore for better shelter. We set ours near theirs and went to join them. There were three of them, my friend Angus James's two sons, Alan and Roderick, both teenagers, and Angus, their next door neighbour who was married to Morag, Mary Ann's sister. The wind was rising fast and having talked to them for about an hour, they then left to try their nets and we stayed a little longer. On our way out, we stopped to see if they had come across any herring. They were busy taking in their nets and said it was a light catch but that it would be enough for them. The wind then was real gale force. We went to one of our nets and began hauling it in to find the herring in it were scattered far apart. We decided to remove it and the other two nets, clean them and reset the three of them again. Before we finished cleaning them, we saw by the light he was showing, that Angus had shot his nets again, some 300 yards to our left, on his way home. We were shooting ours windward of him. His light, plainly, could be seen. It did not take us more than six minutes to throw the three nets out and when we did and looked up, there was no light where Angus was. I did not hear anything, I think because I was standing in strong wind but Peter, whose head was in the boat's shelter did at once say, "Let her go Donald." With my knife already in my hand, I cut the rope tying us to the nets and told them to get the oars out, while I put the rudder on and primed the engine. It started on the second try. I have many times afterwards tested how long it would take to do that distance in a calm sea. I estimated not more than six minutes and with a gale force wind following, it should be much less. It was pitch dark. We had no light and began searching the area where we thought the boat would be. With no signs we then went into the lee shore bay and were nearly washed on the rocks when Alistair saw the foam from backwash and shouted, and I put her hard over. She came round fast and took in a lot of water. Alistair said, "Slow her down or you will drown us." Going out we heard a cry and made for it and we saw the man on the oar, then within ten yards. Fearing to pass or hit him, I slowed the boat. She stopped as near as 9 feet from him. Alistair pushed the oar out and Allan, clinging to his own oar, caught it and we pulled him in and began searching for the other two.

In the very few minutes it took us to get Allan on board, I am quite sure it was dead calm and did not stay like that more than the time we took. After telling us what happened we began searching the bay till we were convinced no-one could survive in that sea and they may well be washed ashore where we could not get to them, so we left and took the boat where we could land. Alistair and I left Allan with Peter in the boat and went to search where they might be. Searching and shouting, all we found was an oar. It was very cold, and fearing that Allan might die of exposure, we called it off and went to the north side of the strait in the slim hope…. Nothing was there. How to break the sad news to their parents on the south side of the loch was a hard decision to make, because if we were to take Allan to our home on the north side, it would be impossible to go to the south side again or to contact the priest to break the news on that wild night. Although Allan was wet after being in the water, he was not any worse than we were. We saw that he was bearing up very well, and it was he who took the bad news to his father, who met us at the shore with Morag, now a young widow with a few months' old baby boy in her arms, lamenting. It was hard to forget that sight. Peter stayed to comfort them. Another cousin and he went out again that night in the hope that they had got ashore and that we had missed them. They found nothing. Peter never got over the hardship he suffered that night and never went to sea again.

Alastair and I took out the boat in the following gale and darkness to the lee harbour, but not being able to see the shore we had a lucky escape at the entrance. Next day was fine. Word went round as to what happened. We went out to the scene of the tragedy. Floats from the sunken boat were on the surface but we could not pull her up. Next day Morag's cousins from Eriskay, with their large boat and gear, came to help, along with the local boats. We got her to the surface. She was full of herring, nets and ballast, nothing else. We baled her out and took the nets and ballast and began dragging for their bodies. Angus's body was found first near the boat, and Roderick's body about 40 yards from the shore he was making for. They were put on board the large boat to be taken to their homes. Peter went with them to pilot them in. I towed the raised boat and moored her in a safe place, and then followed the large boat in complete darkness to where she anchored. I only discovered where when someone on board her struck a match.

My neighbour told me that he watched us coming in with the large boat shining with bright white lights, yet no one in our boat saw anything a few yards behind. That boat to my knowledge was not involved in a fatal accident while she remained on this coast, and the two bodies then on board her had nothing to do with her being lit up as my neighbour saw her. The lights remained a mystery and were much talked about. Later in the war she was taken over by the Navy, where she was used to ferry the dead from ship to shore, and that is thought to be the reason for the lights seen. The way this tragedy happened was told by the lone survivor, Allan, a boy in his teens, who could not swim a stroke. After they had lifted their nets and headed for home, they came on a shoal of herring and cast their nets again. While taking them in full of herring the sea was rough and water was coming in faster than they could bale. A huge wave came over the stern and swamped her and they all went down with her. When Allan and his brother Roderick surfaced, they found an oar. There was no sign of Angus. Clinging to the oar, Roderick, who was a good swimmer, said he could swim ashore and left the oar to Allan. I don't think Angus could swim. Regardless of it being a wild night, and their boat being as capable as ours, it was thought that, had they taken necessary precautions in time by cutting the nets, that is if they were able to do that, the boat would have taken care of herself. The thought of how to prevent it could not have entered their minds because of the speed with which it happened and the sea being so rough. One might say how could it have been prevented when it was already ordained to happen that way, there were many unnatural happenings in connection with that tragedy. Shortly before it happened a local boat, coming home in that area on a fine evening, in a flash saw our boat bearing down on them and almost running into them, yet we were nowhere in the area of the loch at that time. Next day when we took the nets in, they were full of prime herring. No one would use it, not even for lobster bait, and we dumped it back into the sea. For a long time, gloom was cast on the township.

We fished for lobsters till March. When spring work on the croft began, that and peat cutting finished, I resumed working on the house, giving the Clerk of Works of the department the measurements for the house. I ordered and paid for the material required and waited for its arrival. When it did come, after a long delay, I asked the mason what wage per hour he was wanting? "If you give me a shilling an hour I will be quite happy." I said I would and also time and a half for any time he worked more than eight hours in a day. He would not take the over-time rate I offered him, saying straight time was enough, seeing that no time was kept off him if we stopped work for any reason. He was noted as a hard worker, as a tradesman he had built many of the houses in the district. He certainly kept me busy working and that was what I wanted. Building an undressed stone house is very different to cement and concrete-made blocks and takes far less time. In fact anyone who knows how to use a plumb and level can do it. With undressed stone of so many shapes and sizes, each one different, the width of the walls is made to take your largest stones, making it as wide as three and four feet. Mine, on account of the large stones, was four feet when finished, the largest always at the bottom.

Two walls were built and the space between packed with concrete and stone, each stone in the inside and outside wall made to fit. Working hard, if we put on one course in two days we were doing well. The house stands on a site some 200 yards away from the sea and about 200 feet above it. Against that incline, I had to carry on my back all the materials except the stone that went into the building of it. Nearly all the sand used was taken from Eriskay and Glendale. That may seem strange since building sand is in abundance on the west shore within seven miles, but since there was no road within three miles from where I could load the boat, going to Eriskay for it only took one good day, with much less labour. With such obstacles as these, progress was slow, and when we began roofing we found we were short of sarking and much slate, such was the calculation of the clerks who ordered it. However, I got them as a loan from a man who was beginning to build his own home. I offered to pay him then but he would rather that I would replace the slates when he needed them. As it turned out I was by far the loser, however we were able to get on with the slating for which I was grateful.

A man came to the site that I did not know. He was the Sanitary Inspector for the district and Seonaidh knew him. He said, "Is this your house?" I said, "Yes." "Then it appears that you have made a great mistake. I have here a report from the Inverness County Council that a house is being built on this croft without any permission. No plans for the house have been submitted or permission to build on it granted. You have broken all the building regulations. My office has the power to make you take the house down, and if you want to build again you will have to get permission after submitting plans. In the meantime, you are not allowed to do any more work on it." I said, "I was not aware of these new regulations, no-one has told me about them, and since I was the tenant of this croft and building the house with my own money, no loan or any other aid, I was under the impression that I could build my own house where it suited me, without consulting anyone but the builder. He is, as you know, a master builder and tells me a house of this kind cannot be built better. Now I can be made to pull it down?" He said, "It is not me you are up against. It's the department. I know that the house is well built and on a good stance. I will recommend that it should stand and be finished." I thanked him and said, "Whatever the department may do, I shall not take it down. Too much sweat went into putting it up, and anyone with that in mind had better have his life insured before he pulls the first stone out." I am not sure if it was that or his recommendation, but I got an early reply to have a plan of the existing house made and sent to their office. I did that and it came back. They wanted a clear plan and a duplicate before I got permission to continue with the house.

SS Kayeson

The war had started. Soon I got a letter from St. Andrew's House saying how my building was not far enough advanced to make it eligible for any material. I was therefore advised to close it up until hostilities ceased. That was the final blow. There was nothing else I could do but recall the words of Burns 'The best laid schemes of mice and men gang aft agley'. I began to secure the house against the winter gales, filling up windows with stone and had a door fixed. I then made preparations to leave the island. I had beached the boat that spring thinking and planning that the house would be finished before winter and nothing would stop me from getting married. I had also planted potatoes and corn for the cow I planned to buy and the crop was growing very well. Now I had no use for it so I gave it to Peter. I was not able to see the man I got the loan of the slate from before I left home but wrote to him from my sister's house in Oban saying that I was going to sea and if anything happened to me, he was to contact my sister for payment of the slates. I gave him her address. Like mine, his building was at a stand still. In the event of my not returning, I was leaving the house and croft to my nephew, Iain, my sister's eldest son, and the boat to Peter. I left her a paper signed to this effect and stayed in Oban a few days.

During this stay, and since I had known her, Mary Ann and I were in regular correspondence with me growing fonder of her as time went on. The latest setback was a hard felt disappointment, and while I knew there were two others in the running, she seemed as keen on me as I was on her and we promised to keep writing as often as possible.

I arrived in Glasgow and found lodgings. In there was a man that I slightly knew whose name was Roderick MacInnes from South Lochboisdale. Big Roddy, as we called him, told me he was signing on a certain ship the next day and if I enquired for a job on her, I would very likely get it. The last British ship I was on was before the 1914 war. My papers to that effect were long lost but I had my American A.B. certificate plus my lifeboat one. Armed with these I went on board that ship and saw the captain and was signed on. All the sailors except one from Glasgow were from the Uists and Skye. The ship was the *Kayeson* from London. She was then getting a gun fitted on her stern, and as that was where the crew's quarters were, they were now made very confined by the supporting iron pillars of the gun and platform as well as the magazine.

We left with the tide and began swinging out the lifeboats passing Greenock in order to get her ship-shape. One lifeboat would not swing, perhaps something with the davits? The boat was stuck half way out which was a bad omen. We anchored and signalled for burners and welders and they repaired the damaged part. It was morning before we got away, bound for Cardiff, and we had good weather down the Irish Sea till we ran into thick fog. As we were not in a convoy the Captain kept her very close to the shore. I was keeping look out on the fo'c'sle head and visibility was about 100 yards. I saw something white ahead. A moment later I knew it was the breakers on the shore and we were heading for them. I sang out "breakers ahead" but I am sure those up on the bridge saw them first. They were higher up because by then the ship's head was already turning away. I saw no more of that shore. I think the old man knew exactly where he was because he did not reduce speed. On that short passage the sailors were getting to know one another. I was the eldest in the fo'c'sle. The boatswain and an ordinary seaman, first trip to sea, were neighbours from the south end of our island. The ordinary seaman thought, since that was so, he did not have to take any orders from his home neighbour. I took some time to convince him that a boatswain had much authority on board a ship regardless of who he was, but Donald was incorrigible. To the boatswain's embarrassment one day, Donald said to him in our hearing, "Do you remember the day you took our horse and cart to go for a load of peat, and coming back you went off the road and capsized the lot into the ditch?" "Yes, I do. The horse was like you, he didn't want to take orders, so see that doesn't happen to you." Donald was a good enough ordinary seaman before the voyage ended.

We called first at Cardiff for a part load of coal, the rest at Newport. As my sisters, the nuns, were there I was able to visit them the next day and brought them a small present. They were very glad to see me. They thought I was still at home. I spent a few very happy hours with them and before leaving, the one in charge asked me if I would like to leave the ship and stay in Newport? If I did, she could get me a job starting tomorrow as a barman with people she knew well. I thanked her and said I did not like to break any engagement and I would take my chance like the rest. Running away from danger won't save you if that's what you have to meet.

After a fast loading, we left on Christmas Day to join a convoy at Milford Haven. We were delayed for a couple of days as the Chief Officer took ill, but he recovered and a replacement was not required. We left that night in good but cold weather to join another convoy. When daylight came we were in the middle of a convoy of some 30 ships of every description and size. It was an eight-knot convoy; that was the slowest vessel. All had to keep to that speed in order to keep to their station, four abreast about 100 yards apart, with those behind not in the wake but about 50 yards to port or starboard. If to port, the next line went to starboard. These positions had to be kept to avoid collision. It was a nerve-racking situation, more so at night with no lights showing except the small shaded glimmer in the compass. All the convoy turned left or right according to the plan on the steering chart, staying on given points as long as the time indicated on that chart, before putting the ship on another course. This might be three points left or right and back again to your standing course. A bell rang when every course was changed. Ours was a good steering ship but much care and attention was necessary when changing by a few points at any time. There was no room to play with.

One dark night with the one ahead of us steering very badly, I was at the wheel. Big Roddy was standing lookout a few feet in front of me. The old man was on the bridge not far from me, but I could not see him in the dark. The ship was steady on course. I thought I would chance taking the three steps to ask Roddy how far was she away from us. "About three herring nets" he said. I returned at once; the ship was on course. No sooner I felt the captain at my side and in an angry voice said, "What were you saying to the look-out?" "Nothing, sir." "You did say something and I want to know what." "Well sir, I asked Roderick how far the ship ahead was from us. He replied about three herring nets." I expected at least a telling off for leaving the wheel, but instead he said, "That's just what I want to hear, are you both fishermen?" "Yes sir." "Well I think he is about right, I was a fisherman myself at one time." Ever since that night we felt that he had more confidence in us and often talked to us about different ways of fishing. He told me of a certain net, a trammel. I got one made years afterwards and it was very effective. Too much if you landed in a shoal. Dog and kingfish ruined it.

Another incident while at the wheel in that zigzag convoy in daylight, the second mate was in charge of navigation. The bell rang to change course to starboard. The officer was watching the bad steering ship ahead. I put the wheel hard over and the head began to move in response. When the officer saw the direction, he ran over and grabbed the wheel trying to pull it from me saying, "My God man, we are going the wrong way." At the same time he tried to pull the wheel his way, which he could not do, for I was stronger. I said, "I am perfectly sure of what I am doing." At that moment he looked up and saw that the other ships were swinging like us. With drops of sweat on his face he said he would take an oath that I was doing the wrong thing. Two heads are better than one. He remarked how easy it was to make mistakes in that kind of work. Shortly after that we nearly had a major disaster, in broad daylight and calm sea. All the warning bells rang in the ship for emergency stations. We thought we were being attacked. Roddy was at the wheel. We were on deck watching every ship taking evasive action to prevent colliding. By the grace of God, none did, regardless of the many near misses. It all happened when the man, a high-ranking officer on the commodore ship in charge of the convoy, sent out a wrong signal. Some obeyed, some did not, causing much confusion, every ship trying to save itself. When things settled and Roderick was relieved, he looked very pale and sweating; he did well to save the ship. Afterwards, it was claimed that the signal was sent out before the last order was completed. The commander admitted his mistake and congratulated all on their performance in that action. All the same, in the time we were to be under his command, we had little trust in him.

As the sun was going down, the wind was rising soon to gale force. The convoy could not keep their stations and were drifting apart. Before midnight, it was storm force and we hove to, nothing to be seen when the ship rose out of the trench. When daylight came and the storm moderated, we saw a lone small ship about two miles to port making heavy weather of it. Whenever we saw her, she seemed to be making for some African port. There was no sign of the rest of the convoy, we were on our own and glad to be. The gale had died down. We were now well into the South Atlantic and out of range of the U-boats. We were on true course. The rest of the way we had the sea to ourselves, nothing to be seen in clear, calm, sunny weather, except the occasional long range bird and plenty of flying fish. I spent a lot of time watching them and thinking that no wonder the Barra man in his song thought they were birds until he found one of them on board. I did not see any coming on board this time, as the sea was too calm.

All the soldiers and sailors in the fo'c'sle were Gaelic speaking except for an ordinary seaman from Glasgow, and he was a rascal. That came to light when, at the start of the voyage, I noticed that Roderick was not smoking; he told me he was out of smokes. I told him I had plenty of black tobacco and he could have some. He said that he took plenty of cigarettes with him but the Glasgow lad had stolen them. He had caught him at them in his locker and told him to stop it, but he just kept doing it. He said if he had laid a hand on him he might hurt him bad, and if he reported him he would get a bad discharge. He would rather stop smoking than do any of that, but now he had taken nearly all of his soap. Roderick was a giant in body and strength, as brave as a lion, and as gentle as a lamb. I have never in my life seen a man having so much influence on a crowd of hard swearing, cursing men than he had, not by strong arm tactics but by talk and kindness.

Before we reached Montevideo, I decided to make myself a better kit bag, as the one I had was small and borrowed. At the wheel one day I asked the third mate if he would let me have some canvas, twine, palm and needle to make one. He did, but told me not to let the others know where I had got the stuff. I was making a start and had the canvas cut when the bosun came and asked what I was doing. I told him. "Do you know how to do it?" I responded that I would give it a good try. "Alright" he said, "I'll show you how to do the sewing." He began and sewed about a foot then told me to do it just like that. He said he would come back to see how I was getting on. I looked at his work and decided to take the lot apart and began on my own. I was well used to sewing canvas as I had done a lot of it on the lake boats and learned from a Swede. I saw no point in telling him what I could or could not do, because he had already hinted that I was bluffing my way and did not know all I was supposed to know. When he came back I already had one seam done. After inspecting it he said, "Where did you learn how to sew canvas?" I said, "Do you know Donald Gillies, the tailor?" "Of course, he made a suit for me once. He is a very good tailor." "Well, once I took a piece of cloth to him for a pair of trousers. He said they would be ready at the weekend. I went for them but he had not started. Next week was the same. By the third week I must have said something he did not like. In anger he said, "Alright, I'll cut you the cloth and you can do the sewing yourself. I will show you how." He did and I finished them in two nights. Of course, fearing damage to his reputation, he inspected my work and said he could not do it any better, and that was how I learned to sew.

One day the naval gunner we had was allowed to test the gun and fire three shots at a floating barrel that we had put out at about 300 yards away. The first shot went at least 30 yards past the barrel, the second was a near miss, the third smashed the barrel. We all agreed that he was a very good gunner and although in a dead calm sea, we felt much safer that night of the 28th day out from Milford Haven. We sighted the glare from the lights of Rio de Janeiro. From the time we parted with the convoy we saw no other ships and had no news about the war until we arrived outside the beautiful harbour of Montevideo, when we took on board the pilot. A mile out from the harbour we saw a large super-structure out of the water. The pilot told us it was the *Graf Spee,* the famous German pocket battleship, scuttled there. He told us that her master had shot himself rather than face the British waiting for him outside. He also told us about the battle and how lucky we were to have avoided it. It took place two days before we arrived but we had heard none of it. The convoy that the illness of the chief officer prevented us going with, ran into a nest of submarines. Many were sunk, some from the same port as us, which I learned about later on. Learning our draught, the pilot, as arranged, took us straight to a mud bank near the pier, there to part unload with barges. We needed no anchor until she was lightened. A man from the Catholic seaman's mission came on board and took as many off watch that wanted to go ashore with him. It was a beautiful clean city built on a slope around the bay with a high mount at the back.

Our guide took us to the mission building where we had tea, played games and wrote letters. I wrote to Mary Ann and gave her an indication of where I was and where to write to in Glasgow. We got away from the guide who thought he had us converted, and made our way to a tavern that had plenty of fairly good beer and other drinks. At the table next to us sat a crowd of young German sailors in uniform, part of the crew of the *Graf Spee*. After a while we raised our glasses to them. They did not respond. As that country was not then in the war, they were interned for the war and lucky in a friendly country with plenty of food to eat. It took them four days to discharge part of our cargo. The rest we took to Buenos Aires, two days up the river, and there we docked. I think because we had behaved well in the last port, no drunks and no quarrels with the Arabs, was why the captain allowed each one of us to draw a sub to the amount we wanted.

At the beginning of the voyage I pledged myself to spend as little money as possible and save it for the house I left unfinished and my marriage. On account of my age, I was not obliged to go to sea or join any other service. I would leave it and work ashore where there was more money with plenty of overtime. When we got back I would soon be able to buy all the materials I wanted; surely that would be available by the time we got back. I would then be my own master and what a good life that would be. The boys went ashore and went to town. I did not go as I was on watch that night. Some came back very drunk, all except Roderick, who next day saved the ordinary seaman from Glasgow from me giving him a beating for vomiting all over my bunk. Roderick with one hand pulled me away and held me. I pointed to what the red head had done to my bunk. Roderick said, "He is drunk. Leave him alone, I'll clean it up myself." He did and seeing that, I didn't have the heart to do what I had intended. The Glasgow man also brought on board with him a revolver, causing much fear to one of the crew that he did not like, who ran to report the matter to the chief officer. While he was away, I took the gun and opened it. It was empty and useless. I flung it on his bunk. He was the only member of the crew to be disgraced among the sailors at the end; he was given a bad discharge and fined five shillings.

My job as night watchman on the ship, now in Buenos Aires, was to keep anyone without a pass, except the crew, from boarding the ship, ensure that all the lights required were on, and that the gangway was safe. With ships going past there would be a movement in the ship causing the gangway to slip. I had to watch and look-out for anyone walking on the dock beside the ship, because at that time there were cases of fire bombs thrown on board Allied ships, so one had to be on deck most of the time. The naval gunner we had was from Chatham, a very nice quiet man who often entertained us with tales about the Navy. His duties were light, looking after the gun, cleaning and oiling it. Whenever we needed help he gave it. In that way he was accepted as one of us. I often went ashore during the four days we stayed in that city. It is large but not nearly as beautiful as Montevideo.

As soon as we left that port, we began to clean the holds for the cargo of grain and merchandise we were to load at the port of Rosario, some two days against the fast flowing river making the narrowest parts in daylight. Although the river was pretty, it did not compare in beauty with the St. Mary's from Lake Huron to Lake Superior in the fall. Seeing the flowers of every colour in profusion down to the water's edge, I thought what a nice place to stretch myself when she ties up and I am off watch. I did just that as soon as I had the opportunity, picked out where the flowers in short stems looked more enticing, and lay down among the different pretty flowers. There were none that smelt any different from the air around me. What a shock I got when I saw that I was covered with small and not so small crawling beasts, all from the ground. I got up as if I had sat on a hot plate and ran, shaking them off. What a disappointment, a place that only looked so nice and beautiful in the distance. I began recalling my native island, the machair and profusion of different kinds of flowers that sent an aroma from them, the hills in their purple bloom, the many other flowers down to the sea-flowers at the shore. You can sit or lie anywhere without fear of being attacked, although that would happen only on an occasional evening when the midges were not on the rampage. Not much work could be done then but how gentle they are compared to when the mosquitoes are about, whose bite causes swelling, soreness and much irritation.

Loading in that port was slow. The grain came in large sacks, carried by the gang of loaders on their backs from horse drawn wagons to the ship's side, then put in slings and winched on board. I don't know why these wagons were stopped so far from the ship, unless the horses were afraid of the racket the winches were making. The morning before we left that port I, with a few others, went ashore for a last drink at the German pub we used to go to. When leaving, the German owner said that he was well satisfied with the money he got from us. It was the jeering way he said it that made us angry; it was as if he compelled us to part with it. Time was short and he got away with it. We left that port and made a fast passage down the river and anchored at the mouth of Montevideo, where we took on board the ammunition for the gun that they took off us before we entered that port. Also the captain got his sealed orders to be opened after so many hours at sea. When opened, the orders were to proceed to Freetown on our own to wait for the convoy. Our ship was number 14 and the orders wished us good luck. We needed it and it held. The foredeck cargo of old bones we took on at Rosario, though now covered with tarpaulin, smelt bad when heading into the wind. We, in the after quarters, were not getting the worst of it; still we were glad when we ran into heavy seas and most of it was washed over. There was little of it left when we reached Liverpool and no one seemed to care.

On our way back, in the clear sky, we saw our first sighting of the first star in the Plough. It was nearly two days and nights before we saw the second, we were coming nearer to home. Reflecting on that also meant increased danger ahead. One fine day with nothing in sight, a small cloud of smoke appeared on the horizon ahead. Soon, we made out masts and funnel and the shape of a man of war coming towards us fast. D.A., the ordinary seaman shouted, "Let's man the gun" and rushed for the platform. The gunner shouted back "You damn fool, stay away from that gun. It's our only chance." By now the cruiser was less than one mile away and began signalling us to stop, which we did. On the bridge they had trouble making out the signals. At last going through the book, they succeeded. The cruiser wanted to know what port we had just left, where we were going and our number. By this time the gunner knew she was one of our own battleships. She told us to proceed on course to our destination. That was the only ship we saw till we reached Africa. Crossing the equator both times there was no celebration except that we got a double issue of rum.

Certificate of Discharge

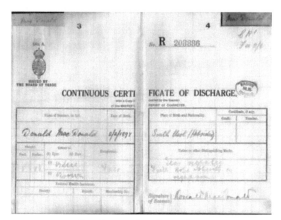

Discharge doc Page 1

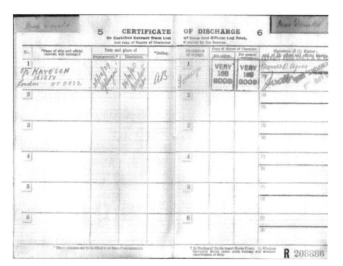

Discharge doc Page 2

Like the Royal Navy, the sailors got a glass of rum every day at sea, a custom very seldom carried out on the merchant ships. The Chief Officer, that none of us liked, had the overtime we worked made out and presented it to us. We did not agree with his hours and we kept a record ourselves. He would not honour them, saying we did not know how to keep a record. Going to the Captain he said he had no record of our overtime; that was part of the mate's work to look after. Although I was not in the union, I went to see the delegate and explained how we were robbed of our overtime. He at once intervened, and explained that new laws now were in force regarding overtime being paid to seamen for Sunday work and holidays. Apart from the money I was glad to hear the chief officer put in his place, as I had had many brushes with him where he under-rated me.

When paying off time came, and all the overtime was paid, we were much richer than expected because of standing up for our rights. We made our way to the nearest pub. I told them

I was having one drink only because I was calling again on my sisters. One said, "Are you going to look for another ship?" I said, "No, I am finished with life at sea, a shore job will now suit me better." I left and was now able to buy more expensive presents for my sisters and the mother in charge. I was received with the usual kindness and hospitality. I spent that day in the happy company of my sisters, and left for Glasgow on the night train, in the blackout. The war was in full swing.

A letter from Mary Ann awaited me in Glasgow. Everything was as before, suggesting that I should take a trip to Oban where she now worked. Before looking for work I went to Oban to see her and my sister and family. The first night there, my sister showed me a letter she received recently from the man I got the slates from, pressing her for payment for the slates he had loaned me. He also said that he had not heard anything about me since I went to sea. Many ships are sunk and he feared that I was in one of them. He had my letter written to him before I went to sea, which said that my sister would be responsible for payment. He then said that he was looking for an early reply to his letter so that he could bill her for the slates. I there and then wrote to him saying I was glad he was now in a position to use the exchange of slates that I owed him. I asked him to write to the Clerk of Works for the price of the slates and the cost of transport to his house. I was happy to send him the money by return of post.

I enjoyed my weekend in Oban, more so because I was most of the time in Mary Ann's company. We talked of everything, including the dark cloud hanging over my efforts to finish the house. I told her I was going to Edinburgh and to St. Andrew's House to see if I could get the material to resume work on it. She told me she was giving up her post in Oban and going to work in Glasgow as cook in a restaurant, with better wages. I did not think the change was entirely on my account. Nevertheless, I was glad to hear it.

Back in Glasgow and before looking for work, I went to Edinburgh and St. Andrew's House, as planned. I found the South Uist place of records. There was only one man in the office. I gave him my name, where from and why I was there to see him. He at once looked for my file, read some, looked at me and said, "You are building a house on your croft but on account of the material situation, you had to leave it unfinished?" I said, "Yes, I now would be glad if you can provide me with some materials. I am prepared to pay for most of it, the rest I am obliged to apply for a loan of £100 and want to make an application for that now." He said, "Are you married?" "No, but I hope to be as soon as the house is finished." "Well" he said, "I am sorry but the situation now regarding building material is even worse. All the stuff we get is allotted to the war effort, for the defence of our shores, and even if we could let you have it, you would be very foolish to throw your money away, as this country will be under German rule in a very short time. My advice to you is hang onto your money or maybe some of it, to be of use to you when Hitler takes over." I did not like his advice and less his attitude of defeat. I was surprised to hear such talk from a civil servant, although it was the time of the Dunkirk affair, perhaps being alone with me was why he let his tongue run away, or was he a fifth columnist? Whatever, I made him take my application for the loan. That cost ten shillings but I never made use of it. I told him I owed a man for 500 slates. "Is it possible to replace that now?" He was not sure but thought, since there would be no great demand, they maybe available. He looked up the price and wrote it down. I took it with me and when I got the bill from the man, the amount was the same. That was the only consolation my trip to Edinburgh gave me.

Back to Glasgow disappointed, but not down hearted, as there was no one depending on me. I looked for a job, which I got the next day as a rigger in Fairfields shipyard. Although I was only an able seaman and had not served my time as a rigger, they said with my knowledge of ships and my common sense that I would manage. I was put in a gang of four with a leading hand in charge. The work was varied, mooring ships, mostly naval, preparing to launch them when built, rigging up poles on battle ships, fitting out destroyers, many jobs of that kind, no chipping, painting or wire splicing. For me it was a strange place to work. We were not wanted all the time but had to be there on call. The 'between times' the foreman would say to clear out and hide under the loft. Sleep if you want to and he would get us if and when he needed us. It was a lazy job. Of course there would be other times when we were kept hard at it, such as putting the outside armour plates on the battleship 'King George' as she was to be named.

One day we were installing a gun and turret on a destroyer with the large stationary crane at Princes Dock. A top engineer from Yarrows was fitting it in. Our job was to place the ship in the right position. That was done and tight to the dock. Still the ship was not where he wanted her. Two and a half inches was required for the plumb, tilting would not do. In more anger he shouted up to the crane drivers, "Raise your jib a little more." "Come up yourself if you think it can be done." We began to laugh. It was then that he realised the crane was stationary. One of us, a common seaman from the islands, said, "If you take the fenders away from the ship's side, it will give you the distance you need when we pull her in." We did and it made the difference and saved the day. The top brass claimed he didn't know that the fenders were over the side regardless of them being in plain view.

One day we were preparing to launch a destroyer off the stocks, the launching platform was ready but not yet occupied till the drag chain was heaved on board. This would be made fast at the top of the spurling pipe to a heavy block of wood across the opening that acted as a toggle. Some careless person had put this block in place before it was to be used. When the drag chain was being hauled up, the vibration caused the untied, unattended block to move. I was working some ten yards away and saw it slipping and ran to stop it, but I was not fast enough. It tumbled down the spurling pipe onto the launching platform and bounced off without hitting anyone, which was lucky for those ready to climb on it.

The next near fatal accident I was involved in was strange and only my own angry stubbornness prevented it from happening. In our gang we had a new leading hand for the day. He was an older man and claimed to be a qualified rigger. The job was to rig up the jib of a rail crane that needed repairing. The two engineers doing that work required the jib to be lifted high to give the two topping lifts plenty of slack. The crane that raised it held it there. We only had to make two new wires fast near the top and bottom. This leading hand measured the length of wire rope we needed in two pieces, also sacking for wrapping round the iron frame. When everything was ready, he told me to get one of the wires and make it fast where he had marked off. When I saw his mark I thought it was far too low and began to make it much higher. He noticed what I had done and anger mounted on both sides till he said; "If you don't undo that knot you made and make it fast where I tell you, I will report you." I had to obey. Suddenly the jib came crashing down, the rod spun high in the air, our two wires sprung backwards and everyone went pale. The leading hand ran to where the wire was made fast, perhaps sure that my knot gave way. I ran after him; both knots had held. Both wires parted a foot below them. I said, "What do you think of yourself as a rigger now? These two men were very lucky they were not cut in two on

209

account of your stupidity." Our leading man Ronnie came in the next day and we were put on the same job. He and I made the wire fast at the top this time and the job was done without incident.

I watched a welder jumping across two three-inch beams, six feet apart, on the open hold of a destroyer we were doing a job on, and trailing two long hoses after him while jumping from one beam to the next with a drop of some forty feet below him. Apparently he thought nothing of it. The ship was in for a refit. One of her masts was too high and they were to cut off the top section, burn off some six feet below and replace the top section on it. Our job was to hook up the crane on the dock to the top of the mast, then rig up lines for a Bosun's chair for the welder to sit on. When every part was tested, we thought the same welder would be doing the work, but he said that he would not risk his life up there for any money. We told him all he had to do was sit in the chair and we would heave him up. He said the rope might break. We assured him that we had tested it for more than twice his weight and that he would be as safe as sitting on the deck. Still he refused to go up so another man had to be found. Strange that the welder felt safe jumping from one beam to the next with a drop of forty feet below him yet would not allow himself to be hoisted up the mast in a chair.

It was about this time when the Germans employed the magnetic mine. We soon had the degaussing gear as an answer, which was effective. Our yard fitted out a small ship full of top secret gadgets to sweep up these mines, when a switch pushed in made the ship safe from that kind of mine. When finished, she was taken down to the lower reaches of the Clyde for trials. Mines had been dropped the night before. When she began sweeping someone forgot to push the switch that would engage the current, and the ship was blown up in a short time. We learned of this through the grapevine. Shortly afterwards, this and other human errors did cost the nation dearly in her war effort. I learned a lot in my stay in that yard, much more than I did on ships at sea. However I was getting tired of being idle much of the time, and the wages were not as good as those with rigging gangs around the docks.

I left and joined the Clyde Rigging. The first week there with tide work, I made twice as much as I could with overtime in the yard. I was getting more tide work than I thought some of the rest were getting. I knew they were there long before me and were good men. I did not think of myself as being that good. Come pay day the boys made for the nearest bar. I, with my fat pay packet, made for home and deposited a good part of it, picturing the bank account growing fatter every payday. Next week I went early to the office as usual. The crowd of Riggers kept coming, some were sent on tide work, some on other special work. I was by-passed. At last, with two others, I was sent to a ship to start painting on a stage over the side. This was paid at flat rate. The old hand with me thought I was a relation of the foreman as I was put on a good job with more money from the very start. A newcomer without pull would not be put on that kind of work. "These are kept for boys more acquainted with the slate." I said, "What slate are you talking about?" "You must know." "I don't." "Well, have you been to the pub at the corner from the office?" "Yes, once." "Then you must have seen the slate behind the bar with names chalked up on it?" "I did and wondered what it was in aid of." "It is in aid of the foreman. Our names are not on it, that's why we are on this lousy job and what's more, until our names are there, with whatever we kicked in, we will always be out at the tail end." "That" I said "sounds strange to me. I have not known the foreman. I have never done him any favours and yet all last week he has put me on these lucrative jobs." "That maybe is right, but remember that was before pay day when he thought you were a soft mark. See what happens to you this week and then you'll

210

believe me." He was right. As neither of us added money to the slate, we were both kept painting over the side and very little of the pay packet was sent to the account that week. The foreman was often incapable of doing his work because of the unlimited supply of whisky via the slate, and some days only the most generous in decorating the slate were taken on.

I got another job working in the docks, loading and unloading cargo from a ship, the *Highland Monarch.* On night shift we had to unload train wagons of goods for the ship and truck it to the ship's side, a distance of about 100 yards. The night was calm but freezing hard in the pale moon. To keep warm we had to work steady. Every two hours we were given coffee and sandwiches. With our job finished, we went on board and made for the dining room where we had breakfast. The Chief Steward was a good sport, gave us a dram and said we worked hard last night. He saw the large amount of stores that were piled on the dock and in addition, another wagonload was to come down. I was told it would be 10.00 a.m. before it would be shunted to the dockside. He asked if we would come back about noon to take that lot down. It would give us a few hours sleep and so we said we would. That afternoon we worked hard trying to get it finished before night and the blackout. The steward was pleased and said he was putting us in for two extra hours overtime.

At the gangway, one of the ship's officers stopped us. He said he was short of men and would we come tomorrow as he had some deck work to do. We said that we would. That night an air raid was in that area and when the enemy planes came over Shieldhall, the *Highland Monarch,* although well armed and guns manned, was not able to fire a shot at the planes going past. The aggravating reason was that other ships with tall masts were moored too near. She was unable to train and fire her guns on account of that obstruction. All the gunners could do was curse and swear. In such circumstances, to fire was to cause more damage. One more lesson was learned. After that raid all ships in dock at night had to be moored a certain distance apart. The fact that no ships were able to fire there that night may well have saved the dock and ships there because no gun flashes could be seen from above. The pilot shot over his target, and dumped his bombs in fields well away from the dock. No damage was done that night in the area. Previous to that when ships arrived in port and were securely moored, their crew was paid off the next day. Two shore watchmen and two of the ship's officers were kept on. One of each, day and night, till the ship signed on another crew. That was the usual during peacetime. Now in wartime, bombing raids, and indeed sabotaging, such a watch was next to useless. It took a heavy raid in Birkenhead to change all that. When ships that were unarmed caught fire, broke their moorings and collided with others, doing as much damage as the enemy did, a law was passed requiring all ships in port to be manned at least by a skeleton crew, day and night, and to get steam-up whenever possible. That's where we as riggers came in, and also for jobs such as what we were doing on the *Highland Monarch*, besides fire watching at night.

I did not go to work at that ship the next day. Instead I went to pay my last fond respects to the remains of my cherished and unforgettable friend Roderick, whom I have already described during our voyage together in South America. His remains were in transit from Falkirk to Hallan, South Uist. After being fatally injured in a ship at Grangemouth, he died on the way to hospital at Falkirk, following a fall from a heavy beam of iron into a ship's hold. The facts of this sad and tragic accident were as a result of a human error. That night I with two of his sisters went to see the body at Falkirk Hospital, lying there with the usual kind expression on his face. It was hard to believe he was dead.

Some months after this happened, coming from work, I met a lady from nearby my home village, and wanted to hear the home news. We decided to meet at a certain pub at 9.00 pm. I went there early. Standing at the bar nursing a pint and watching for my friend at the door, I saw a man come in. The young man behind him had his arm in a sling, his head in a heavy bandage. Still I knew from what I could see that this was Red, the ordinary seaman who was with us on the voyage that I have already written of. He also remembered me and came to greet me, and his friend walked on to another part of the bar. I asked what happened? He said he had been on the Red Cross ship *Lancastria*. She was bombed and set on fire off the French coast. This was him out of hospital. We talked for a little while then he said, "Did you come across the old crew from the Kayeson and when did you see big Roderick last?" "I am sorry to say Red, that he is dead, killed in an accident on board a ship in Grangemouth about three months ago." He looked at me and said, "Big Roderick is dead!" walked four paces to the door, turned, and like a child began crying his head off.

There were not many in the bar but they began crowding around Red; then his friend pushed himself through the crowd with his fists up ready to strike me demanding, "Why had I interfered with his pal?" The rest of the crowd was very willing to join him in sympathy, and for a moment, and until Red raised his good arm to protect me, I thought I was in for some rough handling. He said, "It's nothing like that. This is a good friend of mine. He has just given me news of the death of my best friend." At once the raised fists dropped, and the crowd went back to their drinks. I stood watching Red getting over the worst shock he said he had ever had. I was not greatly surprised at the way it affected him. He had many good reasons to remember Roddy, not least when by his stealing habits he made Roddy stop smoking rather than giving him the thrashing he deserved. I wondered if thoughts of those and other misdeeds were now passing through his mind, causing him the grief that was so apparent. When I offered him a drink he would not take it, perhaps because it was I had caused him so much sorrow. When time was up, we parted on friendly terms. My friend never did turn up that night.

Shortly after that meeting in the same pub 'The Pavilion', I was to hear much more wailing and see another amusing incident. I was working in a ship in the Queen's Dock. On my way home in the evening I often called in that pub for a drink. When I was about three steps from the door the air raid warning went. I carried on. There was only one man inside, the barman. He was an old man with a round face and except for a thin line of white hair at the back of his head he was almost bald. His arms were resting on the bar, his head down. I was touching the bar before he moved. I called for a pint of lager. He came to life and started pumping, overflowing the glass many times. At last he placed the spilling pint on the bar and made no effort to wipe it. While the loud wailing of the sirens was blazing in every direction outside, I put the price of the pint on the bar. Leaving it there, he quickly turned to the shelf with the many bottles, picked one, unscrewed it and put it to his mouth, raising his hand as the contents went down fast. While this exercise was in progress, other customers were crowding into the bar and demanding, with hard knocks, urgent attention, which was completely ignored. I heard a voice above the rest saying the old barman must be stone deaf. What's he doing in a place like this? It was then, after the bottle had been well elevated, that he turned around smiling and saying, "I am alright now. Hitler can go to hell" as if it only took half a bottle of whisky for that decision. Finishing that pint, I left, walking the five minutes to my destination.

Outside the air was full of the wailing sound of the sirens; heavy aircraft guns were in action, windows rattling by the concussion, some spilling glass in every direction. I made the close without being hit by the flying glass. The large window at its corner was intact and the close itself was crowded with people taking shelter. I stayed three flats up. Climbing, I met the Irish lady that lived next door to us. She was always the first one down when the alert sounded, taking with her, always, her rosary and her insurance policy, thereby feeling fortified both spiritually and materially. When I reached the top landing and opened the door, the man of the house and another were standing in the middle of the kitchen ready to abandon ship. I asked where the rest were. He didn't know except that his wife went shopping and should have been back long ago and he didn't know about the children either. He was not long in however and he suggested that the pair of us go to the shelter. Perhaps his wife and children would be there. I said I was going to have a wash first and then something to eat. "A wash with all this going on, who is going to notice you in the dark, there is no-one here to make you a meal." "I'll help myself." "Well, we are leaving now." They left and I began washing and then helped myself to a large piece of roast beef untouched on the table, not having eaten since morning. The rats in the ship I was working at had made a feast of my lunch. This was why I was so hungry.

After a quick meal, I also left the nest, intending to go to the shelter around the corner. The close was fairly safe but crowded, and was supported with strong pit props. Although always in the way, they made that close much safer, with standing room only. In the dim light I saw and heard the Irish lady reciting her rosary, unashamed. I could also hear the Lord's Prayer said aloud. I was not a stranger to scenes like these under many conditions, but I was a total stranger to those I saw and heard in the shelter I was going to. Making my way through the crowd at the mouth of the close I nearly collided with a man in a hurry, coming in. He said, "Where are you going?" I knew by his tin hat and white armband who he was. I said, "To the big shelter on Watt

Street." "Stay where you are, don't go outside now, too much glass flying." I turned back with him. Seconds later, or before the large bomb fell on Morrison Street and the co-op, the large window beside us, and where I would have been if the warden hadn't detained me, went out in a wave of splintered glass. I know of no way to reason or explain why these lucky events happen to all of us. Except, as I always say, that we are ordained for other matters and when they are done, so are we too.

When the flying glass stopped, I made my way to the shelter. I had not been there before but it was easy to find with the noise coming from within. I did not stay long in that mad house, as a result of all the obscene language and behaviour that seemed to be going on in there regardless of its supposed protection. I decided to go back to the close I had left. Although the guns were in action, the glass shattering had stopped. No more windows to break in that area. In the close, except for some reciting their rosary, all was peaceful. Guns had stopped firing. I went through to the back, the sky overhead was clear and no drones could be heard. I concluded the raiders had left; and now to bed but for how long? The crowd in that close was also leaving, I am sure with the same idea. The 'all clear' went as I climbed the stairs, like many others, and I am sure I said to hell with Hitler.

The room was in darkness as no one from the household had yet arrived. After a while the lights came on. Outside, except in the far distance, was quiet. I saw on the table what I had left of the roast and wondered if there would be enough for the rest when they came in, which I hoped would be soon. I dried the mess I had made washing in the dark. I heard a noise coming up the stairs, and when the door opened there was the household. I was glad to see them safe. They too at seeing me, each one telling his own experience of the night that would stand long in the memory.

Perhaps I should also record another air raid in the close. Never again would I go to that disgraceful shelter. After the day's work, we were all at home, and in the middle of our evening meal the alert went and kept sounding its mournful tone. We all left the table for warm clothes to put on. We heard the Irish lady going downstairs, no doubt with her usual protection, the rosary and her insurance policy. The rest went to a shelter. I stayed in the close. Bombs began to crunch in the distance but were scattered. All the guns in Glasgow seemed to be in action. Shells that did not explode in the air came down to add to the destruction below. After what seemed a long time, the guns ceased firing. I lit a cigarette, cupping my hands. I smoked for a short while keeping the light shaded. I went outside in the back, smoking and trying to make out where the drones were. I was sure they were nowhere near us. I put the smoke out and went back in. No sooner was I inside than the women beside me yelled, "He is a German spy. I watched him outside signalling with his cigarette to the planes above us. Let's grab him before he runs away."

Before I could protest, they had me, pulling me apart. They soon had me down with some on the top of me. I knew this was no joke but even in that position I did not want to hurt them. I kept arguing, "You are making a mistake, a great mistake. I live in this close in the top flat." The one that was pulling my hair and not getting a good hold because I had it cut that day, said, "Don't believe what he says. I saw him showing his light waving it up and down and sideways. What other reason for doing that?" I must have been down getting pelted and pulled for 3 or 4 minutes when the Irish lady spoke when she heard 'top flat'. "That's not a German spy. I think I know that man, has anyone got a light?" Someone had, and they shone it on my face for a while for the Irish lady to say that she knew me. "That's MacDonald the lodger staying with my next door neighbours, he is no more a spy than you or I, he is an old soldier, let him up at once." They did and began to apologise. Although the incident was amusing, had it been that the lady did not know me, I am sure I was in for a rough time. Amusing still was the way that they crowded around me when the guns opened up again, as if being an 'old soldier' meant protection, but then we all like to cling to any straw when in danger. Air raids were nerve wracking periods, when one had to leave one's warm bed many times; six was the most I had to. Many times more in other seaports and I felt sorry for them.

The Blitz in Govan

The morning after the raid I had made my way to see my girlfriend, fearing and walking in ankle deep glass, that I had lost her. If I was lucky, I would ask her to marry me there and then, not considering whatever else that was involved. I was, of course, cooling down when I saw the area where she stayed had not been damaged. I pressed the doorbell. It was herself that answered. One look and we fondly embraced. Entwined like that, neither made an attempt to kiss the other as if the feeling of our arms compensated. It could not be because we were both shy. She was the first to speak. "Are you coming in?" I said, "No, I have to be at work soon. Is everyone here alright after last night's raid?" "Yes, we were all lucky and no damage was done. I was never so frightened in my life. I thought I would never see you again. Did all the people at your place escape? We could hear bombs going off in your district." I said, "Yes, as far as I know. Before going to work I will call to see if my relations in Plantation and Maclean Street are all right. Are you working today?" "No, this is my day off." "Then can I see you tonight at the usual place?" "Yes, what time?" I told her and that was about all the conversation between us then. Fearing the next raid, we did not forget to kiss when we said goodbye. As I made my way back on broken glass, to me it was like a carpet of roses such was my elation at finding her safe and well.

Nearing my cousin's place, things looked grim. Many buildings were destroyed. Walking on the other side I saw beds hanging out where the front had crashed to the street. I hoped no one was in them when the blast came. Although strange and sad, it was amusing to see the bedclothes hanging down and flapping in the wind. When I located my cousin Red John, the story was not so grim, not in keeping with the destruction I had just seen. No one killed although some injured, was then all he knew and when I said, "It was a pity about the buildings that were destroyed", he said, "Not at all, they should have been down long ago. Just hovels with one shared stair head toilet that smelled bad as you climbed that stairway, and made worse by eternal argument as to whose turn it was to clean it. If it was not for the loss of life, I would see all the street flat." I think anyone knowing the area would agree. It was demolished years later.

After the meal, John invited me to his favourite pub where we had much to talk about, because this was Red John of my young days at South Lochboisdale. It was with him that I often played pranks on people, including the incident with the bag of cuddies we spilled over the heads of the man of the house and his friend who was leaving for home. Now John and I recalled it with amusement as we did on recounting many other stories from our past. After a dram and reminiscence, all of which we greatly enjoyed, besides not seeing each other for many years, we covered much of our early days and now, at closing time, we had to part.

I went to report at the office because my last job was finished. There I was told to be on board a certain ship at Merkland Quay to work, standing by day and night till the ship was ready to sail, most probably at the weekend. They said, "She is moored alongside another ship at the river side, in a dangerous place when ships are moving up and down the river. It is very important that a good watch is being kept. A shore watchman will be with you at night but will have nothing to do with your work. Sinclair will again be your leading hand." They then explained the hours and the pay and that I was to be there by 5pm. I called on Sinclair to see if he knew of this job. He did and was going to call on me and the other two. Very few or none of the working class could afford a telephone at that time.

Being told that everything was okay, by-passing my lodgings I called again on Mary Ann to cancel our date for that night. On enquiring, she was out shopping and would soon be back. I said I would meet her coming. I did, and she was surprised to see me so soon. She said, "Is there anything wrong?" "No, just calling to let you know that I have to work tonight and I'm not able to keep our date." "I am sorry. Will you be free tomorrow?" "No, we are going to be on duty day and night on a ship for a week." "Are you going to sea again?" "No, this is just keeping watch. I will see you next Sunday."

The other three were on board when I arrived. Our first job was to fix the makeshift gangway which was always coming loose whenever a ship passed up or down, causing ours and the one we were tied to, to range back and forward, so collapsing the means of getting from one ship to the other. This bridge was made of boxes on each deck and of two planks across to walk on. They were not lashed down, and at times not very safe. We put a section of beams on number 1 hatch before it got dark, then washed for our six o'clock meal. We didn't expect that to be so good or so plentiful. I am sure it was much better than hotel fare at that time, all free to us and with no meal tickets required. There was no traffic on the river on account of thick freezing fog, which was very dangerous. No one went to the pub for the carry-out as intended, we just played cards till bed time, to sleep undisturbed until the mess boy called us for breakfast at 7.00 a.m. Another surprise, three fried eggs, three rashers of bacon and fried potatoes, after porridge and plenty of fresh milk. The mess boy did the cleaning up and made the beds. He also would run small errands for us, very obliging, for which at the end of the week he was well rewarded.

Sinclair, a Barra chap, was as I said our leading hand. An experienced old-time sailor who loved his work, and also he knew how and when to talk. Shore engineers were on board doing repairs to the ship's engine in daytime, no light being allowed at night. A donkey boiler was used to keep steam on deck. We did no work on deck next day, except replacing one parted wire and attending to the gangway. The fog had cleared and there was much traffic then, keeping

217

us on the alert watching the moorings as the ship strained them, for our bow and stern chain rope were made fast on board the ship we were alongside. Sinclair was not happy with this arrangement. Better he thought to have these two thick ropes made fast, with our wires taking much of the strain. One rope amidships should hold them together. We agreed, but did not have the authority to change them except in an emergency.

While we were fixing the gangway a man was waiting to cross over. When both ships were steady we put the two planks on and told him it was quite safe and if he intended coming on board, now was the time. He took a few steps and said that it wasn't safe, and asked where the handrails were? He was told that it didn't need a rail, and so he came on board but did not look satisfied, either with what we were doing, or us. Without any more words, he went to the engine room. We thought he was some kind of inspector. Later, we saw him going ashore. He had a good look at us sitting around doing nothing but did not say anything. The fact was there was not much that could be done while the ship was in her present state. We were replacing a parted wire when the deputy harbour master came on board to see that all was well. We told him the number of times a wire had parted, and we thought that if the bow and stern rope was to the shore instead of the ship, there would be less strain to our wires. He agreed, and so we changed it so as to have slightly more strain on the wire when weight came on.

That night the freezing fog came down thick. We were in the galley having coffee. The old shore watchman was watching the plank gangway. Although it was very cold, we had to call him in twice for hot coffee. Drinking that and sitting around spinning yarns, the door, without a knock, was flung open and in barged the troublesome man. "What the hell are you doing here?" Sinclair spoke up, "Drinking coffee as you can see. Who are you to barge in here without knocking?" "I am the captain of this ship, I was bringing my wife on board but she saw that your gangway is not safe. She had to turn back. I find you all in here doing nothing, as usual, when you should be watching that thing you call a gangway." Sinclair said, "There is nothing wrong. I checked it only ten minutes ago. No ship has passed up or down since. It's safe enough to take a ton of weight and you came across it safely. If you wife weighs more than that, she was wise not to try it." "Are you trying to insult my wife? I have good reason to order the bunch of you off my ship right now, for being useless and insulting. Get out before I do." No one made a move. Sinclair said, "Whether this is your ship or not, you have no authority over us. We were sent to look after your ship and not to wait on women that might want to board her. We intend doing so till further orders from the boss. If you want to know who that is I think the Harbour Master will help you." He left with one more sour look at us. We knew we had not seen the last of him, not in the rage he was in after the dig suggesting his wife was overweight. Reprisal would soon be on the way. That is why we got up early the next day and began splicing the wires that parted.

We were engaged in that work when our boss came on board alone. He stood watching us for a while, then came over and said, "I see you are working. I understand that complaints from her intended master have been received, that the men looking after her are not capable of doing the work entrusted to them and should be removed without delay." We explained what had happened. and he said that he was satisfied with us and what we had been doing, and advised if that man interfered again we were to send him to the Harbour Master or himself. When the splicing was done and the wires put back on rails ready for use, we knocked off for the day, except the watching. We did not see the captain again and later heard that another master had been appointed. He signed on at the end of the week, although we were kept on for another day helping to get the ship ready for sea. Reporting for our wages, we were paid over twenty pounds, at that time a handsome sum.

While I was working on this ship I wrote to a friend at home regarding the timber that I had heard was coming ashore. I got a reply saying there was much of it but mostly covered with tar and oil and not suitable for my purpose. If any was useful, he would salvage some and let me know. That Sunday I took my girlfriend out. We had a long enjoyable walk and talk, and were able to get a meal without tickets in the restaurant where she was employed as cook. I told her I was thinking of going back home as I had a reply from the Department, saying there was a fair chance of me now being able to get some of the material I needed for my building. I was advised to place my order as soon as possible, as delay may be expected. I took Mary Ann home and said I would let her know soon how things were developing.

Monday, before noon, I took a walk to the employment agency, not expecting anything. Before I actually reached it, a man was walking towards me. He stopped me and asked if I was a seaman looking for work? I told him I was and he offered me a job in Queen's Dock unloading tonnage from a torpedoed ship. I said I would take it and he told me he was the foreman and to get my overalls and be there within an hour. He was going to look for another two men. I was back in time and met the others and we went on board. She was a fairly large ship, about ten thousand tonnes, and having been torpedoed, it was necessary to take out all the insulation which had been required for the frozen and chilled meat that was carried, to make the hold larger. This insulation of grounded cork was 18 inches thick, packed tight, covering the walls of the hold and held in place by an outside wall of wood nailed to upright posts. The cork was first put ashore.

5 North Locheynort after move from North Glendale

Our job was to shovel it into large iron tubs to be dumped into a waiting lorry. Although it was not a very dirty job, we got dirty money for doing it. Although there was much dust, we were

219

surprised to find the cork so dry after the ship had been torpedoed. The reason was that the torpedo struck a few feet from the stern and did not explode. It buckled a plate, and although much water came in, the chain locker bulkhead held it back so no water got into the rest of the ship, with no damage to the cargo. One of the crew, the engineer, told us they were attacked in the Irish Sea and the destroyer escort knew that a submarine was in the area. The sea was flat calm, all hands watching out for the periscope. He said, "We truly saw it not more than a hundred yards away, then the coming torpedo struck. Up on the Bridge they took evasive action, but the ship was slow responding to the wheel. At once the destroyer circled and dropped depth charges. We were busy getting a collision mat over the damaged part when we saw the sub was forced to the surface. The destroyer pounded her with gunfire and then went back to pick up any survivors. We were slowly going down by the head till the water reached the bottom deck where, by plugging and strengthening every opening beforehand, we were able to hold it there. With reduced speed and the ship not steering properly, we were left far behind. By then most of the convoy had left us for their English ports of destination.

There were only four ships for the Clyde. We kept them in sight till nightfall. Then out of the darkness the destroyer found us and stayed with us to the Clyde entrance at Greenock. We dropped anchor for the rest of the night. In the morning we got a shore team of repairmen, divers and welders. When they were finished putting the temporary patch outside, we began pumping out the water, our head slowly coming up till she was dry and then, without a tug, we took her here. After the insulation is removed, and you are finished putting the rubbish ashore, she is going to the dry dock for proper repairs." We asked him if any of the rest of the convoy was sunk? "No, we were the only one, at least to where some of the convoy parted with us abreast of Land's End, for southern ports. We came from the River Plate, Rosario, crossed over to Freetown with a nine-knot convoy of 32 ships escorted by two destroyers and a frigate. We were well protected till those that parted with us took a destroyer and a frigate with them. After more broke off for Liverpool our protection had only four to guard, but even then the sub took a big risk to come so close with her periscope showing. Hitler paid dearly for her mad commander. We were very lucky. We only needed a trip to the dry dock to put in a new plate and have her bottom scraped, which she badly needs. She is wasting a lot of fuel."

We were kept busy with the rush to get her ready for the dry port, but there was no night work on account of the blackout. Towards the weekend we were nearly ready in that hold. I was working making up slings of timber, which a carpenter was tearing down with a crowbar over-head, standing on a platform well away from me at what I thought was a safe distance. This platform was staged at a height of 30 feet, and the wood he was pulling down fell a safe distance away. He was having trouble with a small piece that was nailed with long spikes. Putting much weight on the crowbar, the wood with the spikes came away, hit the platform and bounced off. It struck me a glancing blow on my head as I was bent looking at the sling. I was badly cut and in a dazed shock. They took me to the Southern General Hospital where I had many stitches put in. After testing, I was told I had no concussion and would be alright when the stitches were taken out in a few days. They sent my mate, a Tiree man, along to see me safely home. Next day they sent me my pay in full, and a note enclosed, saying if at any time I was out of work, to call at their office. I never did because that was my last ship to be working on, a long time ago since my first ship, the 'Ivanhoe', that I joined in the early part of 1914 as a young boy.

After the stitches were taken out I began making preparations to leave for home. I saw Mary Ann and we both hoped it would not be for long before we would be joined permanently. I stayed a night in Oban and left early next morning. It was a daylight sailing. The boat had a bar but nothing to drink! When we got to Tobermory, I thought I would nip ashore to have one, but the man at the gangway stopped me. "Pass please." I showed him my pass for Lochboisdale. He looked at it and said, "This is for South Uist." I said, "Yes, that's where I am going." "Sorry, unless you have a passport and reference for Mull, I can't let you ashore here." I looked at him in disbelief. Only then he turned to the crowd following me and said, "Only passengers holding a passport to land here are allowed to go ashore." Tiree was the same as every island where a passenger ship called. Crossing the Minch I asked a member of the crew that I knew if this was a dry ship. He said, "Yes, nearly always going out to the islands, but coming back the bar is open and you can have all you want." I said, "That's funny, how is that?" He said, "Did you not hear of the ship that ran ashore near Eriskay?" "No." "Well this ship was heavily loaded with whisky. Thousands and thousands of cases of it, all the best, with so much of it there it would be a damn shame to come back dry." "Well" I said, "I very much doubt what you are saying because I know a lot of people from that area in Glasgow. I never heard that mentioned. I did hear that a lot of wood covered with tar and oil was coming ashore." "Oh that" he said. "Nobody wants that now since another ship full of timber of every size, coming from America, ran aground not far from the whisky ship. You can see much of it floating when we are near land. The shore is covered with it; we have to keep a good lookout for the floating logs. Perhaps the reason why

Peter and Sarah

221

you did not hear of this is because everyone was warned not to spread any news that may be of use to the enemy." I could understand that might be the reason why I was not informed.

I saw the floating wood on the shore and in every bay there was tons of it. Surely now I could get what I wanted and would begin selecting and gathering as soon as I got settled at home. Arriving at Lochboisdale in daylight, my brother with his car was there to meet me. The pub was open. I asked them for a dram and called for three whiskies. The barman, who evidently knew my brother well, put his hand under the bar and brought out two large white jam jars and placed them on the bar, and then added the third. Getting a full bottle, without any measurement he began pouring into the jars. I thought his hand had lost control and wondered if the pound note I was getting ready would be enough. It was and I got a lot of change back! I was ashamed to count it. Drinking whisky out of a large jam jar is not so easy, but it was really funny seeing the crowd lining the bar, each one with one of these jars over their heads draining the last drop. I asked Peter "When did this style come in? He said, "When all the glasses but a few were broken and could not be replaced, the few that escaped were taken out of service so that no favours could be shown. The occasional jar that was broken by slipping from an unsteady hand to the concrete floor was not considered a loss since there was plenty of them in the midden."

We luckily got home in daylight because I did not have my Wellingtons on and the path, after much rain, was a mess. When I asked Peter if any of that wood, so plentiful down south, came ashore our way, he said, "Yes, plenty of it. I put ashore quite a lot for you thinking that you might sometime need it."

"I do and had I known about it I would have left Glasgow before now." He had the same story of being warned not to spread it. After a good night's rest and breakfast, I walked the half mile out to see my house, and wondered if it's isolation had in any way changed my mind. When the house came into view, I felt as if a magnet was drawing me towards it and thoughts of isolation vanished. When I opened the door I saw in the light a pair of rabbits crouching in a corner. I thought of catching them and then decided against it. I stayed in the shell of that house for a long time in silent contemplation, thinking now that I am here what should I do first. Taking a lunch with me, early next day I went to the shore and began selecting and piling wood above the high-tide mark. When I had gathered a considerable amount, night was near and I was very tired. Tomorrow I would see about the windows and more cement, also doors.

The next day I went to the Department of Works. I said to the clerk that I hoped the situation was much better now and asked if I could get the material I needed. "If it is better," he said, "I have not heard of it." I told him I wanted to order windows and doors and pay for the goods now. He said "Money is not accepted till the orders can be filled, they will let you know when that will happen." There was no point in ordering the stuff now. Another wasted day, but not quite, because I learned a lot about the whisky ship, the *Politician*, now locally known as the 'Polly'. Much of the dry stuff was taken out of her and shipped to the mainland. The ship, and what was left in her partly seawater logged hold, was given up as a total loss and kept on that inshore reef to be pounded to pieces. Some daring local fishermen boarded her and found good pickings. These pickings no doubt helped to spread the news that there was plenty whisky still in her. With each visit, better gear was used for retrieving it. At that time reminders were posted, in frequented places, not to waste anything that could be used for human consumption. Is it surprising that the Islanders, generally considered honest, looked at what came on their shore like they do on a patch of floating seaweed, which they were glad to use for growing potatoes.

When another survey was done, it was found that the ship was not past repairing, and that repairs should be undertaken before more damage by the sea was done. A day and night watch was put on board her, but not before frequent visits were made by day and night. She was under that watch when I first became interested and acquainted. In the pub all the talk, or most of it, was about her.

That night I made plans to put the boat afloat and use it for whatever purpose I had in mind. Wood was essential and had to come first. The boat was made ready for sea again, and with her I towed many rafts of choice timber to the jetty near the house, then carried it on my back and piled it up, Canadian-style, beside the house. That done it was left to dry. I was kept busy laying the foundation for the floor. When I got the ground beams in and level, the rest was easy. The thick planking, 6inch wide and 2inch thick, had to be planed and it was hard work since I did not know how to set a plane. A joiner friend offered me some very good advice and set the plane for me. I learned a lot that day, saving me much sweat.

The weather had settled and looked like staying that way for at least two days. It was a good time to see if the 'Polly' would keep to her promise. Already we knew that inside her, to the high water mark, she was covered in oil from her burst fuel tanks, and every tide added to that. After a visit, all the clothing worn was set on fire, as no amount of boiling and washing would remove the oil. We had good pickings that night, and even made contact with the watchman who, during our conversation, said that a man from Locheynort had greatly befriended him when he first started to work in a hotel in Mull. When told that this man was still living, but too old for this game, and that in fact his brother was along with us, he said "It's getting light now, but come up tomorrow night, and bring me some fresh eggs and I'll have a load ready for you." Before the next night it began to blow hard from the North East. To risk it meant to be storm bound, but for how long no one knew, only that it would be dangerous. We sadly decided to cancel that golden opportunity, with the weather as usual being blamed.

About that time word went round that a ship had arrived at Lochboisdale and was going to take away all the wood that came ashore and commandeer it as Government property. When they had collected all that was there, our loch would be next. Anything of importance, the law requires that it be reported to the nearest customs office, detailing where and when it had come ashore. Some did but most did not. There was a general rush to hide what one needed. It was impossible to hide it all. I used up every good hiding place I knew on the croft, some up the hill, but still there was a big pile left on the shore, too heavy to move far. I also had rafts of it hidden in creeks that could not be seen from a boat at sea. While waiting for that ship to come for the second load, I wrote to the customs in Stornoway, reporting that I had salvaged a lot of timber and would they be good enough to send a man to inspect and measure it. A week passed, and still no sign of that ship. I began to regret that I didn't let sleeping dogs lie. When the man arrived he was amazed at the amount of wood that I had salvaged. First I took him in my boat to where the logs were. He measured them and gave me the receipt for 686 cubic feet. He said to send it to the office and that I would be paid a tidy sum for the lot.

Back to the jetty and the large pile, where I told him to make an estimate saying that I had to go to the house for a moment. There I poured some Spey Royal into a very different bottle. I could see him with pencil and paper making his calculations as I joined him. I said, "It's a cold day, would you care for a wee dram?" "Sure, that's very kind of you." I only had a cup

223

without a handle and nearly filled it. Looking at it and the bottle as if it was lemonade, he tasted it and looked again at the bottle. "That's good whisky, we haven't got anything like that our way." He smiled, took out his notebook, tore a leaf off, threw it away, wrote some more and without a word gave it to me and then said, "That's good wood in that pile. I wish I had it at my house in Lewis." I said, "A steamer is calling in the Loch any day to take it all away. I expect you know all about that already." "No" he said "I am new in the office. I did not hear a word of that. Likely the order went out before I joined them." I was thinking of the stack that I had left uncovered near the path he would take walking back and I did not want him to see it. I think that was why I said, "Have another small one for the road." "Alright, just a very small one." "I am sorry I can't ask you to the house for a cup of tea, I don't live there. I am just building it and I am having a lot of trouble getting material from the department." He said, "At least you have plenty of timber for your house," and I said, "Yes but they will be taking it all away." He said, "They may if you are fool enough to let them. I know what I would do." He thanked me for the hospitality and turned a blind eye to the stack of wood near the path. Putting his hand in his pocket he asked me if I smoked. When I told him I did, he said, taking out his pouch, "Try a fill of this. It's Condor, you may not like it." "I do, better than any" and quickly knocked the old ash out of my pipe and filled her tight, but I did not tell him that I was almost out and no van for the next two days. We parted with him saying he hoped we would meet again. I went back to the planeing, but first to where he threw a leaf from the notebook away. I found it. Comparing his then estimate, I found I was a hundred cubic feet to the good. It's surprising what a dram can do!!

That night I wrote and posted both estimates to Stornoway expecting a handsome cheque soon. I got a reply within a week with a money order for twenty-eight shillings and a note enclosed, saying it was not possible for me to gather and put so much timber ashore, and they felt that the money order enclosed would compensate for the salvage work I had done. Unfortunately the day before I got that letter, the steamer gathering the wood arrived, with a team of workers and small boats, taking everything they saw in the way of driftwood. I tried to bargain with the man in charge to leave me at least some of what was in the big pile. He liked what I offered but said that the others would know and he would be in trouble. He did say, "I'll tell you what I will do for you. We will be finished loading today. There will be some that we had gathered and piled up, left. We may not come back. If we are not back within a week, get it before anyone else does." Thinking of the raw deal I got from Stornoway, I did not wait that long. I made several rafts and towed them to where only a local could find them.

The steamer did not come back because we heard that those in charge of taking the wood away were arrested along with someone in the customs office. I hoped that the man I gave the Spey Royal to was not involved. Regardless of what was taken away there was plenty left for anyone who wanted it. Of course many did, and those stacking it for future use made large piles of it, very neat, one on the top of each other, not knowing that it required air to flow through it as it had been in the sea for some time. If left that way, it would not take long to rot. Having had some experience in a lumberyard in Canada, I advised people what to do and why. Some would not believe me, others took my advice. With much wood destroyed, the steamer did not take away the heavy logs. She had no gear to lift them. Many of them I towed to Lochboisdale for fenders for the pier there. I made some money on that. The county treated me much better than

Stornoway on that account. Whenever possible I worked at the house, and by trial and error I was now finished with the flooring, at least it was level and strong. It was only a small house and all the available space had to be put to the best use. As I had no plan, the planning was done as I progressed. Trips to the Clerk of Works brought me no nearer to getting the windows and doors however, and some wise cracker, after seeing my slow progress, as a consolation said that Rome was not built in a day.

To break the monotony, there were some existing trips to lady bountiful. These were not always successful but exciting, dodging the law, till at last workmen were put on board and thereafter no visitors were allowed. I tried to but did not get as much as a dram, while plenty of the stuff was going to waste. She was repaired enough to be towed to the Clyde by two tugs. Those in charge of that operation would not listen to local knowledge as to the best way and which direction to take, claiming to be well qualified to take her anywhere so long as she was afloat. What they would not accept was the strength of the current along the way they intended to go, and the result of that was the tugs could not hold her, as the current drove her on to a sand bank, there to stay, regardless of efforts made to move her, till she was broken up to below the low tide mark and taken away. The whisky found during repairs, after being under water so long, had turned green and was not fit for drinking, and so ended the ship made famous by Compton Mackenzie's book and film *Whisky Galore.* As far as I know no lives were lost in connection with that wreck, but many of the stories told about her were entertaining and laughable. Many of her cases of 'Spey Royal' and other brands found temporary rest in different peat bogs.

Kate and Sister Barbara

It was now well into spring and there was much need to plant as many potatoes as possible. There was little or no sign of the war coming to an end, and other foodstuffs were becoming scarcer with every passing week. We on the islands were fortunate; there was always plenty of fish and game, provided ammunition was obtained. At the end of the spring work and all peats cut, I decided to prepare for lobster fishing, although there was plenty of labouring work, i.e. road building and putting up army huts. With another man of much experience, we began fishing. Lobsters were fairly plentiful and the price was not bad. For those that reached Billingsgate alive, we had to depend on the honesty of the salesmen whom we had to send them to, and as it was easy for them to say that most or some were dead, we had no way of knowing. However, our cost of living was not high as there was little that money could be spent on. Even tobacco and matches were often in short supply or unobtainable. We often had to take a pot of peat fire when going to sea to light our pipes, if we had any tobacco.

A minister once came to me for a lobster as he was celebrating something special. I asked him if he had any matches to spare. He said he was sorry he didn't smoke. I said I would send him the lobster the next day and sent him three large ones. A man came to see me the day after with a packet of safety matches and offering to pay a high price for the lobsters. We told him that the matches would more than pay for them and we hoped the minister would enjoy them. Apparently he did because many times after that he very kindly sent us boxes of matches wherever he was getting them from. We did very well at the lobsters and a little herring fishing for home use, much better than any other small boat in the area before us.

Mary Ann, Ealasaid and friend

During this time the windows and doors came. I had them installed, also the ceiling, stairway, and the walls plastered and painted. I had nothing in the way of furniture or a stove. A man near the South End was leaving and selling up everything so I made sure to be at the sale. I started off early but had to walk all the way. On reaching the sale, much of the stuff was sold, everything in demand. I managed to get four chairs and two tables and other small bits. When I was taking these things away the next day, the tables fell apart. There was an old bed for sale, but I did not bid knowing that I could make a better one myself.

I wrote to Mary Ann and told her of my progress regarding the house and the bits of furniture I had got. She wrote back saying that many had started a new life with less and that as long as there was a roof over our heads and a place to sleep, there would be no excuse to go hungry there. Considering the truth of her statement, I had no strong reasons holding me back now. I wrote at once saying how glad I was to get her letter and hoped that she was willing to share her life with me. It had been a long road with many bends, now let us both start on a new road. I was very willing and hoped she was too. Please would she let me know soon what she had to say so that I could go up to see her parents to ask them for her hand. If everything was alright, we would set a date. When I finished I stamped and sealed it and felt a sense of elation. The dye had been cast. I walked the double four miles to post it and slept well that night.

After a week I got her reply suggesting a date for our wedding. Soon afterwards, when with my best friend in the boat, I told him that I intended to get married soon. "Well" he said, "That's good news. It's high time you were. I can't understand what's been keeping you." I asked him if he would come with me to see her people on Friday night. I would get in touch with Neil Smith to take us up to East Kilbride calling at Lochboisdale first for whisky, as Polochar may be dry. "I think Smith is a better talker than you; we will have him do the asking for the whisky." Angus said he would go with me willingly and that Neil was a good choice. He certainly has the gift of the gab.

We met at the appointed place and time and when we heard the rattle, this was him and his model T Ford. On the way he had to get out to put more heather in one of his tyres. "I think it will get us there now but lean more to your left side." As this was common, we thought nothing of it and there was still plenty of heather on the hills. As Smith knew Findlay, the proprietor of Lochboisdale Hotel, I asked him if he would ask Findlay for the whisky for me. In the bar I called for three whiskies and three beers. The barman looked at me and said "One round of whisky is all I can give you. There is plenty of beer." The three nips that he gave hardly covered the bottom of the two-pound jam jars; there was not a glass in sight. After a few of these beers, my friend said, "Is there any chance of a bottle of whisky. I want it for a special reason?" "None whatsoever." "Is himself upstairs and do you know if he is in a good mood?" "He is, and I think he is in a good mood. Try him now and you may be lucky. I see people coming here with a line supposed to be from the vet for a bottle of whisky for a sick cow. At first, as himself was fond of cattle, they were getting it. Now even the township bull has no standing. Whatever you do, don't tell him anything like that, he is tired of that excuse." Afterwards my friend told me he just told him the truth and who he wanted it for. He said he knew my brother Peter well and would give me one bottle although he was very low in stock. I was not to mention or show it to anyone in the bar.

Outside Neil checked his lame tyre and said that it was hard enough. On arrival at the house in East Kilbride, Neil parked and we were ready to get out when I said, "Who takes the bottle?" Neil said, "You do, and after we are inside seated, you give the bottle to Angus saying, 'Will you give us all a dram'. While he is doing that I expect the ladies will be busy preparing the tea." The old lady answered my knock, "Is that you Donald and who is there with you?" I said, "Friends. You know Angus well of course and this is Neil." "Come in, come in." The introductions over and all sitting, as told I took out the bottle and gave it to Angus saying, "Will you give us a dram Angus?" Angus stood up, bottle in hand, and called for glasses, which he filled. By the time the weather was discussed, the tea was ready. The table was spread with goodies of every kind, fit for a prince. There was no sign of food rationing here. After grace, said by the man of the house, he handed the glass this time to Neil, who took it, looked at it, then set it down on the table saying, "I refuse to drink any of it until we all know why we are here. I may be a stranger in this house but I am not a stranger to my good friend Donald here. I have not heard anything bad said against him. I have known him for a long time and he is very capable of making a good living, from both land and sea, for himself and for anyone that he wants to be with him in his home and surroundings. That 'one' is your second eldest daughter. He brought me here tonight to ask her parents for her hand to marry him. He would, I am sure, like to know if you have anything against this intended marriage taking place. Do you willingly give him your daughter's hand?"

The father spoke, "They have known each other for a long time, and if they have decided to marry we have nothing to say and no reason to be against it. We feel that Donald will look after and care for our daughter to the best of his ability, the same as we have done. We wish them the blessing of God." Neil said to the mother, "Are you agreeing with what her father said, "Yes." Turning to me he said, "Then I want to congratulate you Donald, and wish you health and happiness." I thanked him and rose and kissed my intended mother-in-law. I shook hands with the father. Next Neil filled the glass and gave it to the father who wished that everything would go well with us, and then down the hatch it went, without batting an eye. The same followed with the others, each offering their congratulations and good wishes. Then we began on that delicious meal, after which we began talking about days gone by and about fishing, and lamenting that fish is not as plentiful as it used to be. When you went out, you always caught nearly as much as you wanted, never disappointed. The conclusion of our talk was that the Minch should be closed to trawlers, and a chosen time put on herring fishing from the 10th January to the 10th May. If that had been adhered to fish in this area would be as plentiful as ever.

If I was describing the fishing condition now, in 1980, and comparing it to what it was when this event was taking place in 1942, I would have to say there is hardly any fish left in our area, all because of wastage and bad management of a sea that was once bountiful. Now we are paying for that most dearly and no hope of it ever being the same.

We left, giving and receiving firm hand shakes and the blessing of God, and passed Polochar without giving it a thought. The tyres were holding up and we didn't have to stop to feed them anywhere. When we parted company at the end of the road, it was fairly dry. In the moonlight I enjoyed being alone with my thoughts and indeed felt very happy. The wheel was now set in motion. When and where it would stop no one could guess. The next day I went into Bornish to see the priest about the banns. He was on the point of leaving the house when he saw me coming. He greeted me and invited me in, judging that this was not a sick call. He began talking about the weather and what was I doing out there? Was I still fishing? I said that I was but that the lobsters were now getting scarce. Then laughing, he said "When are you getting married Donald?" He often made fun of me in that way. I knew he had no knowledge of why I was there. I said, "That's just what I want to see about Father. I am putting in the banns today, to be announced at mass tomorrow," He grew serious then. "Forgive me Donald. I was just joking.

Are you in earnest?" "I am Father." "Then I congratulate you. Do I know the girl?" "I am not sure. She is from the south end, East Kilbride, and is now working in Glasgow." I told him of her people. He knew of them and said that they were very good and fine people.

This priest I particularly liked. He was fairly good in a boat and very fond of fishing. Many a good sea outing and fishing I had with him. I saw him lucky one day that he did not lose some fingers. The sea was flat calm. We were trailing three casts, fish slow to take, and he twisted his line round his fingers and sat waiting for a small tug. A large basking shark surfaced behind us and got caught in his gear. There was no way to let go of the line and no time to take the twists off. Before much damage was done the line broke, teaching him something to remember. Over the tea he said, "You are very lucky Donald finding me at home. I intended to be on the machair and shore since the day is so fine. I don't know what had kept me. Then I saw you coming and thought, something urgent. "Well Father" I said with a smile, "I cannot say I am sorry for spoiling your afternoon's pleasure." "No, I cannot say that either, it is always a pleasure to attend matters of this kind. I hope the bachelors over your way will follow your lead. It's a good place to settle in." "It would be ever so much better, Father, if we had a road that cars would run on. As it is it takes courage for a girl to come and live there." "Never mind Donald, I am working on that now. I will not give Inverness peace till you have a new road both sides of the Loch." Many before him had tried but gave up the struggle. If you are any time driving out that way and enjoying it, he is the one that you should thank for that pleasure.

17   Tackety Boots, Wedding Bells and Babies

We arranged to marry in Oban and have the celebration at my sister's house there. With things as they were then, rationing and a shortage of everything, it could only be a small party. I already had a new navy blue serge suit for the occasion, but I needed a pair of new shoes. In the shops at Lochboisdale the only pair that would fit my size eight was a brown pair of brogues; the uppers were nicely leather tooled in a flowery design, the soles were thick and stitched with strong string. I examined them and found nothing wrong. I tried on one, stamped on it and found it comfortable. I said, "How much are they?" He said, "They are dear, only toffs wear those kind of shoes, but they are well worth the money and will last you a long time without re-soleing them." I had to ask him again. "Well, since I have had them here for some time and with not that many toffs around, I'll give you a bargain, two pounds ten." I looked at the thick soles and thought, 'after this mission is over, they will wear well on the rough road to the church.' I took and wore them on my outward journey and for more than a day in Oban. I caught my sister often looking at them and thought she was admiring them, as there was nothing so posh in Oban.

Mary Ann arrived from Glasgow. I had already been to the chapel house to see the Priest who knew me, as I had some time before taken him out fishing. He greeted me kindly and put me at ease. He also introduced me to the Bishop whom I already knew when he served in Daliburgh. They talked of everything but my marriage and even asked in a joking way if I still had some of the 'Polly' left. I said, "No, there's not a drop left in Uist. That's why I am getting married in Oban." "Well according to what I hear, there is a dry spell in Oban too." Talking like that and, after a while, the Bishop said, "Father Morrison will marry you tomorrow Donald, with nuptial mass at ten in the morning. Would you like that?" "I would indeed and thank you for it." "Well, it's simple and easy, you will be alright." The Priest said, "Will three o'clock be alright?" "Yes, that will be splendid." "Well", he said, "We will have a rehearsal later today."

Mary Ann and I got ready for the rehearsal. Sarah had another look at my brogue shoes but still did not say anything. She is the kind of person who wants to see everything done right. I am not sure if that was why she came with us. We waited in the pew just long enough to say a short prayer. The Priest came out, and after a few words began explaining what we had to do. The cathedral was empty and we were sitting at the back. He told us to walk side by side slowly up the aisle to the communion rail and stand. "I will be waiting there for you." It was while walking up the aisle that it dawned on me why Sarah was so interested in my studded brogues; the noise they made was as if part of that solid building was coming down. After we had gone through that performance twice, the Priest said that we had it perfectly and it was as if we had done the same many times before.

When we got back to the house, with yet another look at the offending brogues, Sarah said, "Is that the shoes you're getting married in tomorrow?" I said, "Yes, anything wrong with them?" "Yes, plenty, the Clydesdale that goes round collecting rubbish makes less noise than you did in the church today. If people were there you would have made more headlines in the Oban Times. You are coming with me now to the Co-op for a descent pair. I'll pay for them myself." "Look here sister" I said, "These were the best on sale in Uist, the man said that's what the well-to-do and toffs wear but the toffs had left. I thought they would be wintering in Oban and I would be acting one for a week." "How much did you pay for them?" I said, "Two pounds ten." "You could have bought the same pair here for thirty shillings. They are only worn for hill climbing." "Well" I said, "After that stroll I took down town I can understand your point. I didn't see anyone wearing them". "No" she said, "If there were any, you could hear them plain enough. Come on before the shops close." I went willingly. The kind she picked for me would have made a Red Indian proud when tracking. No chance of anything hearing him. Going home in them I thought I was bare-footed. However, I did not regret taking them for the occasion.

After the mass and the marriage ceremony was over, Sarah invited the Priest to breakfast with us and, once back at her house, Iain, Sarah's husband, made a short speech and after the congratulations and a drink we had a very enjoyable breakfast. After the meal, glasses were again filled. We did get a small bunch of congratulations telegrams, which the Priest read out.

Father John Morrison, now a Canon, left us shortly after that enjoyable meal. He is a noted preacher and a very kindly man. He also made a name for himself as a staunch opponent of the Rocket Range being placed on South Uist, when that idea was in its infancy, claiming that it would do away with the peace and tranquillity of the island and in the end would bring disaster. Meetings to that effect were held in different schools. I went to one of them, and while I was a 'yes' man, when he married me I now had strong reservations in regards to the Rocket Range, reasoning that while peace and quiet was in itself a good thing, it would never fill a man's belly. The proposed millions that were to be spent on the Rocket Range in Uist could not take place without many, perhaps all, the locals that wanted getting work. Fishing was at a low ebb and stock from the croft was in poor demand, was it then reasonable to go against an opportunity that hopefully would make life much better? Of course there was the fear of what we might be involved in. There is still that fear. I well remember as a small boy listening to stories at ceilidhs told by the very old folks. These were often of the prophecies of the Brahan Seer; in one he claimed that the rivers in Benbecula would yet be running red with blood. These stories were brought forward, giving rise to fear when rockets were first talked about. Of course the Rocket Range went ahead giving work to many local men and women. The good Father also scored, for he earned himself the name of 'Father Rocket', and as long as the rocket range is there he will be remembered

I was fortunate enough, despite the semi-dryness of that town, to be able, with the help of Iain, my brother-in-law, to get all the refreshment needed for the wedding party. For music we had the then top Pipe Major of the town whose wife was with him. The guests had arrived and after the wonderful meal Sarah had provided, the party warmed up with songs and dancing, although there was not much space. The Pipe Major's wife and I were brought up beside each other in South Lochboisdale, and this was our first meeting since before the First War, so we had much to say and recall. The party continued until the small hours with much singing, dancing and reminiscing of days gone by.

We stayed for a day in Oban, then went to Glasgow for a few days' honeymoon, picking up bits and pieces for the near empty home. After much searching we were able to get second-hand, pots and pans, crockery, cutlery and an old black stove. On our first night back we stayed at her parent's home. The next day I went down to Locheynort to get the place warmed up and tidy, and having brought enough food with me, I stayed there that night. Next day, when the tide was in I took the boat and went into the end of the road at Bayhead hoping that my wife, if she had got the expected transportation as planned, would be there and she was. It was a beautiful evening when we got back to the house. My brother and his wife had a good fire on and tea almost ready. I had managed to get some whisky in Glasgow, which was still in the case for this occasion. Polochar was still dry. We enjoyed that house warming and the meal, more so since it was our first together in our own home. After the other two left, we sat for a while looking at each other. This was the end of one dream and the beginning of the next.

Donald's father and friend

Donald's Boats in harbour

Mary Ann did not expect to find the house so tidy and liked the view from the window, although she said it needed curtains. She had material with her, and the curtains were up when I got up early next morning. The window looked much better dressed like that and, knowing that she was up a good part of the night, I let her sleep and went to the shore to gather a fresh supply of scallops for breakfast. She was up when I had them ready for cooking. With them she cooked eggs and bacon. Scallops were then plentiful near the house and the loch was teeming with fish. Rabbits would come almost to the doorstep in the mornings before we got a dog. Although we had these things in plenty, we lacked others. The grocery van called twice a week at Bayhead if there was anything to sell, but most of the time there was nothing left even if ordered the week before. We would walk the three miles to Bayhead over muddy paths in all weathers to find next to nothing left in the van. It is unbelievable what the people of the township had to suffer from lack of a road, mains water and electricity, all of which came much later.

We were like that, a forgotten people, only to be remembered when taxes and rates were due. It was to a place like that I had brought my young wife to set up a home and hopefully to raise a family. The weather was good enough to enable us to get the goods we brought from Glasgow to the house, but the stove was a disappointment as far as the smoke went, although the oven worked surprisingly well. We had plenty of our own peats. After a while I was able to make some improvements to the house, and as time went on we added something new to it. It is surprising what one can do when there is no other way. Necessity is often the mother of invention and we needed a lot of mothering. Spring was coming and time or season cannot be held back. Although you are supposed to be your own master on a croft, in reality you are not. You must conform to the season at hand in order to obtain the benefit you hope for. Mindful of that I began looking for a suitable place where we could grow potatoes and vegetables.

Breaking in virgin soil for a garden is a hard and laborious task. The more you dig and rake, the better will be the results. That first spring together we made a garden and sowed oats for the cows we hoped to buy in late summer. I erected a byre-cum-barn from wood I collected from the shore, costing me only the price of the nails. When all the spring work was done and peats cut I began fishing lobsters again.

There was no sign of the war coming to an end and the destruction at sea by submarines and mines was making itself felt everywhere, though we were not as hard off as many. There were always the hills for rabbits, the sea for fish and there was no scarcity of food. One day, with another man, we went to search the shore after a few weeks of onshore wind. In one bay we found many boxes of lard and butter. We put a few on dry land and took some with us to see if the women folk would use it. At first they were afraid to, but after testing it on the animals, they regretted having wasted so much.

Further along that bay we came on a wire coming out of the sea and leading up into a high hill. We began pulling it ashore. We took about 50 yards of it when it stuck. We followed the other end up the hill, not knowing what to expect over the hill. I said to John, "Have you got a knife?" "Yes." "Well get it out, open it and have it ready in your hand to defend yourself if you have to." We crawled onto the ridge following the wire that went down the other side. We then thought it had nothing to do with the sea or what was at the sunken end. We got braver and braver and exposed ourselves. In the far distance, that is about 250 yards, we saw a large grey heap that we knew was not there before. We approached it slowly. When alongside it, I made it out to be a large grey barrage balloon of the kind used by ships in convoy; this one, used to prevent dive bombing, was trailing so much wire that it must have broken its cable near the ship or run off the spool while being let out. The wire itself was not of much use as it was too hard to untangle. The nylon balloon was different, although greatly torn. We made good use of what was left as oilskins were not to be had. What we made out of that nylon was light wind and waterproof, with a long life. I also made table oilcloth covers with it. First they were painted yellow, then stippled with many colours and varnished over. They lasted long after the war was over.

Mary Ann went visiting one day and came back the owner of a grown-up pup. Although mischievous, he was added company and showing signs of becoming a good hunter. Mary Ann got some hens from friends, and these we fed well and they laid more than we could use. After having the grown-up pup for over a month, one Sunday, going to mass, we left the pup loose outside the house with a dead rabbit to play with, thinking he would not follow us. We sometimes called into houses on the way home from mass. This day, not sure that the dog would stay round the house, we did not make any calls. When we came in view of the house we saw the dog running to meet us. He had something in his mouth. I could see it was a bird. I said, "I told you that he would make a good hunter, see, he has a wild duck in his mouth." When he came nearer Mary Ann said, "That's not a duck he's got, that's one of the hens." Wagging his tail he dropped it at our feet. Rushing off to see if he had touched any of the rest she found five of them in a heap on the doorstep, some were not yet dead. She was fuming with anger. It was the first time I had heard her swear. My laughing at this disaster was no help, and because of it I endured as much telling off as the dog got, only I did not catch a slap of the stick she had when the dog came near to admire his day's work. She told me I would have to make a muzzle for him. After all his crime was bringing something different to eat to our doorstep.

Scot, as we called him, was watching us closely and did not seem to be afraid, but kept from the stick. I was able to make a muzzle to teach him to mind his ways. That done and fitted on under protest, he learned his lesson well and soon. Never again did he do more than look at a hen, but with rabbits he never forgot the habit of bringing them to the doorstep, and to that no objection was raised. That week we dined high on roasted chicken and shellfish.

The dog grew large and strong and never ran away from a fight when other dogs invaded his territory. He was different with cattle, and even hens when he learned his lesson. If any showed signs of fighting, he would jump between them and growl, setting them apart, staying there till aggression ceased. He was good at gathering sheep but not good at driving, always keeping them too close. When we got cattle he would, on his own, bring them from the hills. His sense of scent was the keenest I have ever known. He would follow the scent of a rabbit, if warm, at least a quarter of a mile. A party of game hunters came out one day. Their dogs must have had the distemper and, no matter how hard I tried to save him, he had caught it. It was a losing battle. I didn't want him to suffer and I didn't want to put him down myself after all his faithfulness. I could not get anyone to do it. There was no vet, so I was obliged to perform this very unpleasant task myself, by drowning, and when the bubbles stopped coming up I felt a pang of great sorrow. Losing my best cow would not be so hard felt. We had him for ten years and never again his equal.

We fished lobsters and herring that year and did very well. Money was plentiful but little to spend it on. Our first son was born in January of 1943. When Mary Ann told me she was with child our joy knew no bounds. We were happy before and hopeful that we would be blessed with children, and the joy of that anticipation made the sun shine for us every day and all day. It also brought more care and responsibility and we would do our best to face these. Previously I had arranged a signal with my friend Angus James, on the other side of the loch, for when I needed help. Now I felt I should renew that call to include aid at night. This was done by flashing a torch at a certain place on the shore at a certain time. I told him of the circumstances we were in. Happily I did not have to use it in connection with this occasion. Without crossing the loch, the nearest house to us was three quarters of a mile away and out of sight. The distance to the house that I could see across the loch was about a mile by boat if the tide was in, but it was four miles on foot in weather when a boat could not cross over. However, everything was progressing normally. There was no call for the doctor, who was ten miles away, four of them across the moor if a boat was not available. With the child now well on the way, these conditions were kept constantly in mind. I had made the garden and with seed and plants everything in it was growing well. Mary Ann attended it as long as she was able.

Peter had given me a year old heifer, but late that summer we bought a cow, a seven-year-old light brown shorthorn in milk and calving in early January. The price was fifteen pounds. She was by far the largest animal in the township. The man at the sale I bought her from was quite pleased with the price and gave me 2/6 back for luck. As I had the dog with me, I had very little trouble on the road leading her on a rope, but looking at her huge size I wondered how I was to get her over the marshland, as using the foot path, although we had a dry spell, was not possible. When I reached the end of the road the night was falling. It was too risky to take her further out. I borrowed a rope and tethered her till early next morning, and when I got back to her she was grazing quite happily. I put the lead rope on her and, by making temporary bridges from heather and bracken, managed eventually to make the journey over the very soft marshy ground and soft streams to our home, arriving in the early evening. When Mary Ann saw us on the skyline, at first she said she thought it was an elephant I was leading. The cow looked tired and was muddy to her belly. I got some old hay and heather and cleaned and dried her. I milked her and she was as tame as a pet, never lifted a foot. After that hard day, she gave more milk than we expected, adding to it as she settled and got used to the clean lush grass. We called her Leddy and she produced enough milk to keep us in cream, butter and cheese to December, and presented us with a bonny female calf on New Year's Day. I remember the occasion so well.

I had managed to get a bottle of whisky for New Year. At this time she was in the byre so I stretched on the bench, ready to jump on hearing any commotion, and soon enough she calved. When sucking, I let the calf have its fill and then I pulled it away from its mother and penned it, under protest. Much trouble later could be avoided if the calf was kept off her from birth, if you intend milking her and rearing the calf from the bucket. It is often a slow process teaching it to drink on its own, which involves encouraging the calf to suck your fingers immersed in a bucket of milk, and at the same time encouraging it to drink directly from the bucket. The calf soon gets the hang of it and there is no need for it to suck any fingers. A calf left to suckle will always bring a better price with less labour, but don't expect any milk from that cow. You can't have it both ways. Our circumstances called for the bucket.

It was a very happy New Year for us. Perhaps a cloud of care hung over us by the far more important event fast approaching, but we could not afford not to think of it, or what might happen in an isolated place. There was no maternity unit in the hospital on the island. All patients in need of extra care were sent to the mainland, or the confinement took place at home.

Mary Ann was in good health but we lived in an isolated place, far away from help if that was needed. To lessen that anxiety, we prepared and planned that she would go to her parents' home in good time for the birth. I made arrangements for the car to take her. It was a fine day, the tide high enough for the boat to take her into the car, where her mother met us, and into whose care I left her and returned to look after the house and wait. It seemed and was empty without her. The days were long, the nights an eternity, and no one passed by going to the hill at that time of the year. Up until then I never felt so lonely. The dog Scot was of some company.

Four days after she had left I got a letter from Mary Ann saying she was as well as could be expected, just longing and waiting, which summed up the way I was feeling myself. I wrote by return of post and walked the nearly six miles each way to post the letter. To pass the time, I made a milking stool, and with so much milk I thought of making a churn, which would be a surprise for Mary Ann. I had plenty of white pine free from knots, which only needed planeing and cutting. I plancd and marked the wood and after nailing it together and testing it with water I found it was leaking like a lawn sprayer. We had no lawn but it would do for the garden in the dry summer.

I then remembered Mary Ann doing something with a roll of tape and I thought it might do to make the joints milk tight. I found the tape and used it to seal the joints, and at last the article was finished. I knew it was the best I could do and if it didn't prove right this time, it would be the fire for it. It did prove right after testing it with milk and then boiling water, after which I sandpapered it and painted the outside. When we put it to use, the churning could be done in a quarter of an hour. We never bought or made another one. People we knew who got theirs from the mainland claimed the one I made was much better

Some ten days after Mary Ann had left, I got the long awaited wire in the evening telling me that she gave birth to a son early that morning and both were well. Next morning I was up before daylight, fed, milked and watered the animals, cleaned up and made breakfast. I was on my way before it was quite light. I called at my neighbour's house to ask him to look after the cattle, as I intended to be back some time that night. However, he was deaf and asleep upstairs and no amount of hammering would wake him. I had to leave, but if he had heard the hammering, I knew he would take a walk out. The morning was fine and I kept walking the thirteen or more miles, looking behind now and again, hoping for a lift. Eventually, I reached Polochar Inn and called in hoping that I would at least get something to take with me. I told Brown, the barman, who I was and that I was on my way to see my wife and newborn baby. He knew my brother in law, "Red Michael" (Michael Ruadh), and on hearing that name he smiled, filled my pint, scratched his head and said, "We are short of everything here but screw tops. All I can give you is a flask of wine" and with that I had to be content. I rested over another pint and left walking the mile and so off to the house.

There I saw Mary Ann looking pale but happy, with the baby fast asleep in her arms. I stood for a moment as if in a trance before I stepped over and kissed them both. We talked a lot; she wanted to know how things were back home and how I was managing to pass the time. I told her everything was fine and not to worry about anything, that I was always doing something. She asked me if I could make a cradle, and I thought, if I could make a churn, milk and water tight, making a cradle would be no problem. I asked her what colour she would like, and she said, "Pink inside, pale blue outside."

236

After an enjoyable meal and talk about making arrangements for the baptism, I thought it was time I was heading back home. The baby had wakened and was fed and I had a better look at him. I thought I saw him smile at me, perhaps wishful thinking. I saw him close his eyes, and go to sleep curled up in his mother's arms, next to her heart and indeed he was next to mine. I left them with that picture in my mind.

I bypassed Polochar as it was near closing time. I hoped there would be customers with a car going north, but evidently not, so no hope for a lift. I walked the 9 miles to Bayhead. It was dark when I came to the end of the road and so I called in on Neil, the postman, who was now married to Morag, my sister-in-law. I gave them the good news about Mary Ann and the baby. After tea and a rest they gave me an old lantern that sometimes worked, I hoped it would get me through the worst stretch of the path. The night was dark with a fairly strong wind, but I was making good progress. The lantern was beginning to smoke and when I came to a hollow, it went out. I had a box of matches, but as there was no shelter, before the flame reached the wick, each match went out, till I had only a few left. I knew there was a good shelter nearby; I could light it there. I only took a few steps in the dark towards it when one foot sank into a bog up to my knee; I fell and dropped the lantern. When I was free to stand and search, I found it upside down with not a drop of paraffin left. I had been in a happy mood all day and up to then, but this was taking the edge off it. There was one thing in my favour and that was the moon had risen. It would not be long before it would be above the hilltop, so I waited where I was until I could make out where the worst bogs were. I left the lantern standing in the middle of the path so the postman would see it there the first time he had anything to deliver out our way. The moon had risen and I could now take long steps and even short jumps in safety.

I called at my neighbour's house, and they told me that the dog barking in the morning had wakened them and they knew I had gone up south. They had heard from the boy with the wire that Mary Ann had had a baby boy. He told me that he had been out to mine and that he had seen to the animals and cleaned out the byre, so all was fine for the night. He congratulated me and offered me a hot meal, but as I had eaten at Bayhead I thanked him and declined as I was tired and just wanted to get home. He asked if my feet were sore after the long walk and I told him, "No" as I had strong studded shoes on, the shoes that Sarah would not let me wear at my wedding. I could have started walking back then if there was any need. When I got to the house, the stove was stone cold. Calor gas was then not thought of here, and indeed anywhere on the island. I was not hungry and too tired to break wood and start a fire, so I went into a cold bed and was soon in dreamland.

The next day, after seeing to the animals and getting the house ship-shape, I began looking for suitable wood and planning for the cradle. I decided to make it three feet by 18 inches as I thought that would be large enough. I planed and dressed the wood and paid more attention to making it than I did to the churn, although unlike the churn I knew it was not necessary to make it water tight. I worked at it mostly at nights.

I went to see Father Neil about the baptism and we agreed on the day after tomorrow at 11 am and he would pick me up at the end of the road. I left and made an early start next morning when I got a lift from Kennedy, the Clerk of Works for the Department. I got off at the Co-op at Daliburgh for sweets and chocolate to take to Mary Ann and was served by Scoular, the manager, who, when I offered him the money, looked at me and said, "Points please." When he saw that I was silent he said, "Have you got your points?" I said that I didn't know anything about that. Was that not enough money to pay? "It's more than enough but I must have your points before I can let you have this parcel." I said, "I'll get the points somewhere and bring them here." "No" he said "I would trust you with money. I don't trust anyone for points." He began opening the parcel to put the sweets back on the shelf again and an old lady at my back, who I did not know but who evidently saw and heard what was going on, said in a loud voice, "Give him those sweets he asked for. I have plenty of points here in my bag to pay you." Hearing that, Scoular began making up the parcel again. I was watching him and didn't pay the lady enough attention as her head was bent counting the points that Scoular wanted. She put them on the counter, turned and made for the door, with me not even thanking her, and certainly not knowing who she was, a fact that I greatly regretted for surely I should have shown my appreciation in some way. I never did find out who she was and could not describe her.

I left and expected to be walking, but only a very short distance on my way a car stopped beside me. I knew Angus, the driver, who offered me a lift to Polochar. It was my lucky day as he knew Brown, the barman, and after several drinks with Brown, which put him in a good mood, was able to get a bottle of sherry and a half bottle of whisky for me. I paid Angus while Brown's back was turned.

As Angus was going to Ludag to pick up a man coming from Eriskay, I got a lift to Mary Ann's parents' house and arranged to watch for him coming back to get a lift. Mary Ann was feeling fine and getting stronger every day. The baby was doing very well and sleeping most of that time. I told her about seeing Father Neil and the arrangements for the christening. Mary Ann was glad to get the sweets, but asked where I got that many points as she had all we had with her. I told her about the kind lady whom I did not know. At that moment we saw that a boat had left from Eriskay, but as it was an exceptionally low tide, it took the boat sometime to reach the jetty at Ludag. I kissed them both and said goodbye. Angus picked me up but stopped at Daliburgh for petrol. At the pump, getting his fill-up, was Neil Smith, the very man I wanted to see for tomorrow's transport, and as he was going north I was able to get a lift with him and thanked Angus for his help.

I had just one more task; to let the godfather to be, Angus James, know when and where to meet the car. I would take the boat across as soon as I got home, as the tide would be right. I took the stepping-stones short cut instead of the muddy path, which shortened the distance by about a mile, but only when the tide was well out in dry weather was that possible. There were two of these stepping-stone gaps to cross. The first was known as the Cairidh and the other was called the Strom. Originally the Cairidh was built as a low wall, which the tide covered over to allow fish to come in from the loch into the small bay which formed at high tide, and when the tide went out the fish remaining in that bay were caught. It is believed to be the first method the people had on the islands for catching fish, long before they learned from the Irish monks how to make nets from flax. The flax nets did not however last, and it took a long time to weave them, so they were only used when there was no other way to catch fish, when the landlords ordered, with the aid of the ground officers, that these Cairidhs should be knocked down to prevent fish being caught. If the Cairidh was found to be rebuilt there was a danger of being evicted. Their remains can be seen almost everywhere there is a stream to the sea. They were too dangerous for old and infirm people to use. There is now a road bypassing the first and built over the other. Only the few old folk left in this area know the suffering endured before this road was built.

On my way home, at every house I passed, the people came out to enquire about Mary Ann and the baby and as before, Seonaidh had been out and fed and looked after the cattle. When I arrived home, I checked the hen house and collected the eggs, made myself an omelette, and after a little work on the cradle, went to bed early, tired and with thoughts of tomorrow. The next morning, I made another early start, and having dealt with the cattle and the chores I was ready for the path once again. There was no short-cut that day as the tide was in, and once I reached the main road both Neil Smith and Angus James were waiting for me at the appointed place. The car was running good. He had got the tyres replaced and no longer needed to fill them with heather, so that now we didn't have to lean to one side.

To a Christian, baptism is the most important event in his life, and any man or woman who is a Christian can perform this sacrament in a case of emergency or near death, as well as the Pope in Rome can. Water is so important, but when that is unobtainable, wetting one's finger on his or her tongue and wetting the child's head, or whoever is being baptised, takes the place of the water, and at the same time making the sign of the cross over the one baptised with the saying of the words 'I baptise thee, in the name of the Father and of the Son and of the Holy Ghost.' In the eyes of the Christian church this is perfectly valid, so that if a Christian is at hand there is no chance of anyone in need of that sacrament slipping away without it.

Inside the usual warm welcome was extended. The priest had not yet arrived. The short time till he did was spent in fishing talk. Mary Ann and the baby were well. With much pride, she showed me his christening robe. It was a beauty, lent to her by Sarah who had it for her own family. I watched the mother and the grandmother dressing the baby for this occasion. When everything was done the priest arrived and, after a short talk, he told those taking part where to stand and the ceremony began, lasting no more than minutes. We named the child Archie after my father. At the end of the ceremony we sat at a long table, well laden with good things to eat and drink, and toasted the health of mother and child with a glass of sherry. After that enjoyable meal and dram I advised Mary Ann not to be in any hurry coming home, and when decided to let me know, as the tide may not be suitable. With another fond kiss, I bade farewell and eventually arrived home via the muddy path although, having previously learned my lesson, I had left my wellingtons at the road end and carried my old faithful brogues with me. Their soles were now thin and would never again make offending noises on a cathedral floor.

Mary Ann had taught me how to make scones which saved me walking the miles of muddy path to the van for a loaf of bread, which was often mouldy. I only went to the van when I ran out of tobacco, tea and sugar. One day my brother Peter came out. I was busy finishing the cradle, and before he left he inspected it, saying it was good and strong but he thought the rockers were too high and the hood too long. I agreed and altered it to make it safer. I also bored small holes where Mary Ann could put a string through to hang a lace curtain. It would keep the flies off while outside on a sunny day. Mary Ann was delighted with it and after serving our children it was passed on to others in need.

Mary Ann's stay up south was longer than we had expected, but towards the end of the week I got word that herself and her mother and baby were expected to come down the next day, and if it was not raining not to bother with the boat. Thinking of the long, uncomfortable way to carry a baby in arms, I thought of how to make a carry kit. I cut a part out of my sailor's canvas kit bag and sewed shoulder straps on, and a hood, and filled it with a torn piece of a woollen blanket. I thought with that and whatever other garment they had, he would be safe and warm.

239

At the appointed time, I left the house having giving it a good tidy as Granny was coming for the first time. I also put on a good fire and left the kettles full. When I met them, Mary Ann fitted the baby into the carry bag and said it was very good, warm and handy, and asked if I had found it on the shore. I told her I made it from an idea I had, having once seen an Indian carrying her baby in a papoose. I said, "You wrap him well and I'll carry him as the path is still not so good, but you won't need your wellingtons."

We called at Morag's for a cup of tea and a feed for the baby and left for the path. Granny seemed to be enjoying her new adventure. We did not call at any of the other houses as I was concerned about the large fire I left, and wondered if I had pushed the dampers in far enough. Long before the house came into view I had a whiff of a foreign smell. It was soot from the chimney. I hurried in front and met Scot barking, and whatever he was trying to convey it had to be something unusual. Coming nearer the house the smell was becoming stronger, yet I could see no fire. As soon as I opened the door I knew what had happened. The peats we used were nearly as good as coal, and it was not long before the two kettles boiled over putting most of the fire out but causing a lot of smoke. When it got going again, the same thing happened, till the fire was completely out. Testing the kettles there was still a little water left. No damage done there. I built a fire outside till I had the stove cleaned out. Mary Ann left the baby in the carrying kit in the new cradle till we got the house warm again. Because of the good peat that did not take long. Once the fire was going, she made a splendid meal of fried eggs, onions and scallops that was much enjoyed. Wee Archie was quite content, even after his many bumps along the path, and he soon fell asleep.

Granny enjoyed her first visit to Locheynort and I hoped she would stay with us for some time. She would have done except for some unexpected event that took place in the family. We were then on our own again, although with a new baby, and as it was well into the spring much outside work had to be done in preparing for lazy beds, extension to the garden, putting up new fences and making new peat bogs. While working on these things that were necessary, I was not earning any money, and unemployment benefit was not available because I was self-employed while fishing. Much of what we had saved went on buying fishing gear for the coming season. However, as the main part of our living came from what we had planted on the croft the year before, we had potatoes, vegetables, eggs and milk, fish and shellfish, of which there was plenty but no market for them. There were many things the house needed and for these cash was needed. I thought of gathering whelks as it was said at one time they were plentiful on our shores. I would gather them in the daylight at spring tide, and at night I would work on the fishing gear. I walked long distances to do that if the boat was not available owing to bad weather, but contrary to what I heard, the whelks were very scarce, no matter where I searched. After three weeks of searching and aiming to fill a three hundredweight bag, I gave it up before then and sent them to Billingsgate to a salesman I used to send the lobsters to. Totalling up what I got in return, and the time concerned in the actual work, it came to less than nine pence per working day. That was less than what we as boys made gathering them in the winter of 1911 and 1912, when herding cattle was not needed although there was no other work to be had. I gave it up as a waste of time.

A near neighbour with five of a young family and on the means test, got a job with the county roads department, breaking stones for the roads. He had to break a cubic yard of stone to earn 2/6d. Most days he could not do that, depending on the hardness of the rock. Even if our resources were reduced to that state, we would not qualify for that work because we had only one child. Such were the conditions in Uist in 1944 and 1945. It was early in September before we again began lobstering. To do so sooner would be a waste of time, at least on the Minch side of the island.

About this time we were expecting another addition to the family around mid-September. Preparations as in the case of the first child were made. Mary Ann was to go, as before, to her parents' home. Everything that was required had been sent ahead of her, but taking wee Archie with her, however. Alex Iain, as he was christened, decided the calculations were wrong. Near dawn on 4th September, Mary Ann woke me complaining of stomach pains. I said that I would get up and make her a hot milk drink. She drank the hot milk and said she felt much better and was soon asleep. It was well into daylight when she again woke me saying the pain was getting worse. "I am afraid it's labour pains. What are we to do?" Getting up and dressing, trying to show as little concern as possible I said, "You are strong and healthy. Nothing can go wrong. Drink more of that hot milk. I'll go and get Jane, Seonaidh's wife, to come out to make tea and keep you company, and I will be back as soon as I can get word to the doctor."

I spread a bed sheet at the emergency place and ran to waken Jane. I told her how Mary Ann was and that she thought she was in labour. Jane left willingly, saying she would do her best. As it was a post day, I carried on to meet Neil, the postman, who turned back to wire the doctor and nurse. I knew it would be impossible for the old doctor to come out without a boat, but with mine high and dry I called on Peter, as the tide was right for his small boat to get to the head of the loch, and when he arrived he met the nurse who told him the doctor was out on another case, and as the tide was against Peter returning, the nurse said she would walk out.

Kate at rations van

Kate's Cow
Locheynort

When I got back to the house, Kate, my brother Peter's wife was there helping with Mary Ann who was not any worse. Looking across the Loch I was glad to see Angus James, who had seen my emergency signal, coming over in his fast motorboat. I met him at the nearest point and asked him to collect the doctor who should have arrived at Bayhead as the tide was by then well in. I went home. Jane was still there. She had fed and changed wee Archie. Mary Ann was much the same and not complaining. I assured her that the nurse would be here soon and that Angus James had gone with the boat to meet the doctor. Soon afterwards I was very glad to see the nurse walking fast with her black bag.

She asked me if I had everything prepared for the birth, but I told her that everything had been sent up south where Mary Ann intended, as before, for the birth to be. She was to go there this week; but tell me what to do and I will do my best. She told me to put a good fire on and two pots of water and keep a look out for the boat with the doctor coming. I was glad to be doing something. When I got her alone I said, "How is she?" "At the moment she is calm but I wish with all my heart that the doctor would hurry." I felt then that she was worried, more I thought than I was. She said she was afraid the baby might be here before the Doctor comes. I was very relieved when we saw the boat bearing the doctor arriving. The climb to the house was not easy and we had to detour round peat bogs and grassy slopes because of his age.

This was the same Doctor Reardon I had had a brush with in early 1915 when I was home on sick leave after being wounded in France. The Lovat Scouts, who had not yet been to France and had contracted measles, were given an extension of their sick leave, and he mistook me for one of them and did not want to extend my sick leave. When he realised his mistake the matter was sorted.

The nurse met him at the door and took him to Mary Ann. She got a basin of warm water, soap and towel and closed the door behind her. Angus James sat in the kitchen. He was a man with a large family and quite used to such events of this kind. When hearing moaning from inside he seemed to know what was going on. He said, "It won't be long now. You can trust that doctor, he is at his best in a maternity case and well known for that." He was only a few minutes in the room when we heard the first cry from the baby. The nurse beforehand had a basin of warm water, stool and clean towel ready before the fire. She brought him in on the palm of her

242

hand saying it was a boy. I thought how can a man be so small and grow up to six foot and more. She washed him and tied him in her own homemade bandage. Kate made tea, and when the Doctor was ready, a tray laden with home baked scones, oatcakes, fresh butter, crowdie and bramble jam, also homemade, was placed on a stool before him. When finished, I followed him to the boat and paid him his fee of one guinea. He handed back the shilling saying, "Good luck for the baby." I saw him safely on board with Angus James to be landed very near his car.

Kate made a proper meal for the nurse. I knew after an early start she must be famished. I asked her if she liked scallops, "Very much, can you get them here?" "Yes, plenty at low tide." Kate fried an egg and a rasher of bacon along with the scallops, and that with scones, the nurse said, she could not remember when she had enjoyed a meal so much. She said. "You are lucky to be staying in a place like this." I said, "Wait till you come to the mud path when the tide is out and the boat cannot get in and you have to walk, you might change your mind. I'll collect you by boat tomorrow about 9 o'clock." She said she would get word to Mary Ann's people of this event and that she would collect the garments for the baby, which had been sent to East Kilbride. She would bring them back tomorrow, as well as finding out when Mary Ann's mother or her sister, Theresa, would come down. Mary Ann and the baby were very well and she had had a cup of tea and a scone and could eat no more. Till then I thought I could attend to wee Archie myself. Kate stayed while I went to show the nurse the path and walk part of the way with her. I thanked her for the trouble and hoped that it would not be too long before we got a road to the house.

Although we were somewhat isolated, news of events of this travelled fast. When Neil the postman wired the doctor and nurse, someone near Mary Ann's home was in the post office and was told what the wire was about. She at once made haste and got a lift to Polochar, and from there she walked to Mary Ann's people to tell them what she was told in the post office. They had the news long before the nurse and the doctor arrived here. I can imagine the commotion the seriousness of this news caused in that peaceful house. Mary Ann's mother took charge and organised a lift to take her down to Locheynort with a bundle of baby clothes, where I met her and Morag. Before I had gone only a short distance with the nurse, Morag was the first to speak, "How is she? We know it's a boy." "She is very well but how do you know it's a boy?" "I met the doctor when he came off the boat, and he said he didn't want to see any more babies born out there till you have a road where a car can travel." Mary Ann's mother stayed with us for over a week, and I kept collecting the nurse by boat and taking her back every day till she said she was not needed.

The christening this time was to be in St. Mary's church in Bornish; it was then not necessary for the mother to be present. Mary Ann chose the name this time; he was to be named after her father and uncle Alexander John. Our neighbour Seonaidh the stonemason was to be the Godfather, and Mary on the other side of the loch to be the Godmother. We began to arrange a party for the event, and for that we needed refreshment. The two pubs were as dry as ever but there was plenty of beer to be had. I got an eight-gallon cask and cleaned it out with boiling water and left it to dry. Angus James and I went with the boat to Lochboisdale to fill it and get whatever else we could. As I knew the barman we managed to get a bottle of wine and he kindly filled the cask for us. We had a few from the same tap and it tasted good. The bung was hammered in airtight and after another drink and one for the barman, we set off on our journey back to Locheynort. This time we were back early as besides the engine we had the wind and tide following us. After our cargo was taken up to the house, and a meal, I took Angus James home, and then with the boat as far as she could get to Bayhead. I then made my way across the moor and walked the remaining 2 miles to see the priest about the baptism the next day. He said tomorrow about noon, weather permitting for the boat. He gave me a lift to Bornish crossroads, the nearest point to the boat. Before parting with Angus James, I had told him, if the baptism was on, I would put out the usual signal and collect everyone by boat in the morning.

The next day was fine and promised to be good and warm all day long. I got up early, did the day's chores and got the boat ready. The baby was well bundled as if going to the North Pole, his mother had made up a flask of milk handy to fit in my breast pocket for warmth in case he needed fed before returning home. With all on board we got as far as Bayhead and walked across the moor nearly 2 miles to where the priest was waiting for us at Bornish crossroads. After the baptism was over, he took us back to the same place. The baby began to cry and Mary gave him a shot of the bottle. He seemed to like it and soon fell asleep again. We picked Angus James up on our way back and when we arrived at the house most of the neighbours had arrived. Mary Ann changed the baby and gave him a feed. Angus James opened the cask with a corkscrew. It was put on a higher rock for gravitation, with a tube and the milking pail ready, but first when everything was ready and all found a place to sit, everyone had a small drink of wine, and the Godfather proposed a toast for the good health of the baby who was sleeping peacefully.

When tea and home baking, of which there was plenty, was over, someone said that the men might like some beer, and no one objected to that suggestion. We had plenty of tumblers and so the beer was drawn and tasted. One looked at the other wondering if he had lost his taste for beer till someone said, "This isn't beer, this is flat, stale and smells bad. The barman gave you some left-over only fit to dump." "No, it came from the same tap that we drank from. How it changed I cannot understand. I know the cask was perfectly clean and filled from the same tap. The bung was put in air tight and only removed a moment ago. Nothing got near it. I am sure all the rest must be the same but let's run some off to see if it's any better." Deeper in the cask it was not, if anything it was worse. None of us had ever worked in a bar and could not offer any suggestions why it turned flat and sour. The bung was put back in, thinking it needed a rest after the disturbance and the rolling it got in the boat. I also filled two empty screw tops and left them overnight. No change. It was good that we had brought so many screw tops with us, which saved the day and was enough to put Seonaidh in a singing mood. He was a good singer and, had the cask not been so disappointing, I am sure there would be others wanting to prove they could sing as well. The wine was left for the ladies. It was surprising then what good form the ladies were in with only two glasses of wine. I maintain that when the ladies are not in good form, any party is a washout. Regardless of the cask letting us down, and despite rationing I felt all enjoyed it.

Some time after that we were sending away a consignment of lobsters. The same man was the barman. I told him how the cask of beer he filled turned out to be flat and sour. I knew the cask was clean and the beer was good when he filled it. He asked if we pumped air into it before opening it. I said that we just took the bung out, put a hose in and let the beer run. He said, "No wonder it was flat and sour. I should have told you but I thought you knew to put the tap in first, bore a hole near the bottom, insert an air pump there, then pump air in, as much as you can, then turn on the tap and let the bubbles flow till the beer comes in a creamy foam and use it as you need. Very simple, you wasted a lot of good beer."

244

We fished for lobsters and herring all that winter to early spring when it was time to begin the spring work again, and although we were making good money at the lobsters, if we did not plant potatoes in time we might not be able to meet our needs. The effects of the war seemed to be as dark as ever but with our own grown crop and fish we would not starve. The usual rations were cut down and if you did get some, the flour was very dark with much of it stale. There was not much in the way of food that money could buy, simply because there was so little of it, and if living far from the shops you often returned empty handed. We had a good crop of everything we planted that year and also got word from the Department that a road was soon to be built on each side of Locheynort. The joy and satisfaction that news caused around the loch was evident. We knew who was fighting for our cause. At the last council meeting in Inverness, the subject was brought up by the priest, Fr MacKellaig. He was told that by building a new road in a crofting township they would be dispensing with precedent, "Precedents," said the Priest, "were made to be broken. In refusing to grant money to build this much needed road, you are missing the bus. The people will soon be obliged to leave the township for lack of a road, the path that they now have is often knee deep in mud, and they can't be expected to stay there." It was maintained that was the turning point. A grant of £15,000 was passed to build the road, over five miles long, with two causeways and two bridges on the north side of the loch. But there was no free labour as was in force when building the South Lochboisdale road a few years before then.

The only mechanical aid we had while building the south side branch, was the lorry for carrying stone and gravel which, after being dug by pick, was hand shovelled into the lorry. The road was to be nine feet wide with a three-foot verge on each side, and with a six or more inch stone bottom. On the top a load of gravel was spread for the next load of stone, continuing in the same order, except where it needed another load of each. A twelve-pound sledgehammer broke up the stones that one man could not lift onto the lorry. When the road came to places where it had to be cut through solid rock, blasting was needed. Drilling was made by manpower with a steel two-foot rod tempered by a blacksmith at the cutting end, and hammered, or pelted, by two men with an eight pound long shaft hammer, another man sitting holding the drill steady and giving it a half turn with every stroke from the pelters as one followed the other. Picks, shovels, spades, wheelbarrows, iron bars, and the two-ton truck were all the working gear we had on the south side. The County Council gave us a small compressor when we began on the causeway and bridge. It was a great help. For that hard labour the pay was very low. We worked eight hours a day, four hours on Saturday. The wages were one shilling and ten pence per day, paid monthly without unemployment stamp deducted.

In order to help build the road that we needed so badly, Angus James and I gave up fishing to work on it, although knowing we could have made much more money fishing. He lived at the far south end and I at the far north end, and I am quite sure that is why the road did not take very long to build, as our livelihood greatly depended on it. Blasting material was supplied, and we got used to handling gelignite, detonators and fuses. Most would risk setting a blast off, till one man took over that job to become a better judge for the charge needed in different places. Although we had near misses, no one was badly hurt. Nowadays, a battery is used to set them off, safer than the cigarette we used. In view of the conditions and difficulties

245

involved in the construction, I think the most we were doing was 45 yards a day, and when looking towards the end, it seemed it could never be reached. Bit by bit, regardless of the long out of date tools they gave us, we did reach that end sooner than was expected. When we began working on the north side branch, the county gave us a small compressor to blast rocks for the causeway. These large rocks were loaded onto a truck by rolling them onto strong planks with one end on the ground, the other resting on the truck, and then with manpower it was turn by turn forced up into the truck.

It was near Christmas, and one day as I got home Mary Ann met me at the door. I could tell that something was wrong. She told me that Archie had been badly scalded. He was now sleeping after crying all day. No one had come near the house and she could not leave him to send for help. He was naked as he could not bear his clothing on. I had a look at him and saw he was breathing easy. He had been playing on the bench at the window when Mary Ann was bathing the baby in front of the fire; there was a very hot kettle on the stove. When she was drying the baby in her lap Archie tumbled off the bench and brought the kettle down on the top of him.

The dark night was turning wet and stormy and we were worried how to get word to the Doctor. Although he was a young man and had recently replaced old Reardon, it was doubtful if he could make it before daylight. We were sure he could not. I began dressing the burns as I had seen when, as a young soldier, I helped the Ward Sister to dress what she said was the worst burns case she had ever had to handle. I remembered old people saying that olive oil was the best thing you could put on burns and it was the only thing we had to put on. I got a feather, dipped it in hot water, dried it and used it to spread the olive oil. Archie had very few toys to distract him during this painful operation. I had an old double case key winding silver watch that my uncle left me which I had shown to him often and told him some day I would let him have it. I gave him the watch and his face lit up. His mother took the sheet off. It looked painful, but as long as he was kept quiet, he was not in any great danger for one night. With the feather we spread olive oil on, the other held him till we bandaged him. Regardless of the watch he did a lot of crying. At times we had to stop. In the end we did not quite finish it and he lost interest in the watch. After a long while he stopped crying. His mother got him to drink a switched egg and milk and before long he fell into an uneasy sleep.

Next day we got a message to the hospital telling the Doctor about Archie. When he arrived a Sister from the hospital was with him with an armful of cotton wool and bandages. I told him what had happened and how we had bandaged the burns and that we were lucky to have olive oil in the house. We had warmed the oil and spread it on the burns with a feather and then put a light bandage on. I fully expected to be complimented for doing the right thing. But he said, "What did you say, you spread oil on the burns?" I said, "Yes Doctor, I heard long ago that was the best thing if you had it, to put on burns, sunlight soap will cause blisters." "Where did you hear this old wife's tale? That's the worst thing you could have put on and remember that." I said, feeling not so proud, "That was the only thing we had Doctor." "No" he said "I am sure it was not, you had tea in the house did you not?" "Yes, plenty." "Then all you had to do was boil an extra kettle of very strong tea, strain it, don't add milk or sugar to it, let it cool till you felt it just warm, put a coating of that on using a clean feather. If it's drying, put another coat on, then two coats daily and cover with a loose bandage. What the strained tea does is to put moisture in the flesh and also keeps the germs out to allow a new skin to grow.

That is too late now but I have with me a new kind of ointment that is highly recommended. I hope it does the trick."

When the struggle of removing the bandage was over, the Doctor said what a pity that cold tea had not been applied at first, and with cotton swabs he removed most of the oil and the sister put the new dressings on. I think Archie felt better; at least he had stopped crying. The Doctor said he was not very bad, his face and eyes escaped and the rest would take time to heal, but he was not in much danger. The nurse would inform him of the progress made, and if he was needed she would let him know. He was not and the nurse continued to dress the burns until completely healed and Archie thankfully suffered no lasting effects. The doctor, however, wanted to meet me to find out how the new ointment had worked, as it was on test and called the 'Glasgow Ointment', so I had arranged to meet him at Bayhead.

It was Hogmanay and snowing. I waited at the appointed place; no sign of a car and the light was fading fast. I had to get the boat back to a reasonable safe place. I was on the point of giving up when I saw this man coming. I knew by his gait that it was not the Doctor. From my shelter I hailed him and said, "Is that you, Angus James?" "Yes, what are you doing here?" I told him. "Is the boy worse?" "No, he is alright now." "Why the Doctor then?" I explained why I was there and told him if he burned himself to try the cream, as it's good. Angus James put down the parcel he was carrying and gave me a drink from a bottle he had, and as it was Hogmanay we had a good drink together. Angus James asked, "Is it the small boat you have?" "No, the big boat with the engine." "Well it's getting dark and you have many rocks to pass and the tide is getting low, I think it's safer to leave now. Have you got a torch?" "No, I left it at home. I didn't think I would be so late." "When you get home, say in half an hour, flash the torch at the end of the house. I will be on the lookout. It is dark and there is a heavy snow shower coming and if you are not through the narrows before she is on you, I strongly advise you to anchor till she is over."

I left and had got through the narrows but, when the blinding snow came, there was no strong wind. After a short while I slowed down and stopped the engine. I thought I could keep her on course by dead reckoning, as there was no light to be seen on either side of the loch. There was some rope on board. I tied a weight on, let it down to touch the bottom and measured it as five fathoms so I knew I was well clear of the shore. I put on an overhand knot at the water and kept testing, trying to make out the direction of the drift. By this time the open boat had a foot of snow covering it and I could not start the engine because it did not have a clutch. I pulled out a floorboard and using it as a shovel I began throwing out the snow that was sinking the boat deeper, although there was no danger. With the homemade shovel, I was now able to cope and gain on what was coming in. With a good dram of Angus James's White Horse inside me, and by working with the shovel, I felt quite warm. I also had in the boat an oilskin that was meant to keep the spray off the Doctor if he had come. I did not need it then, the White Horse was enough. Gradually, it began to clear from the west and I could feel a very light wind from that direction. Scanning through the falling snow, trying to make out where I was, I saw a glimmer of light on my port bow. Judging by its height I was sure what house that was, but I was far from where I thought I was, so I kept rowing slowly till an oar hit a rock, which was well out of the water and covered with snow. I recognised the rock as one that I could see in daylight from the house, and then at last I saw a pole which I recognised as the croft boundary fence, and I knew where I was and a few minutes later I was at the jetty and able to moor her.

I made my way knee deep in snow, up to the dim lit window almost full with snow. I had to keep touching the wall before I found the door. With much hand scraping before I could knock, Michael, Mary Ann's brother, who had been working on the road and was unable to return home on account of the snow, opened the door and said, "Is it you, are you alive, where have you been?" The kitchen was warm and cosy and Mary Ann was getting the teapot ready. She said, "Where have you been since you left at 2.00 o'clock? It is now seven; we thought you were lost, if not worse. Michael thought no boat could go anywhere but on the rocks on a night like this, although he went out to the end of the house and flashed the torch. Did you see it?" "No." Late as it was, it reminded me of my promise to Angus James. As the snow was now clear between here and his house I flashed in his direction for a few minutes and the answer came as I was about to give up. There were many dots and dashes which I could not read, as Angus at one time was a signal man in the Navy and was trying his hand. I gave him a long flash and went inside and told them why I was flashing having met him earlier.

She said, "Michael was waiting for the boat till nothing could be seen, then thought you would leave her and try and walk around. Did the Doctor come?" "No, but I am glad he didn't as he would not get back on a night like this. I never saw snow coming down so thick, almost straight down, with no wind. I was lost most of the time and took to rowing and sounding for depth, and when at three fathoms I would anchor to decide what direction to go next. That and baling out the snow kept me warm. I found my way to the north side by seeing Seonaidh's light for a moment, and from there I was lucky and found the pole that the croft boundary fence is tied to. The distance from point to point is less than a mile and a half, ordinarily less than half an hour, yet it took me nearly four hours." I know that anyone who has never been caught in a heavy snow blizzard or dense fog on land or sea will not believe it possible.

While this talk was going on, Mary Ann was busy with the tea. She said, "I think I should open the New Year's bottle. There will be no first footers tonight and likely not tomorrow, we might be snowed in for days. We have plenty of food and plenty of peat in. We won't be worse off than the rest. I hope they at home will not be greatly worried about Michael." "No" he said. "they will realise where I am but I'm not happy about the Hogmanay and New Year supply. I intended calling at Polochar after work. Polochar will be closed tomorrow but Brown will let me in any time." I told him to forget about tomorrow, that the drifts on the path would be far too deep and it would be easy to get lost. Before I changed into dry cloths, Mary Ann gave us a glass of the White Horse that put us all in a better mood, and then we had tea with mutton steak and home baking.

The deep snow prevented anyone from going anywhere, so there was much whisky left in the township unconsumed for that occasion. Michael bemoaned the fact that it was the first time he didn't have a bottle of his own for New Year. The old year was fast fading away with only two hours left. The small glass was filled and passed round. The effects put Michael in good form and he started singing some of his own compositions. He was a fairly good bard and was well known for that in his own township of East Kilbride.

At midnight, if the clock was reliable, it was the custom for as long as I can remember, to go outside and note what direction the wind was coming from. Some claimed it always changed at midnight. I cannot vouch for that. If the wind at that hour was from south to west, that meant the next season would be moist and warm, the making of a bumper crop. West to north meant dry cold soil and late growth, north to east meant dry cold wind and poor yield, east to south, light harvest and hard to dry with much lost crop such as potatoes turning black and useless for seed. It was believed those that acted on those signs always reaped the best harvest. We had the last drink to welcome in the New Year, that and a meal ended our small celebration.

After breakfast Michael said he thought the snow would be manageable as he had his wellingtons. He regretted having to pass each house and not calling in with his New Year dram, as he did not have any. When I met him again I enquired if he got home alright, and he said, "No I didn't, it seemed every house I passed had a small bar of its own. At first I did my best to pass unobserved but the dog had ideas of its own. I had to go in for a dram more especially as it was New Year's Day, it would be bad manners and unforgivable to refuse no matter what the circumstances were."

That early spring after Archie's mishap, I had to begin the spring work and stop working on the road which, on account of much blasting, was only making slow progress. During that time there was no money coming in and what small savings we had were fast being used up, but there was no shortage of food. We had plenty of potatoes, two kinds of shellfish and salted herring and mackerel; we also had plenty of milk, eggs and rabbits, as long as they were in season. Butcher meat we seldom had, and by late spring we could get fresh fish, which we shared with the neighbours. I was obliged to cut the peat on my own, not being able to pay for help as by then the bottom of the barrel was being scraped. I was back working on the road again and after working there a whole week I asked for a sub and got it, that tied us over till payday, but wages were barely enough to keep the wolf from the door.

One day while working on the road, a well-dressed man and woman stopped to talk to me about our way of life in this township. They wanted to know about the hardships we faced and how we managed to live in winter, and were keen to hear what difference a road would make. It seemed they were interested in my answers to their questions. They were working on a radio programme about the way of life on the Island, and they asked if I would take part in a small interview in Lochboisdale Hotel, and they would send a car for me that night at 8.00 pm. As all was well at home there was no delay in getting ready. I walked the two miles to the waiting car thinking what I would say in my scant history of the loch, and how important this road would be to the alginate factory to obtain the seaweed growing in abundance here.

The car drew up at the hotel where I met the expected man and his lady friend. We shook hands and adjourned to the cocktail bar where it was whisky all around. They said that they just wanted my story and they hoped to use at least part of it in their script. The conversation, after the benefits that the new road would bring, was on our way of life before then and, on being told of the conditions, they were surprised that people could survive and yet, said the lady, "I have heard more laughter since I came to the island the other day than I would in a crowded city. Yesterday I went on a long walk and I'm sure every person that passed me nodded, smiled and said nice evening or beautiful day." Answering her, I said, "I think it's because the people here are happy and contented despite the hardships and lack of amenities."

I learned there were to be four people on the programme, including the proprietor, and I thought that was why the whisky was flowing so freely as he could be lavish when it suited him on an important occasion. Before the bar was closed, after much talking, the man said he would like to have me on the programme and would let me know and send a car when they were ready for recording.

Shortly afterwards I got asked to attend the recording. Going up in the car were two sisters, also in the same programme. They were to give a talk on wool and what they did with it and how that was done. They had with them a double copy of the script with all the questions and answers on it. I did not get anything like that to memorise what I had to say; perhaps if I had I would have done better; besides there was no lubrication this time and no time for the bar. We gathered in the lounge, the mike in the centre, the recording car outside doing cuts and re-takes. The hotel owner spoke first. His was on music. I was glad to see him being cut off for siding with Bach and nothing said of the Macrimmons and other renowned pipers in that music, giving or trying to give the impression that he was far above the rest of us. He left us when his part was said.

Some were good, others fair. I think I was the worst of the lot although my part was easy, dealing with a boat at sea and under sail in strong wind. I began my part but was not very fluent, which meant a cut outside to start over again till the director said, "What's wrong with you tonight? The last time I heard you, you spoke very well." I said, "I feel my throat very dry. I would be glad to have a glass of water." He said, "Will whisky help?" "I'm sure it would," I said. After a large glass and a retake, the recording car phoned in with the advice 'word perfect'. There was an all round laugh. After that there was no hesitation and I seemed to be doing what was wanted. I think it was on account of the lubrication that I later got a cheque for five pounds but no repeats.

At this time we were finished with the South side branch of the road and starting on the causeway and bridge to the north side. Much stone had to be quarried to build this causeway to the shore seawater mark, at a guess more than 50 yards, with a wide bottom of about 15 feet rising from where there were hollows. There was a slope on each side to a height of some 20 feet or so, and a gap for the bridge to allow the tide and fresh water to flow through. The span of this bridge was about 18 feet and only on each face of the bridge was cement used, the rest of the bridge and causeway was all dry stone, yet with very strong current at Spring tides, no stones had left their original position. There was only one stonemason on the site but others with some skill were also doing that part. At that time we got our first mechanical help to build the causeways and two bridges on this road, in the way of a small compressor for boring holes in large rocks for blasting. It was a great help in place of doing it by manpower.

When all the stones large and small were either rolled or gathered within 25 yards at each side to help fill the wide foundation, the compressor began boring at the nearest rocks where the five-ton lorry could get to. An electric battery set off the blasts. The work force consisted of twelve men and a gaffer, and although he liked to see much work done, he was a good man to work under. Sometimes he would lend a hand, I think mostly to keep warm, other times and often he would visit near by houses for a cup of tea, knowing full well that the work would be going on just as well and even better on account of those who needed the road most.

When we got to the causeway and before the second bridge was built and both sides connected, I had to stop work as Mary Ann was soon expecting our third child. We had a new doctor then, a young man whose roots were in Uist and made sure that the people in Uist got the medical care they were entitled to. There was no maternity unit in the old local hospital and patients were sent to Glasgow. When he came to see Mary Ann, he ordered to fly her there in good time and she reluctantly agreed to go. On arrival at the hospital, they would not take her in saying her condition was too soon for admission. Luckily she had friends nearby with whom she stayed. Next day she did not feel well and went to the hospital again, but they told her after examination that it was too soon to admit her but to keep in touch. Mary Ann went back to her friends still not feeling well and that night she went into labour. Word was sent to the hospital, but before the doctor came, a baby was born, another son whom we called John Joseph. He said both were as well as could be expected. She was not taken to the hospital and she stayed with these friends till both were well enough to come home, saying she would never again go to Glasgow for that reason.

Before I got the delightful wire, I had already taken the other two children to their grandparents and myself back to work on the road till I got them all back home again. While the two were up south, I used to visit them as often as I could. After I got them all home together again and working on the road, I was very happy. They all used to watch for me coming in view of the house, and seeing them watching and waiting gave me such a feeling of joy.

It was the custom at Christmas to kill a sheep, a fat wedder. Sitting at the fire a few days before then, Mary Ann said "What about the wedder you intend to kill for Christmas?" I said, "In a few days, if I can catch it." Mary Ann, sitting with John Joseph asleep, then a chubby large baby in her lap, laughingly said John Joseph would make a good Christmas. Will we kill him Alex Iain? "Yes" and all began to laugh. When that ended I thought no more of it. The day before Christmas we stopped early on the road. Archie and Alex Iain were standing as usual at the end of the house waiting for me to appear. When he saw me, Alex Iain ran to meet me. He always gave me his hand and began to tell me everything that went on since I left. This time, before reaching me he stopped, and when I offered him my hand he would not take it. I noticed instead of the usual happy smile, his face had a sad frown. I knew there was something wrong. I said, "Are you all well at home Alex Iain?" "Yes, we are all well." "And why are you looking so unhappy?" "Is it today or tomorrow that you are going to kill John Joseph?" He was then almost crying. I said, "What has he done wrong now?" "Poor John Joseph has not done anything wrong." "Why then are we going to kill him?" "You said you were going to kill a wedder at Christmas. Mammy said, John Joseph would make a good wedder. Are you going to kill him?" "Do you want me to?" "No, no, John Joseph is a nice baby." "Well Alex Iain, we are not going to hurt him. Mammy was only making fun." At that he ran home as fast as he could to give the good news to the rest, leaving me standing in deep thought. On entering the house, I found them in much laughter. Another lesson learned when rearing a young family.

After New Year, I was at the road again and connecting the bridge. Three heavy iron beams had to go across. My experience as a rigger in Fairfield Ship Yard came in very handy. I gave a loan of three 35 feet logs that I had from the salvaged shore wood. One was set alongside each of the iron rails and a covering of three-inch thick oak planks nailed to them, allowing a loaded lorry to go over. It was used that way till much of the road was finished, when all that wood was taken out and the bridge re-covered with concrete.

About this time, my brother Peter was in poor health and unable to do any work. I greatly missed his company. He was a good fisherman and a first-class seaman and always gave me good advice. He was married to Kate and although they had no children of their own they fostered two boys and a girl from Glasgow. Peter was a giant of a man both in build and strength, reputed to be the strongest by far in this area, but would never show it unless he was obliged to. I recall my near neighbour Donald often telling of the day they both went in a small boat to the head of the loch for three bags of meal, where the van from up south left them. Each bag weighed 140 pounds and Peter picked one by the top, threw it under his left arm and held it there before flinging the other over his right shoulder, before walking with this heavy load down an uneven shore onto slippery seaweed covered rocks. He then waded a few yards to the small boat pushing her out with his head to keep her afloat before carrying his load into her. Donald, who was of average strength, was making slow progress with the remaining bag with a rope round it on his back. Peter took the bag off Donald's back and waded out in the mud to the boat which he took to where Donald could board her without getting wet.

Another story about Peter concerned a pipe. The story on this occasion that Peter told was at the wake of an old lady who had died in this township. The neighbours around were attending the wake in relays. Peter and others were there on the last night. It was a poor household, an old brother and his sister. At one point, Peter took out his pipe and tobacco, filled and lit it. Donald John, the man beside him, admired the pipe and asked if it was new. Peter told him it was but said it was not as good as the last one he had, which had a mercury bowl and amber stem. He said he didn't have her for long as he had lost her. When asked how that happened he said, "Well, it's a long story." "Tell it, tell it, that's what we want in a place like this; the one on the hard boards will not move, and the door is closed anyway. The latch is on this side, so nothing is to disturb her till we put her in the box in the morning."

Peter said, "Very well D.J. I signed on this ship for a three-year voyage, trading between the Far East and everywhere, and perhaps as you know I was never careful with my wages. This time I vowed that I would keep them and save as much as possible and be in a position to marry my girlfriend who promised to wait till I came back. I did not know the voyage would be so long and did not blame her when, half way though the voyage, I got her letter saying she had got tired of waiting, had met a fellow at a dance, and they had grown fond of each other and married a month later.

"At the end of those three years the ship got a cargo for the port of London, Tilbury Dock, where she paid off with overtime. I had a handsome sum in wages coming to me, and after we had been paid, I made my way to Euston Station where I booked my kit bag for Glasgow. I had an hour to wait before the train would leave and went for a short walk intending to buy a pipe, a good one. I could afford to after denying myself so much for so long. I came upon a high-class tobacconist displaying many kinds of pipes, some much higher in price than I usually bought. There was one that took my fancy displayed in the window. I entered and said, 'I would like to see the one you have in the window without a price tag on'. I found that it cost two pounds ten shillings, and although that was nearly half a month's wages, I thought it was better to spend it that way than on a pub-crawl. I said I would take it and also some tobacco.

"On my way back to the station I bought a small case, a white shirt and a tie and a bottle of whisky, as there might be someone on the train who knew me and it was a long journey to Glasgow. I found the Glasgow train and took a corner seat in an empty smoker carriage. I had the carriage to myself until the third stop when I was beginning to think it was going to be a dull journey. I had already read most of the two papers I had bought, and a chance to talk would be welcomed. The door slid open and in came a tall middle-aged lady. She had a fairly large case in one hand and a small basket with a lid in the other, which she put down on the seat. She began to lift the case on to the rack; it looked heavy. I got up and said, 'Let me help you lady.' 'No, I can manage quite well myself. I don't need any help.' She did not thank me for my offer.

"I sat in my corner watching her struggle with the case. After getting one end on the rack, it nearly came down on her head. I did not make a move thinking if it did, it would serve her right. However she managed to push it in the right place and sat down beside the small basket. She picked this up and placing it on her lap she opened it and took out a small pup. She said, 'My poor baby, kiss mama'. The dog put his nose to her mouth and began licking. She began kissing it, and putting her hand in the basket she said, 'You are a good boy, you didn't wet yourself. Mama will feed you soon.' The slobbering went on for a while, and when it was exhausted, I was disgusted and thought of what Paddy said when he saw his neighbour's wife kissing the pig, Well everyone to his own taste.

"I was fed up watching this and thought I would try my new pipe out. I filled her to capacity, lit her up and she was going good and tasting good. I did not mind the price I paid. The window was down and I was enjoying my smoke and now paying no attention to the woman and the dog. The small dog was beginning to protest by coughing and sneezing, and the woman said, 'Put away that disgusting pipe you're smoking, you're making my baby sick.' I said, 'Why don't you take him to a carriage where smoking is not allowed?' 'No, I won't, he is quite happy here with his mama, you put out that rotten smelling pipe.' 'I will when I have had my smoke. If your pup chokes before then, it will be your fault.' At that she stood up, took a pace towards me and put her hand out. I thought she was going to slap my face and if she did, I would not have slapped her back, but she did not do that; instead she pulled the pipe out of my mouth and flung it out through the window, leaving me with sore teeth and very angry. Looking at the small dog, I picked it up and out through the window it went, following my pipe.

"The woman began screaming 'Murder, murder, he has murdered my baby.' That was heard in the next carriages. A man came to the door, slid it open and said, 'What's wrong here?' At once he was told this brute has murdered my baby. 'My god' the man said 'this is terrible. Have you pulled the chain to stop the train?' 'No, but I am going to now.' I did not stop her." Angus said, "How can you stop a train which I heard goes faster than a galloping horse by pulling a chain?" "Never mind him Peter" D.J. said, "He has never been across the Minch, never saw a train." Peter interrupted the story to explain to Angus how the emergency chain worked. D.J. was not pleased at such waste of time, and pleaded with Peter to continue the story that he did not want to miss a word of.

Peter continued. "The train was slowing down. The man at the door stayed while the woman kept screaming 'He has murdered my baby.' Soon the guard came and asked what had happened. He was told the same story. Hearing that he said, 'Young man, I have the power to hold you here till the police come. What made you throw a helpless baby through the window? You must be mad.' 'I am not and that was not a baby. This woman does not seem to know the difference between a baby and a scruffy pup and it was all her fault. This is a Smoker; I was quite entitled to smoke my pipe, which was new and very expensive. She objected, saying that it was making her baby sick. I said, 'Why don't you take him to a non-smoker but she refused and got up, and before I realised it, she snatched the pipe from my mouth and threw it through the open window. I threw the scruffy pup after it.' 'Well,' said the guard, 'if that story is true, you won't be charged with murder but you will be charged with cruelty to animals.' By this time the train was drawing to a stop at the small station. The guard said to the two standing at the door,

'Watch him, and don't let him get away while I get the police.' I said they and more like them could not hold me, if I wanted to leave. I strongly advised them to keep their distance or they might go the same way as the pup did."

There was much tension in that small room as Peter was telling his story and everyone was anxious not to miss a word. However, the kettle was boiling so it was time to make the tea. The two girls got up; my own sister was one of them. They got the large borrowed teapot ready, filled it with boiling water, and listening all the time to the exciting part of the story they forgot to put dry tea into the pot and set it at the fire to infuse. Before Peter carried on with his story he said, "My mouth is dry talking, how about some of that tea. The lamp is going down, the wick needs trimming and the funnel is getting dark. We better have the tea now."

The scones were already buttered on a large tray, baked that afternoon. The lamp had been placed where it would shine most of its light in the closed door with the latch on, only a now and again look was needed. Now, with the light getting dim, it was thought wise to listen often for any strange noise coming from within but of course nothing happened. The light was dimmer while the girls were pouring out the tea. They could not see how strong they had made it or in fact if they had put any dry tea in the pot, and it was too late now. Milk and sugar was added. The tray with the heaped scones was placed where all could reach. The room now was much darker and no one had noticed from the first sip that there was anything amiss. Half way through eating someone said, "This tea is very weak." The large teapot was brought to the light and some tea poured out, but it was just clear water. The girls were asked if the tea was all finished. They, laughing, said, "No, with the excitement of the story we must have forgotten to put it in the pot. There is milk but no more sugar left." "Well" said D.J. "it's better to drink it the way it is than without sugar, besides brewing it again is wasting time. We want Peter to carry on where he left off. I think it must be nearing the end when the police came to arrest him. Is that right Peter?" "Yes, D.J., there are only a few more points to clear up. When the two policemen came I was sitting in the same corner as before. The woman was standing and crying her head off with the same story that I had murdered her baby. The police, watching me and getting the handcuffs ready said, 'Is what this woman saying true?' I said, 'No, not a word of it.' Turning to the woman, one of them asked, 'Did this man assault you in any way – did he hit you or push or lay his hands on you?' 'No, he did none of these things. Did he not do enough when he murdered my baby?' 'I'll say he did. How old was your baby?' 'About a year.' 'Was it female or male?' 'Male.' 'Then it was a boy about a year old?' 'Well, not exactly.' 'What do you mean, was he older or younger than that?' 'Well you know what I mean.' 'No I don't. Was he at the crawling stage or was he able to stand on his own two feet and take a few steps?' I said, 'Ask her if he had four legs and a tail?' The cop, thinking I was being smart and missing the point, said, 'You shut up and talk when you are spoken to and remember, you are under arrest.'

"Turning to the woman he said, 'Where was the baby when this man attacked him?' 'Lying on that seat asleep.' 'Did he hit him?' 'No, just picked him up and threw him out of the window. That's the way he murdered him.' Are you sure he was alive then?' 'Yes, because I heard him barking.' 'Barking? A human baby doesn't bark. Was that a human being or not?' 'Well he was my baby and I loved him as much.' 'But you admit it was a dog, a young pup?' 'If you put it that way, yes. I loved to see him when he wagged his short tail.' Turning to me the law said, 'At least you won't be charged with murder and the pup may still be alive. A search will be made after we take you to the station. Come on both of you. We can't keep the train waiting.' I asked if I could take my small case with me. They said yes and I followed between them, the lady in the rear.

"The station was a small building. In the room where we were taken was a table with an inspector sitting behind. 'What's this you have brought in?' he asked. The officers explained to the Inspector what had happened. 'Alright' the Inspector said 'Detail one of the men to walk along the embankment on that side for at least two miles and tell him why. Also to keep his eyes and ears open and report back as soon as he can.'

"This man left, as our addresses and what not else they wanted to know was written down. They asked me what I have in the small case? I said, 'A new shirt, a tie and an untouched bottle of whisky.' 'Open it.' I did. 'This bottle' he said 'has not been opened. It seems it had no connection with your foolish act. I grant you were in pain and considerable provocation when, as she admits, this woman pulled your valuable pipe from your mouth, taking one of your teeth with it and maybe part of the gum. Perhaps that is where the blood on your face and on your neck come from.' I said, 'It must be. It is still sore.' This was my first time ever in a police station. Would they take that into consideration if the pup was found to be alive and well, and would the woman in her joy in that knowledge be glad enough to pay the five pound railway fine for pulling the chain without reason, or would she still want her revenge.

"The Inspector seemed to be sympathetic; would he quash the whole thing there and then? On the other hand, if no hide or hair could be found of the pup, things indeed looked bad for me." "Well" said D.J. "I wouldn't like to have been in your shoes Peter. Did the cop find the pup?" "No, he had nothing to report when he came back." There was stillness in that room and every eye was on him when he said, "A strange scratch was heard on the outside door. The Inspector said to his nearest cop to go and see what the noise is. He did, and on opening the door his eyes nearly popped out of his head, for there stood the missing pup, wagging his short tail with a good-looking pipe across his mouth, and in he came. When I saw him" continued Peter "I felt so glad that I woke up and realised that the whole episode had been a dream and nearly all the bed clothes were on the floor. That is the end of my pipe story."

All but D.J. had a hearty laugh, regardless of where we were, but he was very angry indeed and said, "You have made a damn fool of me believing every word you said." Not another word did he say before leaving for home in the dark, a thing that was not done from such houses. At the funeral that day Peter said he would avoid D.J. when possible, regardless of the fact that he was once responsible for saving D.J.'s life and that of his two sons and boat when he capsized her. In truth, D.J. was an admirer of Peter and I think that was why he felt bad in being misled.

Another story told by my father about funerals comes to mind. My Father used to tell that at most funerals, he was often appointed as the boy carrying the jackets whenever a fight started on the way to the graveyard and long before the procession reached its destination, another lad had to help him as many jackets were thrown off. Much whisky was carried, one bottle to each man. If there was no track for a horse and cart and if the distance was far over rough ground, as often it was for many miles, it was hard to refrain from touching the bottle. The coffin was carried behind on a bier by six men, 3 men at each end, a man walking at the side conducting the funeral, would call out at intervals of about 60 yards, 'stand out six men'. They would, three on each side, leaving a space between them for the coffin to pass till the spares were taken by the relieving six. That order was kept all the way to the open grave. When the service was over, the

255

grave filled in, prayers said over it, the men lined up and outside the walls of the cemetery, two women with trays of biscuits and cheese, went round. Each man picked up a biscuit and a piece of cheese, followed by two men with a glass and a bottle of whisky each. One began serving at one end, the other at the other end, and both kept on till the end of the line. That way every one in the row got two glasses which was the rule of the Catholic Church, amongst us here at least. When that was over, those in the row at the wall dispersed and made their way home, walking, while the near relatives went to the cart for a dram which was not supposed to have anything to do with the funeral, just old friends and relations meeting and going over the score. The Catholic Church put a stop to that. The Protestants followed, only biscuits and cheese were allowed. When the era of the cars and transport came, all that custom ended. Not very long after, a man who made coffins was heard to say when asked if he was going to the funeral replied: "I don't think so, all the funerals are going to the dogs." Well, we still have them but nobody walks."

When the road was built to within a few hundred yards of Peter's house, sadly he died suddenly and never walked a step on it, yet he and Alastair Steel, a near neighbour, did the most in this township to try to enlist those in high office here to write a convincing letter regarding their plight for the want of a road. They walked long distances, both during the day and at night, to make contact with councillors. This effort went on for years and now, with the help of the others, the road was very nearly at their door, but none of them was able to make use of it. Alastair also took ill, and was sent to a mainland hospital but didn't recover. It is accepted that it was through the efforts of the learned and persuasive Father Neil MacKellaig who eventually forced the issue with the Council.

In the meantime I was still working on the road and always, when coming home, seeing MaryAnn and the children waiting and watching at the end of the house for me, gave me such a joyous feeling, and even now after so many years of hardship, it still comes alive to me each time I pass the spot. Eventually, when the road had been finished for some time apart from the tarring, cars were able to use it. Although the wage was small it was better than the dole. That came to an end with no other work where I could earn any money, and to make matters worse, I was short of fodder. I was over-stocked on account of being unable to sell the oldest cow that I had. I was not prepared to give her away for nothing, after all her goodness in providing milk and calves to us. I hopefully could keep her alive for the next cattle sale early in May, a long time off.

There was no money saved from the roadwork, the dole was only from hand to mouth, and there were more of us to feed now. As subsistence became low, we decided that to apply for national assistance would be our salvation. I have never in my life had to ask or accept charity and I would not now, only for the family as I could not see them in real want, so I went to see the Welfare Officer, feeling that my present state qualified me for some assistance. I got a lift part of the way north to Gerinish where that office was.

The officer, whom I knew, was at home, and when I told him why I had come to see him his expression changed, not to my liking. He said, "I didn't think you would be in any need of assistance. Were you on the dole and was it stopped and when. What other resources have you got?" "My unemployment benefit ended weeks ago. I have a few cattle, none that I am able to sell at this time. If I was I would not be here today." "National Assistance" he said "is only for people in real need." I said, "I claim to be one of those people at the moment." "Very well. I'll take your application and a small draft will be sent to you soon while your circumstances are being investigated." I thanked him and said, "If my application fails, I will be obliged to apply to the British Legion, of which I am a member, for their aid. They already know of my service in both wars." He said, "If what you say in the application is all true I don't think that will be necessary." He was right. In a few days the promised draft came. It was larger than I had expected and in time for the grocery van coming that day, allowing us to buy some of the most needed supplies.

Soon afterwards a man came to investigate my position. He was very reasonable. Not at all like the first who gave the impression that the money I was asking for was coming out of his own pocket. This man, after seeing the children ill clad, only asked a few questions and after MaryAnn gave him a cup of tea he left the house and I followed him outside. He stood at the house and said, "You have a grand view here and are these your sheep down there?" "No more than eight as I told you; my mark is red on the left shoulder and the rest, as you can see, have different markings and belong to different people. This is common grazing." I followed him to his car near the byre where the cattle were waiting to be let in. It was a cold evening. He said, "Is this all your cattle?" "Yes, two cows and two steers, however I am short of winter food and the sale isn't until May."

He was not a native islander and, unlike the first man, did not give the impression that the money was coming from his own pocket. When the money did come, I was able to use part of it to buy half a stack of corn from Finlay Mor from Bornish, although he himself was not sure that he had plenty. I paid him and, feeling grateful, I said, "Do you like salted mackerel?" "Yes indeed. Have you got any to spare?" "Yes. I will send you some when you send me the corn." When I got the corn I sent him a pickle of fine prime salted mackerel. Next Sunday at church he called me aside. "Donald" he said, "you have sent us a lot of fish. I have not tasted better in my life. The same with the family, they wanted me to give you this in return." He handed me a pound note. I made a show of not wanting to accept it, saying the good and generous load of feedstuff he sent was enough and I wanted to show my appreciation. "If any time you find yourself short, let me know and I'll do my best." This was regardless of the many I knew he had already turned down. Fodder was very scarce that spring but perhaps why he acted like this towards me was because I used to take his boys out fishing in my small boat.

Peter, as I have already said, was well known for playing tricks, and he and Donald, who lived on the other side of the loch, were both sharing members in a large herring fishing boat with three others. One Saturday at Lochboisdale they were making preparations for bagging their nets. This drill entailed much labour and was a must every two weeks' fishing, to protect the then cotton nets from rotting. For this task a fire was built under a 50 gallon or more cast iron cauldron standing on stones or bricks at the bottom of a slope, nearly filled with water with a lid on to keep the steam in at a certain heat. So many pounds of bark per net were put in this drum and left to boil and dissolve. A three-foot wide slide, which was water tight, extended from the rim of the drum to a higher platform. All nets were tied in bundles and when the bark in the drum was cool enough to handle, the nets were lifted one by one into the large drum and then pushed up the slide to drain. When finished, all the nets would be piled on top of each other in a large heap, and taken to the boat, where they were all joined together as they were thrown into the hold and carefully laid from side to side.

It was on a day like that, when barking the nets, that Peter played an embarrassing joke on Donald. The skipper, Angus James, always kept a bottle of rum for a dram whenever they had an extra hard time at sea. Only one dram was permitted and that not often. He also kept a large bottle of cascara for anyone in need of medicine. Attending to the slow heating boiler was Donald's job at that point. while the rest were passing the time talking and walking up and down the pier while the skipper, Angus James, was talking to someone at the far end of it. Peter was on the boat and, having filled a large glass of cascara he then took the bottle of rum, took out the cork, went outside, and in a low voice called "Are you there, Donald?" "Yes." "You know where the skipper is?" "Yes, I see him at the end of the pier with someone." "Well jump down quick before he comes, you deserve something. You and I are the only two doing anything."

With the open bottle more than half full of rum, he held it near Donald but handed the glass of cascara to him saying, "Throw that down before anyone comes and don't tell anyone." Donald did and climbed to the pier fast before he felt the bad taste, which was too late by then. Some time after that the boiler was nearly ready for the operation. The crew was called to stand by. Donald was looking pale. Someone asked, "Are you feeling alright?" "Yes, only a little headache." Before the operation began, Donald had to take his first trip to the end of the pier where the loo was. After that there were many short trips with Peter keeping his laughter to himself.

At last the skipper said, "What's wrong, Donald? Why don't you stay at your work like the rest?" "I am not feeling well Angus." "Well I know exactly what's wrong with you. You are in need of some medicine. Go down to the boat, and there you will find a bottle of cascara. Take a large glass of it, that will fix you." Donald left but it was not to the boat that he went. The rest could not understand why Peter was giggling.

I must now return to where I am feeding Blackie, the old cow who had been so good at producing milk and calves. In truth the pound that Finlay Mor returned helped to buy cake, which the others did not get, nor need, for their teeth were strong and they were young and could chew any amount of fodder. I fed Blackie on short cut corn with its seed, oil cake in small parts and sea weed that grew just below high tide, the lot mixed and boiled for half an hour outside in a large iron pot. At first she would not take it. I kept putting a little in a bucket for her till she got used to it; then she could not get enough. I used to add seal oil to it. Within ten days I could see a big difference in her. Come May she was served and in calf when I sold her at the quarter sale for fifteen pounds, a good price in those days for a very old cow.

Archie, the eldest, did not start school until 1951 when he was 7 years of age. This was when the road building reached the Strom and the second bridge was built, and as a result he and Alex Iain, then 5 years of age, started school at the same time. The route was over the two-mile limit for a five-year-old child, but regardless of my efforts to get transportation for any of the children, people with cars, whose speedometers they said were correct, claimed it was less than two miles. I did get the local surveyor to measure the distance, which he did by using a tape measure, but claimed it was a hundred yards short of the two miles required. Had the legal method, that is by chain, been used, always in the centre of the road, I think that that one hundred yards would be down to nothing. I did not question the man's honesty as he was, I am sure, using the method he was told to. Only in the winter and in the wet and stormy weather did I mind them walking it.

Spring work over and peats cut, we began preparation to begin lobster fishing again and earn real money instead of the assistance hanging over me. Fishing was good, prices reasonable and when I got the first payment, I wrote to the assistance office saying I did not need their help any longer. Although I was happy to be standing on my own two feet, I was far wrong and with much worse to come, I was forced to go back to them cap in hand. I was now on the dole and managing quite well, besides the prices of certain kinds of cattle that year were good, and I got the highest price for any beast sold in the township, which was forty-seven pounds, a large sum of money in those days. Prices in general were good that year causing many of the mainland buyers to go bankrupt. The following year prices were so low with most of the cattle left unsold, and those that were sold were at give-away prices. Fortunately there was a good harvest and crofters were able to winter feed them, and if not pressed, to keep them for better times. With that money and the dole we were, for a while, on easy street.

To relieve the pressure on their mother, if the day was good I would take the eldest with me in the boat or working on the land. At that time I was beginning to make preparations to build an extension to our home, as we were getting more and more crowded. Since money was always short, I would do most of the work involved myself; that is the masonry and much of woodwork. I had stored much of the wood that I had salvaged and that would be very useful now. When I earlier submitted my plan for the house we were in, I made it known to the house planning body that I intended, when possible, to build an extension to the house, extending from the back. On the strength of that I did not apply for permission for this intended extension.

The task of levelling the floor space was slow because of its rocky nature. Too near and too dangerous to the house for blasting, while the safe, slow way to wear or break these rocks to the required level was by putting fire on the top. A quantity of broken glass was first put on the rock to give off more heat and a fire of the hardest peat built on the top. The flame was kept downwards by adding more peat or dross and kept burning for at least two hours. The fire was then removed, the ashes brushed off, and a full bucket of cold water poured on the rock, causing much steam and cracking, and these cracks were worked on while hot with a sledgehammer. The treatment continued till brought to the required level, a slow process. With my homemade firepower, I was slowly able to level off the required area. When inspecting it, Mary Ann said that that space would give us plenty of room when it was built. I ordered and paid for most of the material for this extension, which left us with little apart from the dole money and that would before long run out. I had hoped and was ready to start lobster fishing again that winter, but as I was not in good health at that time and afraid to see the doctor in case he would order me to hospital, I cancelled fishing that winter.

It was long after making that decision that I got a letter from the employment exchange in Oban telling me I was no longer entitled to unemployment benefit, but that I might still be eligible for national assistance. They would refer my case to the Stornoway office in Lewis where they would investigate my position. Although I knew this was coming, I was glad that this time I would not have to go cap in hand to the local area office, pleading for assistance, as it would be done through the Stornoway office. After my case had been investigated, summed up, and recommended to the local officer, he came to see me shortly afterwards, with a long list of questions for me to answer. I answered them all truthfully, then he asked, "Are you working now?" I said, "Yes, here on the croft doing spring work." "How many sheep do you have?" "Eight, at the dipping." "Are you selling both steers at the next cattle sale?" "Not sure, it depends on their condition and the market."

Once again, I was left with the impression that the money I might get was coming from his own pocket. Before he left, I saw that the cattle belonging to the three nearest houses were at my byre where his car was. I thought he might be curious so I followed him to his car. He was, and asked if the three cattle belong to me. "No, most of them are my neighbours, mine are the ones I have already shown to you. If you have any doubt, the town clerk will confirm my statement." He left saying my application would be sent to Stornoway as soon as possible. I reminded him, since the dole ended we were now in need of money, and would he treat my case as urgent in view of the large young family. He said, "There are many cases like yours, each are given careful consideration." That statement did not convince me then, or at later times when I had strong grounds to complain, and appeal, as, when the allowance came through, we were no better off. There were frequent visits from that area officer wanting to know if our position had changed for the better, and if he thought that to be the case, my allowance was reduced accordingly. Appealing in that regard always fell on deaf ears.

There was no work and income from small crofts could not provide enough even when prices were fair, so we, like others, were kept on the lowest subsistence. Many a young family through no fault of their own, were reared partly on that aid and here I must swallow my pride and acknowledge that I was one of those people but need not bury my head on that account because I had rendered much service and shed much blood in the defence of my country and for that here I was almost penniless. Now with the small allowance from the Assistance Board, we were surviving, hoping that times would return from worse to the better. Spring work so essential was the main concern, seed and fertiliser had to be bought from the assistance money regardless of how needed other things were.

19   Old Locheynort

Locheynort where I now live and where my forefathers lived until the Highland Clearances, was the port of call for South Uist, in those days sailing ships only. Besides being the port of call for cargo and passengers, it was also a haven for pirates and smugglers hiding from the navy patrolling the Minch for such ships. Locheynort is actually two lochs, joined by a narrow strait between the outer and inner lochs, with currents running through these narrows at eight knots in spring tides. It is no place for a stranger to enter, regardless of navigation aids, when the tide is in that state. Low water is best for entering and leaving as you can see what to avoid. There is plenty of water for a ship of up to 200 tonnes to enter or leave. It is, however, easy to go in or out whatever the state of the tide, if you have the power to do so.

I had heard the story of a naval gun-ship that tried to enter to catch the smugglers and pirates she knew were hiding in the loch. She found a pilot that knew the channel well and yet she struck a rock before clearing it. Any story related to her was lost before we came here, although the crown of her large anchor could be seen above low water where she struck. That large anchor was eventually moved by another local and left high on the shore where it could be seen for years. That story was handed down to us by word of mouth, but in the archives a record was kept of her name, her tonnage, the number of guns she carried, her crew and the reason she was wrecked in calm waters.

In those days, cattle ships did not come into the inner loch but came alongside a natural jetty outside the strait where there was no current, and the wind was light and from the right direction. There was no time or date for their arrival, which was announced by hoisting a white flag on a high hill where the people in surrounding areas would be able to see it. A messenger was sent to the ship to find out the number of cattle she was able to take. That done, word was passed around for the gathering of the cattle. If there was more than the ship would take, that was a settlement between the owners, and the rest of the cattle went to an isthmus past the narrows and were kept there till the wind was favourable for the vessel to be taken alongside the jetty, where a gangway of planks and ropes was made from ship to shore, for the cattle to be driven on board slowly. On board, they were allotted a pen and water and some fodder. Work of loading had to be done fast, no stopping for a meal, for if the wind changed to the wrong direction the ship would have to leave in a hurry to get off the lee shore, whether the loading was finished or not. The journey was not long to Kyle or Kyleakin, and journey times depended on the wind, but when the cattle were put ashore and rested for a few hours, then the long drive to the market at Falkirk began. Many are the stories told of the danger and hardship involved in that operation, hardships from runaway cattle, and the dangers from robbers when coming back home with the money made.

Another old story from Locheynort also deals with a ship and has a supernatural element, and I can only tell it as I heard it from a native who claimed it was handed down as being true. When I said it was strange that I had not heard that story before now, his reply was that there were people in Locheynort related to the woman in the story and for that reason they did not want to talk about it. The supernatural part of it is hard to believe.

261

The story began with a ship that left the Isle of Man to pick up a cargo of potatoes from the Isle of Barra for a port on the west of Ireland where there was much famine and starvation. The ship ran into a southeasterly storm in the Minch, and lost much of her top gear, the main mast and yards along with sails. They hove to, and in that condition drifted northwards, and when the wind abated, she was far to the lee of Barra. With the lost main mast, she was unable to navigate windward to Barra and with Locheynort to her leeward and, as a port, well known to her captain, he managed to take her there with the aid of a rigged-up jury mast. She anchored till able to sail through the narrows to a sheltered place with an almost natural pier. There she was moored between four hawsers, near enough for a gangway to reach ashore. She took the sandy seabed at low tide, and remained there to repair the massive damage.

Above where she was moored a house stood, occupied by a man and wife and his two small children. When work began on the repairs, this man, like others who knew how to use carpentry tools and rigging, found steady work while it lasted. This man, whose wife was very pretty, could play the violin and apparently their family life was a happy and contented one. The captain of the ship did not have much to do. The First Mate was in charge of the work and that left the Captain with much idle time. He spent most of it in the house above his ship and in the company of the pretty wife. This was looked upon as an innocent pastime, the captain being someone to look up to. This went on for some time, with the visits becoming frequent and longer, but when both began taking to the hills, leaving the two young children behind uncared for, people began to sense something far wrong.

Her husband, whose name was John, took his wife Jane to task regarding her conduct with this man. She admitted she was deeply in love with the Captain and that she intended going away with him as soon as the ship was ready. In spite of the row that followed, she would not give in, regardless that the Captain did not want the children and would not take them. What could John, who loved his wife and children dearly, do? The Captain was a much stronger man and whatever law there was, it was sure to be on the Captain's side.

Confronting the Captain on the issue, he was only laughed at, saying he should look after his wife better, that it was her decision, and he was only giving her that chance. John did not of course believe this story. He had a musket and thought of a chance to kill the Captain or at least maim him for life. The first meant murder and hanging, the second, a long term in prison, by which time his wife, if he still had her, and his children, would be starving. In that state of mind, and doing his best to make his wife change her mind, work on the ship was nearly finished. Sometimes, when he knew the Captain and his wife were alone in the house, he would creep up on them, and if he found they were too intimate he was prepared to use the knife he always carried, but he never did. To order him out of the house would mean him being ordered off the ship, meaning losing his job and perhaps whatever money he had coming to him, and he needed that money badly. That was why he was not able to watch the captain and his wife more closely.

At last the ship was seaworthy, and with water and provisions put on board, she now waited for a west or northwest wind to take her through the narrows. There was no change for the better between John and his wife. She was determined to leave him, and despite him asking her what she was going to do with the children, she would answer that they were his as well and it was clear they liked him much better than her and so he could do whatever he wanted with them. John said that he would never desert them, a girl then four and a boy over five, as she was doing.

The day before the ship was due to sail, with the wind steady from the west, the Captain announced that a farewell party would be held on board that night. There was also plenty of grog and provisions on board. It was to be a male party. All the workers including John were invited. With so much grog, the party was loud and merry throughout the night. In the morning, the workmen went ashore and home. When John's wife and children rose, there was no sign that her husband had come home. The wife thought he was still on the ship, perhaps sleeping in some corner. After waiting for some time, she went the short distance near the ship where she saw men working on deck. She called out, "Is my husband still on board?" She was told the workmen had long since gone ashore but that the crew would search the ship for her, and if he was onboard he would be found. After a fruitless search, the Captain reported that her husband must have gone ashore early. The wife went back to finish her preparations for leaving. One of the crew happened to look over the side and there saw the body of a man lying on the sea bottom. The alarm was raised and with boat hooks he was pulled on board. Bad marks were seen on his head. None would claim to have seen him falling overboard. One of the crew said that he saw this man and the Captain quarrelling on deck early in the night, which the Captain did not deny, saying that John was very drunk and falling on the deck and he managed to calm him down and put him in a corner. He noticed that there was a bruise high on the side of his face but no bleeding. He left him there to sleep it off and went to his cabin.

The next thing he knew was when told that a body had been seen over the side and pulled on board. He recognised him as John and swore he had nothing to do with what had happened to him. That was the statement he made at the so-called court of enquiry that was held. The one-sided court verdict was that the suspicion that was attached to this Captain in this case was not proven, he was free from all blame in regards to the tragedy and, therefore, free to leave with his ship whenever he wanted. Although the relationship between the Captain and John's wife was made well known to this court of enquiry, it turned a deaf ear to that statement, claiming that the affair had nothing to do with how John met his death. The Captain's word was more to be believed than any gossip. The now widow felt sure that her husband had met his death at the hands of the Captain, whom she thought she was deeply in love with. Now she had a change of heart. If he could do that to her John, he was capable of doing the same to her when he got tired of her.

Giving him a cool reception when he called to express his sorrow at what happened, she told him she had changed her mind and would not leave the children. "Will you come with me if I now agree to take them?" "No" she said, "for all I know, you may have a wife and children already of your own." "I will give you my word of honour that I have not." "That" she said, "does not satisfy me." Then he said, "You are blaming me for what has happened. Let us face it; we are both to blame, only God it seems knows which of us is most to blame for John's death. A foul deed like a good deed, sooner or later has its own reward, and since that's the way you now feel, it is useless trying to persuade you to change your mind." "That" she said, "is true." "The ship is leaving with the tide tomorrow, early. If and when I call again, will you change your mind then?" "No, never." "Well, goodbye then." They shook hands and the Captain departed. Watching the ship next day disappearing through the narrows, her thoughts were, "May I never see you again", and although these thoughts were nothing to do with the tragedy that followed, the ship, bound for a port on the Clyde, was wrecked passing Ardnamurchan point with all hands lost.

The widow and children were living in hard times, the late husband was a well-liked man in the community and she was blamed for what had happened. There was no money or charity or sympathy shown to her or to her blameless children. Other children would not play with them or come near them and their mother was completely ignored by everyone.

The news of the tragedy had spread far and wide, and as time went on they had next to nothing. There were no signs of the people around relenting in their hate, some saying she may have planned the foul deed. With feelings like that going around it was not so surprising that the people acted in the heartless way they did. In former times, that house was full of safety and warmth and always welcoming, but was now cast into gloom, and people would now go far out of their way to avoid it. If by chance they saw the widow and the children outside, without a wave of the hand, the head was turned the other way. That house was to be in need of pity, regardless of what had happened, and while the three of them were feeling the pinch of hunger, the mother would not swallow her pride and beg of the neighbours, perhaps thinking their plight was well known by now, and if they wanted to show charity they would leave something outside the house.

During this hard time they were not entirely without food. Below the house was a large shallow pool of seawater with stones erected around it. When it was in good order, fish were often trapped inside. It was long out of use because some of the stones had fallen, letting the fish escape, but while it was not perfect, it did hold some back to catch. One had to be there before the birds that were always present, waiting for the tide to go out, dived for the fish. While the pool was emptying itself and many of the fish were leaving, the widow and her children threw stones outside the pool in an effort to stop them, till it was shallow enough to try and catch them. Some days they caught as many as three or four. That and the potatoes they still had a small stock of, kept the hunger away. Unknown to them, there was an extra spiteful person who crept to the pond, knocked much of the wall down and dug a trench through the soft gravel, letting all the sea water run out as the tide receded, rendering the pool useless for catching fish. Now deprived of this source of subsistence, there was little left to live on. There was no bread and the meal chest was empty for days.

The widow had a married sister living in Stoneybridge whom she had not seen for a long time. They fell out once over the head of a man and had never made friends or talked to each other since. A young man often came to do some maintenance work at the house where Jane, at that time, worked, and she grew friendly and they fell in love. This was the late John. After a time they married, but the sister, who also admired John, did not come to their wedding, and they lived a happy life until this fateful ship arrived and she foolishly admired the Captain. She decided to visit her sister, as perhaps there was some pity and forgiveness in her heart. She told the children that she was leaving early next morning, that they were to stay in bed, and that she would boil the small pot of potatoes that was left and leave it warm at the fireside. When they got up they were to peel them and, with the plate of salt on the dresser, dip the peeled potatoes there and eat them with warm water from the kettle. "Don't put too much peat on the fire and stay away from the shore. Don't go near the fish pond there will be nothing there. To pass the time after you wash with warm water without soap, as there is none, if you like, you can take your father's fiddle from the chest and try to play it but see that you don't damage it." "Mother," young Ann said, "when is father coming back?" "Now children, I have told you many times that your father will not be coming back. It is better for you to remember that and try to forget, and

264

through time you will." Looking into the bedroom, both children were asleep so she closed the outside door and left.

The path she took, although five miles, was seldom used. She wondered what kind of a welcome she would get from her sister and could not expect it to be more than lukewarm. After a short rest, she walked to within twenty yards of the door, which was closed. She stood, reminded that once she lived happily there when her parents were alive. The house looked poorly kept now. At that moment the door opened and her sister took two steps outside and stood saying, "What brings you to this locality? I did not think you had the courage to be seen here by your relations and sister. I knew of old, that you are a person without shame. You have as you well know brought disgrace on yourself and your people and now you come crawling to me for help after what you have done. You had a husband that was kind and good to you and your children, but that was not good enough for you so you planned to leave your husband and elope with your grand Captain." Jane said, "My sins are many but the children are innocent. It is for their sake that I have come to you begging." Her sister replied, "You should have been taking care of your brats while you were gallivanting in the hills with your Captain." Jane, growing angry and knowing there was nothing to gain, walked away slowly. Perhaps she did not now have the strength to be very angry and only felt pity for her sister for having to carry such ill feeling towards her kind, whatever the reasons were.

She was in doubt of calling at the next house, but before she came to within talking distance, the door opened. The lady of the house came out waving her hands saying "What a stranger you are. I knew in this distance it was you. How are you keeping? How are the children?" Jane said, "I am sorry I can't say that everything is well with us. Perhaps you know more about us than I do myself." "Well I cannot deny that I have been hearing stories. I don't believe half of what I hear," said the woman. Jane said, "Yours are the first words of kindness I have heard since I have disgraced myself and my relations. Please believe me, no one is more sorry for that than I am myself. I am like a ship without a rudder in a storm, at the mercy of a cruel sea." "Yes", the lady, whose name was Mary, said "I do believe you, and also that you are not the first woman to fall into a trap like that. You better come in, take your boots off and rest on that bench while I prepare a meal. You look very tired." Before the meal was ready Jane was fast asleep on the hard bench.

The good lady thought it best to let her rest, once asleep, while she herself would bake more bread and get a clean sack ready for the meal and other things she intended to give her. Her husband was not at home, but she was sure he would approve of what she was doing, for they had more than they needed, now that their two young children had gone, died of smallpox aged three and five, more than a year ago. They would by then have been a little older than Jane's children. When Jane was showing signs of wakening, she had everything ready for the bag. Mary said, "Would you like a wash to freshen you before you eat? The basin and soap and towel are over there." Jane did, and then sat down to a well-provided meal. After this she left, carrying the heavy bag of provisions to start the long walk home, having thanked Mary, who said she would visit her very soon.

She had to take two rests before she reached her house, where she kneeled beside a stream and offered up a prayer of thanksgiving for what was in the bag, and the generosity of Mary. She took off her boots and stockings and cooled her tired feet in the stream. After that rest and a bite to eat that Mary had made for the journey, suddenly a thick fog came down and she was forced to wait a while until it began to clear. After that she was making better time, and when she arrived the door was closed. She was afraid the children had gone to search for her and got lost in the fog, but when she opened the door and called to them, they called back that they were in bed. "You are in bed early tonight" Jane said, "you better get up for something to eat, you must be very hungry." "No we are not hungry." "Then you must have had more to eat than the few potatoes I left you. Did you eat them all?" "Yes." "Well, that was long ago, you must still be hungry?" "No we had lots to eat since then." "And who was this kind person that gave you food?" "Daddy, he was here long before you came." "Daddy?" the mother said. "Yes" was the reply. "Now children, I have told you many times that Daddy will not be coming back. You are now at an age to be told that your Father is dead and dead persons don't usually come back. Forget about this nonsense that you are only imagining." "No, we are not. He stayed with us for a long time. When we had tired of trying to play the fiddle we went out to see if you were coming. We climbed the hill above when the fog came down heavy. We returned home. We are not sure if we had left the door open. When we came in we saw Daddy sitting on that stool beside the meal chest. He said, "Don't be afraid children. I know you must be hungry. There is plenty of bread and milk in the meal chest. Your Mother will come home when the fog lifts. Come now and don't be afraid of your Father, but don't touch me. I will play you a tune on the fiddle while you are eating." "We were not afraid and I opened the chest" said Iain "and there as he said was the bread and milk. I gave half of it to Ann." Ann said that it tasted like what they had been used to. Jane asked, "What else did he tell you?" "He said we would soon be living in another house where we would not be hungry. He did not say where." "Did he look happy?" "I don't think he was because he never smiled." "He told us to wash our feet and go to bed, that you would be home soon." "Did he tell you not to say that you have seen him in this house?" "No, he only said then that we would not see him again." "Did you see him going away and which way he went?" "No, the door was closed. We did not see or hear him leaving." "Children, are you sure you are telling me the truth?" "We are Mother. What reason would we have to tell you lies?" "I don't know, only I have never heard of a thing like that."

They looked in the bag to find two kinds of meal, barley and oats. There was butter and crowdie and baked bread and also cheese. Wrapped in a clean cloth was a large cake of soap. The children said they were not hungry, it was not long since they had eaten all their father had told them to. "All right, wash your feet and say your prayers and prepare for bed." "We have done that already Mammy. Daddy told us to." She looked at their feet. They were clean, as clean as if they had used soap, which she knew was not in the house. All three slept in the same bed of necessity. "Do you need a light?" "No we are not afraid." "Well, good night. I'll be along with you soon."

She ate slowly. wondering if what the children said could be true. She always found them to be truthful. What made them imagine this story? If they had not eaten, except the few potatoes since morning, they were bound to be hungry, and yet they did not show it when the good things were in front of them. In view of it and what the children had said, she had to admit there was something strange to it. Of course, while the likeness may have been there, it is beyond belief that the Father in the flesh could be there, and very likely that is why he told them not to touch him. Tomorrow she would again question them. Tonight she thought they would have a restless sleep, but when she entered the bedroom, they were fast asleep. Iain at the foot, and Ann curled at the other end as usual. She put out the light and lay beside her. Ann did not stir. She herself, tired, was soon asleep and did not wake until the sun was shining on the window. If the children were restless, she did not feel it. They were still asleep in the same place. Although still early, she was well rested and thought the children would, if not last night, now be hungry and would soon be up.

She rose to make some breakfast and decided not to say a word about last night's affair till that was over and they had settled down. When all were satisfied and things washed and put away, their Mother spoke. "Now children, about what you were saying last night. Tell me truthfully, was it just a story you were making up and do you remember it now? I won't be cross with you, only always tell the truth." Iain spoke first. "Mother, we told you the truth last night, it was as we told you then." "Is that the way you feel Ann?" "Yes, only at first I was afraid till I made sure it was Daddy and he would not harm me." "Well, I want you to promise me that you will not talk about what happened last night unless I am along with you. Will you promise me that?" Both said that they would.

Life for the next few days with plenty to eat was much better, but they knew that would not last long. To help that, Jane herself began digging in the lazy beds where the children always dug. She was sure they were leaving many potatoes behind. It was a good crop and she was surprised at the amount they were leaving behind. While doing that she sent the children to gather shellfish, all of which helped to preserve their stock of food. Nevertheless she knew, with winter coming on, not having any peats to keep them warm they could not stay in that house. The neighbours were as unfriendly as ever. None would cut peats for her in exchange for any work she could do. Where could she go? Her case was known far and wide. She felt everyone but Mary was against her. She could not form a plan to make their existence any better.

Not long after Jane left Mary's house with her load of food, Charlie came home and was told that they had a visitor since he left. Mary explained it was that poor woman out in Locheynort, who people are always talking about. Charlie said he remembered her, and when Mary told him the whole story, both agreed that to help her was the best thing to do, although they knew that to show charity towards them would bring ill feelings and much talk, yet through time that feeling would be forgotten. Shortly after, Mary said, "I want to ask your opinion of a thought that has been on my mind since Jane was here, and after what she told me I feel very sorry for her. We have more than we need so what would you say if, when I go to see them next week, I invite them to come and stay with us, at least until something better turns up?" Charlie was silent for a long time, weighing up all the ifs and buts. At last he said, "Mary, I see no reason why your plan should not work out to their benefit and to ours as well. There is work here that we are not now able for, and that can only get worse. Her children are almost the age ours would have been and if they come here we may never regret it."

Mary prepared a bundle of food early Monday morning, and left on her long journey. Taking the path that Jane had used, in the distance she saw a man with a dog and she thought their paths would meet. The man said, "Hello, you are a stranger out in the hills alone." "Not quite" she said, "I have been out this way, but not often." "I seem to know you, but can't right now place you." "I am Charlie's wife from Stoneybridge." "Yes I remember you well, and Charlie too. Are you going far with that bag? Let me carry it some of the way, you must be tired." "I am, and I will be glad to." "How far are you going?" She told him she was going to Jane's house, as she believed she was destitute and that no one seemed to care for her or her children. He said, "That is true, people here keep clear of them as if they had the smallpox. I

267

think you yourself are a brave woman going to their house in daylight, braving the wrath of the people around here, but then you live far away. I myself have pity on them and only at night time do I risk leaving something, usually potatoes, at their door, but I know those I live with would not approve."

After a while the man stopped, and dropping the bag said, "This is as far as I can go, we are coming in view of the house and I don't like to be seen near it. Here is half a crown for the children." Mary said, "That's very kind of you. I don't remember your name." "Angus MacRae, your husband knows me well, he sometimes comes out to fish with me."

Mary was then near her destination. Arriving there, the door was closed although the day was fine. She heard movements inside and the door was opened. There stood Jane, first with a frown then a broad smile. Without saying a word and with tears in her eyes she threw her arms round Mary and began kissing and hugging her. When she regained her breath she said, "I haven't seen or spoken to anyone except the children since I left your house that day, but come in, we will leave the door open and anybody watching will know that I am not alone and friendless."

The children were sitting at a table having something to eat. "This" said Jane "is Iain and his sister Ann, they are a little shy." Mary looked at Ann for a long time and said to herself how much that child resembled our Katie before asking how they all were. Jane said, "Thanks to you and your generosity, Mary, we are all well in the circumstances, especially with all the food you have given us. I hope you are not leaving yourself short thinking of us?" "No, we always have more than we need, although I did not bring potatoes, they are heavy to carry, but I see you have some left." "Yes, we have, some kind person left nearly a bag full at the door the other night. He did not knock and we don't know who he was but we are very grateful." "I" said Mary "know him. I met him on the hill an hour ago and he carried this bag some distance. He also gave me this half crown to give you for the children. He told me not to mention his name. He said he felt very sorry for the way you are placed, and in view of the latest lies about you, it would be wise to try and find some other place to live. You know him, but I won't tell you his name, not yet anyway."

Jane said, "I know but where can I go? With all that is being said, true and untrue, about me, no one would give us shelter for a night." "Well Jane" Mary said, "last week Charlie and I had thought deeply about your problem, and as we have plenty of room and could do with more help, we concluded that, if you are willing to come and stay with us, we will welcome you and think the move will be to the benefit of both." Jane was silent, then said, "This is most generous of you and a kindness not hoped for. Are you sure that you mean all you say?" "Of course I am, it is partly why I came today to find out what you thought of the plan. Charlie is as keen as I am that you move in along with us, as he is fond of children. We miss our own more than I can say, so don't think we are doing you a great favour. Let us fix a day when Charlie will come out with a boat to take in your belongings. Let's say Wednesday noon if the tide is right. Well then, I'll say goodbye and be on my way before any fog comes down. I'll look forward to seeing you soon." Jane thanked her for her kind offer and said to the children, "Are you happy to be leaving here children?" "Yes, we are, Mother, very happy."

When Wednesday came, Charlie sent two strong lads out with a big sack to carry all the stuff Jane needed, till he was able to take the boat out to collect the rest of her goods, which they packed and left in the house. To make sure no vandals entered the house, as there was no lock or key for the door, a board with the words 'Danger – Smallpox Keep Out' painted in red on it was nailed to the door. Charlie knew that word would soon get around and no one would be brave enough to enter. They left as if in a hurry, for the benefit of any watching eyes, and walked about half a mile, but while the house was still in view they stopped, as Jane wanted to have a last look at the house where once she was very happy and where her happiness had turned to misery. Many unspoken thoughts were passing through her mind.

When they came in view of Mary's house, they saw in the distance two people and a dog coming towards them, and Jane knew it was Mary and Charlie, and when they met they were given a splendid welcome. At their new home, Mary had the table set, crowded with the best food she could provide, things Jane and the children had not tasted for a long time, if ever. The very enjoyable meal over, they all rested before clearing the table. Before the end of that month there was much change in everyone. All the newcomers looked so much better. There was laughter in that house where before there was much silence. The children were well behaved and eager to help Mary in whatever task she was doing. Ann endeared herself so much that Mary often took her on her lap and told her fairy stories, while Iain would be along with his mother, helping Charlie in whatever he was doing.

That evening while sitting together, Jane said, "Mary, I would like to talk to you about something that's been on my mind for some time, and I would rather that you hear it before Charlie. You know that wretched house I left behind. I believe it is still mine." "Of course it is" said Mary. "Well, I want to give that house to Charlie to do with it as he pleases, as a gift you might say. I don't want either of my children ever to live there again. Perhaps Charlie will know of a friend he would like to give it to. It was once a good happy home. Another thing, Mary, I would like to ask you. Did you or Charlie ever hear either of the children talk about their father in any strange way?" "I don't know what you mean Jane. All I heard them saying was that Daddy went away and will not be coming back." Jane said "Sometime soon, when we are all together, the five of us, I will tell you this story, which I myself believe is true. That is all I will tell you now. Don't mention this talk to anyone yet. You will know it when I have the chance to question the children in your presence."

One day Charlie asked Jane "Did Mary tell you of my plan for Iain to get some schooling, he is a bright lad, easily taught? It would be very unwise to waste that ability." "Well Charlie, Iain is with you most of the time. I am sure you know what you are saying. I am in full agreement with all you say, and if you can arrange it, I will be quite happy." Charlie did arrange it with very little trouble and Iain liked school, and no matter what the weather was like, he never missed a day. Mary and Jane passed the time by using the spinning wheel, with one carding and the other spinning, and realised that money could be made by selling what they made. This also kept them and the children fully clothed.

One of these nights, the question of the Locheynort old house was brought up by Mary, who said, "Jane and I have had a talk about it, and she can now tell you, Charlie, what's on her mind." Jane asked Charlie if he would take her house as a free gift, and find someone of his own choosing who may be in need of a house, as she believed it could still be made into a reasonable dwelling. Charlie agreed with her, as it looked well thatched to stand winter gales. The smallpox danger was still nailed to the door, there was nothing disturbed inside. The sign played its part well and they were quite sure someone would be glad to have it. Charlie asked if there was land attached to it and Jane said there was as her late husband kept cows and some sheep but she wasn't sure where the boundaries were.

Charlie said he would try to think of people in need of such a house, but after a time, as he was still undecided, Jane suggested that he visit the Missionary in Benbecula and have him write the names of the three he had in mind on paper, fold them up, put them in a box and draw one out. Whoever's name was on that paper would get the house. Charlie went to see this gentleman and told him the whole story, who, after considering it, thought it was fair and that he would write a paper for Jane to sign and the names of the three people separate, as he did not want to be involved in the draw. The best thing would be to advise the people concerned to be at the estate house on the day and time of the draw. All that was arranged beforehand. The draw was made in full view and in agreement with all concerned. The lucky winner moved in after some repairs and was accepted as one of the community.

One day after school and work, they were all at home. "Mary" Jane said "Some time ago I told you that one day I would tell you a strange story." "Yes, I well remember you saying that, and I often wondered if you have forgotten." "No one could forget a thing of that kind. Actually it concerned the children. I was not there, but I believe the story the children told me. It happened the day I called on my sister, I was not allowed to go near her house, and you called me in and made me welcome and, after a rest, sent me off with a heavy load of food. Before reaching my house, the fog at the back of the hill came down so thick that I did not know where I was and had to wait till it cleared. I was anxious to get home as I knew the children would be very hungry."

Jane then told Mary and Charlie the whole story about the children apparently seeing their father and what they said had happened. She then asked them if they wanted to question the children more on this matter. "No" they both said, "we are sure they told the truth, we have always found them truthful." Jane said, "When they sat down to the good meal you had sent them, Mary, they hardly touched it." "I opened the meal chest but it was as empty as it was for many days. I thought they would be frightened and alarmed but they were not. It was I that was alarmed not knowing if I should believe them. They told the same story every time I asked them, and seemed angry when I showed signs of doubting them or thinking they were making up this story. I told them to be sure not to mention this strange event to anyone. I would like Mary and yourself Charlie, not to mention it, because whoever gets the house might think it is haunted. Anyway, we left there, thanks to you and to the kind person who, unknown to us had left potatoes and fish at the door at night. We never saw him and don't know who our benefactor was." "Well" said Mary "I know who he was, but at the time he asked me not to mention his name. I feel that I can now disclose that that charitable man was Angus MacRae."

Charlie said, "Do any of you know who got that house?" Mary and Jane both said, "No, and if you know you have not told us." "Well" said Charlie "it is strange, almost unbelievable. It was that Angus MacRae who got that house. Of course, it was the luck of the draw. I only put his name down knowing, like the other two, he was in need of a better house, and although I had nothing other to do with the allocation, I admit I am glad that it was him who won the draw. It was him that brought in your chests Jane, and would not accept anything for doing that. He inspected the house and said it was in good condition. He has a good boat and strong children and should be quite comfortable there. He had a look at the board nailed to the door and asked what it was. When told, he said, much better than a lock even if one was on. Perhaps when he gets settled there we won't be short of fish." Jane said, "You did not tell him about the apparition the children saw?" "How could I, it was not known to me until tonight. I will never say a word about it. It has nothing to do with him or anyone now."

270

Life in that home was happy as usual, the harvest was good and the cattle sold well, but Charlie was obliged to sell more as old age was creeping in. One day the Missionary called at the house. He said he wanted to have a talk with Charlie about Iain. He said he had a wonderful gift for learning and was above the rest of his pupils, and it would be a great pity for that to end when there was so much more to learn. "Well" said Charlie "I am very grateful to you for what you have done for him but what else can I do? Between you and me I intend to leave him this place. I have no near relations, and even if I had, that is what I intend to do." The Missionary knew the monks at the monastery in Benbecula ran a school of a high standard; he would perhaps try to arrange for Iain to attend. He would have to live there but he would be allowed home every weekend. He told Charlie that he had to attend a meeting in Benbecula and he would call on the head Abbot to find out the terms. Charlie liked the idea and thanked him, and in a few days the Missionary, after seeing the Abbot, went to convey his news to Charlie and his household. He told them he was received with much kindness, and that he was successful in obtaining a place for Iain. The weekly fee was a shilling, and he would be allowed home every other weekend. He was expected to present himself in ten days' time.

Mary measured Iain for a new suit and went to the weaver for a length of tweed. She took that to the tailor who promised to have it ready in a few days. The rest, such as shirts, she could make herself from material she had. Iain was well prepared for his new life, his only regret was leaving his mother who by now was in poor health. The next day Charlie got the pony ready to take them both to the Monastery. It was a silent house that night. As time went by Jane's health got worse; she was well looked after by Charles and Mary and she died peacefully knowing that her family were well cared for.

Ann grew up to be strong and very pretty. She married and they remained in the house with Mary and Charlie. Charlie had by then given the house to Iain who passed it on to Ann. Iain himself had made so good in the Monastery that the head Abbot sent him to university, where he became a professor and then taught there. Ann and her husband looked after Mary and Charlie in their old age, and when Mary was on her death bed, her last wish was to be buried beside Jane, and near her own two children. When Charlie's time came, he was laid beside them.

This is the gist of the story as Donald told to me. I said, "It's very strange that I have not heard that story from any of the very old people who were here when we settled in Locheynort. We were the first to settle after the Highland Clearances."

"Well" he said "that's the way I heard it from my father, he was an old man then. He heard it from his grandfather who remembered people talking of it, there were so many people related to this Jane who had brought so much disgrace on them. During the Highland Clearances, the people were made to leave the Locheynort district and the story died, but as the children grew up, they never denied seeing and talking to the apparition of their father."

The small island below the house where the hawsers of the ill-fated ship was made fast to, was called Bishop's Island, (Eilean an Easbuig) said to be where the first man of that rank in the Catholic Church landed following the Protestant Reformation centuries ago. Why he landed on that small island was never known. The mass in these days was celebrated in secret not far from this island at the head of the sea loch at the Slochd Dubh. It is a large hollow with a natural altar shelf, well hidden from anybody of men coming from any direction to arrest the priest who if caught, with little time to escape, made his way to where a boat would be waiting outside the narrows to take him to the hideout on the other side of the loch. The people living then on the

271

east side of the narrows were Catholics. So that the priest would not be caught, mass would be said in different places. Word would be passed around as to where mass was to be on a given Sunday. There was a special body of anti-Catholics always on the watch for those few disguised priests. Sometimes a luke-warm Catholic, for a bribe, would give away the place where the mass was to be on the coming Sunday. Knowing there were such men, a watch was always kept to protect the priest.

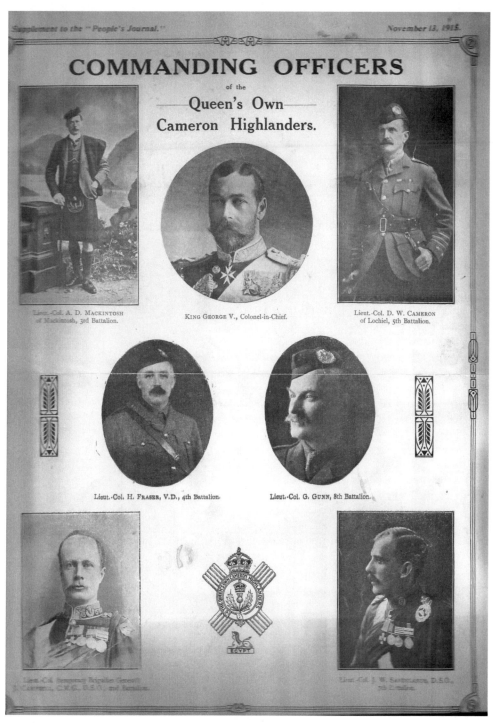

Commanding Officers of the Queens Own Cameron Highlanders

THE FIRST BRITISH CRUISER LOST IN THE
GREAT EUROPEAN WAR.
SUNK BY A GERMAN MINE.

H.M.S. AMPHION.

HMS Amphion

Donald's First World War Medals

Mary Ann's I D card

Mary Ann's ID card

Family Home, 7 North Locheynort

Pollen's hut beside ruined Inn, North Locheynort

Donald and Peregrine Pollen

Donald and Sr Barbara fishing

Kate, Sr Barbara, Sr Paschal and Sarah

Locheynort with haystacks

Donald, Peggy and some of his grandchildren

Donald with grandchildren on his last boat trip

Oil painting of family home by Patricia Pollen

Donald with Sir Walter Pollen's Grandson

Donald in his boat - Locheynort

Stephen & Grandpa 1977

The author at work on his book

I must now go back to my life story after spending so much time telling this old story from Donald. We fished well that season and kept our heads above water, the children were better clad and I had ordered material to build a porch around the door that badly needed done for south west winds. By the time I got the material, the cold weather had set in, with the children small, in and out, I doubted the wisdom of doing it at that time of the year and so cancelled it for a lean-to shed at the end of the house. It would relieve the congestion of the small house where we lived. It certainly did that. A room partitioned off where milk in large basins was set on shelves; much of the rest was used for hanging up spare clothing and other articles not in use. Although still crowded, we were a healthy happy family and Mary Ann was expecting our fourth child. Archie and Alex Ian were at school and very seldom only a bad storm kept them at home. Rain did not matter, regardless of not being clad for it. On a real bad day I used to walk in to meet them and always I would find them making better progress against the strong wind and rain than I did myself, and would be home before me. With that in mind I felt there was no need, but only to please their mother did I sometimes go. Considering how they were dressed and fed, they were much better off than I was in my school days where it was always across a hill bare footed. If any of the children caught a cold, it was either to bed or school, failing that it was a hard task to keep any of them indoors and that seldom happened.

I was working on the Locheynort road and it was December 1948 when Mary Ann went for her fourth confinement to her parents' home. I was obliged to stop working on the road to care for the other three, two were at school, and the youngest was about a year and eight months and was not hard to look after, always in the best of health. Peggy Theresa, our only daughter, was born on 24th December 1948. I was delighted when I got that wire that all was well. We were anxious as the only doctor in South Uist was away on the mainland at the time. However, news spread that a young doctor just newly out of college, was staying in Garrynamonie where his people came from.   He came willingly in the early hours and the baby was born shortly afterwards, both well and no trouble. No one could wish for a better Christmas present than that. The next day I got their young cousin Joan from Bayhead to look after the children and house while I went up south to see Mary Ann and the new arrival, calling on my neighbour to look after the cattle as usual, and promising I would be back as soon as I could.

As it was Christmas time there were more cars on the road. I did not walk more than a mile when I got a lift straight to Polochar. I had a dram there with the driver who would not allow me to pay when I told him why I was up this way. He said, "Let's have one more drink then I will take you to that house and wait half an hour for you. How will that suit you?" I was very grateful for his kindness. We had our drink, and this time I was able to by a bottle as there was no shortage. When we reached the house, I got the usual welcome, I told them I could not stay long as I was getting a lift back and had to get back to the other three children. Mary Ann and the baby were both in the best of health, we spoke about the Christening and decided to call the baby Peggy after Mary Ann's mother and Theresa after that saint which was a favourite Saint of us both who is always shown holding roses.

We hoped she would send down a shower of roses into our garden and that they would last longer than the strawberries I had planted. The first year I covered them with old straw, they grew well and flowered early in May and shortly formed a green berry. They promised a nice crop as they grew to a good size before taking on a reddish hue. I watched them grow with much pride, they looked as good as any that grew on the farms I worked on in Canada where breakfast began with a large dish of cream and juicy strawberries. As they ripened, none got as far as our table and no one would admit to taking any. I could not always keep watch and so decided to pull them out and put a less enticing crop in their place.

After the welcomed tea and drams we said our goodbyes and set off on the road again. Passing Polochar, the driver said, "Do you fancy a pint? It's nearly closed." I said, "I sure do". We had a couple each and I bought a flask to give my neighbour, Seonaidh, a dram. I could always leave the cattle and things in his good care when I alone went fishing and, of course, he always got half of whatever I caught. Although the road was then built to within a mile of the house, the driver was getting short of petrol and he could only risk going as far as Bayhead. I asked him if he liked salted mackerel. He said, "I do very much." "Then I promise to send you some. I will send it with Neil our postman." I did that and he was very pleased with it. After calling on Seonaidh with my dram he told me everything was well and the cattle seen to. At home they were all there, except John Joseph, the youngest who had gone missing and after a short search was found safe and well. After tea it was all questions about the new baby. They wanted to know if it was a girl or a boy, when I said it was a girl they asked what was the difference, I said, "Nothing much, only girls let their hair grow like Mammy, and she combs it every day." "When are Mammy and the baby coming home?" "As soon as the weather gets better. You don't want them to catch a cold in this weather." It was all baby talk till I got them ready for bed and then bedtime stories.

It began to snow that night and by early morning it was very deep. I told the children to stay in bed, that I was going to feed the cattle and milk the cow then I would start making breakfast. The fire, after some poking and dry peats, soon lit up and the porridge, which was easy to make was soon ready. We had no running water in the house, cold or hot, and for years depended on a spring well not far from the house. There was always a large pail of water in the house, a basin with soap and cold water for hands and faces. At night, there was warm water for those who did not have boots. After breakfast of porridge, plenty of milk, tea with boiled or scrambled eggs, they were delighted seeing the amount of snow everywhere. They began making snowmen, even young John Joseph began making one in his bare feet near the door. I began baking scones and when the first batch was ready I saw John Joseph taking one outside I thought to give to the dog. I followed him and saw that he had stuck the scone where he thought the mouth should be, below the left ear. I said he made a good job of it. I took him inside and promised to get him wellingtons from the van the next day. The van had wellingtons and the right size, John Joseph was then very happy playing in the snow with the rest of them.

I got as much as we could afford from the van including a Christmas cake, sweets and apples. I fed the hens, all still inside and afraid to leave their hut because of the snow. Each night I spread a layer of straw on the floor, gathered the eggs and put a small peat fire in an old cast iron pot inside to keep them warm, as was the custom then to keep them laying. Dinner was nearly always boiled potatoes and salt herring with a mug of milk. The cattle were fed and the milking done, some nights I would do some work repairing lobster creels and when the children were older they would give me a hand. The older two, if they had school homework would be kept at it. For John Joseph I would cut up small blocks of wood to keep him occupied. Supper was usually a cup of milk and a scone. It was surprising how soon the nights went in before it was time for washing, prayers, then bed and storytelling until they were all asleep. That was the usual routine. In later years when the family were older, their cousins in Oban faithfully sent the *Weekly News* and the *Sunday Post* to us, mostly with a letter enclosed. There was great excitement each week waiting for this package, which sometimes caused a fight with all trying to get their hands on 'The Broons' and 'Oor Wullie' sections.

While that snow lasted, the cold germ kept clear of this isolated place, perhaps on account of that, the children very seldom took a cold. In that kind of weather I was not able to attend Peggy's christening. The first mail out brought me a letter saying that all went well and they would be home when the weather improved.

Six weeks passed before Mary Ann and the baby at last arrived home. Angus James took them across in his boat, as the road had not yet reached our house. I had the house warmed up for them coming, I had had plenty of time to paint the cradle pink and although long past New Year, I still had a dram left. The eldest two were at school, there would be no delay coming home that day. All were delighted with the new baby, each demanding his turn at rocking the cradle, often over-doing it, and when shown how it should be done properly, would soon lose interest as playing outside was more enjoyable.

As soon as the weather settled and work began on the road, I was back on the sledgehammer again. Blacky produced a bonny female calf, we then had more milk than we needed. Also herring made its appearance in the outer loch and one night when we put out some nets, we got four boxes of good quality herring. We salted as much as we wanted and sold the rest to the locals for as much as we could get. One night after setting our nets, our anchor did not hold and we drifted on the top of other people's nets. Our nets were full and all had to be hauled up by hand. This was hard work, and when our anchor caught in the other nets, I strained myself badly because of that extra weight. I had to see the doctor who ordered me to hospital in Lewis for a hernia operation. The ward was full of patients in need of surgery. There was a bible on the top of every locker and each patient took his turn reading a passage from it and explained its meaning. I was greatly surprised that everyone seemed to be able to read well and somehow they knew that I was a Catholic and was not asked to read. I was told my operation was to be on Monday. The man John, in the next bed who by now I was on friendly terms with, late one Saturday began shaving. I saw that he had a small mirror; I had none. I thought I would shave on the day before my operation. When I began to make my preparations I said to John, "I am going to shave and have no mirror. I saw you using one yesterday and was wondering if you would lend me it?" He looked at me and said in anger "I hope to goodness that you are not going to break the Sabbath by shaving." I said I had forgotten it was Sunday. "Well" he said, "no one should forget that Holy Day, you are welcome to it tomorrow, the next day and any other day but not the Sabbath." They had a strict code in Lewis to keep the Sunday holy. In our southern isles it is not considered a transgression along with other active sports such as games, or fishing for pleasure but to do it for gaining money is strictly ruled out. I had my operation and was allowed out within the week.

The day I left the Lewis hospital the surgeon told me to take things easy for a while. There was much spring work still undone and I was not yet able to do any work. Friends helped me and while I did not cultivate the normal amount, I would reduce the stock accordingly. My fishing crew did the heavy work, they had stopped fishing due to bad weather and no demand. I applied for Sickness Benefit and got it but even with that and family allowance we were struggling along, but within a few weeks I was fit to do most of the work. It was well into the summer and after the peats were cut that I went back to work on the road to earn some money. I worked all that summer on the road, and as there was no overtime, I worked on the croft as long as daylight lasted. If not making hay, it would be gathering and stacking peats but regardless of the long day from dawn to dark, I was happy and contented. There was no illness in the family and the food was wholesome and plentiful. The two in school were doing very well, and the third, John Joseph, was also proving to be bright.

Mary Ann went for her fifth confinement again to her parents' home and took John Joseph and Peggy with her. The other two were at school. I was able to look after them and the housework besides the cattle and haymaking. It was September 1950 and another baby boy was born on 20th September, both well. We christened him Peter Anthony after my brother Peter. When I got the glad news, I got a car and took the rest of the children to see them.

Mary Ann and the baby came back with Peggy and John Joseph in about three weeks time. Peggy was already taking charge of the baby saying, "It's my baby." All was well. The cradle was put back into use again, with Peggy being far more attentive than her elder brothers, which no doubt is the nature of things. This time they got a car within twenty yards from the door. Thanks to the road and the effort we put into the making of it, the days of wading through the mud and slush, always carrying an extra pair of shoes to put on after getting through that mire were gone. Now a bus came round the loch and took us to and from Mass on Sundays and days of Obligation.

We were a happy, healthy family and since there was no money to spare for toys and comics, I used to saw and split small blocks of wood to build houses, boats, bridges or anything with. At night if the stories were exhausted, a quiz would be formed to spot and name things in view in the room. A prize of a penny was awarded for the most correct answers, according to age. This would be extended to things outside, things they would see on the croft or on their way to school. They were rather keen on that form of play. I found that it exercised their young minds and was surprised at the speed they would name an object. As I had no great education myself to pass on, I felt that would be of some help, besides the fun.

At last we were able to buy a wireless and never missed Scottish dance music unless the baby was sleeping. That was the extent of our entertainment together, except on fine Sundays after Mass I would take them for a sail in the small boat and teach them how to row and steer, often taking along a kettle for making tea, scones, mugs and a pot for boiling fish. When enough fish was caught, we would go ashore and build a fire near a burn, clean the fish and boil it in sea water, that meal was always enjoyable and much more was eaten than would be at home. None would be hungry enough to eat when arriving home in the evening. Of course fish just taken from the sea and cooked or boiled in seawater, no salt, tasted different and better.

After Mary Ann came home with baby Peter and the harvest was partly in, we put the creels out again. Lobsters were fairly plentiful, the price was good, a faster and cooler ship was put on the run to Oban so the death rate was not very high, resulting in us doing very well, until a bad storm came and wrecked most of our gear. We repaired what we could and kept on fishing with a reduced fleet of creels. To make good the loss was impossible and so the fishing dwindled to where it was not worth the wear and tear of the gear to continue. While it was profitable, much of that money went to buy things that were badly needed besides clothing for the children. My own Sunday suit was now sixteen years old but still fairly good because I always changed into dungarees when I came back from Mass or any important event such as a funeral. Mary Ann was glad to get a new coat, which was long overdue. When the fishing ended there was very little money left to meet the van's bill, which was small as we had our own garden, fish, milk and eggs.

Mary Ann was an excellent cook. One day she went up to the Co-op and ordered a new stove, a New Rex, the price was £40.00. I was not too happy and thought we would never be able to pay for it because it was the first item we had bought on credit and the prospects ahead were not bright. The cattle sale at which we hoped to sell was far away. After the second payment was made I told the manager although we needed that stove, that I was very worried about being able to keep up its payments regularly as there was no work in view and our last effort at the lobsters was a dead loss. He looked at me and said, "Do you think you can clear it in a year?" "Yes, and much sooner." "Well I am not pressing you, pay me as you can and let me do the worrying."

At that time I was trapping otters and selling their skins, which was allowed in those days. They were large and of good quality, and I got much more for them than I had expected which was a great help to us. I once caught one measuring 6 feet, 3 inches from nose to the tip of the tail skinned. Our method of stretching was by nails driven through the skin on a flat area of wood. That operation ended towards the end of March as the females had their young about that time, and what I made kept the wolf from the door for a while.

With fish at that time of the year being far outside the loch, there was no way for us to catch it. I was again obliged to go cap in hand to the National Assistance area office, where everything I possessed from wife to the six hens we had, was counted. I was warned that any false statement I made would render my application not worth any consideration, and was told an agent would call soon and he would investigate my circumstances. I knew the agent, and this was not the first time I was obliged to ask him for help. In a few days he did come and went over the list of what I possessed, including the hens. I don't think, as they were running about, he counted them, just entered 'hens' and said my application would be posted that day and Stornoway would deal with what allowance was granted to me. When that arrived it was much less than what we expected, I think because we had two cows, a few sheep and a boat, which was beached and not earning anything. It was true the cows were still in milk, but it would be a long wait for the sheep we then had to produce wool for sale. On the better side, there was always plenty of salt fish, potatoes, milk and vegetables.

While that was our main subsistence, many things were lacking in the house, clothing, footwear, and dishes etc. Mary Ann, as I said, was a splendid cook, and as far as good food was concerned, money was not greatly needed, however, much was needed in the way of bits of furniture. New stuff was coming on the market, and those who had money were able to buy and get rid of the old and broken stuff they had. I went over to one of these sales and bought some articles, dry rot and all which later became evident. In order to augment our small income, I decided to begin gathering whelks around the shore of the loch where in the olden days they were plentiful. I would continue until I gathered nearly a bag full or about 3 cwt. It took me three Spring tides, or nearly six weeks, to gather that lot; out in every low tide, hail, rail or snow. A neighbour in his boat took the bag to Lochboisdale where he despatched them for me to Billingsgate, thus saving me the carriage to Lochboisdale. I expected a fair return. When it did come and I added up the number of hours I worked gathering these bags, it showed I was working hard, wet and cold, for the handsome sum of less than nine pence an hour in old money. Obviously the whelks were not improving our standard of living.

I toyed with the idea of giving up smoking, thus making a saving at the van, but by cutting it from three to one ounce a week worked. After a week of discontent, I felt better in myself. I could work much longer without taking a rest. When I gave up gathering the whelks I concentrated on the spring work, now behind on account of the whelks.

That year much was required to make fishing worthwhile, as most of our creels were wrecked the season before, and material for repairing was not to be got. Also I needed parts for the boat's engine and it was doubtful I would get them in time for fishing. My partner Angus James was in poor health. Mary Ann was now expecting our sixth child, and not long after we would have begun fishing. If we did begin, I would lose the assistance allowance, and as the fishing wasn't steady it did not seem to me promising. I thought it wiser to stay on the Assistance, besides I wanted to give Mary Ann in her condition all the help I could in looking after the other five young children, and on being asked, I loaned my smaller boat to the two sons of my friend Angus James and also what creels I had left. I got the parts after some delay for the engine.

When the boat was ready I often took out parties for sea angling and sea trips. Some of these were profitable if the catch was good. If not, and on a rough day, they would be glad to be away in their car before I had time to moor the boat, forgetting they owed me something. I never set a fixed price, saying whatever you think yourself. The most I got was five pounds from an American who claimed that was the best fishing day he had ever had, and he was sorry he had to fly back to the U.S.A. the next day. I was too, with that unexpected tip. Although not regular, it was still a great help along with the Assistance.

As the children were growing, and our small house was becoming smaller, and since there was no prospects of regular fishing that season, I decided to begin preparation for the long awaited extension to the house. I could do all that was required myself this time, unlike before, when most of the sand used to build the house had to be taken by boat from Eriskay. Now, thanks to the road, I could get it by lorry to within a few yards from the site. Much work was needed to level that site. Because of its rocky nature and nearness to the house blasting was not safe. All rocks above floor level had to be burned down with peat fire, taking much time. However, I kept at it and finished that part, ordered the building material and laid the foundation wall, which Mary Ann was very pleased with.

Shortly before then our old Doctor Reardon retired and a much younger man took his place. This young doctor wanted to see that the Uist people got as much medical care and treatment as those on the mainland did. The extension to the old two wards in Daliburgh hospital was still on the drawing board and there was no maternity ward. Patients in need of that were usually sent to Glasgow or Inverness. Mary Ann was on his list. The last time he came to see her she was in her normal good health and fully expecting to be going to her parents' home for the birth, as usual, all safely delivered. "That", he said, "is fine when all is going as it should, but if things go wrong you are a long way from a hospital where that can easily be put right. My policy is always safety first and an hour with an attendant in a plane is worth that." She told him of her experience regarding the Glasgow hospital where she was once sent to for the same purpose, and where they would not admit her, saying she was too early, but that night the child was born in her lodging house, long before an ambulance arrived. However, regardless of all that, both she and the child came back safe and well. The doctor could not understand how a mistake like that could be made. As she was not happy with Glasgow, would she feel better going to Raigmore Hospital in Inverness? It was nearer and just as good. There she consented to go, and so on 28th November 1953, Neil Paul was born.

Shortly after her recent confinement she caught a cold, and although back in bed, it refused to clear up. When in that state, and not responding to treatment, it was decided to test her blood. That proved she needed more blood. In her next letter she told me she was getting this blood next day and was feeling much better. I was happy, as soon she would be well again and back home where she was so much missed. I received her next letter in a few days, and before I opened it I thought this would be telling me the day I could expect her home. Instead, it was to inform me that she did not get the blood she was to get because they did not have her group number, and that they may let her home till that became available. I thought it unbelievable that, among the many blood banks in the British Isles, her group was not stored there ready for use when she was still in hospital. I never ceased to wonder that if that hospital had got and used what they had prescribed, the new blood could have been the means to arrest the coming disaster.

About ten days after that she was sent home and, while not ill, I could see her appearance was not what it used to be after such an event. Before she left for hospital we had arranged that the two youngest would stay with their Aunt Morag while their mother was away. As soon as she came home those two also came, adding more work to their not too well mother, while I gave as much help to ease that as I knew how.

Mary Ann first complained about her fingers. The least scratch normally thought nothing of, would fester and was hard to heal. When other complications began I sent for the doctor. He examined her and said he would send the nurse down the next day with something that would make her much better, and that he himself would come to see her again in a few days time. The nurse came but what she brought with her did not seem to make any difference to Mary Ann's condition. The doctor came to see her when he said he would. This time he took her case more seriously. A week in the hospital where she could get more rest and better treatment was what she needed. I fully agreed. He was a young doctor, not the one that sent her away in the first place, although he was a man well liked and the district felt sorry when he left to practice in Fort William.

The new doctor was an Islander, young and able, and I had great trust in him. He said the ambulance would be down for her tomorrow, I took the two youngest again to their aunt, and this time I told them it's only for a week. Next week I got a car and took them all to see their mother. She was sitting up in bed knitting. After kissing, she said "Whatever you are giving them, they are looking very well. I am much better and, I hope to be back home next week." She looked very well. With much kissing from the children, we left her. I felt the happiest man in the world. We called at the aunt's house where I left the two youngest as before. Mary Ann's sister, Ealasaid, at Lochboisdale, was looking after the baby, so that I only had three to look after and they were attending school some two miles away. At this very small school they never got a meal like in other schools, although they did get a drink of national dried milk at noon.

So it was back to the old style that I knew so well, a piece in the pocket that was often eaten before reaching school. It certainly made them run faster coming home in the evening. After leaving the two young children we made our way home happily. It would be only a week, perhaps less, before their mother would be home, safe and well. Near the end of that week I received a letter from her saying that the doctor had discovered something in her condition that he was not happy about, and since they had nothing there that would cure that condition, he was advising her to go to a hospital in Glasgow where she could get that treatment. He said she would be away only a few weeks. I agreed she should go and took the children up to see her the following Sunday.

When we arrived at the hospital, before letting me into the ward, the nun in charge, the Mother Superior, said, "I want to talk to you Donald before you see her. The children can go in." I said, "Alright Mother." I thought she wanted to tell me they intended to send Mary Ann to Glasgow where in a short time they would cure her. I already had this information and did not feel alarmed. But I did, when I heard what she had to say, and would have been much more had I known what she was talking about. "Donald" she said "I am sorry I have bad news for you." I said, "Is she worse Mother? I had a letter from her yesterday telling me she is going to be sent to Glasgow for some treatment that is not available here." "There is very little change in her since but she is not making any progress. It has been discovered she has Leukaemia." I said, "What is that? I have never heard of it." "That is cancer in the blood," she said. "Is it hard to cure?" "It can be cured, or at least kept under control, if it is discovered at an early stage. Mary Ann may be lucky." At least she gave me that ray of hope. I would pray hard and often that her treatment was to be in time. They gave me a cup of tea and said; "Don't tell her anything about this when you go in to see her, just act as normal as you can."

When I went in she was sitting up in bed looking fairly well, with the children around her laughing. Quietly she said, "Where have you been? What's been keeping you, you look pale." "I have been to the bathroom. I ate something this morning that did not agree with me. How you feel yourself is more important than us." She said, "I don't feel too bad, only I don't seem to be getting stronger, and sometimes I feel very weak. They say they have now found out why I am like that and want me to go to the Western Infirmary in Glasgow to cure that, as I told you in my letter." "And you are quite happy to go there?" "Indeed I am not but what else can I do? I want to be back home as soon as I can. It seems they have not got the treatment I need here, only in the Glasgow hospital can I get that. Two weeks there should clear it. I was longer than that in Raigmore Hospital where I think I got this illness." I said, "Don't worry about us, as you see we are managing fine." Before we left her, Mother Superior told me when Mary Ann was leaving for Glasgow, and the time and place where the ambulance would pick me up, as I would want to go with her to the airport.

I met the ambulance at the appointed day and place. Mary Ann looked well and cheery. She said she felt better already and indeed I did too, walking to the plane with her and seeing how strong and firm she walked. I said, "None could say there is anything wrong with you." "I know" she said, "I don't think there is much myself, and I hope to be back soon." With that we fondly embraced and kissed. I kept my tears to myself. She went up the gangway with a strong step and waved at the top. I fondly waved back and went to the ambulance that waited till the plane was high in the sky and soon out of sight. On my way home I called on the two children with their aunt at Bayhead. Peggy, the eldest, wanted to know how many days Mammy would be away. I said, "Fourteen, can you count to that?" "Yes." "Well, we must also say our prayers for her every day and night that she will get well soon. Before she left she told me she would be writing home often. I will call to see you every Sunday and when I can on weekdays." Peggy and

Peter were never lonely, as the school their brothers attended was only 50 yards away and the teacher, Miss Beaton, allowed them in to watch any time they wanted with their aunt. Kind Miss Beaton also kept an eye on them so that I had no worries there. I left them there for the empty home.

The fire was out, as I thought it would be. It is never wise to leave a big fire on when leaving a house empty and be away for many hours as much can happen. Calor gas was not here in those days, and dry sticks were kept handy for such occasions. Still it took some time to cook a meal, starting with a cold peat stove. The calor gas, which we now have, would have been a blessing, and I often wonder how I got on then without it. But man is an adaptable creature who can condition himself to almost any situation. We sometimes hear the older generation casting doubt on their younger ones; that they could not stand the hardship they had to endure. I myself don't agree with that kind of thinking, as I feel sure they could and would, like their elders, if they had to.

It was late spring, a busy time on the croft, which kept me from too much brooding and too tired at night to stay awake, thinking what her next letter might convey. I got her first one within a few days. It was short, saying she was not any worse and that she did not have much peace since she arrived, answering questions. "They are round my bed like bees and are going to give me a blood transfusion tomorrow. How are you managing and how are the children? Give them my love and I expect to hear from you soon." The letter was short but not without hope that tomorrow's treatment would be what she needed. I answered that day, telling her that all was well with us and she was not to worry as we were managing fine and praying for her.

After I had posted that letter, the local nurse came out to see me. It was from her that I first understood the nature of Mary Anne's illness. How the white cells in the blood devour the red life giving cells by multiplying beyond control, thus eating the red cells till there is not enough left to maintain. "But surely in a place so well up to date as the Western Infirmary is, they can change that condition?" "Yes" she said "if they can get it in time." "Do you think Mary Ann was in time?" "I cannot tell you, but the doctors in the Western can, and I hope and pray will cure her." "Is it a contagious disease? Could the baby she was carrying when she must have had it take it from her?" "No, because he was manufacturing his own blood. We can only hope that they will discover a cure in time for her."

Since then I have read and heard much about that kind of illness which was unknown to me at that time but known to the nurse, regardless of it being rare. Besides writing at least three times a week I also phoned the hospital on Sundays and whenever I could. At first I would be told 'making progress and responding to treatment'. Hearing that made me very happy. It did not matter how long the treatment took, it was a sure sign to me that they had got her in time. Her own letters did not confirm this and despite blood transfusions, she did not appear to be making any progress.

Although her letters were cheerful, wanting to know everything regarding us, reading between the lines I felt she was beginning to lose hope. Needless to say I too was very unhappy but dare not show any signs of it when the children were around. Those of them that could then read went through her letters, those that could not just fondled them because their mother had written them less than two days ago. We then had a daily mail service, communication with Glasgow was good, and when a hopeful letter came I would feel elated, and the reverse when less cheerful news came. I was working as hard as I could outside on the croft and in the house, washing the children's clothes and mending, baking and cooking and all the other chores that needed doing. I did not give myself time to brood on things that might come. As time went on I was becoming less hopeful, till one day over the phone I was told she was taking nourishment, responding to treatment, and at that moment sitting up in bed writing a letter. I was very happy when I heard this good news. Two days after that I saw the doctor's car stopping at the house. I waited outside for him thinking that he would have more good news for me.

When he came near enough I looked into his face but saw no joy there, and without a smile he said, "Hello Donald." I said, "Hello Doctor I hope you have good news of Mary Ann for me." "Well Donald I am sorry to say I have not, and I am very sorry that it's me that has to give you the bad news." I had to lean hard against the wall of the house to keep standing, with my tears flowing beyond control as I tried to listen to what he was saying, that they had word today from the hospital informing them that she was not making any progress, only worsening, that she had not responded to any treatment, and that they were sending her back as incurable to Daliburgh Hospital. "They are to inform us what day that will be. When we get her to the hospital we will do our best for her." I asked, "Is she near death?" "No" he said, "I don't think so. The report I got is that she will last a while, but how long no one can tell with Leukaemia, for if it is acute it can be sudden. A nurse will be attending her on the ambulance plane and our own ambulance will pick you up at the cross road as before, to meet her at the airport. We will let you know in time what day that will be."

Changing the subject he said, "How are the children?" I said they were all well and happy hearing their mother was getting well and would be home soon. "Now I don't know what will happen when she is gone." "I know it is hard Donald. You have been through a lot in the wars and I know you are capable of looking after them. We shall give you all the help we can." With that he left me with my sorrows and no hope, the ray that I held dear had gone. What was I to do? How was I going to break the news to the children when they came home from school? I could not tell them the truth. I told them their mother was slightly better and was coming back to the hospital here where she could get the same care and be nearer home. We went to bed early that night, as I wanted to get away as soon as possible in the morning. There were no stories that night.

It was a restless, sleepless night for me thinking of what should I do, and before morning I thought it best to ask the advice of my good friend, Father Neil, who had guided me many times and who, incidentally it was our pleasure to name the baby Neil Paul after.

After seeing the children off to school, I was on the point of leaving the house when I heard a car stopping near. I looked out and there was the man I was going to see. I said to myself "This is it, she has died, this is the Priest coming to break the news," I leaned on the wall to brace myself and waited for him to come up. When he did, he looked at me and said, "Were you going somewhere Donald?" "Yes I was, I am afraid I am too late now, you have bad news for me Father?" "No, Donald, not any worse than you already know from the Doctor. I phoned the Western and spoke to the doctor who is treating her. He told me they are sending her back on Friday, the day after tomorrow, and the end will not come, at least not within the next ten days." I said, "I am most grateful to you Father for doing this on my behalf." "It's alright Donald, many a good day you gave me fishing. They will let you know from the hospital here when the ambulance will collect you. I'll try and get them to come out here for you." On that note he left me with my mind more at ease. I went to the house after again thanking him, and put peats on the fire that shortly before I had intended to let go out. All things being taken care of, I stretched myself on the bench to rest and think of what lay ahead. I gave in to much needed sleep.

That evening I got word from the hospital that the ambulance would pick me up at my home at 9.30 a.m. to meet the ambulance plane coming in at 10.30 a.m. That day I got up early, got the children ready for school and away, with all the other chores done before the transport came. When the plane landed, the nurse, a nun, and I walked out to meet her with the stretcher trolley coming behind us. The plane door opened and they gently took her down on a stretcher. I felt a shock go through me when I saw the change in her face, as if this was not my Mary Ann. But it was and I knew it. I could see the effort she made to smile. I held the tears back and said, "How are you my dear?" She said, "Not so good as you can see." "Are you in much pain?" "No, but I feel very weak. It is an effort to talk. How are yourself and the children? You look pale." I said, "We are all well. I feel so sorry that you are not well yourself but we must never lose hope. You will feel much better when you are settled in the hospital here." "I am afraid not, but I will be better there than in Glasgow. Will you take the children up? I want to see them all." "Yes, I will tomorrow." With that she fell asleep. She was in a very poor condition when we reached the hospital. After they had made her comfortable in bed I was allowed to see her but told not to stay long. I found her much better, kissed her and said I would see her tomorrow.

On my way out I saw Mother Leonard and asked her if it would be alright for me to bring the children up to see her tomorrow. "Yes" she said, "I think she will be much brighter then." I got a lift down and called on Morag at Bayhead with my news, and for her to have Peggy and Peter ready for tomorrow's bus, as I was taking them all to see their mother. We got the bus the next day and came off at the Co-op store to buy some fruit and milk chocolate for the children to give to their mother. It would please her although I knew she could not eat any of it. At the door, the sister told me that she was a little brighter that day and was looking forward to seeing us. "I'll take you to the ward now but don't stay too long, it will only tire her as she is very weak."

We went in and found her smiling, sitting in bed with extended arms. The children ran to her and kissed her. I said, "How are you today my dear?" "A little better I think." "That is encouraging, every little helps. I hope there will be an improvement by the end of the week."

"I hope so," she said, "If only it would keep up." We talked for a while; she wanted to know what was doing back home, and how the children were getting on at school. I told her that Archie had passed the eleven plus test and that Alex Iain is expected to pass easily next year. "I am very pleased to hear that and I hope the rest will do as well." The sister gave us all tea and sandwiches, and on our way out she gave Peggy a parcel saying "Share this with your brothers." She nodded to me at the door. It was time for us to leave. I said, "The bus will be here soon, we will have to leave you now." As her mouth was swollen, we all kissed her on her brow and said, "It won't be long before we will be up to see you again." She said, "I don't want you to keep the children off school but come up yourself whenever you can manage."

Sadly that was the last time the children saw her. They were not happy leaving, seeing the way she was. Towards the end of that week I went to see her. She was in a worse condition. I had to lean close to make out what she was trying to say. In that way there was very little said between us. I did not encourage her to talk. At one time she smiled and said, "Will you marry again Donald?" "No, never. I am not capable of loving another woman as I have loved you." "But" she said "for the sake of the children." "Well" I said "if it comes to that I will take care of them for your sake and my own. I have gone through much hardship in life before I met you. If I have to bring them up on my own it will not be as hard, but I have strong hopes and pray it will not come to that and may never do." To that she said, "Ealasaid is fond of the baby and wants to have him to herself. I am willing to give him to her, are you?" "Yes, knowing he will be well brought up, better than I could do." "Then" she said, "that is settled?" "Yes, I will never willingly take him from her" and I may add now, I never did.

I left her that day feeling that she knew the end was not far off. I said I would be up tomorrow and hoped to find her much better. On my way out I met the same sister who said, "I am sorry, Donald dear, she is so low and not showing any sign of improvement. I am afraid she cannot last much longer. She is not now able to hold any food and you must prepare yourself for the worst, it could come any time." I said, "Has she had the Last Rites?" "Yes, they were given to her yesterday." I left then and called on the other two as usual when passing Bayhead. I could not give Morag any hope. I told the children their mother was asking for them and wanting them always to be good, do whatever they were told and to think of her in their prayers. They wanted to know when I would take them to see her again. I said I was not sure as she was very ill and it was best not to disturb her too much.

The next day, Saturday, to keep from constant brooding on what I felt was sure to come in the near future, I began cutting peats near the house where I could keep an eye and make a meal for the three children with me. Towards evening I saw a car coming, which stopped at the house, and soon I saw Father Neil coming up. Before he reached, he called out "Drop everything Donald, you are to come with me." I asked if I should take the children and he said, "No Donald it's best to leave them in the care of someone." Kate, my sister-in-law would look after them. I got dressed and put the fire out, and we all got into the car and stopped at Kate's. I told her that Mary Ann was very low, that I was going to see her and may not be back tonight. Would she look after the children? "Of course, Donald, don't worry about them. I will take care of everything."

We left in a hurry with Father Neil driving fast, concentrating on the road, and when we arrived at the hospital she was fully conscious and able to talk a little to me. The screen was drawn round her bed and I sat beside her watching and, having said all she could, she went into a short sleep. I listened to her short breathing and wished with all my heart that I could help her, but there was nothing I could do.

When she opened her eyes again she seemed brighter and her breath was more controlled. She asked if I was staying up tonight and I said, "Yes, that is what I intend to do." "Well I think it is best for you to stay with Ealasaid tonight, you will see the baby and come in to see me early with the Sunday bus." I said, "Perhaps that is the best thing for me to do as I don't think the Nuns would like me to stay with you much longer." The sister took me to a room where she gave me a good meal. It was a long time since I had one like it and I felt much stronger. I told her that I intended to stay at Lochboisdale for the night and come to see her early in the morning, and she agreed.

On that ray of hope I left her for Lochboisdale, a decision I was to regret for many a day afterwards. Arriving there I told Ealasaid that I left her sleeping, thought she was slightly better and that I would go in early in the morning. The next day I left early to catch a lift, not waiting for the bus. I had only walked a short distance when a woman that I did not know met me. I was going to pass her with a nod but when she stopped I did the same. She looked at me and said, "I am sorry I have bad news for you today. She has died this morning at about 4.00 a.m. They phoned us from the hospital to give you the sad message a little while ago. Please accept our sincere sympathy." Feeling stunned, I think I said thank you and turned back to give her sister the sad news. She was weeping at the door, and having seen me talking to this woman, she had guessed what the news was. I told her the message I had just been given and that I wished I had stayed with her to the last. I will always regret I did not, but that cannot be changed now. Ealasaid said, "She has been suffering for a long time with no hope of getting better. She knew that herself when she was in the Western, and told me in a letter not to tell you. We should be grateful she is now at peace and will not suffer anymore."

I had a look at Neil Paul, content in his cot, and Ealasaid said, "I am fond of him and would like to have him to myself. Did Mary Ann say anything to you about that?" "Yes she did. She told me she wanted you to have him if I was willing, which I am, and I know that this is the best place for him." I had a dram in the house that helped to steady me going back to the hospital. where I was met by the same sister at the door, who came with me to the mortuary where my Mary Ann lay looking calm, with a faint smile on as if she was still alive. I kissed her brow, we said a silent prayer, and the sister left me with my thoughts, beginning from the day I had first met her, the five years the war had kept us apart, the short twelve years of happy married life we had together, the treasure of the children being born and growing in the best of health, and the joy and hardship of setting up a home, short of everything but food. When the sister came back we prayed for a short while before retuning to the hospital, where I was given a good meal. Shortly afterwards, Father Neil arrived and we spoke about arrangements for the funeral and for her burial. and after he gave me a lift to Bayhead. I asked Father Neil if the children should go to the funeral but he said, "No Donald, it is best for them to retain the memory they have of their mother as she was when alive. Send them all to school. Tell Miss Beaton to keep an eye on them."

The two children met me and had already heard the sad news as their aunt had been to morning mass where it had been announced. Both her and Peter began wiping the tears away. I told them their mother said they were not to cry, that it would make them and her unhappy. "The best thing to do is to remember her in your prayers always, and now dry your faces and we will go inside." Kate and the other children had also been at Mass and knew of their mother's death. After a cup of tea there I left to face the other three at Kate's, where I found them very sad but not crying. They asked many questions and also could they go to the funeral, but I told them it was better to remember their mother as they had known her, and that almost her last words to me were "That she was sending you her fond love, to remember her in your prayers, be good always and do your best in everything you do."

I told Kate of the funeral arrangements and I said, "Well, I better go home now and take them with me," although I thought 'it's not a home any longer only a place to take shelter'. Kate said, "Why don't you leave the children here tonight?" "That is very kind of you Kate but we have to face it and we may as well begin now. It is not as if their mother had only left home yesterday." I called to the boys it was time to go home. Near the house the youngest broke down, sat beside a rock and began to cry his heart out. There was nothing I could do to comfort him. I left him there, as it was only a few yards from the house. I began to build the fire and told the other two to bring water and peats in for the night. When I went out to persuade the other to come home, he was gone. I called out for him but there was no answer. I found him some 300 yards away behind a large rock still crying softly, but once I promised to buy him a football, he took my hand and we walked home.

Home was a gloomy place that night, hardly any talking, each with his own thoughts. I know mine were on the future. Could I manage to rear them and keep them together? Since their mother left home I was able to look after them. But then there were strong hopes of her coming home well, but that hope was gone. I would face the problems as they arose and do my best. The nights were short then, in the middle of June, and I could not sleep for thinking of all I had to do. I was short of money at that point and decided to ask Ealasaid for a loan till two of the cattle I had were sold. I would get someone to take them to the sale as it was to be held on the day of the funeral. I would also need to call at the Co-op to arrange for biscuits and cheese to be handed out at the funeral, a custom in those days.

I got the children up and ready for school and told them to wait at Kate's if I was not back in time. I milked the two cows, dressed and was leaving, when Angus James came across in his small boat. After expressing his sympathy, he said, "Is there any way I can help you Donald?" I told him I was about to leave, to arrange for the coffin to be taken to the church and to make arrangements for the funeral. Angus James was my best friend and wise councillor in whom I had great trust. He said, "Allan, my son, will be with you taking the remains to the church, and between us we will take your cattle and our own to the sale tomorrow."

I left and caught that bus, got off at the Co-op and arranged for the customary biscuits and cheese for the funeral, then carried on out to Ealasaid, then living in Kenneth Drive. She gave me the usual welcome and said, "Are you up to arrange the funeral?" I told her I was and if possible could she loan me some money for the funeral expenses until I sold my cattle, when I would repay her. She willingly gave me the money and we talked of many things, especially of the future and the children. Kenny, who had agreed to pick up the coffin with his van, soon arrived with Allan. We drove to the hospital mortuary, collected the coffin, and arrived at the church door at the appointed time. Father Neil was there to receive and bless the coffin. Kenny and Allan lifted the coffin and walked with it up the aisle following the Priest. It was put on a rest before the altar and three candles on each side were lit. Short prayers were said and the coffin was left there overnight. Kenny then ran us home and I called at Kate's, thinking the children may still be there. They were not, and the house was empty. I knew she had taken them home, and when I arrived they were all sitting at a meal which Kate had prepared. It was time for mine to get washed, say prayers and prepare for bed. They already knew that they were not going to the funeral tomorrow. They seemed more cheerful than the night before so I did not discourage them. While I myself, if I tried to laugh, I felt something inside me would tear apart.

I got up early to make breakfast, woke the children, and got them ready for school. They did not object going there on their Mother's funeral day. To some it may have seemed harsh or heartless for me to send them that day. Indeed I felt that way myself, but even without the good advice I got, I could not see any other way. I told them when leaving, to give a hand with the cows and to remind Kate to milk them.

Waiting for the bus I tidied the house, anything to keep me from brooding. I found the black tie that Ealasaid gave me and dressed myself. The bus came as I put out the fire, and, as I expected, there were only a few in it, the rest would be at the sale. We did pick up some people on our way and arrived at the church in good time. I walked up to the coffin and knelt beside it. I tried to keep from weeping but the tears kept coming out of control. After the Mass the Priest stood at the foot of the coffin and recited the last prayers, then four men lifted the coffin and carried it down the aisle, with the Priest in front and me following close behind. At the door, others relieved the bearers and placed it in the bus to be taken as near to the cemetery as the bus could get. There, the coffin was placed on a bier and taken up by six pallbearers, who were the nearest relations. That was the custom. If a long distance to the grave, they were relieved by another six men, who laid the coffin down beside the open grave.

At the foot stood three priests, the one performing the ceremony sprinkled Holy Water on the coffin and in the grave. The coffin was lowered into the grave, a spade of sand was handed to the Priest who sprinkled it over the coffin, and then the other priests did the same. I followed, and then the relations and anyone who wished took a handful of sand and spread it on the coffin. When that was done, everyone helped to fill in the grave, as was the custom, and the top turf was replaced. I stood beside the grave, tears of grief flowing uncontrollably.

When the work on the grave was done, the Priest and people knelt around it and offered short prayers. That over, the people left for home, passing through the gate where two or three women were standing with large trays laden with biscuits and cheese, and each person took what he wanted. It was an affront not to take any. That snack was eaten on their way to their transport, or put in their pockets for later. I was the last to go through the gate, Ealasaid was there and we took some biscuits and cheese. She said, "Donald, there are some left over, you better take them with you for the children. I will pack and take them to the bus for you."

Angus James made it to the Funeral Mass, as he did not wait at the sale to see his cattle sold. We heard that it was a good sale, with hardly any taken back. When we arrived at Bayhead the school children were out at play. I told the driver to stop the bus and called the children over. I gave Archie the eldest the package to share among all the children. Kate as usual had a meal ready for us coming back from the funeral, and after everyone had left, I stayed for a while talking to her and reminiscing about the good times. There was some whisky left in the bottle so I called on Seonaidh with a dram. "This" he said "is a sad day for you Donald. No one could wish for a better wife than Mary Ann," and after sharing a dram I left for home.

When I came in view of the house I realised, when at that spot, seeing Mary Ann and the children waiting at the house end, the many times I said to myself, 'there is nothing on earth I would exchange for this'. I think at that time I was as happy as one was capable of, now a cold cheerless house awaited me. I resolved, as far as possible, to act like a man and do my duty as I saw it. I began making a fire and preparing the children's meal for them, coming home from

287

school. I would walk in the road to meet them, and not depend on them calling on Kate, who had her own to look after. Walking in I met Allan coming to me with the money from the sale. "Well" I said, "you have sold them anyway." "Yes, I got a good price for them." I said, "You must be a good salesman." "No, it was not me but those who were keeping the bidding up. The salesman announced who they belonged to at the start and the reason he wanted a good price. I am sure that helped, and I also got a good price for my own which will please my father."

I met the children coming from school, and when we got home I gave them all a small chore to do until I had the meal ready. Of the funeral they only asked if there were any young children there. I was surprised they did not show as much sorrow as I expected, but that was to come later when the shock sank in. I was greatly alarmed, watching that effect, and blamed myself for not preparing them for what was sure to come very soon, instead of pretending that their mother would be home shortly. The result of that shock was frequent shaking of the heads. When I asked "Why" they would or could not tell me, so I treated them with care and patience as best as I could.

There were weeks like that, but slowly things began to improve, and thankfully it ceased and they in time were back to normal. It did not affect the two at Bayhead, I think, because their aunt was always there to talk to them. Next day I sent the children to school as usual, while I went south to pay the funeral bill with the money I got from the sale. When I was paying Ealasaid for the loan I got from her, she did not want to take it, saying "Your need it more than I do" but seeing that it was in connection with the funeral, I insisted that she take it. I called at Bayhead with some sweets and fruit for the children, and I was also able to buy the promised football for John Joseph. It was only a small one, and when I saw the pleasure he got out of it, I thought it was money well spent. That evening the children came home straight from school, knowing there would be something new waiting. There were new sandshoes for all, and the ball for John Joseph, but not a word was spoken about their mother. Inwardly I felt angry, imagining they had forgotten her already, but when finding one weeping and crying quietly on his own, I knew the forgetting part was my own imagination, it was far easier for me to bear my grief.

That week passed without peace of mind for me, and I could not relax, with very little sleep. I felt that perhaps if I went up to see her grave I would feel better. At least for a while I would be nearer. I did that the following week, and kneeling beside it, instead of praying, I began thinking as if I was not aware of where I was. At that moment I felt as if someone was saying, "What are you doing here? There is nothing here for you, go home and look after the children." I don't want to give the impression here that I saw anything, but the grave and I did not hear a word, as all were only my own thoughts. However the effect it had on me was instant, like a heavy load being lifted off my shoulders. My stay beside the grave was much shorter than first intended, and after a short visit to the many graves that I knew, I walked out of the graveyard a very different man, like the sun shining after a rainy day. I wondered if I would have felt the same way if I had stayed at home, but whatever the reason, I was sure I was a changed person. After that day I even found pleasure doing things in the house, and if I was inclined to do a shoddy job, the thought would come to me, "Is this the way Mary Ann would do things." I would try to do my best no matter how hard.

That week I got a letter from the Assistance Office in Stornoway, expressing sympathy and stating that a death grant would be sent and I would get a new rate of allowance for myself and the children. I got a pound each for Peggy and Peter, who were boarded out at Bayhead, and was allowed eight shillings for the baby, all of which was handed over to Ealasaid and Morag. For the three at home and myself, I was getting a little short of four pounds weekly. The family allowance was included in that, and even when things were cheaper it would require a good housekeeper to make ends meet. I was not one of those but I was learning fast. My sister Sarah in Oban wanted to take my daughter, as she had five sons and no girls, but I would not part with her. Word went round that I was giving the children away, and those who believed that lie approached me in the hope of getting one or two. When told that the thought never entered my mind, they were somewhat disappointed and suggested that they should find out who was spreading the rumour. Aunt Morag agreed to continue to care for Peggy and Peter for a while. I called on them every Sunday and paid the two pounds. There were times when, unknown to her husband Neil, Morag would only take one. and I appreciated that kindness very much.

When Peggy was nearing school age, the old lady, Mor Ruadh, who did the school cleaning, spoke to me and said, "Donald, why don't you take your daughter home with you?" I said, "I would if I was sure I could look after her properly." "Of course you can, you are managing the rest as well as any woman could. At her age she is not any different, take her home with you and she will soon be of much help to you." I thought about it that night. The more I thought, the more confident I got that I could do it. I made up my mind to ask her the next day but would leave the choice to her. I found her playing outside and said to her, "Peggy, how would you like to come home to stay?" She asked, "All the time?" "Yes." "I would like that very much, that is what I wanted to do since mammy died but they would not let me." I said, "I cannot take you both now. Will Peter be lonely without you?" "No, he has John Alex to play with." John Alex was Aunt Morag's young son.

I spoke to her aunt, who said that Peggy was able to take care of herself and she would not try to stop her. I said I would like to leave Peter with her, as he was only two, and she said, "Leave him as long as you want, John Alex is very fond of him. He would be greatly upset if he was to leave now, they are good pals and he will look after him." "Well, that's settled. You better get your clothes together Peggy, and we will leave to prepare the school meal. I am sure your aunt has taught you a lot about cooking?" "No" her aunt said "She would not stay long enough in the house to be taught anything, she should have been a boy, you'll see." I did not regret taking Peggy home for she could do many useful small chores in the house. The only problem, at five years of age, I could not risk leaving her alone in the house while I worked on the croft, and the rest were at school. She would happily play outside with Scot the dog, and very seldom took a slight cold.

Archie, the eldest, who had passed his eleven plus test, was in the academic class at Daliburgh High School, so I had to find lodgings for him nearby. For that I was granted an educational allowance, and I thought that would be one mouth less to feed on my assistance. Shortly, the Area Officer came to enquire why I had not reported that one of the family had left the household, was now in school lodging, and I was drawing allowance in respect of him. I pleaded ignorance saying, "The money I was getting in respect of him, I posted to the person he was lodging with, and thought the Education Office would report this matter to Stornoway." He replied in anger, "The Director of Education has nothing to do with this. Your present allowance has to be reduced, and what you have drawn unlawfully will be deducted at so much from each payment. You will be notified of the amount." When he was leaving, he saw Peggy in the house and asked whether she was one of the children staying in Bayhead. When I told him she was now staying with me, he asked whether I had notified Stornoway, and as I had not, he warned me that I was obliged to report any change in the household, and that my money would be cut further. I said, "I am aware that it is impossible to feed and clothe my family on the small assistance I am allowed, to reduce it further will mean much hardship and near starvation for us." He said, "It's not me that is responsible for your allowance, my duty is to report on your position from time to time" and with that, he noted my circumstances, which I had to sign. When the result came it was worse than I expected. Nowhere did it show what I was getting for each child or myself, and my income from the croft was greatly exaggerated. I would be much better off without it, and the only reason I kept two cows was to provide milk for the children, which they would not otherwise get. I appealed against this cut but, like others, it was turned down.

Family photograph, 1955

One thing they couldn't do was to cut me from the bounty of the sea, which I made good use of, as meat, except sometimes corned beef, was prohibitive. I was well used to that stuff in the war years, and somewhere I read there is more nutrition in it than in most butcher meat, and the children liked it. It was easy to make a satisfying meal mixed with mashed potatoes, a ground onion, and a small portion of margarine, all taken with a mug of milk. When milk was plentiful, at night I made carrageen, a type of seaweed found at low tide which, when added to rennet essence, sets into a milky pudding. With practice I became good at making this and all enjoyed it. There was always plenty of fresh and salted fish, besides a good garden, so feeding them was no great problem. But to clothe them was. I was forever patching, sewing and darning. When at sea and in the army, in my spare time I learned to darn, but now as the holes got so large I could only patch them, and while they looked odd but warmer than bare skin, there were no complaints. No doubt at school there would be giggles and perhaps fights.

Peggy was not long at home before she made herself very useful. One day she said, if she could reach the table on which the baking board rested, she would make scones. I said, "Do you know how?" "Yes, I often watched Aunt Morag doing that." "Well, if you want to try, I will make a stool high enough for you to stand on and I will watch over you, a beginner is never perfect at anything." I made the stool about a foot high and showed her how to make the scones. I told her I would attend to the fire and oven, and made her promise she would not do anything with the fire when I was not in the house. She promised and always made a fairly good job. When she tried to milk a very tame cow we had, the cow would stretch her neck to reach and lick Peggy's head, perhaps thinking this was her own calf. However, she would not give any milk and I thought it was because Peggy's hands were not yet strong enough to milk. I remembered the sore time I had learning on the Canadian farm. My only problem with Peggy was that I had to take her with me, even if I left the house for a short time, when the others were at school. That meant her often being out fishing, which she greatly enjoyed and soon caught on till, instead of a hindrance, she was a good help. We would only go out as far as the narrows, as in those days fish were always plentiful; codlings, whiting, lythe and saith, and when we caught enough of those we made for home to gut and clean them, ready to fry or boil for ourselves and them coming home. What was left over we salted for days we could not go out. Time was going past and my sadness was beginning to ease, but I was not yet able to laugh heartily at anything, no matter how funny. If I made the effort the pain inside stopped me. I wondered if I was always to be like this.

Peggy with family friend, Nurse Keeton

In spite of my constant patching, the boys were in need of clothing which I could not provide. Peggy had, in fact, more than she needed, as Ealasaid and Sarah, her aunts, saw to that. I made an appeal for clothing for the boys, and a woman came from some welfare department on a Saturday, and all were at home. She said I was getting all I was entitled to. I said if I was, there would not be so much patching. She asked if that was their best clothing they had on, and when I told her it was, and I couldn't send them to school much longer in those rags, she said she would recommend them for a new issue. She also asked about Peggy, but I told her she was not in need at that moment. She was as good as her word, only, when the goods arrived, three pairs of trousers and three jerseys, they would barely fit the youngest as they were far too small. I was on the point of returning the lot, when Jordan, the Irish packman who sometimes came round, exchanged them for larger sizes for a small sum. They were of better quality than hers, so all had new trousers and jerseys, and the needle and I got a rest, but not for too long as trousers don't last boys that long.

Alex Iain passed his eleven plus test and, like Archie, before going into school lodgings, a new rigout had to be found for him. I had sold one beast at the previous sale, and after fitting him out there was little left for other needy things. When he went into lodgings my allowance was again reduced, as another person had left the household. At that time the Assistance Office, knowing my position that I would be drawing their allowance for a long time unless I was forced to accept employment, wrote to me suggesting, or requesting me, to write to the Oban Employment Exchange for a householder's form, which stated that I was eligible and looking for work. My employment card would be franked while idle, and I would be entitled to draw employment benefit when I had the required number of franked stamps. I wrote back saying that I was not in a position to take any employment until my young family were old enough to look after themselves, and that I was against signing a false statement. I got their reply by return post, stating that if I did not comply with their request, my assistance allowance would be cut off as from the next payment. That was the last straw but, come what may, I would not desert or neglect my young family. I wrote to the Exchange manager in Oban, enclosing this threatening letter along with my own, explaining my position. I got a reply within the week that my case was referred back to Stornoway. I got my allowance as usual, and no reduction, but they were not by far finished.

At that time there was plenty of work going in connection with the army and rocket range. They were informed that my children's aunt lived beside the school, that I could obtain work at the range, send the children to school at the usual time, and then go to work and collect them at the school, or their aunt's house, on my way home. I wrote back to tell them that such a scheme was impossible to comply with, and no sane person would try in the existing conditions. If they had been properly made aware of these, then I was ready to face any court of law to defend my position in regards to my children. I explained, to the best of my ability, what this madness meant to the children and myself, and in a short time I received a letter to inform me that I had to present myself on a certain date before a tribunal court in Stornoway. Although, without flying, it was awkward to get there for that date, I thought I would get a better hearing and decided to attend. I found someone who would look after the children and cattle, and was ready to go the next day, when I got a wire to go to the nearest phone box and phone this number and ask for this name. I did all of that, and on speaking to a man was told my case had now been fully investigated and there was no need for me to attend. I was glad of that, as it meant a waste of time and much expense which I could not pay, and as a result I received a pound Postal Order which more than covered my time. I was let off the hook for a spell. The Area Officer did not call so often.

Peggy had begun to attend school, and I was alone and free to work on the harvest nearly all day, besides I could go on errands. The corn was in small stacks ready to be taken to the stackyard. To make a weatherproof stack needs more than one person, but one fine, sunny Monday morning I decided to try it alone, and carried what would make a large stack to the yard and began the stack. The bottom part was easy and I had it up to about two feet when I saw John Alex, without asking, coming to help me. I was mighty glad to see him. We carried on and were making progress when I saw a white car coming, which reminded me that I had an appointment that day and this was Father Roderick Macdonald coming for me. He parked his car near the house and came to where we were working and remarked that we were busy. I said I was sorry that I had forgotten about the appointment. He said, "Don't let it worry you, I don't think they will ever make a weaver out of you."

He began putting the sheaves in their place and I said, "It's a very strange world, this morning. Not expecting any help, I decided to try to make a corn stack on my own. Shortly after I had started I saw John Alex coming to help me," and then Father Roderick said, "You saw another fool coming." The way he said it must have loosened a chord inside me, that for a long time was till now idle. It made me laugh so heartily that I stretched on the ground unable to stop. They thought there was something far wrong with me, as no simple joke could have caused so much laughter. When the laughter and the pain it caused eased, I was able to stand up and lean against the stack. When asked if I was 'quite well?' I said yes and then explained why I could not stop laughing once I got started, given it was so long since I had been able to laugh. After that I could laugh without pain, whereas before I could only smile.

Weaving had for some time been going on at Gerinish where, after three weeks' training, one was allowed to take a loom home and work there. They supplied the yarn and collected the finished cloth. For some time, since those last efforts to get me off the assistance failed, they were now trying to force me to take up weaving. I was inclined to agree, since hopefully I would earn enough at home to get my off any assistance. That was the appointment that Father Roddy was to take me, to see the weavers about my fitness for training. However, I did go that week, but although the manager was not in, I saw many working on the looms and was told that is was very dangerous where there are young children around. No young child should tamper with the loom as they could lose a finger or a hand, and when not working it should always be under lock and key. There were many empty looms there as business was not what it used to be, and their supply of yarn had been cut. I was told they couldn't see a beginner making a living at it, and that I would be better off on the assistance. I then saw the manager, who explained that my position made it impossible for him to employ me, or consider letting me have a loom to work at home. He wrote to them in this regard, and I heard no more and was left alone with no reduction in assistance money.

Peter was still staying with his aunt and was soon to begin attending school. His aunt did not want to be responsible for him any longer, as he was like every child of five, sometimes up to mischief. Morag's husband Neil, a nice, kind man, was for years a foot postman. However when he learned to drive he was given a red van, and would often pick up Peter playing on the road while making his deliveries. Peter enjoyed these rides and took advantage of Neil, until one day he was nearly struck by the van, causing it to swerve and end up in the ditch. For this reason we decided Peter was old enough to join the rest of us, so I went to Bayhead and asked Peter if he would like to come home with the rest. He was happy with that which meant that, apart from Neil Paul in Lochboisdale, the children were now together.

Although he missed his joy rides with Neil, it was not a hard task to look after him while the rest were at school, and not long after I was let off that hook, as Peter started school. It was about that time the district nurse came to see me and told me that I was granted a home help, three hours a day, six days a week, as soon as someone was found to do it. I said, "On my present allowance I could not pay her." "You don't have to pay anything, deserving cases like yours on low income don't have to pay for this service. I will call on Kate, your sister-in-law, and ask her to take it on." Kate took it and I was free to do more work on the croft, my allowance was reduced on that account, nevertheless it was good to get away from housework.

Kate had no children of her own, but had three boarded out children paid for by the Glasgow Corporation, at that time aged between 7 and 10, the youngest being brother and sister. Having been partly reared near our house, the children got on well together, and I was beginning to feel the joy of living with much less care on my shoulders. Archie and Alex Iain were doing very well in high school with John Joseph soon to follow. The family was getting the name of being good scholars and their attendance at primary school was good.

As a result of the building of the Rocket Range in Benbecula, we daily heard and read that Germany was sending troops to the island of South Uist, to be trained in rocket firing, which aroused much animosity as the war was not yet forgotten. Panorama was doing a TV documentary on how the islanders felt about it. There were many who had reasons to be bitter. A crowd was selected to air and record their views for and against such a prospect, and I was one of those to be interviewed. I was advised of the day for the interview and I wondered what I, a mere nobody, could say in this matter that so many were against. I thought to myself that I should tell the truth on how I felt, regardless of what other people said or thought.

It was very windy the day they came. The three large cars and a crowd of men stopped a few yards below the house and began pouring out and snooping around. At least that's what I thought. It made me very angry that they did not come straight to the house, instead of looking around the croft, especially as they did not ask permission to wander about private property as they liked. The children were at school and soon it would be time to be getting their dinner ready.

I was standing at the door, and no one came to speak to me until at last a man came over. He did not introduce himself, or offer his hand, and I did not offer mine. He said, "We are the recording party, just looking around in search of the best place where we can get the best view. You are, I believe, Donald MacDonald, who we are to interview." I said, "I believe so. I hope you have found the best place for setting your machine." He said, "We have decided now to place the recording machine on the road." Seeing the mood I was in was why I think he asked if I had any objection to this interview, to which I said, "None whatever." With that we all moved down to the road where their recording machine, on a tripod, was set up. The interviewer asked if I was Donald MacDonald and had I lived here all my life. I told him "No," that I had been to the mainland and other places, and I was in the 1914 war from start to finish and for a spell at sea in the last war." He asked whether I had been wounded at any time and I said, "Yes, three times, 1914, 1916 and 1918." He asked if I was up against and saw many Germans, and if so, how did I feel about German soldiers coming to the island for training? I said, "I have nothing against them coming here, or as a nation, and after the 1914 war I worked and stayed with many of them, making good friends and comparing battles in which we fought."

I continued by saying, "Now that they are on our side, I think they should be trained in modern weapons like all our own service men, otherwise we lose their good fighting qualities." He then asked, "Do you not hate them for the pain they have made you endure?" to which I replied, "No, I may have caused much more to them." He continued, "I have been told your wife died and now you are bringing up a large family out here on your own. How do you manage? Do you find that easy?" "No indeed I don't. It's hard enough with both parents looking after them, but alone one can only do his best as nothing holds time back. I think in the circumstances they are growing well, although lacking in many things other children have."

The day was cold and wild, and at that point the interview ended, and they packed up their gear and departed in their cars. Less than a week later the whole thing was shown on the *Panorama* programme and my sisters, who were nuns in Newport, Wales, saw it on television. Others, who had television, also saw it, including Sir Walter Pollen, my dear friend, who was not a native of the island although he very much liked visiting. Of this charming man I shall have more to say when I come to that period of my life, although he eventually told me that he saw the picture and thought I had done very well. He had people enquiring who I was, and that I was the best speaker giving the right reasons why the Germans should be allowed to train here, and that my experience of them as a nation seemed to allay some of the animosity against them coming here. "You know" he said, "many on that programme were against them coming here, and did not like the way that you spoke, but could not deny your experience." For that short service I got a cheque for six pounds, and a later repeat for three pounds, a very handsome sum to me in those days.

For those attending high school at Daliburgh, lodging allowance did not begin till October until April. Before that they had to walk the three miles to the school bus. Seeing they had to carry a heavy weight of homework books, I applied for a grant to buy bicycles. This was granted, and although second-hand and hard to keep in repair, they were much appreciated and time saving. When all the children were at home it was always hard to make ends meet, which meant more work when the weather was rough and no fishing.

One incident I will never forget. There was only a little meal and some potatoes left when, towards evening, there was some appearance of herring in the loch in front of the house. With Archie's help, now in his teens, I thought I could manage to set a net. We used the small rowing boat, as there had been no fuel available for the large boat for some time. However, after hard rowing, we got to where to shoot the net, and it was easy coming back. I made him promise not to tell any of the others that we had set a net, and that the two of us would lift it at dawn. I would wake him before them, and he was to be very careful not to wake the rest. After a short story we all went to bed early. I put the alarm on for long before dawn, made a cup of tea and woke Archie. Archie was sleeping with Alex Iain but managed not to wake him. After the tea, on the point of leaving, someone was coming downstairs. This was Alex Iain and he was dressed. I said, "Any of the rest awake?" "No." If there were, I would wait till daylight. "Well, get a cup of tea and make no noise, you can come with us."

We left, and I stood at the door listening to any sound from the rest. All was quiet. The first two were ahead of me at the boat. Before we got in we heard a cough and cry "Wait for me." This was John Joseph. I said, "Are the other two asleep?" "Yes, fast asleep." "Alright, we'll take you, but you must stay quiet in the boat." We all got in. It was then getting partly light and the wind had gone down a lot. A short distance from the shore we heard a cry, "Wait for me, come back." I knew it was Peter. I backed the boat in. "Is Peggy with you?" "No, I left her sleeping." "Are you sure?" "Yes." "Well if you promise that you will stay seated in the boat where I tell you, we will allow you to come." Peter was eager to promise, but keeping it was another thing.

We had got further from the shore this time when we heard the dog barking and someone crying. This would be Peggy. What was I going to do? Leave her to cry on the shore where the risk of her being frightened could be dangerous, perhaps more than over-loading the boat. To quieten her down I said, "What's been keeping you Peggy? Peter thought you did not want to come with us." "He knew well but did not want to wait for me." I said, "It is now daylight. Would you rather stay here with Scot till we come back than risk going in the boat? I am afraid I can't take you. The boat will be overloaded when we take in the net and any herring we may catch. Hearing this Peggy began to cry. I said, "Alright, stop crying I'll take you." She did and scrambled on board. Scot stood barking. He usually was the first to jump aboard. This time, seeing he was to be left behind after I had shoved the boat off, he made a long leap to the boat and fortunately for us he did not quite make it. We rowed fast. He made for a rock and stayed there.

We rowed to the net, and I think it was the only time that I have ever hoped there was little or no fish in it. Before hauling the net in I told everyone where to sit, and to lean to the opposite side from where I was taking the net on board, and all would be safe. When the first few yards came near the surface I could see many heads and bits of herring in the net. I knew well what had done that. I did not say anything, although I could see many whole ones also coming up. When these were nearly onboard, the children made a dive to that side. Before I had time to let go the net and jump to the other side, the boat had leaned over with water coming in, and was near capsizing. Two of them came over to my side, and despite the water she took in the boat slowly came back to an even keel. I told them not to be afraid, and to sit in the centre while we got her baled out. We had about six inches of free board. The sea was flat calm and we were safe as long as that balance was held. I raised the stern platform to allow baling. Archie did that with a large bucket till he had her near dry, and then I began taking in the net. This time there was no need to tell them what to do. I hauled in a large dogfish, which was tangled in the net and had done much damage. I told them not to touch it, as it was still alive.

Fr Roddy and Donald out fishing

Back at the jetty Scot was waiting for us, regardless of leaving him on the rock to sink or swim. He always gave us a great welcome, fish or no fish. When we touched the shore I told them all to go home and get the fire going, and to make sure the chimney did not go on fire. I would be up with the gutted fish after cleaning the net and getting rid of the dogfish. We had

297

breakfast of fresh herring split and dipped in oatmeal, tea and scones, and those who wanted went back to bed. Our catch of good herring was almost half a fish box. The rest was thrown away on account of the damage done by the dogfish. Had we been out before daylight, much more would have been in the net, besides what the dogfish ate. In our case we were lucky that only a little was left. Regardless of the near mishap, they were all keen to be out in the boat again, but certainly not in those conditions. When I shot a net no one was allowed to come with me, they had learned their lesson.

Most Sundays after Mass, if the weather was suitable, I would take them all out in the boat, and after catching all the fish we needed, we would go ashore at Bolum, it was their favourite place when they were young. While I cleaned the fish, they gathered dry wood and soon we would have a good fire going. When we had our fill of fish, tea and scones, we would head back for home with some more fishing on our way. These days were very enjoyable, and did not cost anything. We were also able to give a fry to the neighbours. Besides teaching them to fish with mackerel gut, they would also take turns at rowing, with the older ones soon learning how to handle a boat. If out on these joy trips, when whales and sharks came too near, I always made for the shore, taking no chances when the children were with me.

It was about this time that the school at Bayhead closed due to the shortage of pupils, and the few remaining children were transferred to Kildonan School, a distance of nearly six miles from us. The children were then made to walk almost the same distance as they did to Bayhead, and from there a car took them to Kildonan. The one good thing in connection with that school was that the children were provided with a good dinner. Mine were happy there and doing well. and when they were given homework I was very strict in making sure they always finished it before being allowed out to play.

While they were all still at school, the alginate seaweed factory on the Island was keen to get as much seaweed as they could handle. Strong boys during school holidays always wanted to earn a little money and mine were no different. I bought them forks and cutters and they teamed up with nearby boys. I was to tow their day's cutting to the south side of the loch where it could be loaded into a lorry and taken to the factory. Things worked fairly well the first few days, although I was busy at the hay and couldn't stay with them for long. For those few days' work they cut about six tons. My boys offered to give me half of the money from their share. I said, "No, all the money you earn is your own, but don't spend it on useless things. You need clothing and footwear. Attend to that first, and the rest you can keep as pocket money. You know it is impossible, on the assistance I am getting, to provide better things for you." Next spring tide Archie and Alex Iain decided to work on their own, and at first it was suggested that all the weed would be sent up to the factory in my name, and that I would share the money with the cutters when I got the cheque. I would have nothing to do with that plan, and I was to be glad of that decision later on. Before the next spring tide John Alex, their cousin, an old hand at seaweed cutting, began cutting with my boys. I used to give them a hand when working near the house as I had the other three to look after and cook for.

One day when I was going home to make the dinner, the Area Officer arrived in his car, I was in a muddy state, and there was no hiding that I was working at the seaweed. I told him I was helping John Alex. He said it did not matter who I was helping, as long as I reported the money I was making to Stornoway. "Have you done that?" "No, we have only worked at it for three tides and we did not get it all away. We don't know how much was made, and until then I

298

cannot report to Stornoway. I am entitled to claim expenses, and, as you know, the gear needed to do that job is not cheap. The younger children at home must be looked after and fed, and until I find out what was made, reporting to Stornoway would only be guess work." "All right," he said, "When you do find out you must let Stornoway know." I said I would and fully intended to.

Shortly after we sent that seaweed up to the factory, the manager of the factory came to see me and told me that the Area Officer for the Assistance had been to see him, and wanted to know how much money the factory had paid me. I told him I could not give that information without written consent from you. I just came to warn you they are after you." I told him I would give that written consent, but he would not find my name anywhere on his books. The seaweed we cut has always been sent to the factory in John Alex's name, and as he is not on the Assistance he doesn't have to give the Area Officer any information in this matter." "Well Donald, in that case he will never find out, but I think you should tell John Alex what to say should they call to enquire." I did that.

In a few days the Area Officer came back. He wanted my permission to see the pay books in the factory. I said I would happily give that permission, and that made him appear happy as much as to say, "Now I've got you." He wrote down who I was, and that he had my consent to enquire into any money the company had paid me in connection with seaweed cutting. He read them out and asked if I understood everything. When I signed he looked very pleased and said, "This will settle things, you will hear from us soon." He left in a good mood; I had a chuckle to myself, and thought it would be some time before he came pestering me again. I was wrong. He came back the next day, very angry that he did not find my name in the factory books. I said that I had never suggested it was, and I had told him I was only helping John Alex, and the children were also helping him. He could call on him to check that out. "Although he is not obliged to tell you how that money is to be shared out."

After I had put John Alex in the picture, I wrote to the Assistance Office in Stornoway, putting my side of the story and saying what I had earned. Less than a week later, when school had begun, one afternoon a car stopped at the house driven by the Area Officer. Two men got out. When I saw the driver I said to myself 'more trouble'. The two came to the house and they said they were from the Assistance Office, Stornoway. They explained that they were not quite satisfied with the report I had sent them. It did not tally with the information they got from the Area officer. "Well" I said "To the best of my knowledge my report was correct," and I gave them a full report of all that had happened between me and the Area Officer, and they thought about it for a short while and then said "Well, after we take all into consideration, you may hear from us." As they were leaving they saw the children coming home from school, and saw that they were all in need of clothing. I told them that I had promised the children any money they earned at the seaweed would go towards buying them new clothes. I thought they were in a better mood when they left, and I was kept on the same allowance, with no reduction, regardless of the efforts the Area Officer had made, several times here and to the factory, seeking the information that would prove me guilty. That local Area Officer appeared to me a very hard man, as he was well aware of my circumstances, and yet he continued to check on me at every turn. Perhaps that was his way, as I was not the only one in need to suffer as a result of his dedication to his job.

As it happened, I was not finished with the Assistance and that Area Officer as, when nearing retirement age, I was granted a reduced pension because I did not have enough employment stamps. I wrote back, saying I was refusing the offered reduced retirement pension, on the grounds that it was impossible to take employment while I was on my own, and looking after my five young motherless children, and for that reason I was short of these stamps. I felt because of that I was entitled to a full old age pension. I was then called to a tribunal at Lochboisdale School, when the Area Officer began reading what the Tribunal was all about. I was told that, by signing a form, my present allowance would not be reduced; that I would be on supplementary pension, getting the same money as a full retirement pension, and when that was increased, the supplement would also increase. With that kind of persuasive talk, I was inclined to think that I would not be worse off by signing this document, not understanding that I was being led up the garden path by those false promises. For every time there was a rise in retirement pension, I got that rise but not any rise in supplementary. I was, therefore, worse off than when on the Assistance, till the Social Security Act was passed, and I got some of what was due to me back.

For some time past I was suffering from bleeding stomach ulcers, for which the doctor many times advised me to go to hospital. I refused because it meant scattering the children, and relied on baking soda for relief. My sister Sarah was staying with us for two weeks' holidays at the time, and after seeing the amount of baking soda I was consuming every day, she strongly advised me to see the Doctor. He was sure to give me something better, and she would look after things for a while. I did go, but on the way there I took a painful turn, and was obliged to ask him for something to ease my almost unbearable pain. He did, and I felt better. When he again examined me, he said he would not be doing his duty if he allowed me home in the condition I was in. He phoned the hospital and said, "I am taking you there now." In the morning I was feeling good and wondering what I was doing there. I was kept there for a week and was feeling fine when I got home. The rest had done me much good. Sarah was glad to see me back as she could now go back to Oban to her own family. I took the pills and powders they gave me whenever I remembered, and for some time I could eat and keep the food down before going back on the home made cure. The inner condition was getting more disagreeable as time went on. Often when sitting at the table I would be obliged to leave without touching my food, other times I was much better and refused the Doctor's advice to go back to hospital.

Before Mary Ann died I had made a start on the extension I was to add to the house, as it was becoming smaller and smaller every year. Having got the material, cement and timber, when she died all that went to waste and I did not care, and some was given away for nothing such was the state of my mind after her death. At last the world looked brighter, and I made another start as the foundation was already laid out. I got the cement, shingles and sand, without the need for a boat journey to and from Eriskay thanks to the road, which now reached the house. I could not afford a builder and was doing it on my own. I still had salvaged logs, which I sawed to make shuttering and standards. I made the wall 15 inches wide to take small stones, making a saving in cement, but as I had to do all the labour myself the job was slow with childrens' meals and washing to be done, cattle to attend to and sometimes, when hungry, a snack for myself. When the wall got as high as 6 feet I always found, in the mornings, that the standards were out of plumb as the children had been climbing over them while I would be milking the cows. Much time was lost in the morning re-building, but despite those hold ups, which did not happen every day, the building went up slowly till the roof was put on and windows put into place. Then the wall from the original house was knocked down, floors made, walls plastered and painted and the ceiling the same. We made it into a dining place and scullery, with calor gas and a sink. It was a sink without a tap, as the water supply for the township was not granted till years afterwards.

It was some time after the scullery was built that I got around to getting fresh water to the house. Above the house on the hillside a small wet patch always appeared on a soft flat rock. I thought water must be near the surface, so I tried with hammer and chisel, and the stone, which was soft and brittle, came away easily. I did not dig more than six inches when water, which had a reddish tinge, came trickling out. I continued to dig, making the hole larger and deeper. One side of the rock was solid and the other brittle and easy to wedge and hammer out, baling the water out as I dug deeper. I thought, if a working well could be here, I would apply for a grant to construct it. Before that could be granted, a plan had to be submitted to the Department of Works, and a sample of the water sent to Edinburgh for testing to see if it was fit for human consumption. When the result of that came, it had passed the test and I was given permission to start work. When the project was finished and approved, I got a grant of 75 per cent.

I did all the work myself before taking the pipe inside to the sink and testing it for pressure. I felt everything now was plain sailing. The well I made was watertight. I disconnected the pipe, plugged the well and began digging the 18-inch deep trench to the house and under the wall; I then made a shallow trench under the floor to the sink. When I had both ends connected, I turned on the tap expecting a good flow. Not a drop would come through, and after a few attempts, when I discovered an air lock was to blame, I tried again and heard a loud swishing and bubbling noise and watched dark, murky water coming through, gradually increasing in volume and in clearness. After a while I turned it off and let it stand like that, then turned it on again to find flowing water as clear and cool as one could wish. When all that was done we were the talk of the township as being the only house with water piped in. It was no joke going to a well for a bucket of water in rain and storm. It would not now be a problem, if the cash was there, to have the hot water as well, since most of the heat from the fire was wasted up the chimney.

New Friendships, a Hut, Whales, the Family and Final Memories

About that time an unexpected, extraordinary favour came my way, when a Land-Rover stopped at the house, and a lady whom I knew came up. She said, "A gentleman wants to see you Donald." I said, "Tell him to come up." The house was not in a good shape. I went outside to meet him and he introduced himself as Captain Pollen, and said "I believe you are Donald MacDonald and this is your croft." I said, "Yes, I have the two crofts, the other goes out past the ruined inn." "Well," he said, "That is why I came to see you. I like this place and would like to put up a small wooden hut on that croft." I told him he could put it wherever he wished and if he wanted, I would build it for him. He said he would come back the next day and we could both walk out and choose a site. He did come the next day, and he chose a site at the east end of the ruined inn. I said, "Alright, but nothing has been served there for the last hundred years or more." He said jokingly, "It didn't take you that time to drink it all?" "No, but I expect my great grandfather had a few hangovers on its account, as whisky was not taxed then."

He told me that the hut was in crates on the pier at Lochboisdale, and the local garage man would take it to the end of the road, as the sections were too heavy to be manhandled this distance. He asked if I could float and tow them out, and I said I could when the tide was right. We had a long look at the remains of the ruin where the whisky was distilled, and I told him I thought it was long before the Highland Clearances, and that it was King James VI of Scotland who had it built. Locheynort was one of the ports of call for ships carrying cargo and passengers to and from South Uist, and there were other inns built at Polochar and Carinish and other places throughout the Islands. It is said they were the only houses on the islands at that time built with lime. He said he had to leave the island soon and his friend, the Master of Works at the new Benbecula airport, would help me with anything I needed.

It is surprising the amount of material that a hut 18 feet x 12 feet. requires. However I was fortunate that I had some pit props that I could use as rollers. The launching down the slope to the sea and making it into a raft was easy, and was done in our spare time. With the help of Alex MacAskill from Ormiclate and the older children, work began on the hut. The front was to face the hill with the back to the sea. Alex was a handyman, but like myself, no tradesman. And the site where it was to be was far from being level, but there was plenty of stone in the old ruin for that.

We decided there were no problems we could not master, and the next day Alex came out with two bags of cement that we took to the hut by the small boat. The hut was to rest on three stout planks on top of the levelled walls, and to make it more secure, we put bolts through those planks embedded in concrete, with a washer and nut screwed on the top at intervals. After the flooring was in we erected the walls, and I got my son Archie to help put the roof on; being young and agile he was a good help. At last it was finished all but the painting. I was sent enough white and green paint to give it more than two coats.

I always kept track of the hours I worked and we came to an agreement regarding payment which I was very happy with. The hut was creosoted to preserve the wood from the sea spray, then two layers of roofing felt put on. The roof was then tarred, and wooden 4 inch slats nailed on from ridge to eaves, four feet apart, then tarred again all over, to stop the inside air from moving the felt. I then did the painting and fencing which Captain Pollen had asked for, allowing as much ground inside as he wanted where he planted many different kinds of flowers.

One day Captain Pollen came with his friend for me to take him out fishing. He himself had something else to do. I found this man very pleasant and no stranger in a boat, and he also knew something about fishing which was very successful that day. Sir Walter Pollen, as he was later called when knighted, was waiting for us at the jetty, and was surprised at the amount of fish we had caught. He said that he would come out to see me the next day about something he wanted done at the hut. Water M. Pollen, like myself, was a soldier in the First World War. There he rose to the rank of Captain, winning the Military Cross for heroic bravery at the opening of the Battle of the Somme in July 1916. I was not at that battle then but knew it well, too well afterwards, and how anyone could come out of that carnage alive, for there surely never was an area of its size, that due to combat was so thickly populated with its dead.

On one occasion, we got to talk about the War and he asked if I had been there. I said I was involved in both wars. Further conversations led us to discover we were in sectors well known to us both, and although not in the same regiment, the talk on each sector brought back memories. Those who were there never forget the Somme, and we were both there at different times. We were both at Castel Maison; we spoke of the tall crucifix standing alone in what had been the churchyard for the village. I said, "I was one day as near as a few feet from it while they were still shelling the area but not very heavily. There were a few scratches on the wooden part of the cross, but on the figure of Christ hanging on it I could not see a single scratch or a bullet mark, yet the churchyard and the large area around was littered with the bodies of young and old."

Sir Walter Pollen

We talked much about different sectors of the line that we once knew. After the War he was appointed Governor of some African state where he stayed for many years. He stayed in Barra before coming to South Uist to stay at Grogarry Lodge, then to Ormaclate where he rented a big house beside the ruins of Ormaclate Castle, before moving to Balranald House in North Uist. While in Ormaclate, and on visiting Locheynort, he decided to build a hut there for rest and peace. It was as a result of this that I got to know him and his family well. His wife Lady Pollen was not on the island at the time but was no stranger. She had been coming to the Lodge during the war years and had been on the MacBrayne's mail ship 'The *Plover*' when a German submarine shelled it. The crew were ordered to take to the lifeboats and some did after firing some shells over her. The submarine submerged and was not seen again.

The hut was finished and the planted shrubs and flowers were in bloom. When Lady Pollen came she admired the hut and its surroundings. Her only questions were about roofing shingles, which she would have preferred, and if there was a well near. I said that I had not yet located the old well that the Inn had been using. Sir Walter sent up a pump and all the one-inch pipe I needed. I dug, cleaned and re-built the well, and piped the water to within three feet of the hut and connected the small hand pump. As far as the roof shingles were concerned, Sir Walter arranged for the materials to be delivered, and with the help of my eldest son Archie and his cousin Donald Joseph, who did most of the work, with me watching and directing from the ground, the shingles were put on. The Pollens also wanted a porch added to the front of the hut, and also the windowpanes at the back of the hut, from where there was a view of the bay,

Lady Rosalind Pollen

replaced by one large pane of glass. I myself was quite happy to do all the work, as money was needed for the children for better footwear and clothing as winter was approaching. As before, Sir Walter provided all the materials and the work was eventually completed.

One day, after lunch at the hut, we went looking for seals, and Lady Pollen enjoyed seeing so many and so near. It proved an exciting day for her and she asked if I would take her some day out fishing. I said I would be pleased to, any day suitable to her and the weather. It would help if she could let me know a day or so ahead, so that the boat would be afloat and ready. She said she would let me know in good time, and asked if she could bring her two grandchildren. I said it would be safe enough to take them and I would take the small boat, which would be best to get near to the seals. They arrived on a nice warm day and I had all the gear ready. I found the two girls, Rosalind and Annabel, very nice and not a bit shy or awkward in getting on board. We had a most enjoyable day out in the boat, and saw many seals and other wildlife, and that was to be the first of many such trips.

I took so many of the Pollen family and friends, young and old, out fishing and sightseeing over many years, it is hard now to recall who I was along with on any particular occasion. No one was ever hurt or badly frightened, the nearest I can recall to have been in a tight corner was once when out with Peregrine, Sir Walter's son, and his wife Patricia. The outside loch was full of basking sharks, porpoise and whales and seldom, if ever, have I seen so many in such a small area. The sea was flat calm and we tried fishing but nothing would take. I was not surprised, although I knew there were plenty there but saving themselves from the raiding big fish was more important. I felt it would be wise to clear out of the loch as there were so many between us and the open sea. There was no sign of them clearing out and more kept coming in, so I suggested we try the inner loch, although fishing there is never as good or as big. The tide was about half on the flow, and coming to the outer narrows the reef in the middle was covered. I gave Peregrine the tiller and a point to steer for. I thought no shark or whale would venture into that narrow part. I also wanted Peregrine to get to know the place better. It is only by a person himself steering can the places to avoid become familiar.

We were almost at the inner end of this reef when a large whale began to surface across our bow, a few feet away. The reef was on our port side, and it too was only a few feet away and it was doubtful if there was enough water to pass over. I was not sure if Peregrine saw her in time for him to put the boat hard to starboard, thinking he would clear her, that is, providing she was making a turn to go back to the outside loch. In that moment, rather than chance the reef, I shouted to Peregrine to put the boat hard to port, repeating "To your left side." It was evident that's what he had already done, as the boat was coming over fast in that direction. Once on the top of the reef it was too shallow for the whale to follow, if she intended to, but perhaps it was a case of 'keep clear of me and I will not harm you.' Just the same, I was grateful and proud of Peregrine for the fast way he had acted even before I called, for to stay on his original course he was sure to have hit her side, and it is anyone's guess what then would have happened. We passed over the reef just touching it, no damage done. The whale half surfaced and made for the open sea. I could not tell if it was a killer. I do know that my shirt was wet with sweat but dare not show to the other two that I was not as brave as them, who seemed unconcerned, or were they like me, hiding it. To finish off that evening with Peregrine and Patricia, we made for the inner loch where, at a deep spot, we got a fairly good catch of whiting, codlings and lythe. On the whole an exciting trip still remembered.

Some time after the big pane of glass was put in the window of the hut, we were sitting in comfortable chairs and taking in the view, when in the calm bay a large whale surfaced not far from the window, diving and going round in circles. I think she was after a shoal of mackerel that came in. She stayed in that area for at least half an hour, till I think she had driven most of the fish out towards the narrows. There were other times watching seals and the occasional otter, but none as spectacular as watching the whale. Besides being well paid for any work I did for the Pollens, it was a great pleasure to know them. They were most considerate, given our different standards of living, made me feel like one of their own, and I always looked forward to seeing them. Sometimes they would wire when they expected to come fishing, but often the wire would come after they had gone. That did not greatly matter as they took things as they found them. The boat was nearly always afloat, but if not, by the time I had the gear ready, she would be. Strangely, when little preparation was made, fishing seemed to be always good.

305

It was after hearing parts of my life that Sir Walter and Lady Pollen began to persuade me to write my memoirs. When I told them my education was very limited, they said, "Your experience in life is not, and telling it in your own way makes it more interesting." It took a lot of prodding before I eventually made a start. Sadly, Sir Walter died and did not see any of it. He died suddenly after taking a massive heart attack at his home at Balranald. He was up to see me a few days before then and when I got the news I was stunned. I had lost a dear friend. Alec MacAskill took me down to pay him my last respects, and my condolence to Lady Pollen and the family. For himself I prayed "May the good Lord be as kind to you as you have been to me and us." They took his body away by plane that day for burial at his own place in England. I followed the coffin to the plane. It was the last service I could do. I shall always have fond memories of him as a man whom I had good reasons to admire. One day he said to me, "Donald, I'll give you anything you ask of me but I know you are too proud to ask." I said, "You have already given me much work on the hut, that was a godsend to us. You could have got it done by a proper tradesman."

I also felt that the hardship we both went through in the First World War had much to do with our friendly relationship, yet we seldom talked of the horrors of the War. Lady Pollen was a very charming person and at first I felt embarrassed at a titled lady coming to my home. I need not have been as she soon put me on the same level as them, and when I suggested making coffee, she said "That will be nice Donald, I'll make it myself. Just show me where you keep the gear, then you two can talk." I think from that moment I liked her. I took her out fishing many times, as she was fond of watching the seals and birds, and I also got great pleasure in taking her grandchildren out fishing, and found them very easy to teach in the boat. She too was very generous to me and to my family, as was her son Peregrine and his wife Patricia, who was kind enough to undertake the hard task of typing my life story. I recall every Christmas a large hamper arriving with a turkey and food items that we could only dream of. One time, while the children were at school, a very large box arrived. It was full of all kinds of toys, and I felt there was too much to give them all at once, so I hid the box in the byre and covered it with hay. Every so often I would take a toy up to the house, which caused much pleasure and excitement amongst the children. After some time they became curious and wondered where all the toys were coming from. They saw me coming up from the byre and raided my plank, which was by then nearing the bottom of the box. The younger children have fond memories of this.

Archie, being the oldest, was the first to leave home to attend Lochaber High School in Fort William, closely followed by Alex Iain who went to the same school. About this time, John Joseph also left home to begin his five years' apprenticeship as a yacht builder with Magruer's Yacht Builders in Clynder, not far from Helensburgh on the River Clyde. Peggy was a great help at home but it was not a place where a young girl could learn the ways of modern life. I certainly did not know how to teach her, and it would be selfish to keep her at home. She grew up doing the same things as the boys, using tools as they did, but regardless of that, she needed training of a different kind. She had by this time left school and was asked by the Nuns from Daliburgh Hospital if she would like to go to work there as a maid. She did and within a year was put to work on the nursing side. I was sorry to see her go but I knew it was the right thing for her. When Peggy left, and with Peter in winter lodgings, I found myself in an empty house, and while it would have been a great help to have some of the family staying at home, I always said I

306

would not hold any of them back, and hoped they would be able to travel the world if they wished, as I had done, but without the danger of war.

Having suffered from stomach ulcers for some time, my suffering continued and my makeshift cures did not help. One day I was very low, and Alex Iain was home at the time and that evening he left to go to a dance. I had the usual stomach pain, no worse. After he left, the pain became worse and the medicine I took was no use. Suddenly, I felt terribly thirsty and made for the sink, feeling I could drink a bucket of water, but before I reached it I collapsed with a massive haemorrhage. Alex Iain, for some reason, decided not to go to the dance and came home and found me in that condition. He at once went for the doctor, but the public phone, nearly three miles away, was out of order. The night was wet and stormy, and he eventually got the doctor who came in a hurry. After a short examination he said that there was no time for an ambulance and he would take me in his own car. I could not stand, so between him and Alex Iain, they carried me to the car.

In bed they gave me injections, took a blood test and found two ulcers. I think it was early next morning they began giving me pints of blood. I was in a bad way, not in any pain but did not know where I was. All I could see was thick white fog and forms of people moving around. I remember asking them to open the window and let the fog out. They said it was the injections causing that and there was no fog. I was parched with thirst, and with much pleading and begging all I could get was a half cube of ice, and that only every half hour. After I had been transfused with the new blood, I felt stronger. The fog cleared and I could recognise my own daughter from the rest. I had to stay perfectly still on my back, and began to recover slowly and was moved to a ward with three patients, where I was much happier and progress was better.

Sometime before, Peggy had been on holiday and stayed with her Aunt Ealasaid, who by then had moved to Lenzie, outside Glasgow. While there, she saw that Stobhill Hospital was fairly close to her aunt, and she decided to apply to train as a nurse there. She was accepted and moved to Glasgow to begin her training. In due course I was told that my ulcers would require an operation and I would have that done in the Western Infirmary, Glasgow, to which I was transferred by ambulance plane. A few days later I was operated on, and after the operation I was back in my ward when things began to happen. First pneumonia, then pleurisy, and it was touch and go. Peggy, then training at Stobhill Hospital, was called, but when I rallied the call was cancelled. From what I remember it was a very painful time, with every cough hurting, but I was making slow progress and eventually was transferred to the Discharge Ward, where there was a T.V. set, the first I had ever seen. Owing to the many would-be mechanics trying to fix it, the picture was not always clear. But it was a far cry, as I earlier mentioned, from the first time I heard that such a thing would yet be made possible. I heard this from a fellow passenger on a ship coming from the States, who claimed to be experimenting with this idea. He offered me shares in their company and I now regret not listening to that advice. I left that hospital in good shape, with no more stomach trouble, at least of that kind. In the meantime, at home, I was becoming stronger and began a little work on the croft.

My son Alex Iain, who by then was attending Strathclyde University in Glasgow, was home for the summer and Peter, who was still attending school and in winter lodgings, was soon to leave school.

Archie, having been the first to leave home to attend Lochaber School, joined the Air Training Corps, I think with a view to joining the Royal Air Force later, and he also joined the mountain rescue team. Afterwards, he worked for a time at the Loch Awe hydro scheme, which was then being built, and eventually he was accepted by the Met Office and in due course went to a weather station at RAF Kinloss. He met and married Angela, from Johnstone near Glasgow, and lived in Forres where their first child, my oldest grandson, was born. During his time with the Met Office he worked in Stornoway and in Benbecula, from where he retired. Over this period two other grandchildren, a boy and a girl, were born.

Alex Iain was the second to leave home. Like Archie he went to Lochaber High School and after to Strathclyde University, where he passed with a B.Sc. in Electrical Engineering. He found work with Ferranti at Bracknell involving computers. After some years there he was sent to the rocket range in Benbecula, where his firm installed a computer system in connection with the Rocket Range, and to train army personnel. He was often called back when things did not work as they should, and also was sometimes sent abroad to do maintenance on projects that he had worked on. Needless to say I am very proud of his achievements considering the humble circumstances he was brought up in, a credit to himself.

John Joseph completed his apprenticeship in Clynder, and after finishing his training there, he was considered to be one of their best tradesmen. He stayed with that firm till they went into fibreglass yacht building, which he did not like. He came home and began boat repairing. When his work became known there was a great demand for him for that kind of work and also for installing new engines. He also successfully fishes for lobsters, and was cutting seaweed for the factory when it was operating. During his many years with that firm in Clynder, he made many friends, many coming to Locheynort for their holidays yearly. A couple, Norrie and Ivy Sutherland, come here regularly, both very fine people who seem to like this place and our way of life. Also a very fine lady by the name of Liz Todrick, who had a small yacht, the *Ayrshire Lass*, and was well known on the lower reaches of the Clyde for her expert seamanship, sailed here regularly. She had won many races and cups for her type of vessel, which she claims is over 90 years old, the oldest yacht on the Clyde and still very sound in timber. Liz, then at over 60 years old, sails alone across the Minch to islands in the Inner and Outer Hebrides. She was also a first class boat builder, and worked for many years with John Joseph at Magruers Yacht Builders. Usually one of my sons would sail back with her, depending on the wind, as the boat had no engine in her. She spends her yearly holidays that way and stays on-board at night. The family have enjoyed many sails on the *Ayrshire Lass*, myself included.

Peggy is now married to a Sergeant in the Police Force. They have two boys, their own home in Bishopbriggs outside Glasgow, and are expecting their third child and come here every year for their holidays.

Peter had originally enrolled in the technical college at Inverness where he spent a year, before taking up the building trade as an apprentice bricklayer with the firm of Campbells of Inverness, with whom he served three and a half years as an apprentice. The year spent in college stood him in good stead, as he passed his City and Guild's Certificate and then the Advanced Certificate. Shortly afterwards he began to work with a small family building firm in Gairloch, Wester Ross, where he now lives with his wife, Dyllis, a nurse from Huntly and their two boys.

The youngest of the family, Neil Paul, was only seven months old when his Mother died. His Aunt Ealasaid and her husband Joseph, a sea captain, brought him up along with her own children, all of whom loved to visit Locheynort and enjoyed fishing trips and playing with their cousins. We were like one big extended family. Ealasaid was a great help to me when the children were young. Neil Paul, after leaving school, went to sea, starting off working on the Puffers, before joining MacBrayne's. In due course he went deep sea as an ordinary seaman, till he became Able Seaman going to many parts of the world on the Ben Line, mainly to the Far East. After a spell in that line, he joined B.P. oil tankers where, after much studying, eventually he achieved his Masters Certificate, a proud achievement.

John Joseph, having returned home, and while repairing boats, also kept the work on the croft going. In the meantime Archie, having been transferred to Benbecula, decided to settle in Locheynort, and as I had two crofts I gave Number 7, including the family home, to John Joseph and Number 8 to Archie who began clearing that site without any mechanical aid, made all the thousands of concrete blocks required, and worked on that throughout the winter, not missing any time from his work in the Benbecula Met Office where they work on shifts, sometimes 24 hours on duty. He placed a large caravan on the site, and his wife and children lived in it until his house was finished. Peter, his brother, by then a qualified builder, came on holiday with his family and provided some professional help. Anyone passing by there a few years later would think that such change was not possible for one man and his wife, without any mechanical aid, to make such transformation in such a short time.

I recall the time while Archie was building his house and Peter and his family were on holiday from Gairloch, when Peter helped him with the house. At the same time Peggy, David and their family were also home on holiday. Locheynort being such an isolated area was a haven for wildlife. As it was such a lovely calm day, John Joseph and David had gone out in John's boat and taken several of the older grandchildren with them. While they were out one of the youngsters shouted, "There's a shark." He had seen something sticking out of the water. It was in fact the fin of a killer whale and, as it turned out, there were four of them. They had come through the narrows and were swimming west along the loch. John Joseph, with his knowledge of the area, knew that they would soon turn back to leave the loch and so they headed to the narrows to wait for them at a safe distance, having lost sight of the whales.

One group of two whales reappeared and passed the boat by, some distance away, and headed out through the narrows. Suddenly, without warning, the other two whales surfaced very close to the boat, one passing it by but the other diving underneath and surfacing right next to the boat, where its fin scraped the keel causing the boat to rock. They said it was so close they could see its blowhole opening and spraying seawater into the air. While all this was happening I am told there was a seal, which they saw leave the water and, as they described it, 'ploughed a furrow up the hillside until it reached the heather'. The seal is a fast travelling creature under water and yet very scared of a killer whale, and will drive himself ashore and climb as high as he can to avoid them. A colony of seals can nearly always be seen basking or fishing between the two narrows.

Peggy and Dyllis with the younger children were watching all this from the shore. They had seen the whales coming in and were very concerned for the safety of those on the boat, especially the children. While they were walking up and down the road, shouting to the boat to come back, they met a man who told them he was a naturalist. He had been holidaying on the island and was to leave the next day. He had come to Locheynort in the hope of spotting an otter, but was amazed that in the space of two hours he had seen four killer whales, some otters, lots of seals and a buzzard sitting on the fence beside our byre. It had made his holiday and I'm sure he would relate his story to many people afterwards.

I missed all this display and doubted that seals were forced to take to dry land till I remembered the day, many years ago, while looking for driftwood in Corrodale Bay, that I came across a dead seal, some 12 feet in the bracken above a high shoulder of the shore. It was a large seal, I would say over 6 foot and dead for at least a week. The bracken was not high, and I saw it when a few feet away. I got a shock, thinking it was the body of a man who had died there or been washed up in a gale, still alive and crawled there. I stood spellbound, before going nearer, till I saw the back flippers. I knew then what it was, but how could it get there, no tide or wave could have done it. Had it been above a low part of the shore, a high wave might have washed its dead body ashore, but that was impossible where it was. How it got there was a mystery I could not solve, and I could only conclude that it had died there. This later killer whale event must be the only solution to that mystery.

This event brought to mind an incident of a similar kind. While fishing near the reef at the narrows, with John MacIntyre, a local man, we were using the old method, six or more rods spread from the stern and held under a strong board resting across the boat's stern. The lines, with hooks made of feathers, trailed almost on the surface, where fish would only take when the sun was almost setting. This was some 40 years before the mackerel cast appeared here.

The sea was flat calm when the fish began to take, keeping the man at the rods working as fast as he could. All of a sudden they stopped taking and began rushing away from us, jumping out of the water like mad. We could not understand the reason. I was at the oars and happened to look over my shoulder, and there I saw, some fifty feet to my right, a huge mound of sea rising. Before I had time to shout a warning to John, the back of a large whale was out of the water with almost a covering of small fish cascading down its side to the sea. I was then able to say, "My God John, look at the whale!" John turned, and what he saw made him stand and make a grab at me as if that was protection. I glanced to see if she was coming our way. She was, and I am sure with not more than 18 inches of water on her back. We waited, hoping she would turn away at the last moment. She did not, but kept coming very slowly towards us, as if studying which was the juiciest. It was clear she had no thoughts like that, as she moved slowly under us till she was clear, without us being touched. We drew a deep sigh of relief and rowed fast the few yards to dry land.

She submerged at the end of the reef in deep water, between that and the inner narrows, and surfaced there among three others of her kind. We were glad to be on dry land watching, and thinking they would now do an about turn. They were moving very slowly, four abreast. but instead of turning back, they closed near each other, stayed like that for a moment, then one moved towards the mouth of the inner narrows, the rest waiting their turn to follow. It was an awesome sight and amazing how they kept away from the shallow rocks and the jutting out points that I knew so well. Only echo power could have guided them so well, and that must be how the first passed under us without touching. We did not leave our safe place till they all turned left to the inner loch, then we took the boat further having left the rods standing in the sea, knowing there was a fish on every one. But the thought of losing good gear was not worth the risk. It was nearly high neap tide; the rods were sure to be in their way when the whales decided to return. No saying how soon that would be. We left the boat in a safe place and climbed a small mound to keep watch on the whales. We lived on the other side of the loch but dare not cross it while they were in charge. At last they began cruising back and I thought, no matter how

310

good the navigator or his chart, he could not improve on the track they were taking, because I have fished it so often that I claim to know the bottom to within feet.

On going through the narrow channel we thought it impossible for them to miss getting tangled in the rods which we had left standing in the sea. We expected to see the whales putting on more speed and to see the last of our rods. Unless you were there to see, it is hard to believe that, instead of spreading out, they stayed single file and, when near the rods, each one cleared them, as far as we could see, without touching them! The proof of that amazing navigation was seen when they had cleared to the open sea, and we ventured out and found our rods safe, with a small dead fish on each hook, which we threw to the birds.

For some time I was suffering from bladder trouble with much loss of blood. I was again sent to the Western Infirmary in Glasgow for an operation. Some days after that three doctors, making the rounds, stopped at my bed and between them began discussing my case. I did not know what they were referring to, but I had a feeling they were not satisfied at the progress I was making, and so they decided to operate. I was downhearted, seeing some that came in a week after me now leaving for home, apparently quite well.

It was the wedding day of my son Peter, and when I saw a smiling nurse coming up the ward with a huge bouquet of pretty flowers, which she placed at the head of my bed, I knew they had not forgotten me. That cheered me up and I began to improve, and soon was discharged and went to stay with my sister Sarah in Oban for over a week, and gained much of my strength back before I set sail for home. Soon after I arrived, I reported to the local hospital, where the doctor, after a short examination, told me I was nearly alright, but not to do any heavy lifting for some time, and to come and see him again whenever I thought I should.

It was some time after that when I was obliged to see him again, as one day, swinging a heavy bag of peats onto my back, I felt something inside me giving way. I knew the symptoms and in a very short time I knew I had given myself a hernia, a nasty thing to have. I saw the doctor and told him how it happened. He said, "I told you not to lift heavy things after your last operation. Now you're in for another." I had my minor operation and, after the outside stitches were taken out, I was soon back home with warnings to take things easy for a while. That was my last operation, ten as far as I can remember, some of them major.

My next admittance at that hospital was some years ago, through a bad lingering cold I took, turning to bronchitis and asthma. I was in a bad way and late at night the doctor was called. He gave me some injections, saying that the ambulance would come for me early next morning. The injection worked wonders. I was able to breathe and get a little sleep. In the morning I was admitted to hospital where I was put on oxygen. I don't remember how many days I was in that state, but the spells of coughing became wider spaced and less painful, and eventually the oxygen was taken away. It took me quite a while to gain my strength, but even then the doctor was not keen to let me go home. When there was talk of me being let home, Peggy, my daughter in Glasgow, wanted me to stay with them for the winter. The good doctor knew, that even with home help, I would be most of the time, day and night, alone and not capable of making a meal or attending to the fire, and in the circumstances he strongly advised me go and stay with Peggy where I would not be at any time alone and sure of every comfort. I took the Doctor and Peggy's advice and arrangements for my travel were made. Peggy, David and baby Stephen were there to welcome me. I was put in a wheel chair and taken to their waiting car. The drive to their house took nearly as long as I was in the 'plane. There I was given the usual loving kindness that I

311

always got from Peggy and David. Baby Stephen was at the learning to walk stage. We two became trusty friends with him sometimes pretending to hide.

It took me many days, practising walking with the stick, in the back garden and driveway, before I ventured to the sidewalk, gaining more confidence with every walk. Where they stay is a few minutes walk to a park, where I often walked on the grass as I found it much easier as the pavements were very hard. There were also seats where I could rest, and I gained much benefit from these walks. I did not wander far as I found that area easy to get lost in, but I soon learned the short cuts to the local pub about a mile away, where I took a long rest over a pint of lager, which I enjoyed but dared not take more. Spring was well on now and I was gaining strength all the time.

It was during the early part of my stay there that Peggy began to persuade me to begin my life story. She knew that years before then Sir Walter and Lady Pollen had made many attempts to get me started on it. Sadly, Sir Walter died before I got started. Lady Pollen read part of it and said she found it very interesting. Patricia, her daughter-in-law, Peregrine's wife, also said the same and that she would type it for me, which she did and for which I am very grateful. It is to those fine people that I owe so much for the interest they took in my story or memoirs. They planted the seed and Peggy encouraged it to grow, first by recording it on tape, which I found did not work because I was not used to recording, and so I began writing and remembering as I went along.

Stephen, after many falls, was now running around, and I was surprised to see how careful he was to keep out of my way when I walked with the stick. Other times he would hide and I would pretend not to know where he was! I had lots of fun with him. I regretted not being able to play with him or any of my other six grandchildren, the eldest being twelve. That is the penalty of marrying late in life.

I had now spent a very enjoyable winter, spring and part of summer in Bishopbriggs. I felt the craving to see the familiar hills, loch and shoreline with the tide in and out, fighting against it under sail in the old days, hard as they were, I found pleasure in remembering them. Perhaps nowhere lingers longer in the mind than when one was young, playing and active. I announced that I intended to head back home soon. They tried to persuade me to put it off till they would be coming in August, saying there was plenty of room in the car. But, regardless of their pleading, I wanted to see again as much as I could in the summer of Uist. I took the aeroplane home and enjoyed every minute of the journey. Archie and Angela met me at the airport and took me to their home, where I stayed for a short time before moving back to my own house. John Joseph had made some alterations while I was away, which made it more comfortable. The home help, Nellie, also restarted that day, and although not as comfortable, I felt contented to be back, and by then could walk at least a mile, but only at a snail's pace with the aid of two sticks. I could even do a little at the peats, which I had craved to do. It made me sleep better at night.

In 1923 I sailed on the *Metagama* with my dreams and expectations of a bright and prosperous future, and I can't deny that my time in Canada and America provided me with a wealth of life experiences. Due to post war days, and such as the Depression, like many other islanders my experiences did not live up to my expectations. Having returned to these shores, and, with hindsight, over the years, despite the heartaches, I have been more than happy and content since coming home and I take great pleasure in enjoying the views, remembering the

312

past and enjoying visits from the family of whose achievements from a very humble and hard beginning I am very proud.

I feel that it is time for me to draw this narrative to a conclusion. Except for the stories I heard as told by others, the rest is what I remember of my own life, although through lack of memory, I am sure parts have been left out. If so, I don't think these were very important. It is far too late to say had I been better educated, my telling of this story could be more interesting.

-o-0-o-